# VANESSA REDGRAVE

# VANESSA REDGRAVE

## An Autobiography

HUTCHINSON

London Sydney Auckland Johannesburg

This edition first published in 1991 by
Hutchinson

**Random Century Group Ltd**
20 Vauxhall Bridge Road, London SW1V 2SA

**Random Century Australia (Pty) Ltd**
20 Alfred Street, Milsons Point, Sydney, NSW 2061, Australia

**Random Century New Zealand Ltd**
PO Box 40–086, Glenfield, Auckland 10, New Zealand

**Random Century South Africa (Pty) Ltd**
PO Box 337, Bergvlei, 2012, South Africa

**British Library Cataloguing-in-Publication Data**
Redgrave, Vanessa
Vanessa Redgrave: An autobiography.
I. Title
920

ISBN 0–09–174593–4

Photoset by Speedset Ltd, Ellesmere Port, S. Wirral
Printed and bound in Great Britain by
Mackays of Chatham PLC, Chatham, Kent

# Contents

| Chapter | | Page |
|---|---|---|
| 1 | ................................................... | 1 |
| 2 | ................................................... | 19 |
| 3 | ................................................... | 27 |
| 4 | ................................................... | 39 |
| 5 | ................................................... | 50 |
| 6 | ................................................... | 59 |
| 7 | ................................................... | 68 |
| 8 | ................................................... | 78 |
| 9 | ................................................... | 89 |
| 10 | ................................................... | 103 |
| 11 | ................................................... | 113 |
| 12 | ................................................... | 123 |
| 13 | ................................................... | 135 |
| 14 | ................................................... | 150 |
| 15 | ................................................... | 162 |
| 16 | ................................................... | 172 |
| 17 | ................................................... | 188 |
| 18 | ................................................... | 197 |
| 19 | ................................................... | 206 |
| 20 | ................................................... | 214 |
| 21 | ................................................... | 223 |
| 22 | ................................................... | 232 |
| 23 | ................................................... | 243 |
| 24 | ................................................... | 258 |
| 25 | ................................................... | 272 |
| 26 | ................................................... | 287 |
| Index | ................................................... | 301 |

# Illustration Acknowledgements

SECTION I

Paul Tanqueray (*p1/centre*); Hulton Picture Company (*p2/left, p3/ top*); Rex Features (*p4/top & bottom*).

SECTION II

W. R. Ayling (*p5/top*); Rex Features (*p5/bottom, p6/bottom left & right*); Camera Press (*p5/bottom right, p7*); Hulton Picture Company (*p6/top, p8/top & bottom*).

SECTION III

Rex Features (*p9/top, p12/top & bottom*); Hulton Picture Company (*p9/bottom*).

SECTION IV

Hulton Picture Company (*p13/top, p14/top, p15/bottom left, p16/top & bottom*); Rex Features (*p13/bottom, p14/bottom left, p15/bottom left, p16/ centre*).

SECTION V

Rex Features (*p17/top & centre*); Hulton Picture Company (*p18/top & centre, p19/bottom, p20/centre & bottom*); David Hurn/Magnum (*p18/ bottom*); Camera Press (*p19/top left & right*).

SECTION VI

Camera Press (*p21/top*); Phil Cutts (*p21/bottom*); Mander & Mitchenson Theatre Collection (*p22/top*); Hulton Picture Company (*p22/ bottom right*); Donald Cooper/Photostage (*p23/top left*); Rex Features (*p23/top right*); Inge Morath/Magnum (*p23/centre*); Mikki Ansin (*p23/bottom*); Rex/Richard Young (*p24/top left*).

## SECTION VII

20th Century Fox (*p25/top*); Rex Features (*p25/centre, p26/centre right & bottom centre, p27/top centre, left & centre right*); Camera Press (*p25/bottom, p27/bottom right*); Eve Arnold/Magnum (*p26/top left*); Rex/Warner Pathe (*p26/top right*); Hulton Picture Company (*p26/bottom left*); Inge Morath/Magnum (*p27/top left*); Mikki Ansin (*p27/top right*); Donald Cooper/Photostage (*p28/top & bottom right*); Mander & Mitchenson/John Haynes (*p28/bottom left*).

## SECTION VIII

Hulton Picture Company (*p30/top*); Camera Press (*p30/bottom*); Mander & Mitchenson/John Haynes (*p32*).

Whilst every effort has been made to clear copyright, in some cases this has not been possible. The publishers would like to apologise in advance for any inconvenience this might cause.

The extract from *The Tiger and the Horse* by Robert Bolt, published by Faber & Faber Ltd, is reproduced here by kind permission of Margaret Ramsay Ltd. All rights whatsoever in this play are strictly reserved and applications for performance etc should be made before rehearsal to Margaret Ramsay Ltd, 14a Goodwin's Court, St Martin's Lane, London WC2N 4LL. No performance may be given unless a licence has been obtained.

The extracts from *Actor Prepares* by C Stanislavski are reproduced by kind permission of Geoffrey Bles (Publisher) Ltd.

# 1

I was born in the middle of a snowstorm on Saturday, 30 January 1937. My mother was in a maternity clinic in Blackheath, London, at the time, about six o'clock in the evening, and my father was fighting a duel with Laurence Olivier at the Old Vic. Laertes versus Hamlet. Someone signalled to my father from the wings 'It's a girl', and at the curtain call Olivier stepped forward and announced to the audience that Laertes had a daughter. My father was quietly rather proud of this story. He told it to my mother, and according to her Olivier said, 'Ladies and gentlemen, tonight a great actress has been born, Laertes has a daughter.'

The earliest memory I can recall in sharp focus, with sound and smell, is of an early summer morning in August 1940 when I was three years old. I am alone in a garden, eating a bowl of milk and Kellogg's Rice Krispies. The sun shines, the air smells cool, sweet and damp with the moisture from the grass and the leaves of a large chestnut tree. A few midges and flies hover; their buzzing and the popping noise from the Krispies are the only sounds breaking the silence. Suddenly a vast wailing fills the whole sky. A wooden sash-window on the top floor bangs up. Dulcie Shave, my baby brother's nurse, thrusts her head out and shouts 'Vanessa! Come indoors. Come indoors AT ONCE!'

The wailing came from a siren sounding the first air-raid warning I ever heard. My mother, Rachel, remembers us spending that afternoon, and every night for a week, in the basement while the bombs fell on the City and the densely populated East End of London. Rachel laid out mattresses on the floor, told stories by candle-light and sang baby Corin and me to sleep;

Golden slumbers kiss your eyes,
Smiles awake you when you rise.

Sleep pretty darlings, do not cry,
And I will sing a lull-a-by.

Soon after the bombing, Corin, Rachel and I left the rented house in St John's Wood and Daddy, whom Rachel, when she was very happy, used to call 'Mikey' or 'Misha', to go to Bromyard in Herefordshire. Michael was performing in the theatre every night in *Thunder Rock* by Robert Ardrey, waiting for his call-up papers to serve in the Navy.

In 1938 Prime Minister Neville Chamberlain had returned from a summit meeting in Munich with the Chancellor of the Third Reich, Adolf Hitler. He waved a piece of paper and said he had brought 'peace in our time'. Some years ago, I asked Rachel, 'What did you think when you heard that?' 'We didn't know what we know now,' she said. 'I was just so relieved that there wouldn't be a war for a little while longer. We knew there *would* be a war, but I was so thankful that we would all have a little more time together before it started.'

Rachel and Michael fell in love in 1935 while they were performing in a season of repertory plays in Liverpool. At twenty-four, Rachel had been a wage-earning actress for two years and had played Juliet with great success in her very first engagement at Stratford-upon-Avon. Her father, Eric Kempson, was a schoolmaster who taught science at Rugby, and later became headmaster at the Royal Naval College at Dartmouth. Her mother was Beatrice Ashwell, the youngest of a homoeopathic chemist's three daughters. A beautiful name, and a very beautiful woman in her youth, but rather melancholy and disappointed when we knew her. Married life, my mother told us, had not come up to Beatrice's expectations. My mother adored her father, and found her mother rather a trial, especially after Eric's death in 1948. 'If ever *I* become like her,' my mother used to say, 'please warn me.' 'You *couldn't* become like her,' we reassured her. Mother's family was beset with strange inexplicable feuds, fierce likes and dislikes, and arguments that simmered on for thirty or forty years, long after some unforgivable, absolutely unspeakable thing had been said or done. We thought it very funny, and never asked the reason why.

Michael and Rachel were married, a year after they met in Liverpool, in 1936. Lilian Baylis then asked them both to join her Old Vic Theatre Company in London. The leading actors,

2

Laurence Olivier and Edith Evans, were already great names in the theatre. Others, like Alec Guinness, were playing their first small parts that season. Michael had only two years' experience in repertory behind him, but he was given some of the best parts to play. By the end of 1936 he was playing Orlando in *As You Like It*, with Edith Evans as Rosalind, and Mr Horner in Wycherly's *The Country Wife*, with Ruth Gordon.

By August 1940, when my first memory begins, my father had become the most popular film star in Britain. Alfred Hitchcock had cast him in *The Lady Vanishes*, and he had played David in Carol Reed's *The Stars Look Down*. Reed's film, adapted from A.J. Cronin's novel about a miner's son who leads a strike against a private coal company, was a great success when it was first shown in 1940, and must have contributed to the growing demand amongst miners during and after the war for the coal industry to be nationalised. I saw the film for the first time when it was screened on British television one Sunday afternoon in January 1987, almost fifty years after it was made. I was watching it not long after the year-long strike of the National Union of Mineworkers, and was struck by one scene in particular. An elderly miner is asking the middle-class anti-union butcher for some beef on credit. His wife is sick with pneumonia. The butcher abuses him and threatens to call the police. 'Yes!' shouts the old miner, 'You call the police as if you own them, you and your lot!'

'Michael Redgrave At Home' was a special feature that appeared in *Picture Post*, one of the best magazines for photo-journalism of its time in 1940. In the interview, Michael talks about his interest in Equity, the actors' trade union, and what he hopes the theatre will be like after the war. '*All* theatre must be subsidised, that's the only way it will attract new audiences and new writers.' There are photographs of Michael and Rachel singing at the piano; Rachel walking upstairs with a cup of tea; Michael, in a smart double-breasted suit, watering a pot of geraniums with his three-year-old daughter, Vanessa. But by the time the photographs appeared the blitz had begun and we were separated. Sadly, leaving Michael in London, Rachel, Nurse Dulcie, Corin and I went in a taxi to Paddington station. Enormous monster engines spouted columns of steam and smoke up into the arches and iron columns of the Great Western Railway terminal. Amidst the soot, steam and smoke, masses of people were packing into the railway carriages.

3

Criss-cross adhesive netting covered the windows to protect passengers against bombs splintering the glass. We travelled via Rugby, changing trains at Worcester and finally descended at a small branch-line station, Bromyard in Herefordshire.

A man in a peaked cap and navy-blue raincoat met us at the station, and we climbed into a small car which smelt strongly of old leather and petrol. We drove through the small market town, up a very steep hill, and turned left through some white gates, coming to a halt before a large grey front door and a small elderly woman. 'Ah! There you are, duckies!' cried Lucy Wedgwood Kempson, cousin of Grandpa Eric, welcoming us to her home, Whitegate. We went through a porch smelling of damp rubber galoshes and wellington boots. Cousin Lucy showed us her barometer, an old aneroid instrument which she would tap whenever she passed it, to see whether the air pressure was rising or falling. As we stepped into the hall the scent of rose-leaves and toast greeted us, and a loose tile in the parquet floor 'plocked'. After tea we climbed a large staircase to the top floor of the house where Corin, Nurse Dulcie and I were to share a bedroom.

Cousin Lucy always called Rachel 'Rachel-ducky', and Corin and I were 'Corin-ducky' and 'Vanessa-ducky'. At first sight she seemed quite ugly, with a large mole on the side of her nose and thick spectacles over her pale blue eyes. But she was full of energy, always interesting and always interested in us. Before her retirement she had been Warden of Bedford College in London and was one of the first women to have studied at London University.

It was summer-time when we arrived in the countryside and still light in the evenings. But when autumn and winter came the large house was chilly and dark. There was no electric light on the landing. To save electricity and help the blackout we used small wax night-lights on the landings and in our bedrooms. All the windows had regulation black blinds beneath the curtains, and the lights that we were allowed to use were very weak. Corin and I were frightened at night so we were allowed to have the night-light burning until Nurse Dulcie came to bed. When the wind blew from the west – it blew in from the Welsh mountains which, on a clear day, we could see from our bedroom window – the blinds rattled and creaked and the night-light quivered, casting sinister shadows on the walls and ceiling. As the house was at the top of a hill, an old engine in the basement was needed to pump water up. The age of the water system, combined with coal rationing, meant that both water and heat were in short supply. The basin taps provided only cold water, very slowly. Stone hot-water bottles were placed between the sheets when the weather grew cold and a copper warming pan filled with hot cinders would be placed in our mother's bed when she came to stay. She came from London, probably more frequently than it seemed to us then. Time had only one meaning for us. When Rachel was away the minutes went like hours. When she was there, the hours went like minutes.

It was in November of 1940 that I and some grown-ups looked out of a top-floor window and saw a fierce red glow on the south-east horizon. The city of Coventry was burning after a raid which killed more than 2000 people. In the early 1980s I read *A Man called Intrepid*, about William Stephenson, founder of the British Intelligence Service MI6 and the Central Intelligence Agency. It tells how a team working in Bletchley, England, had broken the Nazi Enigma machine code and learned of the plan to firebomb Coventry, and the date of the raid. On Churchill's instructions the city was not evacuated. The reason given in the book was that this would have told the Nazis that the Enigma code had been cracked. But what was the point of breaking the code if not to save lives? I had never felt fear of the war until that night. For years afterwards I had nightmares. Fires started out of sight, miles away. When I raised the alarm, friends and relatives told me not to worry: 'The fires will never reach us.' But in the dreams the fires raced inexorably nearer until they engulfed our home.

Cousin Lucy would invite Corin and me into her sitting-room every evening at five o'clock. She used to read to us, and taught us to play cards – Beggar My Neighbour, Happy Families and Pelmanism – and after cards we would have a round of Snakes and Ladders. At five minutes to six, whatever the state of the game, she would turn on the wireless and we all sat silently listening to the weather forecast. 'Attention all shipping in Rockall, Fastnet and Shannon. Winds slow to moderate, force 2 rising Force 3. Winds east, veering to nor'-nor' east.' The tones of the announcer were solemn and measured. The names of the shipping areas, Rockall . . . Malin . . . Faeroes . . . Hebrides . . . Cromarty . . . inspired pictures of unknown islands in unknown seas, surrounded by birds and shipwrecks. Rachel's brothers, Uncle Nicholas and

Uncle Robin, were both in the Navy, serving on armed merchant-cruisers protecting the supply convoys across the Atlantic. 'Viking, Cromarty, Forth, Tyne . . . Winds moderate, rising to Gale Force 6 . . .'. Our daddy Michael, whom I barely knew and of whom Corin had no memory, was an ordinary seaman.

When I began to write this autobiography, Uncle Nicholas lent me a scrapbook my grandmother Beanie, Rachel and Nicholas' mother, had kept to record Uncle Robin's career as an actor. There is a photograph of Robin lying in a field with some friends, picnicking. Under it she wrote one word: 'Crisis'. Then, just below she added, 'Sunday, September 3rd 1939, England and France declared war on Germany.' There is a photograph of Robin's first ship, HMS *Salopian*, and near it are news articles about Dunkerque, where Robin assisted the evacuation of the British troops from Normandy. One report stated that HMS *Turquoise* to which Robin had been transferred had been hit.

Robin was wounded and suffered a nervous breakdown and shell-shock. When he was given sick-leave he came up to Cousin Lucy's to recover. I remember a tall man with blue eyes, a wide smile and red hair, playing a hilarious game with us in the fields at the bottom of the garden where there was a small hillock. 'Get *Down* you dirty rascal!' Vigorous shoving followed, and the challenger either toppled the king, or found herself rolling down the hillock. He was still at Whitegate when Michael and Rachel visited us for Christmas Day.

It had snowed heavily and we had a huge Christmas tree in the hall. Rachel dressed me in woollen trousers and gaiters and a pair of red wellington boots, and we set off for a walk down the middle of a country road, deep in snow, to Birchyfields. Rooks were cawing in the birch trees which lined the drive leading to the house where my grandfather, Grandpa Eric, had lived as a boy. He was then in Dartmouth, and I could tell that she was missing him. As we turned away she started singing to keep our spirits up –

> Good King Wenceslas looked out
> On the Feast of Stephen

Her voice was high and very sweet, quavering a little on the top notes when the page answers the king –

> Sire, he lives a good league hence,
> Underneath the mountain
> Right against the forest fence
> By St Agnes' fou-n-tain.

I thought her courageous and gallant, singing as we tramped through the snow. I didn't want to go home, I wanted this walk and her singing to last for ever so I stumbled and fell. 'Don't fall down again,' she said, 'or you'll be soaked through and we'll have to go home.' She was so sweet and loving as she picked me up and brushed the snow off that I fell down twice more, deliberately. And yet the last thing I wanted was to go home. How can you explain such contradictory actions when you're very young? Rachel did not slap me, she never would. I am sure she was upset that our last moments together for a long while ended with me doing the opposite of what she or I wanted.

On Boxing Day morning Rachel and Michael left, and soon after Robin went to join the destroyer HMS *Prince of Wales*. Grandmother Beanie, continued to paste photos in her scrapbook following Robin and the war. When the *Prince of Wales* was torpedoed off Malaya on 10 December 1941, the Admiralty sent a telegram written in pencil: 'Very glad to state your son Lieutenant E.J. Kempson RNVR safe'. But no more news was heard of Robin, and Beanie and Grandpa Eric lived in sorrow and suspense until one day in 1945, when a survivor, Stoker Farron, told them what had happened.

Robin had reached Singapore, and had begun commando work behind the Japanese lines, running motor boats through the mangrove swamps of Malaya to evacuate British soldiers. In mid-February 1942, he evacuated from Singapore in a tugboat as the Japanese were advancing. Two Japanese destroyers spotted the tugboat and fired. The skipper and Robin put the seriously wounded into a raft they made with lifebelts. But there were not enough lifebelts for Robin and an army officer, they were 15 miles from land, and Robin's right arm was useless for swimming as he had dislocated his shoulder some time before. Nevertheless, the two men struck out for land, Robin turning to wave and shout 'goodbye and good luck' to Stoker Farron, who had a belt. Stoker Farron and a friend made it to the shore and spent the rest of the war in a Japanese prisoner-of-war camp. Grandpa Eric had a small book printed in six copies to commemorate Robin. It has an epitaph from Homer's *Iliad*:

Hector, of all my sons the best beloved. Thou in thy life wert dear to the Gods and even in the doom of death they have shown care of thee.

Rachel's father, Grandpa Eric, as I first knew him, inspired awe. He was extremely tall and wore a monocle in his left eye. Sometimes, when he sat in a chair looking at Corin and me rather gravely, he would suddenly lift his left eyebrow and out would fly the monocle. His grave face would crease with mirth and he laughed, more of a shout than a laugh, until he cried. 'Do it again,' we pleaded, even more fascinated to see how he could keep the monocle in place than how he made it fly out. At some point during those early years, I remember him taking me out in a rowing boat down the River Dart in Devon. He moored the boat on a sandy bank, made me hunt for twigs, put a kettle of river water on to boil and made us both a cup of tea. He was famous for his skill with boats, especially the long, flat-bottomed punts. He and another old boatman who taught him were the only two people in England who could take a punt up the rapids of the River Wye at Simmons Yat, Rachel told us. He called Corin 'Bread and Butter' or 'Towser', and took us for walks which were runs for us. Like all the Kempsons he walked very fast and upright, never slowing his pace.

In the days when his family had lived at Birchyfields, Grandpa Eric's father had been bankrupted. So he left school and became a bank clerk, studying in his spare time for an engineering degree at Cambridge. He took jobs in a steelworks and a woollen mill, and for eight years he taught science at Rugby School. His favourite story from Rugby was about the housemaster's wife who used to order meat by telephone from the butcher's:

> '. . . and three pounds of your best mince, please.'
> 'Three pounds, ma'am? For the boys?'
> 'Not for the boys, of course. For the dogs!'

Grandpa Eric served in the First World War in Palestine, where he won the Military Cross, and then returned to teaching until, like many other teachers, he lost his job and had to take a post as a schools inspector. The salary was very low and there was hardly enough money to pay the rent for a tiny terraced house in Kew. He taught Rachel to drive a car, and at seventeen she left home to take a job as a companion to an elderly lady in Dorset. Then, in 1935, he got the post of headmaster at the Royal Naval College and moved to Dartmouth in Devon.

Simple physical descriptions and memories cannot convey the sort of man he was; and sometimes you do not know the people you are closely related to for many years. Rachel told us many stories about Eric, his life and his marriage. But I never felt I really knew him, until Uncle Nicholas lent me a box of small books and albums, amongst which I found a loose page from the *Pottery Gazette and Glass Trade Review*, dated October 1943. Eric had given a talk on the BBC Radio Home Service, and the trade magazine had printed it.

From the standpoint of an educationalist, Eric saw British society with its rigid class system as 'arch-conservative'. And as a socialist he was acutely aware of the enormous contrast between the living conditions of the rich and poor throughout the country. He realised how most working people were deprived of an academic education, while academics and industrialists, who knew nothing about labour at first hand, made decisions affecting the workers' lives.

Eric proposed a school curriculum in which half the time would be given to books, and half the time to practical work: 'The present one hour to art, one hour to music, one to carpentry is just so much time wasted for it is a sham. What is done on the practical side must be taught by those who really know.' He also proposed a compulsory period of National Service, 'with pay, of not less than three years. Labour by hand, or with machines, in factories, workshops, farms, mines, on the railways or at sea, to come between school and university . . .'.

Eric was one of the last honest descendants of Robert Owen, the English utopian socialist of the 1840s.

Where would my proposals lead us? To this: instead of over-academic public servants handing out what they are pleased to consider benefits to the common man – we should have the work done and controlled by men and women who knew it from the ground up. Conditions of work would be good, not because some politicians had a conscience, but because the best men and women were in the work and knew what was wanted and how to get it. Men would be good citizens not because they had attended a course in Civics, but because their work was worth doing, was well done and had made them happy.

But the Labour government he voted for at the end of the war did not share his views and devised an examination that streamed off the 'bright kids,' the 'academic' ones from the 'non-academic'. The latter were given technical courses for manual labour, while their 'academic' counterparts were groomed for college or university.

Thanks to Nurse Dulcie and Cousin Lucy I could read by the time I was four years old. My first book, *The Bird Talisman* by Henry Allen Wedgwood, was a gift from Lucy, inscribed to 'Vanessa, with Cousin Lucy's love, Xmas 1942'. Lucy was a Wedgwood, and Henry Allen was a grandson of the original Josiah Wedgwood, the master potter of Etruria, Stoke-on-Trent. If I look at the book now I can hear Lucy's kindly, rasping voice, and realise that her early influence on us as children, her books, her questions and her answers, spurred me on subsequently as I struggled through the boring hours of Janet and John and their wretched cats on mats in my reading primer. Children would undoubtedly learn to read much earlier, much faster and with real pleasure if the subject matter was not limited to lambs, bad wolves or three dreary little pigs.

In 1943 Corin and I and a new nurse, called Kathleen Randall, returned from Cousin Lucy's and Bromyard to London on the train. The worst of the blitz was over, though bombing still continued and Rachel, who was pregnant, wanted us to be together in a new flat in Putney. We had sandwiches for the journey, a thermos flask of tea, home-made biscuits, and best of all a new book, a present from Rachel. As the train started to move I opened my book and began the most enthralling story I had ever read – John Bunyan's *Pilgrim's Progress*:

Then said Apollyon, 'I am sure of thee now', and with that he had almost pressed him to death, so that Christian began to despair of life. But as God would have it, while Apollyon was fetching of his last blow, thereby to make a full end of this good man, Christian nimbly reached out his hand for his Sword and caught it, saying, 'Rejoice not against me, O mine Enemy! When I fall I shall arise'.

As children we never went to the cinema and did not have television. There were no entertainments like *Star Wars* to inspire us with mighty exploits. There was only war, and the reports of the war which we heard each day on the radio with no explanation being offered of why we were at war nor what Fascism was. *Pilgrim's Progress* provided me with a perspective on the world of 1943, and a longing that the good – my father and my uncles – would triumph over the bad, Hitler and the Fascists.

We came home to our parents' new flat in Putney overlooking the Thames. The London sky was filled with great grey barrage balloons with ears like giant mice. At night the searchlights criss-crossed the sky on the other side of the river. We reached our flat on the sixth floor by lift. In the nursery Corin and I shared was a rocking-horse with a real horsehair tail. Our next-door neighbour was a kind old lady who would occasionally beckon us into her flat for a tiny brick of delicious vanilla ice-cream, or a square of Cadbury's milk chocolate. But then, out of the blue I fell ill.

'Have you got a mate?' asked a young girl's voice. I guessed she was about my age, six years old. Where was it coming from? I was alone in an isolation ward in the Middlesex Hospital, covered with scarlet fever. On 8 March my sister Lynn was born, and I looked forward to a visit, but no, 'I'm afraid you might infect her,' said the nurse, and it seemed my mother couldn't come for the same reason. The days were long and lonely, so the voice from the other side of the wall cheered me up. 'What's a mate?' A friend, she explained, someone you can share everything with. She told me she was a real cockney, born within the sound of Bow bells, and she taught me 'Knees up Mother Brown' and how to speak in cockney rhyming slang. 'Do you know any songs?' she asked. I sang a verse of 'Good King Wenceslas'. 'Do you know this one?' she asked. Her clear, loud voice rang through the thin partition, Vera Lynn's song –

> 'There'll be blue birds over
> The white cliffs of Dover
> Tomorrow, just you wait and see.'

And then she left. And just as I was about to go home, as I sat waiting on the edge of my bed with my suitcase packed, the matron looked at my face and said 'What's that?' She brought a doctor, who looked at my chest and told me to get undressed again. He was sorry to say I wouldn't be leaving for a few days yet, I had chicken-pox.

The days seemed longer than ever, but one afternoon I heard a voice from the room behind my pillow. A man's voice. I was wildly excited, and now that my cockney friend had taught me not to be afraid of talking to strangers, I lost no time in introducing myself. He was an airman. I sang him my new song 'The White Cliffs of Dover' and told him all about myself. I drew pictures for him and wrote him letters. 'I wish you could see them.' 'That's no problem,' he said. He made a gap in the partition, with his clasp knife, of about two inches so we could see each other and exchange drawings. He was dark and even more handsome than I had imagined. When his wife came to visit he showed her the gap and then closed it so that they could have some privacy. I was filled with jealousy and talked all through her visit. She was very kind and understanding and didn't lose patience even when I kept interrupting her with: 'Are you going yet?' 'Not yet.' 'Isn't it time for you to leave?' 'Not yet.'

One night matron came into my room before we had time to close the gap. I knew that the thin line of light would give us away and I tried everything I knew to distract her attention. But she was not to be fooled. The panel was nailed up and the next day my airman was discharged. Later that afternoon, still covered in scabs, I was pronounced free of infection. My homecoming was worth waiting for. My baby sister was in her crib. That evening I watched, fascinated, as Rachel breast-fed her, amazed that a tiny creature could suck so strongly. Corin, at three years old, had been very put out by her arrival, and still showed little or no interest in her. For a while, he had hidden under the dining-room table, in protest. At length he was persuaded to come out and cradle her in his arms. 'Be careful,' Nanny said, 'you mustn't drop her.' 'Would it matter?' he asked.

Michael had bought me a two-storey doll's house and painted it himself, with hollyhocks and delphiniums round the front door and red and white roses trailing up beside the windows. The oil paints made the roses stand out, so that you could touch their petals.

Michael called me 'Van' at this time. Later it was 'Vanessa', or sometimes 'V'. At six I was already tall for my age, and my hair was long and straight like Tenniel's illustrations of Alice. I longed for those times when we could be together, he and I, reading, talking, or painting, which was our special hobby. But although he had been discharged from the Navy with a wounded arm which wouldn't straighten properly, his work, on tour in the theatre, kept him away from home for long stretches of time. But about this time Michael did something for me which established a close bond between us for ever. One morning I was whining to Nanny Randall, 'I'm bored, I've got nothing to do.' 'I'll teach you to be bored,' said Nanny, who never stopped working from the moment she got up in the morning until she went to bed at night, and didn't understand the word 'bored'. She picked me up, put me in my room, and shut the door. 'That'll teach you to be bored.' My father surreptitiously opened the door a crack. Then he went to the piano and started to play some beautiful music. Nanny Randall must have had built-in radar. She stomped out of the kitchen, slammed my door shut, and I heard her ticking off my father. I knew she was right to teach me a lesson, but none of that mattered now. I glowed with the music and the knowledge that Michael had played it for me. From then on I adored him.

I first saw him on the stage when I was five, in a melodrama, *The Duke in Darkness*. I cannot recall much of the story, but I vividly remember that at the end they threw Michael's dead body over a parapet at the back of the stage. Michael took me back stage before the performance and showed me the mattresses he fell on, so that I shouldn't be frightened.

I loved going to the theatre, but best of all I loved pantomime. For a Christmas treat Granny Margaret, Michael's mother, had promised to take us to a pantomime and for months before the planned outing we lived in a charged state of excitement and anticipation. Granny Margaret had begun her career in pantomime in the chorus of *Babes in the Wood* at Aberdeen, though no one would have known it. She never appeared in public without a dead fox on her shoulders, and had a very deep, loud voice. She called Nanny 'Nurse' and me 'Van', the only person besides Michael to do so. But when she started life on the stage she was 'Daisy' Scudamore.

Daisy Scudamore left her home in Portsmouth at the age of fifteen to try her luck in the theatre. Her mother wept, and her father William Scudamore, a shipwright, cursed her as she left and said 'Thank God you're no daughter of mine!' In London she went straight to see an agent in Maiden Lane, who took one look at her and said 'So *you* are little Scudie.' He gave her the address of an actor-playwright-manager called Fortunatus Augustus Scuda-more, William's cousin. 'F.A.' lived in Barnes, and when he saw Daisy on his doorstep he threw his arms around her neck and cried, 'If you are not my daughter, then I don't know whose daughter you may be!' Daisy lived with F.A., his wife and his actor son Lionel for some years. She became his leading lady, and had some success at the theatre he managed in Mile End. But one day she made the mistake of siding with Lionel in an argument, and worse still she left the flat threatening she would not go in F.A.'s play that night. Next morning she returned to make her peace. She had of course not kept her threat to miss the performance the night before, but she knew she had hurt the old man. She knocked for a while without getting an answer and, growing alarmed, called the caretaker. They found F.A. on the floor. He had died of a heart attack having turned all her photographs to the wall, except one. To reach the last one he had needed a step-ladder. His body lay at the foot of the ladder.

By the time Corin and I knew Granny Margaret she had become Mrs J.P. Anderson, wife of a wealthy retired tea-planter, although she was still a working actress. Michael never told her full story in print – probably because he wasn't entirely sure how much was truth and how much invention – but he often spoke of it to Corin and me.

When I was eight, Granny Scudamore took us to see *Cinderella*. Evelyn Laye played Prince Charming in a dazzling white satin coat. Suddenly a giant tea-cup descended from the flies with a song printed on it, and Prince Charming invited all the little girls to come up on to the stage and join her in the chorus. Cinderella asked for all the little boys. Corin was very brave and dashed down the aisle to be with Cinderella. I was longing to follow but I did not dare. Then we all sang the chorus, which was something like 'Oh I do like a nice cup of tea, oh, I do like a nice cup of tea!' In between the scenes an act drop was lowered and a long stream of little boys and girls ran out in front of the footlights. The Terry Juveniles performed three numbers during the show. In one they were dressed as snowballs, tap-dancing on the tea-trays they carried on. Their finale was an amazing display of handsprings and double somersaults. At the end all the little Juveniles lined up in a series of back-bends to form an arch and the lead girl, after the customary tension-building drum roll, leapt over their ten bodies, landing with a somersault and a flourish on the other side. My hair stood on end with excitement and envy. I longed to be a Terry Juvenile. I never thought, however, that I might work in the theatre until my seventh birthday. Rachel had given me a book called *Curtain Up* by Noel Streatfield, which told the story of three children who were separated from their parents during the war and were sent to drama school. It had never occurred to me that there were schools where children could learn ballet, acting and acrobatics. I found out there was one called the Italia Conti Stage School for Children, and it became my aim to enrol at it.

When the V-1 rockets started we had to queue up at Fulham town hall for our gasmasks. For Lynn there was a gas cradle. She was laid inside and the lid closed down over her so that she resembled a miniature Snow White through the glass window. Corin had a gas mask like Mickey Mouse. Nanny growled and prowled like a bear in her mask. Thinking it was very funny we never asked what the masks were for. The doodlebugs and the later V-2s thumped down day and night. We saw strange men with yellow diamonds sewn on the backs of their brown overalls clearing away the rubble in the streets. Nanny said they were 'internees'.

In 1944 Nanny took Corin, Lynn and me away from London again and back to Herefordshire, this time to a small cottage in Bromyard which belonged to another Kempson, Cousin Joan. There was a wireless, and every afternoon at five o'clock a programme called 'Children's Hour'. 'Uncle Mac', David and Elizabeth became almost as familiar to me as my own relations, and soon I had another ambition: to broadcast on 'Children's Hour'. Not long after the war, Corin and I wrote to Uncle Mac at the *News Chronicle* where he had a regular column, asking for an audition. He replied that he would be happy to see us. He was a nice old man – not unlike Grandpa Eric, except that he wore an eye-patch instead of a monocle – his voice so uncannily similar to that familiar voice on the wireless that it was like talking to a ventriloquist. He explained that he no longer broadcast himself, except on special occasions, but he arranged for us to audition for 'Uncle' David. We both duly auditioned – mine was a piece in several languages and accents to show my versatility – but for some reason best known to themselves 'Children's Hour' never employed me, though they gave Corin a small part in a Christmas play.

During this second long visit to Bromyard we made firm friends with a ten-year-old boy called Stephen Croft. His parents had nothing to do with the theatre, but Stephen was even more theatre-struck than I. He had a magnificent model theatre that he had made himself, with tiny electric light bulbs for footlights and numerous different stage designs. He started our drama group. There were three members: Stephen, the dramatist and director; Corin and myself, the actors. Our first production was called 'Shipwreck'. We rehearsed in the playroom on the top floor at Cousin Lucy's house 'Whitegate' and charged a halfpenny admission, all proceeds to be sent to the Merchant Navy Appeal Fund. My first entrance as a shipwrecked lady began with a long speech enumerating the possessions I had saved from the wreck. I stepped forward into the middle of the room, lost my nerve, forgot my list, and came to a dead halt. Stephen prompted me, but I was paralysed before the dozen or so spectators sitting in rows a few feet away from me and looking me straight in the eye. Stephen stepped in front of me, furious. 'Ladies and gentlemen, I must apologise to you. We must start the play all over again. Vanessa's gone and bished it all.'

We met regularly to discuss further dramatic presentations. Eventually I claimed my right to take my turn as group dramatist. I wrote some scenes, which the boys obligingly rehearsed. I enjoyed this experience so much I wanted to prolong it. 'The play's not finished yet. There are a few more scenes I forgot to tell you about. We'll rehearse them tomorrow.' The next day we ran through my material very quickly, so I started to improvise the outline of what was to follow, but the boys had got my measure and told me firmly enough was enough. From the age of six or seven onwards I developed my passion for acting as Corin and I were dependent on plays as our main form of entertainment. When we didn't actually put on a play for an audience we rehearsed and performed for ourselves, but usually we would find some friends or relatives to watch us.

While we were staying at Cousin Joan's Corin and I attended a class which included the sons and daughters of the local doctor, chemist, vicar and grocer. The local Bromyard parents had obtained a large school room in a country house, about three miles outside Bromyard, to which Westminster School had been evacuated. Corin and I walked to the schoolroom every day, setting off from her cottage across fields, through some woods, and across a plank that spanned a narrow stream, some six feet below. I was always frightened and Corin had to encourage me over to the other side. It is only now, as I write, that I recall Lillian Hellman's story about crossing the stream with her friend Julia. Corin was my Julia.

The governess who ran the class was a sadist. Her daily target, the doctor's eldest son, was a quiet, gentle and rather plump boy. He suffered dreadfully from her bitchy sarcasm and occasional raps with a ruler. I had already read *Jane Eyre* by Charlotte Brontë, and this woman reminded me of the cruel Miss Scatcherd who killed poor Helen by making her stand in the wind and rain at Lowood, the charity school.

In 1944 I read another terrible story but this one was true. It appeared on the front page of Nanny's Sunday newspaper, the *News of the World*. First I saw the picture of two small boys, Neil and Terry, aged nine and seven. They were evacuees from London who had been cruelly beaten by the farmer they were billeted on. They worked in the fields for the farmer. He starved them, beat them, accused them of being lazy, then punished their 'laziness' by locking them up at night in the pig-sty. Desperate with hunger, they went into the fields and scraped up some of his turnips and ate them. The farmer found out and beat them with a strap so badly that Neil, the elder boy, died.

More than twenty years later, in 1970, I was reading to my daughters, Tasha and Joely, from a children's comic. One story was about a group of children who were evacuated to a farmer during the war and were forced to work in the fields. I realised that Neil and Terry were not so exceptional, and that many children like them must have been forced into labour gangs. Later still, in 1982, I was talking with a Glasgow bus driver about the Thatcher government's cheap labour scheme, the Youth Training Scheme, for unemployed school-leavers. This scheme meant hard labour at menial, unskilled work at £27.50 wages, for five to six days' full work and no job at the end of six months. As the driver looked about forty-five years old, I asked him if he knew anything about child labour during the war. 'Oh, yes,' he said, and told me his story:

'I'll never forget it, it was scandalous. It happened to thousands of working-class children from the cities. It happened to me and my brother.

17

We were evacuated from Clydeside. We were herded with loads of kids into a church hall. We were told to stand in lines for inspection. The farmers came in and went down the lines inspecting us, to select the boys they wanted to take on. One farmer came up to my brother and started pinching his arms and legs to feel his muscles. Then he opened his mouth and looked at his teeth. Then he said 'I'll have him.' He said he didn't want me. I was too small. I began bawling and hollering because I didn't want to be separated from my brother. I made such a din, I wouldn't stop until he gave in, walked away, and chose another lad instead of my brother. All that was Ernest Bevin. He was in charge of that.'

When Winston Churchill formed his wartime National Coalition government in 1940, he asked Ernest Bevin, Chairman of the Trades Union Congress, to become Minister of Labour. Bevin and his Labour Party colleagues drew up special regulations. It became a crime for a trade unionist to call for a strike, or organise against the regulations covering hours, conditions or wages. That didn't stop the strikes. But the conditions were harsh, basic democratic rights were denied and some of those who organised went to prison. Many larger farmers and landowners made handsome profits from the conscripted labour, as did the coal-owners and the steel and shipyard owners. That is the other side of the war, the history of these working-class families and their children. Many books have been written about the war, but I have yet to read one that tells their story.

One wet afternoon Corin and I walked with Nanny and Lynn, who was in her pram, down Bromyard High Street into the market square. It was raining hard. A van was parked with its back doors open and a huge crowd had gathered round. We went closer. Inside the van was what looked at first like a window. In the window, or beyond it, we could see more crowds. Suddenly, we saw a woman in a headscarf rush up to a soldier and embrace him. Then her face became very large and she turned her eyes in our direction and wiped away her tears. She waved at us. Corin and I waved back. Nanny laughed, and so did some of the others standing by. 'It's a film,' Nanny said. 'There's nobody there. It's just a newsreel.' The war was over; as was our stay in the country. We returned to London, and our parents.

# 2

An enormous heap of boxes, broken furniture and planks was piled up in the middle of the road in front of our flat in Putney. At night the bonfire was lit, sending sparks and smoke flying past our sixth-floor windows, while down below small figures ran to and fro, clapped their hands, and threw more fuel on the flames. No more searchlights criss-crossing the skies, no more sirens, no more bombs. In the Underground, wooden bunks still lined the platforms and posters warned us to beware of idle talk. But in the narrow back streets behind our block of flats home-made banners of white cotton were slung from house to house, bunting everywhere, and above the front doors – 'WELCOME HOME BILL', 'WELCOME HOME TED'.

I read the headlines in Nanny's *Daily Mail*: 'HIMMLER SUICIDE'. Nanny had forbidden me to read it and stuffed the paper under the seat of her armchair, but as soon as her back was turned I pulled it out and read the whole story. The chief of the Nazi Gestapo had been captured but had committed suicide, biting on a cyanide capsule. The concentration camps were being liberated in Poland and Germany. Thousands upon thousands of starving men, women and children, tens of thousands of dead, starved bodies. Rooms full of spectacles, shoes and hair. Later I read that 6 million Jews had been murdered by the Nazis and I was filled with horror. I began to perceive the real world I lived in: 450,000 British and Commonwealth soldiers, sailors and airmen killed in the war; 300,000 Americans; 7.5 million fighters from the Soviet Union, killed on the battlefields. Many times more civilians. I have heard people say 'numbers don't mean anything to me' and I could never understand why. Those numbers were human beings who had once been alive like me, with their families, their homes, their hopes for the future. All were gone. The artist Feliks

19

Topolski, a close friend of Michael and Rachel's, came back from the USSR. His war sketches showed something of the fantastic hunger and fortitude of the Russian men and women. He told us about the 900-day siege of Leningrad, and the families who ate wood and paper to keep alive.

With thousands of other families we lined the London streets or watched from our windows as the parades went past, and waved when Churchill appeared in his siren suit. Churchill's leadership had won the war. So said the *Daily Mail*, and now a grateful nation must reward his Conservative Party with a landslide victory in the general election. Without a doubt I was very much influenced by Nanny's *Daily Mail* and her worship of Churchill. But the soldiers returning from the war had longer memories. They were determined never to return to the mass unemployment and misery of the 1930s, and it was their determination for change which prevailed over all the patriotic fervour. They knew that the National government had brought in the means test in 1931, and that a National government under Churchill in 1945 would do the same or worse at the first opportunity. And so the National government had to give way to a general election which neither the Conservatives nor the Labour Party wanted. The Communist Party was also opposed to an election. Their leading theoretician, Palme Dutt, was arguing in April 1945 that Churchill's Coalition government should continue to rule 'in the transition years following victory in Europe'. Only when it was certain that an election would take place in July did the party change sides and campaign for a Labour victory.

'And how are you voting?' The woman on the pavement had her car door open, ready to offer us a lift to the polling station. 'Labour,' said Rachel. I clutched her hand more tightly. I knew it was the wrong answer. Sure enough this woman's angry red complexion became redder still beneath her blue-rinsed grey hair, and she pushed her face to within a few inches of Rachel's, arguing furiously. I felt embarrassed that Rachel would not agree to vote Conservative. Not because I thought she was wrong, but because the Tory woman was so intensely annoyed with her and I didn't want my mother to be unpopular. The *Daily Mail* was predicting a landslide victory for Churchill. But notwithstanding the barrage of Fleet Street propaganda, and with only one newspaper, the *Daily*

*Herald*, supporting the Labour Party and presenting its policy, the landslide went the other way, against Churchill and for a 100 per cent Labour government.

Labour won 396 seats out of 640. The National Health Service was established so that medical care was provided free by the state. A massive housing programme was launched, and the locally elected councils, mostly Labour, were given a statutory obligation to find accommodation for every family in the area. The coal mines were nationalised. So were the railways, steel, electricity, gas, civil aviation, cable and wireless communications. None of this amounted to socialism. The old coal-owners were paid a hefty £600 million in compensation. All the nationalised industries were burdened with debt. The drug companies remained in private ownership and could charge the National Health Service whatever they wanted for their pills and their medicines. Still for millions of families this Labour government seemed like the beginning of a new era.

Lindsay Anderson, the film director, told me that he was in the Army, stationed in India, when news of the Labour victory came through. He and his friends ran up an improvised red flag over their headquarters. Working class families cheered when the National Health Service was announced. Miners hoisted the red flag over the pits on Vesting day, the day when nationalisation came into force, in 1947.

Michael voted Labour. He never talked about politics with me or Corin until the last years of his life. But he must have noticed how heavily influenced I was by the Tory press – the *Daily Mail*, the *News of the World* and the *Sunday Empire News* – and he attempted to interrupt this process. 'Have you read this?' he asked one morning, thrusting a copy of the liberal *News Chronicle* at me. 'Try this for a change.' At other times, when I would thoughtlessly echo some snobbery or prejudice from a schoolfriend's Tory parents, he would stare at me and say rather sharply. 'What do you mean "uneducated people"? Why haven't they been educated?' And once, to my horror, after I had made some particularly obnoxious remark he pushed his plate away and declared he would not sit with me if I really meant what I had just said. In his library were several pamphlets by Lenin, and one in particular, *Socialism and War*, had been heavily underlined and annotated. One day, Corin and I were looking through his collection of

21

gramophone records and we came across a 10-inch 78 r.p.m recording with 'Workers' Music Association' on the label. ' "A New World Will Be Born" – Michael Redgrave'. His singing was strong and clear, beautifully phrased, but it was the song and its chorus about the new world which would see the end of exploitation and suffering that puzzled and amused us. We must have played it for the fourth time, very loudly, when Rachel came in and asked us to turn it off. 'Don't play that, for Heaven's sake. It'll upset Daddy.' 'Why?' 'Don't ask him. It'll only upset him.'

Why would he be upset? I couldn't understand why he should not want to talk about it. I often wanted to ask him, but remembered what Rachel had said, and I didn't. We talked about everything under the sun, but not that. Later, when I joined the anti-nuclear protest movement in the 1960s, I couldn't understand why he wouldn't discuss that or why he began to tremble as he urged me, slowly and quietly, to concentrate on my acting. Only in the last years of his life, after his long struggle with Parkinson's disease had finally forced him to give up full-time work in the theatre, so that he could start again the autobiography he had left unfinished years before, only then did he begin to speak about his political experiences. The reasons for his silence and his fears, as he explained them, were of central importance in shaping his life, and mine.

Like so many artists of his generation, who grew up in the 1930s, his political horizons were dominated by the menace of Fascism, the horrors of Nazi Germany, and the defeat of the Spanish revolution. At university, many of his friends were members or supporters of the Communist Party. Guy Burgess designed the set for his production of J. M. Barrie's *The Admirable Crichton*. Anthony Blunt, a postgraduate art historian, was his co-editor for a literary journal, *The Venture*. Though he never joined the Communist Party, he saw it as the only hope for defeating Fascism. Once, reading through a book of his press cuttings and Rachel's from the pre-war period, I found an interview in which he called himself a 'red hot socialist'. No doubt the expression was the interviewer's, not Michael's. But he was certainly a socialist.

In September 1940, whilst he was waiting for his call-up papers, he was sent a petition from the People's Convention for a People's Government. It consisted of a six-point programme and was published in the *Daily Worker*, the newspaper of the British Communist Party, on 28 September. These were the six points:

22

1. Defence of the people's living standards.
2. Defence of the people's democratic and trade union rights.
3. Adequate air-raid precaution, deep bomb-proof shelters, rehousing and relief of victims.
4. Friendship with the Soviet Union.
5. A people's government, truly representative of the whole people and able to inspire the confidence of the working people of the world.
6. A people's peace that gets rid of the causes of war.

Michael thought the petition a 'good socialist document', and signed. He was not against war with Fascist Germany. A war to defeat the Nazis – yes. But as to Britain's aims in the war, as to what the war was *for*, that was a different question. The petition's first three demands were very popular, because so far little attempt had been made by the wartime government to protect the people. It was only after a popular outcry that they were allowed to use the Underground stations to shelter against air raids. The fifth and sixth demands seemed to accord with his hopes, as a socialist, for the kind of world that might be built after the war.

He and Rachel attended a number of meetings, and he sang in a concert to raise funds for the Convention. It must have been about this time that he recorded 'A New World Will Be Born' for the Workers' Music Association, which became the campaign song for the Convention. Two more points were added to the programme: nationalisation of the banks and basic industries, and national independence for India. Michael agreed wholeheartedly with both. In the last week of February 1941, he received a letter from the British Broadcasting Corporation asking him to come to Broadcasting House for an interview. A senior executive and a BBC solicitor told him that the governors had decided that those who supported the People's Convention should not be employed any more by the BBC. 'They asked me if I would write a letter to the organisers of the Convention withdrawing my support and send a copy to the BBC. I replied that my personal views were none of their business,' he wrote in the *News Chronicle*. 'Of course I didn't write any such letter. I asked them directly if this meant that I should not receive another BBC contract and they replied that this was so.'

When this story, and Michael's letter, were published on the front page of the *News Chronicle* on 5 March, Lesley Howard and other actors working at the Denham film studios wrote a resolution denouncing the BBC's ultimatum. Altogether twelve artists had been banned. Rachel, as loyal to Michael as she would be to Corin and me many years later, went to several protest meetings. One of these, called by the Council for Civil Liberties, was attended by Edith Evans and many other artists. The speaker, E. M. Forster, told the BBC that he was immediately cancelling two contracts for radio talks in protest against the ban. Ralph Vaughan Williams, the composer, wrote to the BBC that since they were refusing to play any music by Alan Bush, he was withdrawing permission for one of his new works to be broadcast.

The BBC was unmoved: 'The policy of the BBC is not to invite any person to the microphone whose views are opposed to the national war effort.' But the protest was so vehement and widespread that Winston Churchill made a statement to the House of Commons on 20 March that the BBC had withdrawn its ban on Michael and his co-signatories. Michael was profoundly shaken, not so much by the ban, or threats that his film contract might be in jeopardy, but by the nature of the People's Convention itself. The more he argued in support of the Convention's programme, the less he found himself able to defend it. 'The more I thought about the People's Convention, the more ambiguous it seemed. What was its attitude to the War? What would it advocate supposing we were invaded by Germany? How could one answer the charge that it was a Communist Party front, on orders from Moscow, following the line of the Molotov–Ribbentrop pact?'

The programme of the People's Convention was in fact thoroughly equivocal, and the reason for the equivocation was the Stalin–Hitler non-aggression pact, signed in Moscow on 23 August 1939. Stalin undertook to provide huge quantities of raw materials for the Nazi war machine, in return for a promise of non-intervention in Finland and the Baltic States and a treaty for the partition of Poland. German Fascism was greatly fortified by the pact, militarily and politically. The Soviet Union was terribly weakened. Stalin's confidence that the treaty would protect the Soviet Union against attack proved to be criminally light-minded. Communist parties everywhere were completely compromised. Obedient to Moscow's orders, they opposed the war with

Germany, whilst still appealing to the instincts of those, like Michael, who wanted to fight capitalism and Fascism.

One of Michael's friends who was a member of the Labour Party told him that the Communist Party would drop the People's Convention like a hot potato the moment they had no use for it. Michael sought reassurance from a friend in the CP. Would they do such a thing? 'Probably,' said his friend 'and so what? Why shouldn't they?' News of his worries and his questions must have reached the CP leadership, and a meeting was arranged with D. N. Pritt at his country house outside Reading. Pritt was a successful barrister, a King's Counsel, and a well-known apologist for Stalin's regime in the Soviet Union. He had reported the Moscow trials for the Labour weekly *New Statesman*, describing them as an impeccable model of socialist justice. He was charming, relaxed, talkative. The Dean of Canterbury, he said, had also had his doubts, but was 'still staunch'. Probably, when all this commotion had 'blown over', Michael would be awarded the Order of Lenin. As to Michael's fear that the CP would drop the People's Convention, when it seemed opportune to do so, he too replied, 'well, so what?'

The *Daily Worker* published a reply to Michael's letter: 'The People's Convention is not a "stop the war" movement. It is not a movement for a deal with Hitler or for "peace at any price". All supporters of the People's Convention are irreconcilably opposed to Fascism or to any victory of Fascism . . .'. The last sentence was true. Yet the statement as a whole was a lie. The People's Convention was *based* upon a deal with Hitler. Its *raison d'être* was the Stalin–Hitler pact; and it was clear that the Communist Party was *not* calling for the defeat of Fascism.

On 16 March Michael wrote in his diary:

To the Royal Hotel for Convention. A long depressing day, full of disappointment and dismay. I can see very well why the movement is charged with revolutionary defeatism. Everyone who speaks, airs a grievance. . . . I long several times to get up and say, 'But what about the War? What is our attitude to the possibility of defeat? Friendship with the USSR certainly – but England must do better than that.'

Politically, Michael was completely undermined. The programme of the People's Convention was a complete falsification, a parody of revolutionary defeatism, the policy first advanced by Lenin and the Bolsheviks in the First World War. Against all those 'socialists' who called on the workers to support 'their' government, join the Army and win the war, so that socialism could be built 'after the victory', Lenin and the Bolsheviks said: 'This war is not our war. The enemy is at home. Turn the imperialist war into a civil war.'

The essential content of revolutionary defeatism is international, the political struggle to unite workers all over the world to overthrow capitalism. Without the strategy and perspective of the world socialist revolution, the People's Convention was a fraud. It could give no explanations to those, like Michael, who genuinely opposed Fascism, and who believed that the war was being fought against Fascism and therefore had to be supported.

On 22 June 1941 the Army of the Third Reich invaded Russia. From that day, as Michael had feared, the British Communist Party dropped the People's Convention and began mobilising support for the very same government they had said 'must go' only a few weeks before. Workers who fought for trade union rights and basic working conditions – as the programme of the People's Convention had demanded they should – were denounced as Trotskyists who were sabotaging the war effort.

This was why the Communist Party opposed the demand for a general election in 1945 in favour of a continuation of the National Coalition government led by Churchill. D. N. Pritt especially spoke out against those who called for the election of a 100 per cent Labour government. Michael and Rachel were among the millions that voted for that Labour government, but Michael never spoke on a public platform for socialism again.

# 3

A year after the war's end, in 1946, we moved from the flat in Putney to Bedford House on Chiswick Mall, the first house our parents ever owned. 'The Mall', as its inhabitants called it, was a long road of beautiful eighteenth-century houses overlooking the Thames. Swans swam down it at high tide in the spring and autumn, when the river overflowed its banks and flooded over the river gardens, the road, the front gardens, and down into the basements of the houses. Tugboats plied up and down the river, towing long lines of barges loaded with coal or steel girders, and there were pleasure boats in the summer. From our nursery window we could hear the commentary of the guide, through his loudspeaker, pointing out our house where 'Michael Redgrave, the film star' lived.

Round the corner from the Mall was the Cherry Blossom shoe-polish factory, and when the hooter went at half past four, scores of women in factory blue overalls and headscarves ran out of the gates and home down Devonshire Lane, where little children played in the gutter in bare feet. At the other end of the Mall was Miller's Bakery, where the men in white hats, their faces whitened with flour, lounged against the wall in the lunch breaks in summer-time, whistling at any girl who passed by. Further up the road, beyond the Upper Mall, was the Bemax factory, and at the bottom of our garden was the Griffin brewery of Fuller, Smith and Turner. The smell of hops poured over the garden from the brewery funnels, reminding me of the Herefordshire hop fields where we stood in the long lines of pickers on the Adams's farm every summer, giving a 'helping hand' for a few days.

Chiswick after the war was a Labour constituency. But Chiswick Mall, where I spent my childhood and teenage years, was home for well-to-do people in the arts and professions. Mr Edwards, at Red

Lion House, was the curator of the Victoria & Albert Museum. Next door were the Trevelyans; beyond, the Lousadas, Anthony Lousada and Jocelyn Herbert, the theatre designer; A. P. Herbert and his family; and at the further end of the Upper Mall, George and Sophie Devine. The world of my parents and their friends, that of the theatre, painting and music, dominated my early childhood, and the only hints of a world beyond were given to me by the Home Service on the radio, the *Daily Mail*, and our governess, Miss Glascot.

For a year after we moved to Bedford House, Corin and I walked a mile or so to the state primary school in Sutton Court Road. I was neither happy nor unhappy there, simply a fish out of water. I was far ahead of my class in reading and way behind in mathematics, and although I and my classmates tried we found little we could share in common. What I read and thought about struck no chord with them, and though at first it seemed that having a film star for a father might help, their interest waned when they realised I had seen no films to speak of and had no autographs of my own to exchange with theirs. I was lost and out of my depth in everything except reading. So Miss Glascot was found.

'School' became the vicarage, next door but one to our house. Now our classroom consisted of two tables placed end to end in a back room on the ground floor. Round the tables sat Corin and I, Matthew Guinness, Alec Guinness's son, the vicar's two sons, the Lousadas' two daughters, Caroline Westmacott, and at the head of the table, Miss Glascot of the Parents' National Education Union. Why this handle, with its initials PNEU should have stuck in my mind I have no idea, except that Miss Glascot made it sound impressive when she mentioned it from time to time by way of a credential. Whatever it was, it had in her a formidable exemplar. She taught us everything – English, French, history, mathematics, natural history, art and scripture.

Our history lessons in 1947 were based on an out-of-date illustrated text book, *Our Island Story*. We read about a fortunate island, Britain, whose history was made almost exclusively by its kings and queens, their generals, and latterly, to a degree, by their prime ministers. The task of the historian, and his illustrator, was to distinguish between the Good, the Bad, and the Ugly. There was 'brave' Boadicea, defying the Romans (neither Good nor Bad), and scything the legs of legionnaires not nimble enough to leap out of the way of her chariot. 'Courageous' Richard the Lionheart, the 'Bad' or 'Wicked' King John. 'Great' Queen Elizabeth, 'Unwise' and 'Autocratic' King Charles I, 'Tyrannical' Oliver Cromwell, and 'Merry' King Charles II. Young Queen Victoria, we noted, promised to be 'Good'. Early in her reign there were some signs of autocracy, but they were soon curbed by Prince Albert. Queen Victoria knocked at her husband's bedroom door one night, demanding entry. 'Who's there?' asked the Prince Consort. 'The Queen.' 'Who?' asked the Prince again. 'The Queen!' This exchange was repeated many times, with the Prince stubbornly refusing to open the door until at last she repented and said, 'Vicky.' Thereafter all was well. History consisted of stories such as these, punctuated by an occasional visit to a museum to look at the clothes, furniture, weapons and transport of the times we were studying.

But when it came to the Napoleonic wars, Miss Glascot cast aside the textbook and told the story in her own terms, which were dramatically different from those in *Our Island Story*. You would have expected her to revel in the victory of Nelson at Trafalgar, and of the 'Iron' Duke of Wellington at Waterloo. Quite the contrary. She was heart and soul pro-Napoleon. She made us weep with her description of Bonaparte going amongst his troops before a battle, fraternising with them, calling them by their first names, astounding them by his memory of each one, his family and his problems. How different from the brutal disciplinarian Wellington, whose troops were 'the scum of the earth'! Waterloo, in Wellington's words, was 'a damn close run thing'. In Miss Glascot's version it was a tragedy. How this neat, kind, punctilious, patriotic spinster came to cast aside her patriotism and embrace the cause of Napoleon and France we never knew, or thought to ask. Perhaps she had once fallen in love with a Frenchman. Perhaps some earlier generation in her family had shared Byron and Shelley's love for Napoleon in his revolutionary days. For the whole term devoted to her hero, we ceased, temporarily, to think as Little Englanders.

There were long nature walks, gathering specimens of yellow ragwort, campion and rose willow beside the pavements in the grounds of Chiswick Park. She taught us to take a blade of grass and, holding it between our thumbs, cup our hands and whistle through it. We learned how to draw a profile and then a three-quarter profile and, one thrilling day, how to mix a flesh-coloured tint with the waterpaints to make the painting of a face more lifelike.

Books were expensive and we didn't know about lending libraries. An elderly friend of Michael's gave me twenty-five massive annuals from her childhood: *Little Folks* dating from about 1880. There were long serial stories, competitions with prizes promised and long since awarded, scientific titbits and – always – news and stories about the crowned heads of Europe and their families. I was so hungry for reading I devoured them, burying myself in them day in and day out. In my thoughts I lived at the turn of the century. 'Bookworm', my brother called me. 'If you don't stop poring over that book you'll wear your eyes out,' said our Nanny. In fact, I already had. As a result of reading so much, often in bad light, by torchlight under my blankets at night and in the early mornings, I was already badly short-sighted.

From the time when Nanny Randall first stepped off the train at Bromyard station one sunny afternoon in 1943, she lived with us until she retired in 1961.

> Kathleen Randall
> Ran around the candle
> and couldn't find the handle.

She was born in the village of Mattishall near East Dereham in Norfolk, where her father George had been a small farmer and this is where she lived again when she retired. I never went to Norfolk until I stayed with her in her bungalow after her retirement, but long before that I had become more familiar with the names of its towns and villages from her stories than with any other county in England. Her story unfolded gradually, in episodes told many times over until we knew them by heart and loved them all the more for that.

When we had colds, flu or bronchitis, she would smash an onion with a spoon to extract the juice until her eyes poured with tears, then she mixed glycerine of thymol and some sugar into the juice and gave us a teaspoonful. She had false teeth, top and bottom, and was proud of them. Her teeth had been perfect until at twenty-one she went to the dentist and had a tooth drilled without an injection. 'I told him never again,' she said, and asked the dentist to remove all her teeth. She had a misshapen big toe which she had broken in an accident on a staircase. It had not been set properly and made her other toes bend, causing corns, and her shoes hurt every time she put them on.

Her first job had been as a nursery maid to a Norfolk gentleman who would wait on a landing on the back stairs and waylay all the kitchen maids and the nursery-maids. She told him she would 'soon put a stop to that', and resisted him so fiercely that he did stop. But he disgusted her so much that it had put her off marriage for ever. Her greatest day came with another family when she nursed four children back to health after an epidemic of diphtheria. She was still a nursery maid but the family doctor had told her employer, 'This one should be your head nurse,' and she was promoted to be in charge of the nursery. She loved all her children, especially those who were naughty and rebellious, but best of all she loved a boy born with Down's syndrome, and her saddest day was when he was taken away from her at the age of ten to be put in a home.

Much later, when I saw Shakespeare's *Henry IV Part I*, I recognised Nanny Randall in the extraordinary character of Falstaff, and again in Hotspur's furious description of a 'certain Lord'. She had absolute hatred and contempt for snobbery, for anyone who gave themselves airs and graces. 'Who does he think he is? Lord Muck?' On the subject of any strike she would mutter through clenched teeth, 'I'd put them up against a wall and shoot the lot of them,' echoing the political sentiments of the gentry she had worked for all her young life. She sang when she was contented and clenched her teeth and looked extremely grim when she was upset. If we did not hear 'K-K-K-Katie, K-K-K-Katie, she's the only little girl that I adore' as she scrubbed the washing or made the beds, we knew she was troubled. She made skirts, knitted stockings and jumpers for us, mended and darned. She made us say the Lord's Prayer on our knees before we got into bed, with a 'God bless' for all our relations and a 'please make me a good girl, amen', but she never went to church herself, except at Christmas. 'I don't need some vicar to tell me how to pray,' she would say, and 'what makes him think he's better than I am?' She could not tolerate being 'bossed about', and had long feuds with every female member of her family, as well as with her best and oldest friend, who was also a nanny. During these feuds she would not speak to or see the relative or friend until they had apologised, which they usually did because she was implacable. 'That'll teach them to keep their nose out of *my* business.'

31

Once a week she had a night off to go to the local whist drive. She won many prizes – tea-sets, trays, tablecloths – and these were all kept in trunks for the day when she would retire to a bungalow. Her legs and painful feet had been up and down stairs every day of her working life, and they longed never to climb stairs ever again.

For much of our childhood Nanny was mother and father to us, as our parents were often away. She loved us all and was scrupulously fair with her favours and punishments, but she loved Lynn best, because she nursed her through her early illnesses and because, as the youngest, she missed her parents most and needed most love.

When she retired to her bungalow we promised to visit her often, but 'often', as it often does, meant sometimes. Once I was filming near Yarmouth and realising how near I must be to Mattishall, I took a taxi and knocked on her door, unannounced. She opened the door and for a second or two we didn't recognise each other. Her hair had lost all its perm, which she hated, and I realised she could no longer afford a perm except for special occasions.

She had a stroke and partly lost her memory, and in the hospital in Norwich they would sometimes find her in the corridor at night looking for Lynn. Lynn was then married and living outside Dublin with her husband, John Clark, and they found a hospital run by nuns, who looked after Nanny until she died, two days after her seventy-ninth birthday. I will never forget her, especially her hands, and if I picture her hands now, I want to cry and laugh. Cry, because they were so cracked and worn with hard work, and laugh because her big hands were so gentle and comforting.

Our first winter at Bedford House in 1946–7 was the coldest that anyone could remember. The newspapers called it the 'Big Freeze' – and blamed the Labour government for the fuel shortages, the universal rationing of clothes and food, and the harshness of Chancellor Sir Stafford Cripps's 'austerity'. In reality there was a measure of social justice in rationing, except that the rich could buy their way out of it through the black market. Michael had bought a little pre-war Morris 8 saloon car. He refused to drive himself – had never driven, in fact, since the first day of his marriage – but Rachel was a fine confident driver. And then the squat brown little Morris that Corin and I were so proud of disappeared and was replaced by a great, black gleaming Rolls-Royce, vintage 1936, with a window between the back seats and the front and a telephone to communicate with the driver. Off we drove to Richmond Park, scattering the sheep as the speedometer swept past 60 miles an hour and up into the nineties. Rachel was now in the passenger seat. The driver was Kenneth, the new chauffeur.

At a time when cinema audiences were larger than ever before, or since, Michael was making two or three films a year, earning a lot of money, saving none of it and employing, besides Kenneth, Birdie, the cook, Ella and Mary, the housemaids, Mr Owers, the gardener, all of them living at Bedford House. In 1947, Michael, with Rachel following shortly afterwards, went to Hollywood, and we children stayed at Bedford House and continued our lessons with Miss Glascot. Our life settled into a routine, a word I shall always associate with childhood where sometimes routine is comforting but more often it means waking in the morning with an awful foreboding that nothing will ever change. Lessons at the vicarage, walks to Chiswick Park, hair washed once a week.

Lynn is six years younger than I and nearly four years younger than Corin. As a small child she was very anaemic and suffered from many attacks of bronchitis, which made her breathless and unable to walk far. Her frailty combined with the gap between our ages meant that she could not share in the games Corin and I played together, or more truthfully, that we seldom wanted her to. My most abiding memory of Lynny as a child is of the little girl who trailed behind us crying 'wait for me'. Only when she too became a professional actress and had her second baby at the same time as I had my last did we transcend the gap and become close friends.

The vicar's sons were fun to play with, but apart from them we had no other friends, so Corin and I were dependent on one another's company for long hours of the day, and for entertainment we invented our own games or put on plays. There was one in particular, our favourite, which we called 'The Game'. We had begun it at Bromyard, during a long convalescence from measles, when we were forced to lie in bed day after day with the curtains drawn and nothing to look forward to except meal times and a teaspoonful of Dr Lewis's sticky pink medicine in between. Joe Louis, the Brown Bomber, was the heavyweight champion of the world, and Bruce Woodcock the British champion. We became their sons, who were somehow close friends, and we would swap stories about our supposed fathers and other boxers by the hour.

Perhaps these imaginary fathers made up for our own father's absence or perhaps it was an expression of the wartime alliance between British and American troops that we had heard so much about on the wireless. At any rate, the Game lasted until 1947 when a real fight took place, an eliminator for the world title, between Woodcock and another American heavyweight, Joe Baksi. The *Daily Mail*, and all the other papers were blowing the trumpet for the British contender, 'our' Bruce, and we confidently expected him to win, though we knew it would be a hard fight. But in the event Baksi pounded Woodcock into a terrible defeat, knocking him out in the seventh round. Worse still, we read the next day that Woodcock, who had boxed very bravely but was heavily out-punched, had suffered a broken jaw, probably in the fifth round, and had fought the last two rounds in agony. So boxing was out. We could no longer be the imaginary offspring of champions.

We created a new scenario, in which I was the President of the United States, and Corin the Vice-President. At any spare moment, in the garden, or on a walk, or at night-time in the bedroom we still shared, long and complicated adventures un-folded, with endless twists and turns. It makes me laugh now to wonder why on earth we selected such characters. Neither of us wanted to be these people, or knew anything at all about the lives of US Presidents; if we had we probably wouldn't have wanted to play the game at all. I guess we chose them because by assuming their identities we could fly all over the world and meet whoever we wanted to in our imaginations. Like the producers and writers of 'Dynasty', 'Falcon Crest' or 'Sins', we wanted a social milieu where we could be on a ranch one minute, or in New York the next, or could suddenly fly to Paris or Rome, run a newspaper or ride our own horses and win the Derby.

When Corin went away to boarding-school in Malvern Wells at the age of eight we were separated for the first time. He hated the school and a year later Dad took him away, but meanwhile I had started at a girls' day school called Miss Spalding's in Queen's Gate. 'Your husband Michael,' Miss Spalding told Rachel, 'is one of the intelligentsia.' But whatever the intelligentsia was in Miss Spalding's vision, it was not to be hoped that any of her pupils would ever join it. We were back in a routine I remembered well from the two terms I had spent at Putney High School during the war in between our stays in the country. The piano thumped, 'How many flowers are there that grow', we had prayers every morning and a hymn. In the afternoon we formed a crocodile, two by two, to walk from Queen's Gate to Kensington Gardens for netball and rounders, and in the winter we played lacrosse. Queen's Gate, like most schools, had a yearly school play. This, combined with my having always put on plays with Corin, particularly when we were in Herefordshire, meant that I had a lot of time throughout my childhood and teens to work at acting for the sheer fun of it with plenty of encouragement and without any pressure to succeed. I played the Tin Man in *The Wizard Of Oz* when I was twelve, and Mole in *Toad Of Toad Hall* when I was thirteen.

My best friend was a girl whose grandfather had been the foremost Persian scholar of his time. Maria Browne and her parents lived in the nineteenth rather than the twentieth century. Her books were the books of her parents and grandparents. She talked the same language, shared the ideas and used the same vocabulary as the public schoolboy in Rudyard Kipling's *Stalky & Co.* She used the same expression of contempt – Foo! – and said 'Nothin'', 'Somethin'', and 'Anythin'', without sounding the 'g'. Her parents' house was still and quiet, with heavy curtains, silver candlesticks, and volume upon volume of books, including every edition of *Punch* back to the 1860s, and all the stories of E. Nesbit.

Maria and I read E. Nesbit together, and passed our weekends building temples of heavy volumes of the *Encyclopaedia Britannica*, with silver candlesticks for pillars. She had read Samuel Butler's *Erewhon* and most of Walter Scott, and regularly got 'A's for her history, English, Italian and French tests, always coming first or second in the class. She left school after the school certificate exams to have special tuition for her entrance examination to Oxford.

Tasha Kalin, my other friend, was the daughter of a Russian aristocrat. Her father had been killed in the war and her mother had a small pension from a trust which had been set up for Tasha. They lived in a bed-sitting-room near the school. Tasha, like Maria, was brilliant academically. I adored her, and when Maria left she became my best friend until I left school, a year before she did, in 1954. Tasha introduced me to Tolstoy, and together we read *War and Peace* and *Anna Karenina*. Then she and her mother moved into a friend's house, where the son of the house had a treasure trove of American comics, and where food parcels would arrive, containing peanut butter, something I had never tasted before. We thought ourselves very 'advanced'. When our turn came to stand as candidates in the sixth form mock elections, we chose to stand as communists and quoted *Das Kapital* in our election address. We thought our lessons very boring. As indeed, many of them were, especially English lessons, from which I remember nothing but an abbreviated version of *David Copperfield*, and Robert Louis Stevenson's *Kidnapped*. Now and again things would liven up, when we came to a passage of dialogue and the teacher would ask us to read it aloud. 'Now who is good at accents?' she would ask, and my hand would shoot up, certain from hours of listening to the wireless that I could produce any accent required, Scots, Welsh, Irish, or what our teacher called 'a rough accent'. Dad had taken us to David Lean's film of *Oliver Twist*, and I could copy Robert Newton's accent as Bill Sykes, or Kay Walsh's as Nancy.

Clothes were a problem. We wore brown lisle stockings, 'sensible' skirts and jumpers in the winter, and ugly cotton dresses in the summer. At thirteen, we longed for boyfriends, and were very conscious of wanting to look better. I yearned to look like Genevieve Page, a young French actress who was appearing with my mother in a play at the St James's Theatre. She was the most beautiful and elegant woman I had ever seen. She wore a beret at an angle, and silk stockings which she would stroke her hand up, now and then, in a slow, gentle way. I thought this incredibly sophisticated and told Tasha. We howled with laughter as we sat stroking our wrinkled brown lisle stockings.

Together we went in search of life and adventure to a dance at the French Lycée, round the corner from our school. I wore a dress that a friend of my father's had sent from America. A blue and green silk skirt, a blue velvet bodice, and a blue and green stole. Tasha borrowed a skirt from her mother. I thought my dress was beautiful, and we came into the hall full of hope. A band was playing bebop, and we looked aghast at the girls, all in sweaters and wide skirts, all bebopping and jiving. I stood at the side of the room and no one asked me to dance all evening. Tasha was asked once – at least she wasn't wearing a stole.

It was 1950, and I was attending classes at the Ballet Rambert four times a week. My father had taken me to meet Madame Rambert when I was ten. He expected that I would want to act, sooner or later, and knew that I would be very tall, so he wanted me to learn ballet. But I had seen Margot Fonteyn dance the

Sleeping Beauty, and wanted, more than anything else, to be a ballerina. Now, at thirteen, I could graduate to Madame Rambert's own Saturday morning class. I worked extremely hard. I could dance well although I failed to do good work with the block shoes. Madame Rambert encouraged me and raged at others but I soon realised that she raged most at the student who was most promising. One day she was so furious with our stupidity she tore her green bead necklace off and threw it on the floor. The beads rolled everywhere and the boys ran to pick them up. I loved her for it. I admired and worshipped her angry, passionate fight for high standards, her emotive explanations of the content of the music and the gesture. She would make us repeat and repeat an exercise until we were exhausted, and then repeat it again.

Thanks to her training I became aware of the significance of physical movement and physical space, of extension and relations of bodies in space. Aware also of tempo, and that while the music may have a certain regular beat, the form of the movement will sometimes take a different, longer tempo than the beat that sustained it. While in my daily life I was round-shouldered and stooping, so much taller than my friends and self-conscious about my height, in class I stretched upwards and ceased to think about myself. One day Madame Rambert said, 'You are a tight little rosebud, but you are beginning to open.'

I thought I knew what she meant. I was beginning to be able to give myself over to the music and movements; they were opening me up and stirring me. I was filling with life. I had been almost entirely introspective and more interested in dreams of the past than the present. In early adolescence I was still very much in my own world, only leaving it when I thought about the boys I might meet and fall in love with. One Saturday morning after class we were chatting in the changing room, wiping down sweaty feet and pushing lamb's wool in between our toes to protect them from blisters in new, hard blocks. A new girl had joined the class. She had a part in a film, someone said. I looked along the bench, jealous, admiring and excited. She had large dark eyes and a wonderful big mouth with a beautiful smile. 'That's Audrey Hepburn,' my neighbour whispered. I went to see *The Lavender Hill Mob*, a marvellously funny film with Alec Guinness. There she was, in a scene about two minutes long, with one line of dialogue. A lovely girl with a tray, selling cigarettes: Audrey Hepburn's first appearance in a film.

At the age of fourteen I was as tall as my father when I stood on points, and he was taller than any of his friends. For some time I had resigned all hopes of becoming a prima ballerina assoluta, like my idol, Fonteyn. What Helpmann, what Soames could possibly lift my 5 foot 11 inches above their head, or catch my 9½ stone? For a little longer I clung to the hope that with a neatly regimented line, as in the vanguard of the Grenadiers when on parade, I might still pass muster at the end of the line of the back row of the *corps de ballet*. But that hope was soon extinguished. Overgrown, as my Nanny used to say. Too tall for anything. Too tall for Walt Disney. Not that Disney himself had objected. He had sent for my photograph for a film he was planning about Lewis Carroll's Alice, and I had made sure to put my height on the back so he wouldn't be disappointed when he saw me. But apparently he approved, and asked my parents to send me to Hollywood for a test. I was ready and eager to go, but it never happened, because at about that time I started to have black-outs and fainting fits, and also alarmed my parents by sleepwalking. Doctor Mary Nelson next door, a dear friend of Michael and Rachel, said it was because I had grown too fast and needed time to 'grow into' my height. No Hollywood. And now, no ballet. I should have to be an actress.

Michael and Rachel came to see me in school plays but the first time I remember being aware of them in the audience was when I was fourteen and played Saint Joan. Michael and Rachel loved my long Alice in Wonderland hair but I had finally persuaded them to let me have it cut quite short. I had my picture taken by Angus McBean, the photographer, in Saint Joan's trial costume with my newly-cut hair for a magazine article. We did three performances of Saint Joan, and my school friends loved it. They sent me bouquets and little notes. The morning after our last performance the headmistress gave a sermon at prayers saying that while we should all be very glad at success there must not be any lionising of particular pupils. Even with the glow of being in her words 'lionised', it was not until many years later when I was appearing with Michael in *A Touch Of The Sun* in 1959 that I can remember thinking that I really could act.

# 4

In 1951 Michael went to Stratford-upon-Avon to play Richard II, Hotspur in *Henry IV Part I*, the Chorus in *Henry V* and Prospero in *The Tempest*. Besides playing these four parts he directed *Henry IV Part II*. It must have been hard and often exhausting work, but Michael was exhilarated. I think he was happier during that season than at any other time.

Rachel, Corin and I went to join him for the opening of the season in April. It was the spring school holiday and we were to spend a whole week at Stratford. We began preparing for the visit months before, polishing our bicycles, which were to be sent up to Stratford by train, and fitting them with dynamos in case we needed to cycle home at night after the theatre. We saved our pocket money, making one purchase only – a map, one inch to a mile, on which we marked out every village within a 20 mile radius of Stratford.

We drove to Stratford in Rachel's Hillman Minx with its canvas hood which howled in the wind when you went at any speed. There were no motorways or bypasses then so the journey seemed interminable. Rachel stopped our boredom by telling us about her first season at Stratford, before the war, when she had played Juliet.

'Who was Romeo?'

'John Wyse. I adored him.'

'Did he adore you?'

'Not at all. He paid no attention to me at all. But I adored him just the same.'

And there was another actor she adored, a legendary barn-stormer called Anew McMaster who told her: 'You're very good in your tin-pot way but remember, it's me they want to see!'

Rachel, like all the Kempsons, has a loud infectious laugh and we laughed so much on that drive and were so giddy with exhilaration at the prospect of Stratford and seeing Michael that night in the dress rehearsal of *Richard II* that I pulled Corin's cap off his head and flung it out of the window. It caught the wind and sailed away, coming to rest, forlornly and incongruously, a bright green school cap with a red Maltese cross, in the middle of the highway a hundred yards behind us. *'What* did you do that for?' asked Rachel, crossly, slamming on the brakes. She was hardly ever cross.

But nothing could dim my excitement. The Memorial Theatre smelt exactly as I thought a theatre should smell. There was no curtain. Tanya Moiseivitch's wooden beamed set, with side stairs, a balcony, and rushes on the floor of the stage, was the setting for the whole cycle. Leslie Bridgewater's theatre band struck up what sounded like a medieval march – it was in fact the overture from Bizet's *L'Arlésienne* – the doors at the back of the stage opened, courtiers and soldiers came on, and when the lights went up Richard was seated on his throne:

> 'Old John of Gaunt, time-honoured Lancaster,
> Hast thou, according to thine oath and bond
> Brought hither Henry Hereford, thy bold son . . .'

The plot of *Richard II* does not thicken. It is thick from the very outset, clarifying and simplifying as the play progresses. But at the beginning there is a mass of allusions and a tangled web of intrigue surrounding Woodstock's murder, at the centre of which stands Richard, charming, cruel and despotic. Michael's appearance was startling. He glistened, like a golden sovereign – golden hair, golden beard. When he banished first Mowbray and then Bolingbroke you didn't know whether to laugh at the brilliance of his trickery or to cry at the certainty that he would be caught by it himself. Not many Richards make you believe that in boyhood they confronted Wat Tayler, tricked him into abandoning his rebellion, and then slaughtered the rebels, but Michael's did. Counting that first dress rehearsal the night we arrived I must have seen *Richard II* at the least half a dozen times, usually standing at the back of the stalls for half a crown. Fourteen is an impressionable age. But years later I stood at the side of the stage at Liverpool Playhouse and watched Michael play the great central scene, Act III scene i, of Richard's return from Ireland. Illness had made his

40

Daisy Scudamore,
Michael's mother, aged
about seventeen (*above*);
Roy Redgrave in a 'Bush
Drama', Australia circa
1909 (*above right*);
Michael and Rachel,
1940 (*right*); and Eric
and Beatrice Kempson
at Whitegate with me
and Corin, 1939.

Father and daughter in the garden at Clifton Hill, St John's Wood, August 1940 (*top left*); Cousin Lucy Kempson (*top right*); in our front garden at Bedford House, Chiswick, 1950; and (*inset*) Michael Redgrave in Saigon filming *The Quiet American*, 1956.

Playing my father's Bechstein at Bedford House, 1950.

With my best friends Sue, Maria and Tasha on the balcony at Queen's Gate School, 1954.

With Claudio, in love with Italy, 1954 (*inset*); and Corin and Lynn in Rome, 1956.

On the lake at Wilks Water, Rachel's cottage in Hampshire. In supporting roles, Lynn's pony Rosalinda and Rachel's favourite Labrador, Barney, 1960 (*above*); and Lynn and I on Rosalinda.

voice quieter, though it still had an extraordinary range and flexibility. He was seventy-four, and writing his autobiography. He said that when he came to play Richard he used some of John Gielgud's phrasing because 'to this day I can see no way of improving on the dazzling virtuosity of phrasing and breathing which was Gielgud's'. I could see no way of improving on Michael's playing of that scene. Richard's sudden wild flights of optimism, his violent spasms of rage against the favourites he thinks have betrayed him, his horrified contrition when he learns they have been executed, all were grounded not only in my father's imagination, which included a vivid sense of the reality of betrayal, but in his historical sense of the period in which the absolute monarchy was coming to an end.

We returned to Stratford in the summer holidays. Every afternoon we played tennis, or hired a boat to row on the Avon. We played endless sets of tennis with the actors William Peacock, David King and Robert Shaw, who befriended us during our summers at Stratford. Bob Shaw invariably strove to win every point. He was intensely ambitious to succeed in everything he did, and his straightforward, non-actorish voice and the aggressive, clenched-teethed manner in which he spat his words out brought a note of reality and freshness to every part he played, whether it was Dunois in *St Joan*, or later, when to many people's surprise, though not to mine, he became a very popular film star playing parts like Quint in *Jaws*. I liked him very much, and *Cato Street*, which he wrote in 1970, is one of my favourite plays.

Every evening we went to the theatre. Richard Burton was playing Prince Hal and I, like all my generation, became his passionate fan. He was the only actor I have ever seen whose voice and eyes literally compelled the audience to listen and observe his every move. His eyes were fascinating. When he turned his deep, steady gaze upon the audience his eyes seemed to search you out, so that even in the furthest row of the stalls or the back row of the circle you felt close to him. His raw, resonant Welsh voice, sorrowful and sometimes harsh, his physical stillness, and that steady piercing gaze, were unique. I longed to meet him, and only managed it once, by chance, as I was leaving the stage door with Rachel and he came running in. He stopped and looked at us, as though he thought he should recognise us, and I found his face, which was heavily pock-marked, even more attractive than I had

41

remembered it on stage. 'You must be Rachel,' he said, and leant forward to whisper in her ear. 'What did he say?' asked Corin, as we drove back to the flat Michael had rented in director Anthony Quayle's house on the banks of the Avon. Rachel seemed not to notice. 'What did he say?' Corin persisted. Once he had decided to ask something he would not be put off until he had the answer. 'He said, "You're so beautiful I could eat you," ' Rachel laughed. 'What did you say?' asked Corin.

We went back to Stratford again, two years later, in 1953. It became part of our young life, as much loved and longed for as Cousin Lucy's in Herefordshire, or our cousins Ralph and Sylvia Carr's farm in Northumberland. Rachel was in the company that season.

She played Elizabeth Woodville in *Richard III*, Octavia in *Antony and Cleopatra*, and Regan in *King Lear*. She loved acting, and especially loved acting with Michael. She taught us to punt, which she had learned from Grandpa Eric, showing us how to trail the pole behind in the water so it would act as a rudder and stop the boat careering helplessly from bank to bank. She took us to tea at the Lygon Arms in Broadway, told us about the deer in Charlecote Park which Shakespeare was said to have poached, and seemed as happy as I had ever seen her.

Like so many actresses, Rachel's progress had been interrupted by having children. She had played the Princess of France ihich she had learned from Grandpa Eric, showing us how to trail the pole behind in the water so it would act as a rudder and stop the boat careering helplessly from bank to bank. She took us to tea at the Lygon Arms in Broadway, told us about the deer in Charlecote Park which Shakespeare was said to have poached, and seemed as happy as I had ever seen her.

Like so many actresses, Rachel's progress had been interrupted by having children. She had played the Princess of France ihich she had learned from Grandpa Eric, showing us how to trail the pole behind in the water so it would act as a rudder and stop the boat careering helplessly from bank to bank. She took us to tea at the Lygon Arms in Broadway, told us about toan in 1954 at the tiny 'Q' Theatre where she played Joan opposite Robert Shaw's Dunois. She was brave, eager, direct, and very moving. In Chicago in 1977 I watched my sister Lynn play Joan with the same eager, brave directness. Lynn must have been eleven years old when Rachel played St Joan, old enough for it to affect her own performance years later, just as

Rachel's performance was surely affected by her memory of Sybil Thorndike in the first production of the play that Rachel saw, as a schoolgirl of fourteen.

Michael, when he had a large part to play in the evening, seldom enjoyed company or talked much. It was not that he 'lived' the part during the daytime hours, rather that he kept himself in readiness mentally, like a boxer before a big fight, or an athlete before the race. And because he was never satisfied to repeat what he had done the night before, he was often abstracted and sometimes irritable. There were other troubles that season, though we knew nothing of them at the time. Bailiffs were hounding him for unpaid bills. Corin and I watched the dress rehearsal for *Antony and Cleopatra*, aghast. He seemed to forget every other line, and yet the next night he was triumphant. His best and most creative work was done that season, as Antony, Lear and Shylock. He revised the lectures he had given the year before at Bristol University for a book *An Actor's Ways and Means*, which was published in 1953, and began work for the Italian producer Filipo Del Giudice on a film script for *Antony and Cleopatra*.

His Shylock was fierce, funny, anguished and awe inspiring, combining a real ferocity in fighting for his rights under the laws of Venice, with the pride and burning anguish of the Jewish patriarch, isolated in the ghetto. Forbidden to trade, Shylock is forced into money-lending by the laws of the rich mercantile state whose merchants despised the Jews with the racist contempt and envy of the newly and fabulously rich. The play has not been fashionable for many years, and that is understandable. But I did not think the play anti-Semitic then, and I do not now. Robbed of his daughter and mocked by the anti-Semitic yuppies of Venice, Shylock loses his mind with grief. The pound of flesh, a bitter joke against the merchant Antonio, becomes a symbol for Shylock of those rights under law which he, as a Jew, has been denied. Many of the productions I have seen, including that one, idealise the merchant society of Venice. But Michael's Shylock transcended this. His speech, 'Hath not a Jew eyes?' was a furious denunciation of anti-Semitism, and he wore the Star of David – 'The badge of all our tribe' – on his cloak with defiant pride.

I was fifteen and almost dying with excitement when I went abroad for the first time. Tasha and I, with four other schoolfriends, set off by train to Italy, with 'Mademoiselle' Eleanor

Tassarty. I had a new grey flannel suit, two berets, cherry pink and grey, and a red blouse and blue skirt I had made myself in the dressmaking class. We crossed the Channel at Newhaven and were sick.

At Paris we changed stations, and sat in a French café, eating croissants and drinking French coffee. 'I'm in Heaven,' I thought. Half asleep, half awake at the frontier station of Domodossola when Italian customs men came on the train to inspect our passports. Down to the coast at Genoa. Standing in the corridor, looking out of the windows I talked to an Italian soldier. He kissed me and I felt an electric shock run through me. When he left the train I told Tasha, glowing with pride and silly with excitement. We got out at Florence and gasped – we had never seen such beauty – the glowing terracotta tiles on the roofs, the Duomo, the bridge across the Arno, the slopes of the hills up to Fiesole, covered with olive orchards. We strap-hung in the long buses, tramped up the 350-odd steps to the top of the Duomo, and giggled whenever our bottoms were pinched. We saw Botticelli's 'Birth of Venus' and the originals of all the reproductions on the walls of our school.

On to Rome, and then Bologna and Ravenna. Here we ate with Mademoiselle Tassarty's family friends and I sat next to the son, Franco. Our knees touched under the table. He passed me some sweet wine and said 'sweets for the sweet'. He was the first man I'd ever met who wore cologne, Pino Silvestre, and it smelt marvellous. I gave him my address and he told me he would be coming to England for an English course to help him with his commercial studies. I noticed his hair was going thin on top, and when Tasha teased me I became very tight-lipped and refused to talk to her. I was fifteen, but said I was sixteen and sweated with fear in case my lie should be discovered. We were English girls, nourished on overboiled cabbage, watery, boiled potatoes and tough, tasteless meat, and like countless English girls before us we had fallen head over heels in love with Italy, its life, its noise, its warmth, its colour, and the beauty of its cities.

1954, my last year at school, consisted of study, arguments and endless games of racing demon. I shared a small study with my three closest friends, Tasha, Sue and Sarah. We were the first girls at Queen's Gate to sit for and pass A-level examinations. Others, like Maria, whose parents had set their hearts on a university education, had left school for special tuition before going on to Oxford. But we wanted to stay and study together, so we

44

demanded and received tuition for A-level history, French, Italian and English, with art and Spanish as 'extras'. We argued for hours over the meaning of T. S. Eliot and Ezra Pound, and the French symbolists Sue was studying. Our mission was to love life. We were taught to praise poetry which 'affirmed' or 'enhanced' life. We all wrote poetry ourselves, and our final-year contributions to the school magazine were steeped in sorrow, old age and death. 'Falling, the ground that met him was a grave,' wrote Sue that summer in a poem called 'Dissolution'. 'Blindly he stares ahead, but his heart drags back through the wake, and his young eyes are clouded already with age-old regret,' wrote Sarah in 'Release'. Both were very superior to my own contribution: 'As the sun disappears, its last glow fading from the villa, I see Death appear, embodied in this house.' We were all seventeen years old. I finished school at the end of the summer term, proudly listing the twenty-four plays, ballets and concerts I had seen.

That summer, Dad paid for me to spend two months staying and studying with an Italian family, the Minettis, in Tuscany. As a young man he had been sent by his stepfather to study in Heidelberg, and knew that this was the most enjoyable way to learn a language. But he also must have known, from his own experience, and certainly deduced from my ecstatic postcards, that it might be the surest way to learn absolutely nothing. After one wonderful month at the old villa in Tuscany with four generations of the Minetti family I received a postcard from him: 'I very much want to hear when you have started your lessons. Your ever devoted Dad.'

Stung into action, I found a teacher in the nearby town and immersed myself in selected cantos from Dante's *Inferno*. I learned most of Machiavelli's *Il Principe* by heart. I walked with Carlo Levi through the poverty-stricken villages of Catania in his classic *Cristo si è fermato a Eboli*, and disappeared for hours on end into the lives and times of Franco Maironi and his wife Luisa in Fogazzaro's *Piccolo mondo antico*. Set in 1852 when Italy was under the political, military and economic occupation of the Austrian Empire, this book opened a window on to the lives of Italian men and women who lived under constant surveillance by the secret police and the threat of arrest and imprisonment. These were the years of reaction, following the defeat of the revolutions that swept across Europe in two weeks in 1848. That 'little, ancient world' slowly became as real to me as the hot sun, the cicadas and the hospitable,

45

happy Minettis. I remember every small incident in the lives of Don Franco and his wife as vividly as my own early life, and as intimately as if I had lived every moment of domestic and social detail. That 'little, ancient world' became my world, its hopes, my hopes. The wind and rain of Lake Como lashed my face. I wept with Luisa when her little girl was drowned. I shared that last solemn, silent moment with Franco and Luisa in their hotel room in Turin, and walked with them to the steamboat which would take Franco and his young friends to the battlefield against the Austrians.

'These young men spoke of fighting with enthusiasm, but without boasting; they spoke of the future of Italy with a good deal of silliness, but one felt they didn't think their lives were worth a dried fig unless they could liberate this great old country.'

From the moment I first learned to read I had always retreated into my books and lived long hours in my imagination. But what stirred me in Fogazzaro's novel connected with my world in 1954 and made me look at it more closely. On 7 May 1954, after a 55-day siege, the Army of the Vietnamese League of Independence had finally routed the French Army, backed since 1945 by the American government. The French military chiefs and government were forced to the negotiating table. On 8 May, for only the second time in my life, and as usual in the *Daily Mail*, I read a political news story from beginning to end, on the fall of Dien Bien Phu. I was ignorant of the history of French imperialism in Indo-China, but I knew immediately that I was very glad the Viet Minh had won. But as I read the history of the long Italian struggle to liberate and unify their country, moving on from *Piccolo mondo antico* to Silvio Pellico's *Le mie Prigioni* (My Prisons), I learned how a national liberation movement suffered, and in that sense, thought I knew all I needed to know about the Vietnamese struggle for liberation. The French were defeated, the Vietnamese League of Independence had won, and the war, on 21 July, was officially declared to have ended. I thought it was the end of that cruel period.

Three years later, in 1957, Michael was in Saigon filming Graham Greene's novel *The Quiet American*. Vietnam had been partitioned. Two countries, North and South Vietnam, had been artificially created as the result of the international 'peace' conference whose co-chairmen represented Britain and the Soviet Union. A puppet regime, backed by American money and the CIA, had been installed in the South. One evening the American film crew were shooting scenes of the Indo-Chinese New Year in the streets of Saigon. It was a religious demonstration. Suddenly the Vietnamese interpreter began shouting at the cameraman and gesturing at the placards carried aloft in the procession. 'What's he saying?' asked the director, Joe Mankiewicz. 'He says we should cut,' yelled the cameraman, Robert Krasker. 'He says they're anti-American slogans.' 'What the hell,' said Mankiewicz, 'No one'll know what they mean.'

When Michael arrived in Rome to film the interior scenes for *The Quiet American*, at the Cinecittà studios, I was on holiday before my last term at drama school, renting a room in a small *pensione*, and I saw him every day. He showed me some sixty black-and-white photographs he had taken from the window of a Dakota flying from Saigon to Cambodia. A knot gathers painfully in the stomach when I look at those photographs. The year before, at the Edinburgh film festival, he had seen some of the very earliest film shot by the Lumière brothers. 'Somehow it's awfully touching,' he wrote, 'when you see a moving picture of a small boy running across the road in 1890, to think that if he's still alive he must be a very old gentleman.' Dad's black-and-white photos are curled round at the edges, from being kept in a box rolled up in a plastic band. He was a keen photographer, and often pasted his snapshots into a book. But I suppose he never found the time to paste these up, and I never have. Far, far below the plane, almost beyond the range of the Leica lens, are rice fields, small roads, woods and villages. Somewhere along those roads small boys are running to their friends, or their families. A little, ancient world where life was not worth living unless that great old country could be liberated from the Deuxième Bureau, the Paris Bourse, Wall Street, the CIA.

In Tuscany I knew no more of Vietnam than I could imagine and interpret from my studies of Italian history, but they set me thinking. The year before, 1953, I had heard about the Rosenbergs' execution by electric chair. I knew the United States as the country that had no rationing during the war, the country of Hollywood and the hilarious Danny Kaye, of Broadway and Ethel Merman in *Annie Get Your Gun*. When I heard they also tortured and killed people in an electric chair, it seemed impossibly barbaric. The Rosenbergs, like Paul Robeson the great black American singer and actor, were communists.

I am sure it was thanks to Paul Robeson that the anti-communist witch-hunting of the Eisenhower years failed to brainwash me. Amongst Michael's records I found all of Robeson's songs, and played them over and over again on an old wind-up gramophone someone had given Rachel for a wedding present. He sang fiercely and proudly, 'Let my people go'. In 1955 the government took his passport away, and made Robeson a prisoner in his own country. The United States, the strongest country in the world, was so afraid of this great man, and the power of his songs, that they had to take his passport away to stop people overseas from hearing him! It was thanks to Robeson that the terrible lies published about the Kenyan Mau Mau liberation movement and its leader Jomo Kenyatta equally failed to convince me. I knew nothing then of the tortures and killings in the infamous Hola Hola concentration camp, of Africans dying in the ditches they were forced to dig, without water to drink, like the Jews in the Nazi concentration camps. Reports of those atrocities came much later, but I knew what I read in the press about the Mau Mau could not be believed.

Finally there was Garibaldi. On the mantelpiece above the fireplace at Bedford House stood a six-inch-high china figure of Il Generale, mass-produced by the Staffordshire potteries when Garibaldi received that tumultuous welcome in London from the thousands of workers and their wives who came to greet him on his visit in 1864.

'I am not a soldier,' he said at the Crystal Palace to the Italians who presented him with a sword, 'and I do not like the soldier's trade. I saw my father's house filled with robbers and snatched a weapon to drive them out. I am a working man, I come from working people, and I am proud of it.'

Dida Minetti's grandfather, Doctor Sambalini, told me to buy Alexander Herzen's memoirs, *Pasato e Pensieri*. Herzen, a political exile from Tsarist Russia, wrote a long entry in his diary about Garibaldi's visit to London and his meeting with Mazzini, founder of the first Italian liberation movement, the illegal Carbonari organisation. Mazzini lived at Teddington, two and a half miles down the river from our house at Chiswick, at a time when London was the centre for all the political exiles and refugees from Europe.

All the poorer classes of Teddington had crowded round the railings of our house waiting from early morning for Garibaldi. When we drove up, the crowd rushed to greet him in ecstasy, pressed his hands, shouted 'God bless you Garibaldi!' Women caught at his hand and kissed it, kissed the hem of his cloak – I saw this with my own eyes – lifted their children up to him and wept. Suddenly, an old Italian, an emigrant from days long past, a poor fellow who made ice cream, burst through, caught Garibaldi by the skirt of his coat and stopped him, burst into tears and said 'Well, now I can die. I have seen him, I have seen him!'

An Italian novel, some black-and-white photographs, some gramophone records, the diaries of a Russian exile who died in 1870 and a pottery figure – this was how the political struggles of past history became known to me and guided my attitude to the political struggles of the 1950s. The seeds are scattered far and wide, and taken one by one seem so insignificant, so powerless. But all that is required for the seeds to germinate is a new wave of political struggle which involves millions of people.

Twenty-three years later I stood in the refugee camps in Lebanon and saw Palestinian and Lebanese women lift their baby sons to greet Arafat, crying, 'Allah bless you, Abu Ammar,' just as Herzen says the poor Italian emigrants in London greeted their hero Garibaldi.

# 5

I passed the Italian exam with distinction and my father glowed with pride when I told him how the oral examiner, a lady in her sixties, had offered to recommend me for an interpreter's job. Throughout the autumn, while studying, I had taken a bus twice a week up Abbey Road for singing lessons with Jani Strasser. Jani and his wife Irene were Hungarian and very close friends of my parents. Michael met Jani when he needed coaching for the role of Macheath in *The Beggar's Opera*, which he performed at the Haymarket in March 1940. Jani was a superb singing coach and developed Michael's light baritone into a very good voice. He was on the teaching staff of the Young Vic Theatre School formed by Michel Saint Denis and George Devine, and later went to Glyndebourne Opera House.

Jani sat before the grand piano in the teaching room, the light dimmed by the heavy wet trees outside and the 60-watt electric light bulb inside. All the surfaces in the room were covered with pictures and small silver objects he and Irene had brought with them to London from Hungary. I knew so little history when I met Jani that I never asked him about his early life or how he left Hungary because of the Nazis. His enormous intelligent eyes shone with vigour behind thick spectacles, and I have never forgotten what he taught me. He gave me a number of physical exercises to loosen and strengthen the muscles around the small of the back and the ribs. We worked up and down the scale with Ds and Ms and up and down with sung phrases.

'Winter, summer, autumn, spring! All the little birds are on the wing.' (Chord up a semi-tone.)

'You must feel as if you have diarrhoea.'

'Stop listening to yourself! Stop listening to the sounds you make! If you listen to the sound you start correcting the sound. You have a lot of little poodles, you see. If you keep them on a lead and keep pulling at it they can never do anything on their own. They are very clever little poodles. But if you keep pulling at them they can only do what you tell them, they can never show you what they can do. You must only think of what you are singing about, why you are singing, what your feelings are. Singing is just the same as speaking, only your feelings are so strong you just have to sing.'

Whenever an actor asks me to listen to a reading of a line, I want to explain about the poodles. I believed what Jani said, because he spoke with the kind of authority I trusted absolutely, but it took me years to understand fully why he was right, and to let my own poodles go free, never to plan how I would say a line, only to think of the situation, and listen to the other actors. The pressures of film and TV schedules are intense. Directors get nervous if they don't see and hear something that 'works', or, on the contrary, if they see and hear something they are not expecting, and that does not accord with the sounds they think they ought to be hearing. So actors get nervous and start checking and controlling. Skilful actors acquire great expertise, and the greater the expertise the more difficult it becomes to give Jani's poodles a free rein.

His advice stays with me and has been invaluable throughout my professional life as an actress. Acting means working to be alive and alert to the incident and the moment, to the director, the other actors and the script. What is hard, and really has to be worked at, is being able to go with whatever comes up from other actors or the director at each moment of a performance and to try not to force a repetition of something that went well the day before. I love reading around a role – finding out about the times when the writer wrote a play, the social conditions, the literature and the culture. It is exciting to make discoveries through reading, and while this takes time, particularly when you are married and have children, I don't regard it as hard work. The real work of acting is letting go and unleashing Jani's poodles.

At home, every Sunday afternoon, Michael would sit down at the piano. He played well, both classical music and American songs with a syncopated rhythm. He and Rachel sang through *The Beggar's Opera*, Schubert – especially the dramatic 'Erlkönig' – Benjamin Britten's setting of 'Little Sir William', Noel Coward, Jerome Kern's *Show Boat* and, a regular favourite, Judy Garland's

'The Trolley Song', which Corin, Lynn and I sang with gusto. 'Buzz-buzz-buzz goes the buzzer! Ring-ring-ring goes the bell! ZING ZING ZING go my heart strings . . .' The exhilarating tempo, the words tumbling, pouring out, caught us breathless, scrambling to keep pace with that wonderful trolley. Before growing too tall Michael had made me learn ballet; now he wanted me to train for musical comedy. He urged me not to go to drama school but to concentrate on singing and modern dancing. He told me about Noel Coward's star, Gertrude Lawrence, saying that an actress who could sing and dance would have a big career. He paid for me to take tap lessons at Buddy Bradley's school in Denman Street, Soho, just behind the famous 'we never closed' Windmill Theatre where the showgirls played five or six performances every afternoon and evening.

Buddy Bradley, whose very name conjured up the lights of that mysterious, glamorous, faraway place in New York called Broadway, did not teach beginners. In fact I never saw him. Twice a week I joined seven or eight other debutantes and we tapped up and down the rotting floorboards behind an agile instructor who never took his eyes off his reflection in the big mirror. The landlord wanted Buddy Bradley out and so refused to repair the floor; it was a major victory to tap through six bars of music without stumbling on the broken boards. Soho, the squalid Avenue, smelt of urine, beer and stale whisky. The tiny dirty name-plates of film companies in Wardour Street were not alluring, only frightening.

If there had been a brilliant modern dance teacher in London, I would probably have taken Michael's advice and pursued musical comedy. As there was not, my admiration and yearning for the lights of Stratford-upon-Avon, the plays of Shakespeare, and Peggy Ashcroft remained steadfast. I doubted if the Memorial Theatre would ever invite a musical comedy actress to join the company, so I told my father I wanted to go to drama school, and attended an audition and interview with Gwyneth Thurburn, the principal of the Central School of Speech and Drama.

Gwyneth Thurburn looked at me over the top of her desk, and told me not to expect anything noteworthy in the way of employment in the theatre until well into my thirties. My height, she said, was a handicap I would not overcome until the onset of middle age. I was neither alarmed nor discouraged by her view. I accepted it as my fate. To make matters worse, at the age of fourteen I could still play tennis without spectacles but by now I had to wear spectacles all the time. Rachel was very sensitive and always knew when I was depressed and discouraged, when she would exclaim, 'Oh! my beautiful daughter!' with such total conviction that for a moment I believed her. My morale was also sustained by Ellen Terry, that great Shakespearean actress who had written in her autobiography that her main ambition was always to be a useful actress. If that was good enough for Ellen Terry, it was good enough for me.

On 11 January 1955 I took the Underground to Gloucester Road station, where I had descended every morning for six years at 8.30 a.m. for school, and walked up the tree-lined Queen's Gate to the Royal Albert Hall. Central had its theatre, main rehearsal room and a registrar's office in a section of the vast corridors that ran round the enormous circular concert hall. For my first day I bought black tights, a leotard, a copy of Miss Thurburn's book, *Voice and Speech*, and a one-inch-long piece of whalebone with a groove at either end – Miss Thurburn's bone prop for voice and speech training. In my bag was *The Oxford Book of English Verse* (a required textbook), a towel, soap and a hairbrush. I was handed a typewritten page of Elizabethan prologue. For the spring term all the studies would be concentrated on voice, mime, movement, verse-speaking and the delivery of a prologue from Restoration drama.

Speech therapy was one of the courses provided at Central. We did hours of consonant and vowel practice with the bone prop between our front teeth. I found concentrating entirely on technique limiting. Weeks spent listening to sounds and correcting them, with no work on a scene or situation from a play, on subject or character, made students nervous. My own voice strangled with self-consciousness. I compared this with Jani's method, but I could not analyse what was going wrong. The mime classes were still of the old school, 'pretend you have a tea-cup and saucer in your hand', but in my delight at being a student I was not in a critical frame of mind and accepted on trust that I was getting the best training possible.

Four years earlier the Young Vic Theatre School, run in conjunction with the Young Vic Theatre by the great French director, Michel Saint-Denis, Glen Byam-Shaw and George Devine – all close colleagues of Michael and Rachel – had been closed down. The Treasury refused funds to the organisation which at that time included the Old Vic Theatre Company. The Arts Council drama director Evellyn Rees was hostile to the work he saw the students were involved in. 'I went into a class of Saint-Denis,' said Rees 'and these boys and girls were all being animals; it was like going into a lunatic asylum.' When Michel Saint-Denis took my father round the school for the last time he was crying.

Before the Young Vic, Michel Saint-Denis had run another school, the London Theatre Centre, for four years. And he had persuaded Litz Pisk to join him. A brilliant young Viennese woman who had fled from the Nazi *Anschluss* in 1936, Litz was working at Dartington with Michael Chekhov, Anton Chekhov's nephew, when Michel found her. As a young girl in Vienna she had studied painting, design and movement from the most advanced generation of artists. At Dartington she taught movement and painting. When I later worked with her in the 1960s, she told me that one of the tasks she set her students at Dartington was to find a hundred different red textures, and make a collage of all these reds. The challenge and excitement of such a project took my breath away. Animal mime, clown techniques, music hall, Noh masks, improvisation, the work of Isadora Duncan, Meyerhold, Stanislavsky, Picasso, Cocteau – all were embodied in the theatre outlook and the concepts of Saint-Denis and George Devine. When they were denied funds and resigned on a point of principle, all this work was brought to a halt.

Thinking back now I can understand why my father urged me not to go to drama school. No single glimpse or reverberation of this kind of work and these great cultural achievements existed in the training at the Central School. When I went there in 1955 Michael and Rachel told me the story of the scandalous closure of the Young Vic School, but I was unconscious of the implications and still failed to recognise either the depths of English middle-class philistinism, or the extraordinary creativity of the European, Soviet and American artists my parents and their colleagues admired so much. I was amazed when an Israeli student in my year bitterly and angrily criticised the training at Central. I could understand neither what he thought was missing nor why I did not know what I was missing.

This may have been why Michael gave me two tickets for a production by a new company in the East End of London. Theatre Workshop was presenting *Richard II* at the Theatre Royal, Stratford

East, directed by Joan Littlewood. The company had toured all over England for a few years and, thanks to Peggy Ashcroft and many of her friends including my father, they now had a permanent home for the first time. I sat in shock through the performance. The stage was grey and black. King Richard II was accompanied by a group of sycophants, liars and careerists and he was clearly a man of similar character. He spoke like an ordinary man. Bolingbroke spoke with an accent, in fact none of the nobles spoke or behaved like either actors or aristocrats. The old theatre was shabby, dingy and threadbare. My shock turned into pompous effrontery. I took the Underground train home elated with indignation. My father was waiting for me and invited me to sit down and eat some scrambled eggs with him.

'Well, tell me about it,' he said.

'Oh, it was dreadful – well, interesting – but dreadful.' I took a deep breath and let out a tirade of prejudice and ignorance. When I had stopped to breathe and take another mouthful of scrambled eggs, I looked up at my father. He looked back in silence with grave, troubled eyes. He did not speak for quite a while. Then he said, quietly, his voice deep and tremulous with emotion:

'Never, never speak like that. Never, never go to a production with your head full of what you like, and then come away full of what you don't like. You must always begin with what is the aim of the production. Then you can speak about what the production achieved, and only then can you speak about what it failed to achieve, what the mistakes may have been.'

He said more than this, but that is what I remember, and will never forget. I was shocked and agonised. I was made to think.

I went back for the next production – *Edward II* – with Amos, the Israeli student. My prejudices had been rocked by my father's criticism and a feeling that Amos knew a lot about life that I did not. This time I understood more about Joan Littlewood's company and their approach. The courts, the church and society of these medieval monarchs were cruel, vicious and criminal. They and their barons were basically feudal families fighting ruthlessly for absolute power. They were not supermen appointed by God. Neither were the churchmen, who were weak, greedy and treacherous. The more poetic their language, the more it served to cover up their actual lives, deeds and ambitions.

That summer Michael asked Joan Littlewood if Corin and I could watch rehearsals of a Ben Jonson play, *Volpone*. We watched the energetic, forthright Joan working on improvisations with her company, stripping away every cliché that even her actors sometimes fell into: 'No, let's get rid of that crap!' Her actors treated her as familiarly and directly; there was no false diplomacy and no egotism. The play was staged in semi-Elizabethan costume but included a variety of hilarious anachronisms. Mosca, Volpone's pimp, fleeing from his pursuers, swam down the Grand Canal, which was the orchestra pit, with a snorkel tube and flippers.

Michael introduced us to Sean O'Casey's plays. I remember vividly sitting in a room in Notting Hill Gate called the New Lindsey Theatre. At the other end of the room, with no curtains and no effects, a group of actors opened our eyes, ears and minds to the tragic stories of the Irish struggle for self-determination. The performances were so powerful that, sitting on hard benches, we forgot who we were and where we were.

That July, in 1955, Michael opened in the Jean Giraudoux play *Tiger at the Gates*, directed by Harold Clurman. Corin and I watched all the rehearsals, thanks to Clurman's kindness. Robert Shaw played a sailor, Diane Cilento, later Sean Connery's wife, Helen of Troy. The theme of the play, written in the 1930s, was anti-war. Its original title was *La guerre de Troie n'aura pas lieu*, *The Trojan War Shall Not Take Place*. Hector, played by Michael, was doing everything in his power to prevent Troy going to war with Greece. For the first time Greek and Trojan history came to life before our eyes; we had both plodded through pages of Homer's *Iliad* at school without excitement. Diane Cilento with her Australian accent was beautiful and sexy, and Harold Clurman cast her knowing the play would transfer to Broadway if it succeeded. An English director would never have cast her, and she was perfect. She had an extraordinary speech in which she foresaw her own future, old and wrinkled, covered with make-up, eating sweets by the fireplace.

Harold Clurman was a founding member of the Group Theatre of the 1930s in the United States. He had often visited the Soviet Union, where he met Stanislavsky and had been inspired like many other Americans by the extraordinary work of the Moscow Arts Theatre Company. The vigour, precision and energy of his direction, and his attention to detail during rehearsals, were thrilling. We could often see how actors' chief problems would occur when they lost sight of the demands of the situation and the story as a whole, and focused on their 'feelings' about what was right for them as individuals. The production was a big success. It was taken to Broadway. That Christmas my father paid for me to join him in New York for three weeks.

I saw Arthur Miller's *A View from the Bridge*, with Van Heflin; Shirley Booth in *Come Back Little Sheba*, and Julie Harris in Anouilh's *The Lark* and *A Hatful of Rain*, with Shelley Winters, Ben Gazzara and Tony Franciosa, developed from improvisations at the Actors' Studio. Every morning for a week I was allowed to attend Lee Strasberg's famous Actors' Studio.

Here I saw professional actors working on scenes, which they then analysed with Lee Strasberg and their fellow actors. The Actors' Studio had become world famous because many of the greatest American actors – Marlon Brando, Julie Harris and Eli Wallach – worked there, and studied 'the Method' based on Stanislavsky's teachings. It was housed in an old church hall, with wooden benches ranged in tiers around an acting area. Strasberg sat in the centre, by a table, sometimes taking notes. After a scene had been played or improvised a discussion would begin, with Strasberg and other members putting questions to the actors. His comments were often fascinating. On Shakespeare's Richard III – 'His deformity is basically a spiritual degeneration, something inside the man. He exaggerates its physical effects, to win sympathy, or strike fear in his opponents. Probably his hunchback is not actually very noticeable physically. Look at pictures of David Garrick in the role and you will see, he hardly padded his costume at all.' Then, 'You must be very careful with illusion on stage. For instance, if the scene is set in an unswept, untidy room, like this [he gestured at the studio, and we all laughed, because it was], and you beat a carpet or a cushion and real dust comes out, the whole audience will sneeze, you'll stop the performance.'

Watching one scene I thought there was a problem. Unlike the method of Stanislavsky where the actor must start from the given circumstances of the play, the Actors' Studio started from the 'feeling' of the individual actor. An actress was having difficulty; I felt she had decided to concentrate on her feelings of cold, fear, and so on, and had forgotten the situation of the play. I thought she would find the answer to her problems if she paid more attention to the given circumstances so I asked Strasberg if this might be the problem. Strasberg said this was not the issue. The truth of her feelings and her own conviction were the task at hand. I was not convinced; I felt that both would develop from her consciousness of the given circumstances. But I admired him and his colleagues for recognising that development is not only a question of sufficient practice, it is first of all a question of what outlook or approach is guiding the work, and that continuous and serious analysis is required to overcome problems. Without such work an actor's craft must degenerate into repetition of effects that 'work' or, as Stanislavsky said, 'empty stencils'.

That Christmas I also saw Strasberg's daughter Susan in *The Diary of Anne Frank*. I cried and cried, marvelling again at the total conviction of Susan, Joseph Schildkraut and the rest of the cast. One of the members of the Actors' Studio, Fred Sadoff, had become a close friend of Dad's. I had long discussions with him about the Method, and watched him work on a scene with another actress. One day we were in the Actors' Studio when an actor said to Fred, 'Look, there's Eva Marie, isn't it great how beautiful she looks now she has a job.' It was Eva Marie Saint, who played Marlon Brando's wife in *On the Waterfront*.

In New York I experienced the glitter of the city's thousands of lights in the skyscrapers and in the expensive stores. But I also saw the actors' world, always treading between unemployment, hunger and the 'big success' with ovations at Sardi's restaurant. The actor who spoke about Eva Marie Saint was excited and proud that one more hungry actor had got through, and I knew what he meant when he said she was 'looking great' because she had a job.

I got back to England in January 1956 crammed with impressions of what I had seen. I had been given a new perspective on the actor's work, so different from everything I had been taught at Central School, and I longed to share it with others.

# 6

Clive Goodwin, a student in the third year at Central School, listened to my description of my experiences in New York. The more we talked, the more we convinced ourselves that we should publish a magazine where work of the kind I had seen at the Actors' Studio could be discussed.

Neither of us had any knowledge or experience of writing, still less of editing or publishing, a magazine of this kind. But neither, for that matter, did anyone else. There was no magazine or periodical at that time in England which seriously discussed and criticised work in the theatre. So *Encore*, which began as a quarterly in the mid-fifties and soon became a monthly, found quite a substantial readership.

The new life I had sensed in New York, and which had invigorated and excited me so much that I wanted to tell everyone about it, was not really so new. It had begun with the Russian revolution, and the impact of that revolution on a generation of writers, actors and directors in the American theatre of the 1930s. But suddenly, it seemed, some of this new life was springing up in a London which, when I began my training, had seemed a desert. At the Royal Court Theatre in Sloane Square, George Devine formed the English Stage Company, dedicated to the work of new writers and playwrights such as Bertolt Brecht, whose work had hardly been performed in London. Rachel was a founder member in 1956, and the company included George Devine himself, Rosalie Crutchley, Kenneth Haigh, Alan Bates, Michael Gwynn and Robert Stephens. The top salary, earned by four members of the company, was £30. Four were on £20, four on £15, and another four on £10 a week. The assistant stage managers, who were students, were paid £1. That was the wage Granny Scudamore had earned, had just survived on, provided she walked to work, when she joined Sarah Bernhardt's company in London as a lady-in-waiting and an extra in *Hamlet* and *La Dame aux Camélias*. In those days, she complained, the London theatre was hidebound in snobbery and outworn tradition. So it must have seemed to most young writers in the 1950s, until the English Stage Company began.

I was in the theatre one morning, watching a final rehearsal of *Look Back in Anger*, the third play of the season. I cannot remember why or how I came to be watching that rehearsal. From my seat at the back of the circle I recognised the director, Tony Richardson. He had come to our house in Chiswick the year before with an introduction from George Devine. 'He's just down from Oxford,' George had said to Rachel, 'and he's very clever.' Now he was George's associate director at the Royal Court. I could see him down in the stalls, talking to Kenneth Haigh and Mary Ure. The Royal Court is a tiny theatre which seats about 400 people, yet I could hardly hear a word that was said. An hour passed, with not more than five minutes' rehearsal on stage; the rest of the time was spent in whispered discussion. The play was to open in two days, and I crossed my fingers. I knew that the finances of the theatre were precarious, that one failure could jeopardise the whole season, and that the entire company were anxious for the success of this new play by a young author, himself a member of the company.

*Look Back in Anger* opened on 8 May 1956, and was greeted with a near-unanimous howl of scorn and abuse by the critics on the daily papers. One of them coined the phrase 'kitchen-sink', meaning that here there were no maids or butlers, and the penniless young men and women who lived in bed-sitting-rooms washed their own tea-cups. But that was the whole point as I saw it, that was how most of my fellow drama students, and thousands of young people all over the country, lived.

Sunday came, and Kenneth Tynan, the drama critic of *The Observer*, said he doubted he could fall in love with anyone who didn't like *Look Back in Anger*. Another Sunday, and Harold Hobson, the elderly and much respected critic of *The Sunday Times*, declared that he had seen the play a second time and had changed his mind: it was a masterpiece.

I don't think of John Osborne's play as a 'masterpiece'. I loved it because its principal character, Jimmy Porter, was funny and defiant, utterly scornful of middle-class society, its values and hypocrisy. Arthur Miller's *The Crucible*, which was the second play the English Stage Company performed, fully deserved that praise. I was enthralled by it, though I didn't recognise its greatness, nor its contemporary significance. I knew of Senator McCarthy, and the House Un-American Activities Committee, I knew that Miller himself had been interrogated by the Senate subcommittee and sentenced to jail for his refusal to name names; that all Paul Robeson's records had been removed from shops and libraries, and that hundreds of American artists and writers had been blacklisted. But Senator McCarthy's star was on the wane, or so we were told. He was to die a year later, and *The Times*, in one of its most pontifical and elegant obituaries, remarked that the passing of such a vulgar, unscrupulous demagogue would hardly occasion much mourning. What the obituary didn't mention was that those who had been ruined by the McCarthyite witch-hunts remained blacklisted, or were forced to work at a fraction of their former salaries under assumed names. Nor did any of the obituaries point out that the spectre of communism which had haunted America in the 1940s and 1950s had also haunted Britain.

So when I saw *The Crucible* in 1956 at the Royal Court, the then of the seventeenth century witch-hunts in Salem, Massachusetts, was separated in my mind from the now of the twentieth century, and I saw it more or less as a historical play, powerfully written and acted, but without its universal implications.

When the autumn term began at Central, my class was to perform Angus Wilson's *The Mulberry Bush*, which had opened the season at the Royal Court that spring. I was given the part of Rose Padley, the elderly matriarch of a family of Fabian socialists. I knew that I could never understand this woman and her family from within the limits of my imagination. She was modelled on Beatrice Webb, so I borrowed every book by the Webbs which I could lay my hands on, read George Bernard Shaw's diaries, found a reference there to Eleanor Rathbone, the Labour MP, and then, in a biography of Miss Rathbone, found to my delight a reference to our dear old cousin, Lucy Kempson. Now Rose Padley began to come to life. In her speeches I could hear Cousin Lucy's characteristic flat vowels, and the forthright, emphatic rhythms of her speech. Our director, James Roose Evans, encouraged us to improvise, analyse and discuss our characters. One night he organised a dinner party for us at his flat. Each of us had to arrive 'in character' and stay in our role until we left, some hours later. Jimmy was a breath of fresh air. We began to think that our training was making progress.

When the Bolshoi made their first visit to London in 1956, a group of us slept all night under the back portico at Covent Garden in order to be first in the queue in the morning for gallery tickets. Nowhere, not even in New York, had I seen a stage filled with such life and dramatic conviction as the Bolshoi presented in *Swan Lake*, *The Fountains of Bakshisarai* and *Romeo and Juliet*. The legendary Ulanova danced Juliet. She was said to be fifty. When she ran across the stage to meet Romeo in Friar Lawrence's cell, there was the kind of silence in the audience I had never known before. I became one with Ulanova, knowing or rediscovering what it was to be sixteen and desperately in love in a hostile world. She transcended her years, the centuries, and the limits of the stage itself.

When I got home I pasted my ticket stub for *Romeo and Juliet* in my scrap book. When I married, seven years later, that scrapbook, together with boxes full of cuttings, old photographs and every copy of *Encore*, were gleefully chucked on a rubbish heap by my husband. 'What did you do that for?' I wailed, half in admiration of such a radical solution to the problem of clutter. 'Those are my memories, for when I'm old.' 'If that's all you'll have when you're old I feel sorry for you,' he said. So I lit a match under them. But I still have – or rather I have my eye on, since it belongs to Rachel – Ulanova's ballet shoe. It was presented to Michael at the Soviet Embassy in London, from Ulanova, in honour of the first visit to Moscow by the Shakespeare Memorial Theatre Company.

The press notices were unanimous in admiration of the Bolshoi, and we students were aglow with love for the Russians and their artistry. We hoped and believed fervently that this cultural exchange would bring about a closer understanding between people in England and the Soviet Union. We were convinced that great art like the Bolshoi's would not only overcome barriers but break them down. We did not know, as we went home that Saturday night, that the Hungarian revolution had begun.

On Tuesday, 23 October, the Petofi Circle, a group of Hungarian writers and poets, had demanded freedom of the press, free elections and changes in the government. Ten thousand students had demonstrated at the Kossuth Memorial in Budapest and marched to the radio station demanding that it broadcast a 17-point programme. Workers from the giant Csepel factory joined them, and soon 100,000 workers and students had gathered. The AVH secret police fired on the demonstrators. Stalin's statue was pulled off its pedestal, and detachments in the army handed out arms to units of the workers and students. Gero, First Secretary of the Hungarian Communist Party, called officially for troops to be sent from the Soviet Union, but when the first regiment arrived they began to fraternise with the Hungarian workers' units, and soon a general strike had spread throughout the country. Workers' Councils were formed and demanded the immediate disbandment of the secret police, the AVH, and the withdrawal of Soviet troops.

On Thursday, 1 November, I woke early and went to the kitchen to make a cup of tea. I picked up Dad's copy of the *Guardian* from the kitchen table and stared with horror at the front page – a photograph of a huge column of smoke rising from the city of Port Said. Eden had ordered the RAF to bomb Port Said, Suez and Cairo, and invade the Canal Zone. The paper said there had been many civilian casualties.

That July President Gamal Abdel Nasser had nationalised the Suez Canal in order to finance the Aswan Dam project which was to provide electricity for the whole of Egypt. At the beginning of the year the British and American governments and the International Bank of Reconstruction and Development had agreed to lend Egypt the huge sum required for the project. But six months later they cancelled the agreement. Meanwhile Israel had been stepping up its raids into the Gaza Strip. So Nasser nationalised the Canal, taking over the Compagnie Universelle Maritime de Suez.

All year, and especially since July, the British press had been lashing out at Nasser and the Egyptian government, whipping up war fever. Leader writers recalled Anthony Eden's pre-war resignation in protest against Chamberlain's policy of appeasement. Nasser was compared to Hitler, and racist cartoons depicting him with a huge hooked nose became the stock in trade of every newspaper. The press realised, of course, that the Tory government was preparing for war, though the actual preparations were made in such secrecy that most of Eden's Cabinet were kept uninformed. And since all the British newspaper proprietors have connections with the security services, they may have known about the MI6 plot to assassinate Nasser. Eden initially approved the operation, according to Peter Wright, and suspended it only when the French and the Israelis agreed to a joint attack.

The Israeli Army launched a full-scale invasion of the Sinai. The Egyptian Army counter–attacked to protect their territory. This was

the prearranged cue for the British and French governments to issue an ultimatum which they knew must be rejected: Egyptian troops must withdraw 10 miles from the Canal Zone, allowing British and French troops to occupy Port Said, Suez and Ismailia, 'to separate the belligerents'. To maintain this fraud, the ultimatum was simultaneously conveyed to the Israeli government, which of course accepted it. It had already been agreed that the Israeli Army would halt its invasion outside the 10-mile 'exclusion zone' so that it could accept the ultimatum and hold its troops at the ready.

On the same day, Thursday 1 November, fresh Soviet troops entered Hungary, replacing the battalions which had disobeyed orders and fraternised with the Hungarian workers. The following morning Premier Imre Nagy appealed to the West to intervene. But this same West – Britain and France – was engaged in the military conquest of an Arab country, Egypt, whose people had dared to fight for their independence and claim their rights.

I could not understand this contradiction, and no one I knew was able to explain or clarify these events. I listened to Eden's radio broadcast that weekend, and marvelled at the sincere and plausible way he delivered his speech based entirely on lies. I knew that Britain, France and Israel were committing a crime, and that the same brutal colonialism which had tried and failed to conquer in Kenya, Malaya and Vietnam was in action again. I knew that none of them, no matter how earnestly their spokesmen appealed to international law, had the right to claim a single yard of Egyptian territory as their own. And I knew for the first time what Israel was: a state whose rulers shared the same kind of racist and colonialist outlook as Britain.

I must have walked miles that weekend, arguing with myself, questions tumbling round in my mind, searching in vain for an explanation. Why was the Soviet Union invading Hungary, and yet supporting Nasser and the Egyptians? Why was one socialist country invading another? I no more believed the official Soviet explanation of events in Hungary than I believed Eden's speech.

Why did the United States oppose the invasion of Egypt, and refuse Imre Nagy's appeal for help? I read the newspapers every day, but everything I read presented the same contradictions with no explanation.

Hard work, I thought, will provide some relief, so I threw myself into preparation for *The Mulberry Bush* and dashed off letters to Cousin Lucy, seeking her advice. 'I don't think you could have found a better introduction to the state of mind and opinion which generated social reform than to read about Eleanor Rathbone in Mrs Stock's life of her,' she replied.

E.R. worked unceasingly for refugees and Jews in the Hitler days of hideous oppression. Eleanor killed herself literally with overwork and most rigid rationing. I can tell you more about her when we meet. . . . To trace the history of social reform one has to go back into the 19th century, when the social conscience was awakened. You read Dickens and earlier than that the work of Mrs Gaskell, where you realise the conditions of child labour in the mills, the hideous poverty of the old, the frightful treatment of the insane – and I *think* that the awakening was due to two main causes, the Liberal spirit tradition that made itself felt increasingly in the second half of the century – Lord Shaftesbury and the 'ragged school' etc. – and the doctrine of the perfectibility of human nature. It all derives really from the 18th century and the French Revolution and all that. But one really cannot go back too far at the moment. . . . At present one can think of little but Hungary. . . .

And that was true. I wanted desperately to go to Hungary and join the revolution. But I had no skills that would be useful, and I knew from Lajos Lederer's reports in *The Observer* that only those who brought supplies of medicine or food were likely to be allowed to cross the frontier posts, which were controlled by detachments from the workers' and students' brigades. Then I read a letter in the *Guardian* from a Hungarian organisation in Ladbroke Grove, appealing for volunteers to help sort and pack clothes for the refugees pouring into Austria from Hungary. I told my parents I must leave Central at once. It was the autumn term, 1956, the start of my final year. Michael was in New York, having just opened in Terence Rattigan's *The Sleeping Prince*. I knew he would be alarmed and I tried to reassure him by telling him that Gwyneth Thurburn had said I could return the following term if I wished to, but I knew too that nothing he or Rachel might say could dissuade me. I was adamant.

A red, white and green Hungarian flag hung over the front door of the address in Ladbroke Grove. I was shown upstairs to a room full of clothes and was told to sort them into piles – trousers, skirts, shoes, coats, gloves, children's clothes – and put them into hessian sacks. I worked with the other volunteers from first thing in the morning until late at night, with a plate of goulash for dinner at midday. Every morning, before catching the bus, I would pore over the newspapers. The workers were forming councils, which in effect were soviets. A letter in *The Times* confirmed that real authority in Hungary for the past few weeks was 'in the hands of the workers' councils, now outlawed by a regime which is supported by nobody except the invading Soviet forces'. I went along to my first political rally, at the Albert Hall. It was a huge gathering, very subdued, and I remember nothing of what was said nor even the names of the speakers, only the freedom fighters who came on to the platform, wearing black hoods to prevent identification.

'One feels quite desperate at being so helpless,' wrote Cousin Lucy, 'but one must cling to the fact that we *are* doing what lies in our power, little as that is, and I think the Hungarians know it. It is for *Europe* to pull together and that is exactly what they are *not* doing. Then there might be a solid body of opinion to which even Russia might pay some attention.' Signing herself 'your loving old cousin', she added a comforting postscript: 'And I *do* think you are doing all you can to help.'

But it was no comfort, though it was kindly meant. I had no wish to disparage my work, nor my fellow volunteers who worked every bit as hard as I. But surely it could not be all that could be done? The Christmas lights and decorations in the shops around Knightsbridge and Kensington seemed grotesque. Training to be an actress and planning a career seemed utterly secondary, of little or no importance. Reality, in the form of the Hungarian political revolution, had burst through the limits of my student life and my ambitions. Worse still, it confronted me with the poverty of my knowledge. I sorted clothes, I traced maps for students I met in Ladbroke Grove and later in the house of an anti-communist Hungarian woman in Elizabeth Street, but I could go no further. The Hungarian revolution was crushed, the British and French troops were forced to withdraw from Suez, and I could not understand what could be done politically because I could not understand these contradictions, and I knew no one who could explain them. Dear old Cousin Lucy, aged eighty, the most intelligent, thoughtful and caring of all my relations and friends, was typical of the caring Liberals of her day and could understand nothing and could therefore do nothing. She wrote of 'Europe pulling together' – a phrase which bewildered even my political ignorance – and of 'Russia', bowing before the weight of public opinion, in terms which reminded me of nothing so much as the old *Punch* cartoons I used to flick through at the top of her house in Herefordshire.

The inability to resolve contradictions runs like a thread through the whole of English philosophy and forces it into empiricism and scepticism. So it was in my case. Too many questions were piling up, and unable to answer any of them I fell back into the life of a drama student. Get on with the things you know about, I concluded. Leave politics to the politicians.

## 7

'Our year' – Judi Dench, Jill, Amos, Bob, Chip, Sally, Bridget, Anna, Ken, Rod, Pam, Trudi, Jeremy and about ten others including myself – graduated from Central School on 4 June 1957, at a public matinée at Wyndham's Theatre in the Charing Cross Road. Our teachers had selected roles and scenes for us to perform before an audience of producers and their assistants, directors and their wives, casting directors and their secretaries and, of course, several hundred mums and dads, sisters, cousins and aunts.

What a strange ordeal. It seems incredible now that our three years of training and our prospects for a career in the profession we had chosen should be summed up in one hot afternoon's perform- ance in June. But we were so conditioned to accept that our profession was a lottery in which the odds were heavily stacked against us, that I doubt whether any of us thought what a wretched waste of training and of talent it was to be thrust out upon the world in this way. In one respect at least we were more fortunate than those who came after us. At that time, if you were lucky enough to get the offer of a job when you left drama school you could take it, wherever the job might be. Four years later, British Actors' Equity introduced a policy known as 'restricted entry', which meant that only a small quota of jobs was available to students leaving drama school. The West End theatres, and many other areas besides, were out of bounds to anyone who did not already have a union card and previous experience. It was an iniquitous policy, discriminating against the young, those who were trying to enter the profession, supposedly to the advantage of those who were already in it.

Each of us had sat for a portrait photograph and had it copied, postcard size, to send to every management in the country. Mine was by Paul Tanqueray, who had a little studio in his flat in Thurloe

Square. He had taken pictures of Mum and Dad, and my Uncle Robin, who had started acting not long before he joined the Navy and was killed at Singapore. Paul Tanqueray's friends called him 'Tank' – a most unsuitable nickname, as nicknames go, since he was slight and gentle. He flitted and fluttered around his camera, changing the setting and changing it back again. I tried to look thoughtful and serious, capable of playing the 'older woman', which I was sure I was destined for. I was twenty, and my main role in the public matinée was that of a forty-five-year-old society mother. I was disappointed with the part, but well prepared to swallow the lump in my throat and do my best.

Strangely, I cannot remember the play from which my scene was taken, or anything about the other characters, or even the name of the character I was playing. I must have played many such parts in my last year at Central and in my memory now they have merged into one. I thought I knew all about how to make-up for such parts using the fat, hard sticks of Leichner greasepaint which were the tools of the trade. How to use the palm of the hand as a palette, smeared with a dab of Crowe's Cremine, which the warmth of the hand melted, rubbing the sticks of No.9 and No.5 into the warm, greasy palm to make a flesh tint of 9 'n 5. A touch of No.3 and a dab of one of the slender carmines brought a blush to the cheeks. For the lips carmine, mixed with white No.20, produced a pink suitable for Shakespeare. For modern parts you used vermilion, or a real lipstick if you could afford it. To curl or wave our hair we used kirby grips or pipe cleaners. There were no electric tongs or heated rollers then, although I did possess three giant American metal clip rollers that I had brought back from my trip to New York.

For the older woman, as a rule I used a generous sprinkling of Johnson's baby powder for my hair. But as this was our final show we who played the older parts were allowed to hire wigs. I chose an absolutely white wig with a blue rinse, short and waved. My own mother was forty-five and if she had any white hairs one never noticed them. But I drew no conclusion from that. If I were to convince an audience that I was a society woman of forty-five I had first of all to convince myself, and that meant a white wig.

I looked at myself in the mirror. The woman who looked back was satisfyingly different from myself, and certainly considerably older. I patted my blue-rinsed white wig from behind with the palm of my hand. Society women have their hair dressed every day.

They make such gestures, half unconsciously, reassuring themselves that every hair is in place. But still there was something about that woman in the mirror, my reflection, that was disconcertingly like myself. Of course – my glasses! My wretched, pebble-thick glasses. If I took them off, all that remained in the mirror was an indistinguishable blur. It would be many years later that I acquired contact lenses and could finally see my reflection unadorned with glasses, could apply make-up without a hand mirror a few inches away from my face and, most important of all, see the other actors on stage.

Half an hour still to go before my scene. In another hour it would all be over, my three years' training at Central. In those three years I had played scenes from Shakespeare, Beaumont and Fletcher (Jacobean), Wycherly, Congreve and Farquhar (Restoration), George Bernard Shaw and Ibsen (Modern Classics), J. B. Priestley (Modern), and several plays you could forget as soon as look at them because 'that's the kind of play you'll be doing in weekly rep'. Nothing by Tennessee Williams, or Arthur Miller, or Eugene O'Neill. No French drama, except Anouilh's *Ring Round the Moon*, in which Judi Dench had been wonderful, and no German drama at all. In other words we had been trained for the English theatre as it was.

In the summer of our first year we performed scenes from *The Merchant of Venice*. I was allotted Act I Scene ii of Portia, Judi Dench the final scene, coming home to Belmont. We shared the same costume, which made us laugh for a lifetime – she is just one inch over five foot. The wardrobe mistress Mrs Fox, still in wardrobe when my daughter Natasha went to Central in 1980 twenty-three years later, did a brilliant job with a false hem. I copied Peggy Ashcroft and Richard Burton alternately. I loved Peggy's work and her spontaneous joy as she performed. I hated my voice, which didn't sound right, because I didn't sound like her or Burton. I was nervous, self-conscious and my throat tightened hard when I came to speak on stage, far worse than any other students. I looked at Judi and was both admiring and jealous. She was confident enough to speak in her own voice; she skipped and hopped with pleasure and excitement up the stairs, down the corridors and on to the stage. She wore jeans, the only girl who had them, a polo neck sweater and ballet slippers that flopped and flapped as she bounded around. When I came back, after the Easter holiday and joined the crowd round the noticeboard with the plays and cast lists, Sue in my year turned and saw me. 'Oh you. You haven't changed.' My heart sank like a stone. I wanted to change. I felt unattractive and old-fashioned. My hair wasn't sleek like Judi's. It crinkled and fuzzed in the damp air. I screwed it round into a sausage roll and clamped the coil on to my head with Kirbygrips.

There had been one chance to do something different, and I had seized it. In our second year we were invited to submit proposals for a student production. I asked my father's friend Fred Sadoff for advice, and he suggested Federico García Lorca's *Blood Wedding*. I read it and was astounded. Why had no one at Central ever mentioned this great poet? Obviously, because they had never heard of him. Fred explained that Lorca had been murdered by the Fascists in Spain because he was in sympathy with the revolution, and also because he was homosexual. I was wrong. The Central staff had heard of Lorca and, what was more, they accepted my proposal and told me to go ahead.

Every night after school I sat up late and then rose at 5 a.m., copying the refrains of Andalusian peasant songs from a book I had found in the local library and plotting the physical positions and movements of the characters with figures I had made from plasticine. I looked everywhere for books and photographs of Spain at the turn of the century. I knew that Lorca's poetry had to be grounded in the physical representation of a hard-working, superstitious peasantry in the Spain of the 1900s. The bride's family sat stiffly and formally on four black, wooden high-backed chairs in an empty pink room dominated by a large, black wooden door centre stage. The bride was dressed to meet her husband in a tight, corsetted black satin bodice and skirt with long sleeves and a high collar.

'And why did you dress the bride in *black*?' It was the day after the performance and we were getting our 'crits' from a member of the drama staff, seated in a circle of chairs whilst he methodically ticked off each note in his pad. Days and weeks of study, argument, hope and frustration were ticked off one by one in his notepad, our enthusiasm draining away as he talked and ticked, without a hint of excitement in his eyes and voice. Spain at the turn of the century, the civil war in which Lorca wrote and died, all faded away, and we were back within the familiar prison of the English Southern Counties. 'And why did you dress the bride in black?' He hardly paused for an answer, and even if he had, I no longer had the heart to tell him how I had discovered that the bride in a Spanish peasant family wore a magnificent black, not white, dress which she would wear again and often, because she had only one wedding but there would be many funerals. And when the song in the text referred to 'the bride, the white bride', it meant that she had lovely white skin and was a virgin, not that she wore a white wedding dress. But he wasn't interested in knowing the answer, and I was furious that he assumed so dogmatically that there could be no valid reason for dressing her in black.

All the while our teacher was ticking off his notes I could see my Israeli friend Amos grinning at me, as if to say, 'What did I tell you? Now do you believe me?' I had often listened to his bitter, passionate criticism of our training at Central, and the standards of playwriting and acting in the London theatre. He was much more knowledgeable, thoughtful and critical than I was, with my English disposition to be fair-minded and see the other person's point of view. Amos had done his military service in the Negev desert. I listened uncomfortably to his stories of ambushes and patrols, and I noticed that when he spoke of the Arabs it was as if they were an alien, even inferior, race, in much the same way as I had heard some English people talk about the Jews. He never talked of the Palestinians, only Arabs, and I, knowing nothing of these people at that time, hid behind my lack of knowledge and deliberately forbore to ask Amos any questions in case his answers might disturb me and make us disagree.

Quarter of an hour to go. Butterflies were chasing each other in my tummy, and my legs began to feel as though they belonged to someone else. I lay down on the floor of the dressing room, resting my head on a towel to protect my wig, and propped my feet up on a chair. It's an old trick, but quite effective. Having your feet above your head increases the circulation of the blood to the brain and makes you feel more clear headed. Then I got up and jogged a little from foot to foot, letting my arms and head go limp like a rag doll.

Maître Harmer Brown taught us acrobatics and fencing. He had his own school somewhere in Pimlico, Salle Harmer Brown. French is the language of fencing. The parries are prime, seconde, terce, quarte, quinte, sixte, septime and octave. All except the last two are pronounced in an uncompromisingly English accent. Quinte, for example is 'kwint', like the dead manservant in Henry

Playing Jack in *Mother Goose*, the Christmas pantomime at Leatherhead, 1959, with Nyree Dawn Porter (*right*); with Tony Britton in *Behind the Mask*, my first film, 1958 (*below*); with Michael in N.C. Hunter's *A Touch of the Sun* at the Saville Theatre, 1958, my first part in a West End play (*below right*).

With Derek Godfrey,
Bill Travers and Peter
Hall at the opening of
the Royal Shakespeare
Company's season in
1962. My Yorkshire
terrier, Marvellous, was
a present from Tony
Richardson (*left*); as
Rosalind in the Forest of
Arden with Rosalind
Knight as Celia, 1961
(*below left*); and as
Katharina, with Derek
Godfrey as Petruchio, in
*The Taming of the Shrew* at
the Aldwych, Stratford's
London theatre, in 1962
(*below right*).

Rosalind in Michael
Elliott's production of *As
You Like It* at Stratford,
1961 (*right*).

Michael and Rachel's
silver wedding
anniversary, 1960
(*above*); and as Nina in
*The Seagull*, with Rachel
as Polina, 1964 (*right*).

James's *The Turn of the Screw*. At least, so it was pronounced by Maître Harmer Brown, who was totally English, and since he was a very good teacher we all copied him. He had taught Corin who as a schoolboy had won the All-England Schools Sabre championship, and would go on to fence for Cambridge before giving it up for study and for acting. Maître Harmer Brown was very rueful about Corin, saying that he had lost his best pupil, who could have fought for England at the 1960 Rome Olympics if he had dedicated himself to the sport.

I was only passably good at fencing, but I thought it was an excellent training for actors as well as an exciting sport. You had to be very alert and watch you opponent the whole time in order to anticipate what he would do next, so sharpening your reflexes. I was never very good at acrobatics, but I shall always be grateful to Maître Harmer Brown for what he taught us, and for one trick especially. He showed us how, if you kept your legs perfectly straight, and your spine straight, you could bend at the waist and fall backwards on your bum without hurting yourself. I tried it, aged fifty-two, when I played Lady Torrance in Tennessee Williams's *Orpheus Descending*, and it worked.


I stood in the backstage darkness in my long green, satin moiré dress and white evening gloves borrowed from my mother. The dress had been made for her by Victor Stiebel, and seemed just right for my part. I wished she could have been there on the audience, and my dad too, but he was in Rome working on *The Quiet American*. Rachel had spoken to Olive Harding at MCA, which was a big theatrical agency in those days, and Olive had said that Kenneth Carten would be there. And maybe, somewhere in the audience, was a producer who would have room for me in his next season. None of us had a job to go to, except Judi Dench, who had already been cast to play the Virgin in the cycle of Mystery Plays at York Minster.

I looked down at my hands, which were trembling slightly, and concentrated all my attention on smoothing my gloves over each finger, and then along my wrists. Stanislavsky, the great Russian actor/director, describes how in an agony of nerves before an entrance, he saw some nails on the stage and bent down to pick them up. One small physical action, kneeling down to pick up some nails, concentrated his attention outside himself, calmed him and enabled him to think.

I had discovered Constantin Stanislavsky's great textbook on acting, *An Actor Prepares**, for myself. No one had recommended it to me, not even my father, who was, says Professor Jean Benedetti in his biography of Stanislavsky, 'perhaps the only major English actor of the twentieth century to have applied the system consistently'. Well, my father had written about Stanislavsky in his book *An Actor's Ways and Means*, so perhaps I should have taken the hint, but I hadn't. No member of the staff at Central had ever mentioned him, or said that here, in *An Actor Prepares*, was the first serious study of acting as a process, the first analysis of a method of work with which an actor can overcome the problems that arise in the course of developing a part, and developing his work. So I discovered him for myself on my father's bookshelves.

The simple introduction penetrated the bewildering, confused and jumbled empirical experiences that were the sum of my knowledge, like a road map on a dark, rainy night in the streets of London.

Since the modern theatre came into existence, something like three centuries ago, conventions have accumulated, outlived their usefulness, and become hardened, so that they stand in the way of fresh art and sincere emotion on the stage. For forty years the effort of the Moscow Art Company has been to get rid of what has become artificial, and therefore an impediment, and to prepare the actor to present the externals of life and their inner repercussions with convincing psychological truthfulness.

I disappeared into my chair. Chapter 2, 'When Acting is an Art':

Because the very best that can happen is to have the actor completely carried away by the play. Then regardless of his own will he lives the part, not noticing *how* he feels, not thinking about *what* he does, and it all moves of its own accord, subconsciously and intuitively.

The next lines had been marked with a red pen:

Salvini said: 'The great actor should be full of feeling, and especially he should feel the thing he is portraying. He must feel an emotion not only once or twice while he is studying his part but to a greater or lesser degree every time he plays it, no matter whether it is the first or the thousandth time.'

My heart was beating with the excitement of discovery: *'Moreover, and this is of primary importance, the organic bases of the laws of nature on which our art is founded will protect you in the future from going down the wrong path.'*

I read on and on, unable to put the book down. Surely this was what every actor wanted, to analyse problems from the standpoint of the natural processes of life? Why on earth was this book, a real handbook, unknown at Central? It was the third term of my second year, and no one had even mentioned it. It was not as if there were no provision in our curriculum for history and theory. We studied the history of the theatre, from Greece to modern times, its architecture and its methods of staging. So why didn't we study Stanislavsky's unique contribution, on the basic processes of the art of acting? I was so impatient to get to Central and tell them all that I could hardly sleep that night.

As it happened we had a student–staff meeting the next day. I sat amongst the students, tapping my feet and quivering with impatience. Why were we all floundering about, sometimes getting it right, and all too often getting it wrong? At the first opportunity I jumped to my feet. 'It's all here! IT'S ALL HERE!' I shouted, waving the book at them. Some students looked amused, others bored, or as if their infinite tolerance was strained to the limit. The staff's response was discouraging. Of course they had read it and felt it might certainly be of interest to students but we should remember that there is room for all kinds of methods or none at all. If it worked for Vanessa, fine, but each individual must decide for himself. No one suggested a reading or a group discussion, and I was too deflated to suggest one myself. It was my first real encounter with ingrained English eclecticism, and I was astonished and maddened by it. I little realised then that this open-minded acceptance of the equal validity of all methods concealed a real hostility to any method in particular, and especially to such a method as Stanislavsky's, which based itself upon objective processes in nature and society as the source for all development in art. Nor did I understand the social roots of such an outlook. But my eyes were beginning to open.

75

It was about this time, 1956, that I attended a Sunday-night meeting at the Royal Court Theatre organised by George Devine, on the theme, 'What is Wrong with the English Theatre?' The audience was made up mainly of young writers, directors and designers. Marilyn Monroe, whom I knew attended the Actors' Studio in New York and studied with Lee Strasberg, was also there. Her husband Arthur Miller was one of the speakers. His play, *A View from the Bridge*, had just avoided the Lord Chamberlain's censorship by being presented for 'club members' at the Comedy Theatre. Quietly and very clearly Miller explained that the problem with the English theatre was that its themes and characters were all based upon the narrow, prejudiced limits of English middle-class life, and a total evasion of all the problems in society as a whole.

I took a deep breath and concentrated on my character's self-satisfaction with her elegant appearance in her brilliant green dress and blue-rinsed white coiffure. I boldly seized the door handle, shouted my entrance line and strode on to the brightly lit stage of the Wyndham's Theatre.

I had won the Sybil Thorndike prize, and begun to search for a job. Directors held auditions each summer at the Dinely Studios in Marylebone Road. I prepared monologues and managed to get two auditions, but these turned into interviews so I had no chance to show how I could act. In response to my letters to every repertory theatre in the country I received three polite rejections at my parents' flat in Hans Crescent. Michael had sold Bedford House in 1957 to pay income tax bills. So when a small brown envelope arrived through the letterbox containing a letter dated 4 June 1957 from Peter Hoar at the Frinton Summer Theatre and an offer of work, I leapt at it.

Dear Miss Redgrave
I was unfortunately not able to come to Wyndham's this afternoon, but my wife came and enjoyed your performance. We should very much like you to come to Frinton. I could offer you a salary of £7 a week. The season opens on July 11th, and rehearsals start on the 4th.
Yours sincerely.
Peter Hoar.

I ran into my mother's bedroom shouting, 'I've got a job!' and telephoned Peter Hoar, brimful of gratitude. It never entered my head to wonder whether £7 a week would be enough, or to think that I might ask for more. I went to work at a coffee bar in the King's Road, Chelsea, hoping to save enough in the four weeks before rehearsals began to buy myself some clothes, which I knew I should have to provide for a ten-week season of modern plays. Espresso coffee had just arrived, and the coffee bar had the first Gaggia machines to be imported from Italy. I earned a pound a day, plus tips, and was entirely happy, dreaming about the season to come.

# 8

Frinton was not in the front rank of repertories. Some seaside towns, such as Worthing, had theatres which played all the year round. Scarborough had a theatre 'in the round', where director Stephen Joseph put on new plays as well as classics. When we opened there in July 1957 Frinton had to be content with a summer season programme of ten plays in ten weeks, which meant about five days' rehearsal for each play. Thursday morning would be the first read-through, and all the moves had to be plotted by Saturday lunchtime. On Sundays we learned our lines. Mondays and Tuesdays were run-throughs, Wednesday afternoon was the dress rehearsal, and Wednesday night was the first night. That way, or so it was hoped, the holiday-maker who spent a week in Frinton might see *Dial M for Murder* on Tuesday and *Witness for the Prosecution* on Thursday. In practice this was probably wishful thinking since Frinton's town council appeared determined to discourage holiday-makers by putting every possible obstacle in their way. Coaches and charabancs, for example, were made to park on the outskirts of the town, so that no day trippers would disturb the residents' peace. There were no noisy fights between Mods and Rockers in this very quiet English seaside resort. But it was 'a job', and I was so thrilled to have it, so proud to be a professional actress paying her own way that I saw nothing to complain at.

I soon found out that surviving on £7 a week was only just possible. Mrs Branch, my landlady, charged £4 a week for bed and a large breakfast. That left £3 a week for food and everything else, which included make-up and clothes for the plays. Each member of the cast was responsible for all his or her costumes. Every Sunday the company met at the theatre for a communal lunch, a great cauldron of spaghetti bolognaise which filled us up for the rest of the day and most of Monday. I think the leading man and leading lady were paid £10 a week; we were all in much the same boat. Equity, the actors' union, which we had all joined, had been in existence for just over a quarter of a century, but it would be another thirteen years before the 'living wage' campaign secured a basic minimum wage of £30 a week.

Half-way through the season Corin came down to visit me. I was playing Miss Pringle, an amiably loony lady botanist in her sixties who offered learned and useless advice to anyone within earshot. In the play the leading man's father has apparently gone berserk, tearing off his clothes and alarming the neighbours. 'What can I do?' asks the leading man. Slight pause, whilst the other characters scratch their heads in bewilderment. 'You could try blowing up his nose,' suggests Miss Pringle. I got a big laugh from the audience on that line, though I think I was much helped by our leading man, Gawn Grainger, who did a long, slow 'take' when I said it. Miss Pringle goes on to explain that she discovered this particular piece of fieldcraft on her last safari to Africa when a native porter recommended it as the best way to deal with a maddened rhino. The leading man looks incredulous. 'Yes, yes,' insists Miss Pringle, and is about to launch into a breathless account of how she faced the charging rhino when the upstage door bursts open and on comes the father in his underclothes, brandishing a poker. The leading man offers a silent prayer, tries to blow up his father's nose, and is nearly decapitated with the poker. 'Not like that!' says Miss Pringle, and proceeds to demonstrate, holding the old man's face very close to her own, before applying her lips to his nose. The old man's expression changes from apoplectic fury to moonstruck adoration. He flings his arms around Miss Pringle, who sighs beatifically and swoons. Curtain.

Corin was very proud that I had made the audience laugh so much. I don't think it had occurred to either of us that I could be funny although my father used to say, before I went to Central, that I should be a comedienne. Certainly I had plenty of practice in my ten weeks at Frinton. In our opening play, *The Reluctant Debutante*, I played the heroine's spotty friend and after that a long line of parts, aged between fifty and seventy, for which my experience with Johnson's baby powder came in very handy. I was never a very quick study, but none of my parts were long, and I don't recall having to struggle hard to learn them. Pauline Murch, our leading lady, and Gawn Grainger performed wonders every week in order to be word perfect on the first night, somehow managing to look different in each part, and always well dressed.

The last play was John Osborne's *Look Back In Anger*, a surprisingly adventurous choice for Frinton, and a wise one: every seat was sold. Half-way through the season Geoffrey Edwards, our director, had promised me the part of Helena the actress, and I began to study it there and then. I knew my father would come down to see me in it and more than anything else in the world, I wanted to show him what I could do. He had first seen me act at Queen's Gate School when I was fourteen, as Shaw's *St Joan*. As we drove home that night he told me that his mother, Margaret Scudamore, had been a favourite actress of Shaw, and later he showed me a postcard Shaw had written to her in 1938 from Ayot St Lawrence: 'What!!! So Michael is *your son*? I must rewrite Coriolanus for the two of you.'

He came by train on Friday, for the second performance, and I met him at the station. He had finished shooting *The Quiet American*. Glen Byam Shaw, Director of the Memorial Theatre at Stratford, had been to stay with him to persuade him to play Hamlet, and Benedick in *Much Ado About Nothing* for the next season. 'Oh, you must, you must,' I pleaded. 'That's what I thought,' said Michael, taking me by the arm. 'So will you?' I asked. He could be very teasing sometimes. 'I shall be fifty next birthday,' he replied. 'What does that matter?' 'Just what I said myself.' 'So, will you?' I persisted. 'Reckon so.'

After the performance he said very little, and I began to fear that he had not been impressed. He had somehow persuaded the hotel he was staying in to keep a late supper for us. As we sat eating I talked without a pause – until I ran out of words and sat miserably looking at my plate. For what seemed a quarter of an hour, my father looked out of the window, or at the space above my head, drinking whisky. Eventually he sighed, wiped his mouth with his napkin, and said, 'Brian Desmond Hurst wants me to do a film about a surgeon. I was thinking of suggesting you for my daughter.'

I met the director of *Behind the Mask*, Brian Desmond Hurst, and the producer, George More O'Ferrall, in a mews flat in Kinnerton Street, Belgravia. All the furniture was covered in velvet and silk; everything looked expensive and I immediately felt out of my depth. The film test, the following day, was a nightmare. I had nothing to do except arrange flowers in a vase, look left, look right, turn towards the camera, and smile. The cameraman was kind and helpful, and everyone wanted to put me at my ease, but I was frozen with fear and felt stupid and ungainly. Three days later a script arrived with a contract for £500. My part, Pamela, was what Stanislavsky would have called 'a stencil'. When she wasn't arranging flowers she was pouring cups of tea. Invariably polite, Pamela was worried about her engagement to an up-and-coming surgeon, her father's chief critic and rival at St Dominic's hospital. But it was a film part, and it never occurred to me to say I couldn't play it, although I knew I lacked the experience or the nerve to carry it off.

Pamela was no different from half a dozen other parts in half a dozen English films that year. There were two stereotypes of womanhood on the British screen in the late fifties. One was the English rose, in a tailored suit, with a handbag and gloves to match. The other was the peroxide blonde bombshell. I fitted neither category. Too tall and too large for an English rose, and certainly no bombshell. Pamela was the English rose, and now since I had accepted the part, I had to try and look it. My father sent me to Dr Goller, a dietician in Harley Street, who put me on a diet of lemon juice, four cups of liquid a day, four ounces of meat or fish, and any quantity of tomatoes or hard-boiled eggs. Fruit was forbidden 'because it turns to alcohol in the stomach', and alcohol was forbidden because of its sugar content. Pills were provided in case the patient's kidneys should rebel at the prospect of four cups of liquid a day.

'Some people have big bones,' our old nanny used to say. 'They can't get thin.' With this theory she stoutly defended my 11 st 2 lbs against all criticism. But my father was very obstinate, and I was determined not to let him down in that respect at least. Nanny's theory proved wrong. I went down to 8½ stone. My bust, which was not large in the first place, shrank commensurably, so the wardrobe compensated by giving me a padded bra, and make-up gave me a big, bright red bow for a mouth. I was so nervous I couldn't smile naturally and when I was told to smile one side of my mouth went up and the other went down. I was told to flick my eyes from right to left when I looked at my partner in close-up. 'Flick your eyes, dear, otherwise they look dead.' I was probably staring through sheer fright, but having to concentrate on flicking them from side to side drove all other thoughts out of my head, and ruined whatever slim chance was left of identifying with my character. A photo-magazine, the *Illustrated London News*, published an article about the film for pre-publicity. There was a picture of a canvas chair with my name on it, and underneath it a caption: 'Vanessa's seat – will it be too hot for her?' I thought it a very fair question.

Michael's next job was a play by N. C. Hunter, *A Touch of the Sun*, and again he put me up for the part of his daughter. This time Caroline Lester was a character I could identify with completely, the daughter of a hard-working underpaid schoolmaster, whose family is invited for a holiday with rich relations in the South of France. My heart lifted. I forgot all about lemon juice and four cups of liquid a day, ate what I wanted and threw myself into work I knew how to do. I saw very little of my Dad after rehearsals, although I still lived at the flat in Hans Crescent. By a sort of unspoken agreement neither of us would wait for the other at the end of a day's work. In any case, when he was working and happy with the work he led a kind of solitary, bachelor existence, eating alone at a club and calling on his friends, always unannounced, late in the evening, and then talking till 1.30 am.

One day, during rehearsals, we did walk home together. 'I felt dreadful today,' I said. 'Yes, and you let everyone know it.' Rather chastened, because I didn't think it had been that obvious, I tried to explain why I felt so bad. I didn't think my character, Caroline, would do such and such, or say such and such. 'Why?' he asked. 'I wouldn't in that situation.' 'But you're not Caroline,' he said. 'Your job is to play *her*.' Because I so respected my father I accepted what he said and didn't argue. But I cannot say I wholly believed him at the time. It was my first lesson in subjective idealism, though my father didn't call it that, and I was far from absorbing it completely. We are so conditioned to start from ourselves, that all too often when we consider a character in a play we proceed from a word here or a phrase there, and instead of considering the character and the given circumstances which make them act in the way they do we are in reality only considering our hastily assembled impressions of the character and ourselves. But in good drama, it is those given circumstances and especially the unexpected changes in their given circumstances which make people act in a way that is *not* typical of them, not expected by others, and least of all by themselves. While I had seen Michael and Diana Wynyard struggle to get their performances right I was very lighthearted throughout the run of the play. I did not have any responsibility for the production beyond doing my part as well as I could, and I just loved what I was doing.

*A Touch of the Sun* opened in Blackpool, in November 1957. I had digs in a house that was so cold and damp with the November air that when I got up in the morning my woollen vest steamed as I held it in front of the gas fire, fed with a shilling in the meter. I shared digs with Thelma Holt who was Assistant Stage Manager, and understudy in *A Touch of the Sun*. We shared the excitement and our problems, and years later when she took over as Artistic Director of the Roundhouse Theatre in Chalk Farm we renewed our friendship and have worked together a great deal ever since. The first night started well. When the curtain rose on the second act, on a huge apparently stone staircase leading up through Riviera palm trees to a wide stone balcony, the audience clapped. Ronnie Squire, a superb comedian, who played my father's elderly uncle, was seated in a deck chair, dozing. Ronnie had been a famously handsome actor in his youth, playing all the romantic parts. He told me that the theatre was so competitive in those days that if an actor was jealous of an up-and-coming rival – and evidently many of them were jealous of Ronnie – he would hire someone to sit in the balcony on the first night and boo the rival off the stage. 'What did you do?' I asked. 'Hired myself a tough,' said Ronnie. 'At the first sign of a disturbance in the balcony, there was a loud clunk. My fellow had walloped him on the jaw and he was out for the count.' Then Ronnie had performed in at least three theatres a night, leaping into a horse-drawn cab, from Act I in Wyndham's to Act II of another play at the Prince's, perhaps ending up at the Coliseum in a sketch at the end of a Variety bill.

Ronnie had a much younger wife, Ursula, All through rehearsals he had looked perfect, with his balding pate, skin that was mottled with age, and a mournful moustache which he tugged ruminatively to 'point' a line. But when the first-night curtain rose on the Riviera, Ronnie was wearing a toupee, quite a lot of make-up and his lips were slightly but definitely pink. The cast looked at one another amazed, and rather horrified. Michael spoke to our producer, Hugh Beaumont. Ronnie must be persuaded not to wear his toupee. 'Binkie' Beaumont spoke to Ursula, who proved herself to be the thoroughly nice, calm, tactful woman she had seemed. 'Don't worry,' she said, 'it's going to blow out of the window.' Whether it did, or whether she spoke to Ronnie we never knew, but the next evening he came on stage without the toupee and the make-up, and no one said a word about it.

We toured Leeds, Liverpool, Manchester, and finally Brighton for the last week before playing at London's Saville Theatre. In Liverpool I had digs just round the corner from Falkner Street where, young and in love, Michael and Rachel had shared their first digs while playing at the Liverpool Playhouse. Like theirs, my bedroom had a real grate and my landlady lit a coal fire every evening before I came back from the theatre. I had a brass bed and a lumpy, faded eiderdown. The furniture was dark brown and on the walls were reproductions of allegorical maidens in Greek tunics. The fire flickered, sending shadows across the walls and ceiling. I thought of my parents in 1935, and of my Granny Margaret – Daisy Scudamore – who had spent most of her professional life touring week by week around the country until she met and eventually married her second husband, J. P. Anderson, Grandpa Andy.

Twenty-seven years later, in November 1985, I caught a sleeper from Euston after a performance of *The Seagull* at the Queen's Theatre, and rang a doorbell in another street, just around the corner from these digs. It was my daughter Joely's first job, playing *Miss Julie* at the Liverpool Playhouse. She was tired and wound up, and we hugged each other tight for many minutes in her bedroom. The next day we went to the Walker Art Gallery and into the Playhouse to see her set still in construction, and her dressing room. Of all the things I had ever dreamed about or hoped for, I had never imagined the pleasure of seeing both my daughters on the stage. Seeing Joely in Liverpool, I knew how my father must have felt when I went on tour with him in *A Touch of the Sun*.

Dad played in *A Touch of the Sun* for three months at the Saville Theatre, now a cinema, in the upper end of Shaftesbury Avenue, before leaving to play Hamlet in the 1958 Stratford season. Rachel was also going to Stratford to play Lady Capulet, and Ursula in *Much Ado*. Michael's part was taken over by Michael Gwynn. In April that year Corin, who had won an open scholarship in classics at King's College Cambridge, went to stay with a family in

Versailles to learn French before he went up to university.

Lynn and I were the only ones left at home that summer in the flat in Hans Crescent and Lynn was in her last year at Queen's Gate school. She said nothing about wanting to act, although I think she secretly did, and I'm certain that if I'd been more sensitive at this time I might have picked up signals and encouraged her. The next year, 1959, she came to Stratford to see me in *A Midsummer Night's Dream*, and when she returned to London she told Rachel, 'That's what I want to do.'

I had fallen in love with the actor playing my brother in *A Touch of the Sun*, my first job in the London theatre. One afternoon I learned it would come to nothing: he was already embroiled with someone else. He had bought an old car, a convertible Jaguar I think, the hood patched together with pieces of sticky tape, and when it rained we got thoroughly wet. But one fine morning in May 1958 he put the hood down and we drove together to Stansted airport in Essex. The Russians were arriving, the first ever visit by the Moscow Arts Theatre to London, and between them the Foreign Office and the Civil Aviation Authority had cooked up a reason to route them to Stansted instead of Heathrow. It was said that their Tupolev plane was 'too big' for Heathrow. The news went round the theatres that no reception or welcoming party had been provided. We were horrified. Thanks to Diana Wynyard, who had found out what was happening and telephoned everyone she knew, there were about fifty of us at the airport, and when the Russians finally landed we cheered, clapped and gave them flowers.

I booked tickets for every Wednesday matinée at the Sadlers Wells Theatre. The Moscow Arts brought three productions, *The Cherry Orchard*, *The Three Sisters* and *Uncle Vanya*. I thought the acting was the best I had ever seen. After *The Three Sisters* I went backstage and for a few moments was able to speak with the actress playing Masha. I asked whether the moment when she watches the humming top on the floor and recites Pushkin's 'The Oak Tree' was created afresh for this production, or whether it was copied from previous productions. She said there had been some changes, but basically this production had been in their repertoire for some time. I didn't think to ask her why the company had brought no new work with them. To see great acting is an inspiration. By that I mean not so much the work of a great actor,

85

exciting as that is, but the collective work of a company. For the rest of that week, and the week that followed when they played *Uncle Vanya*, I thought about the Moscow Arts Theatre and longed to work in such a company. On Sunday I caught the train to Leamington, and then a bus to Stratford, arriving just in time for the start of the technical run of *Hamlet*.

The Sunday technical rehearsal at Stratford was an endurance test for everyone in the company. It was the first time on the set, and too little time was allowed for scene changes, lighting cues, music cues, timing of exits and entrances. One does not go to a technical rehearsal expecting to see a performance, nor anything more than the semblance of the production as a whole. Every few moments a voice will call out from the auditorium and the actors will halt, find a light, take a new move, or wait for some scenery that has mistimed or jammed. The actors' costumes still feel alien to them. The wig is too tight, or too loose, the sleeves too long or too short. The set is totally baffling. Countless technical problems must and will be overcome in the long hours into the early morning. At Stratford in 1958 time was desperately short. Four weeks' rehearsal, Saturday morning the dress parade, Sunday lighting and technical rehearsal, Monday afternoon a semi-dress rehearsal, Monday evening a full dress run before an audience of friends and relatives, Tuesday evening the one and only preview, and Wednesday night the first night with the drama critics from the national press.

My father loathed and feared 'opening cold' at Stratford, without previews or the chance to take the play on tour before showing it to the critics. In his autobiography he claimed to be 'a notoriously slow starter', but amazingly, for a technical rehearsal, the first five scenes ran continuously, without a hitch. My father listened to the Ghost's speech as if the most terrible crime had been committed and his own beloved father had been killed. Agony poured out of him when the ghost had disappeared. 'My fate cries out' was delivered at full power, as if his lungs and heart were strained to breaking point. There were, and are, many fine voices in the English theatre. My father's favourite actor was Henry Ainley, whose voice was legendary, and after Ainley, Robert Loraine, neither of whom I ever saw. But I never heard an actor, other than Michael, who could speak at full volume, without producing an 'effect', a special register. It was awesome, and made the hair rise at the back of my neck, giving me the same tingling feeling that I have when I hear Placido Domingo sing Puccini's 'Che gelida manina'.

The drama critics in England, led by James Agate, had decided that my father was an 'intellectual' actor. And after Agate, Ken Tynan, at whose side the ghost of Agate sometimes seemed to walk. Tynan could be very generous and very perceptive, but he swallowed Agate's opinion hook, line and sinker, as if being an intellectual actor were some kind of handicap or defect. For my part, I never saw any actor, except perhaps in the Moscow Arts Theatre Company, who possessed such capacity for emotion and the appropriate form of that emotion. Michael was unequalled in *Hamlet*, *King Lear* and *Antony and Cleopatra*. Perhaps it never occurred to those critics that only an actor who can think can also feel, to the extent demanded by Shakespeare's tragedies and histories, and moreover without any distortion to Shakespeare's blank verse, and with the form and content of the play so deeply assimilated that Shakespeare's words spring from his mouth with complete spontaneity, as if they had been born in him and were his own.

Later that year Michael and Rachel went to Moscow and Leningrad with the Stratford Company – the first English company to visit the Soviet Union since the war. I have some photographs of Michael, still in his Hamlet costume, moving towards the great smiling figure of Paul Robeson in the corridor of the Moscow Theatre. And one of them hugging each other closely and with great emotion. I found these photos in a trunk I opened the night before I flew to Moscow in January 1985, and called out to my new friend, Paul's granddaughter, Susan Robeson, who was staying in my house in London, trying to find the ways and means to make a feature film about her grandfather. Then we drove over to see my Dad and show him the photos. His eyes shone when he saw them.

That year, 1958, ended with my playing Jack, the principal boy in *Mother Goose*, the Christmas pantomime at Leatherhead Theatre in Surrey. There were no Terry Juveniles and no variety acts as in the big London pantomimes I had seen as a child with Granny Margaret, just the traditional ingredients of a repertory panto- mime: the dame, the pastry-cook scene, the pantomime horse, and dialogue like, 'It's a lovely day, Jill!', 'Yes, isn't it, Jack.' Cue for a song. It had been my ambition for as long as I could remember to play the principal boy, if possible Peter Pan in the annual festival at the Scala Theatre. That I never achieved. But Jack in *Mother Goose* was a good second best.

# 9

In 1959, not long after he had met my father in Moscow, Paul Robeson came to Stratford to play Othello. I was a fairly junior member of the company that season. I walked on in *Othello*, one of the crowd in the Cyprus scenes; played Valeria in *Coriolanus*, and Helena in *A Midsummer Night's Dream*. Denne Gilkes, who taught singing at the theatre, had a studio flat at 18, High Street, which I rented for the season. To be working at Stratford, where I had come almost every summer since I was fourteen, was as exciting as getting my first job at Frinton. Stratford was the centre of the world's theatre, or so it seemed, and this was an exceptional season, even by Stratford's standards. Robeson was playing Othello, Olivier was Coriolanus with Edith Evans as Volumnia, Tyrone Guthrie was directing *All's Well That Ends Well* – it seemed the most amazing good fortune to be working there, in such a company.

Robeson had a commanding presence, and his great bass voice came effortlessly as if from the depth of his whole being. His famous line, 'Put up your bright swords, for the dew will rust them,' was spoken with such majestic resonance that the whole theatre and the banks of the river beyond seemed to reverberate. He was sixty-one and had been ill, spending two weeks in hospital in the Kremlin before his arrival at Stratford. He was under constant surveillance by the CIA, and every speech he made that summer in Britain was reported back to J. Edgar Hoover and the State Department. Glen Byam Shaw, Stratford's artistic director, asked him if he was still a communist. 'Yes, and proud to be,' replied Robeson. But his political ideals, for which he joined the Communist Party, and because of which, when he first arrived in the Soviet Union, he had greeted the land of October as the first country to banish the evil of racism, were undermined and

89

betrayed by Stalinism. Knowing no alternative, he felt he could not speak against Stalin without betraying the Soviet Union. Inwardly, as I learned later, he was in despair. But I count it a great privilege to have known him, even from a distance.

There was a general election in June, which the Tories won with Macmillan's slogan 'You've never had it so good'. I didn't vote. I hardly read a newspaper all summer. I rehearsed my understudy parts, especially Desdemona, with Julian Glover understudying Othello, never hoping especially to 'go on', but longing for the chance to show our director, Tony Richardson, what I could do. I rode my bicycle down the country lanes Corin and I had explored, every inch, eight years before. On Sundays I was part of Sam Wanamaker's baseball team. In August and September, when most of the plays were on, we would play softball with American airmen at one of the Oxfordshire bases. They welcomed us with great hospitality, offering a more bewildering choice of food in their canteens than I had seen even in Stratford's best hotel. They told us about the excitement of flying jet aircraft, which had ten times more power than even the most versatile propellor-driven plane, they said. On their brightly coloured flying jackets they had stitched badges – dragons breathing fire, sharks with mouths gaping, flying tigers – with the caption, 'Aggressor Beware!'

Then in the autumn H. M. Tennant sent me the script of a new play by Robert Bolt. Would I be interested in the part of Stella Dean? My dad wrote a day or so later, hoping I would take the part. It meant I should be playing his daughter again, and perhaps I had other ideas, but – Bolt's play was special, and that happens only a few times in a career. Bolt's title, *The Tiger and the Horse*, was taken from the 'Proverbs of Hell' by William Blake: 'The Tigers of Wrath are wiser than the Horses of Instruction.' Stella Dean's father, a brilliant astronomer, turned to writing philosophy when he married. Stella's boyfriend, Louis, a young lecturer at the university where Dean is a senior Don, says:

'They're beautifully-written, lousy books! Don't commit yourself! Examine your umbilicus! Breathe deeply; turn round in circles and quietly, quietly disappear up your own imagination! He's dangerous, he's off the ground – oh yes he is; when your father walks across the quad you can see light under his boots. That's why your mother's off her head.'

Louis is taking a petition for unilateral nuclear disarmament round the university. Stella's mother says she will sign:

'Largely it's the unborn. The unborn. Radioactivity stimulates mutation; and the chances are astronomically against a mutation being favourable. In other words it produces monsters. Babies that are monsters. I shall certainly sign the petition.'

As I reread these words I think of the article in a women's magazine I read recently in the doctor's waiting room, about jelly babies, products of a nuclear bomb exploded in the Pacific in 1954. Jelly babies have no heads, no arms and no legs, and they die soon after birth. An islander told a conference in London that she had given birth to seven jelly babies. She and her teenage friends were covered with radioactive ash after the explosion. They danced in it and rubbed it over their bodies like sand. All the islanders were removed from the island about ten years later. Then they were returned, and were told the island was free from radiation. Later, they were sent an instruction not to eat fish taken from the northern shores. They had been fishing and eating from these shores for years.

In the summer of 1958 I had argued long and hard with an actor in the cast of *A Touch of the Sun*. He supported the case for nuclear disarmament, and tried to convince me. But since the Hungarian revolution had been smashed by tanks, and Port Said in Egypt reduced to rubble by RAF bombers using conventional high-explosive bombs, I could not see that nuclear weapons were the main issue. Also, I could not accept that marching to or from Aldermaston every Easter would force the British government to halt the production and stockpiling of nuclear weapons.

*The Tiger and the Horse*, and Robert Bolt himself, influenced me immensely. He attended all the rehearsals, never intervening in the direction of the play but talking seriously and deliberately about its ideas. He was a socialist. I started reading a newspaper every day again, where everything indicated an increasing threat of nuclear war.

'It reminds me uncomfortably of the thirties, when, as you remember, the younger dons talked like election agents, and the undergraduates to all appearances regarded their time up here as an extended leave from the Spanish Civil War. They're getting agitated again.'

91

*The Tiger and the Horse* opened in August 1960. After four months, I was released to join Glen Byam-Shaw's production of Ibsen's *The Lady from the Sea* which came into the Queen's in 1961 as soon as *The Tiger and the Horse* had closed after a six-month run, the extent of my father's contract. The cast was led by Margaret Leighton playing Ellida, Andrew Cruickshank as Dr Wangel and John Neville as the Stranger. I played Dr Wangel's eldest daughter, Bolette, and made close friends with Joanna Dunham who played Hilde. Esmond Knight, who had been a comrade at sea of my uncle Robin, played Ballestad.

The newspapers reported that Bertrand Russell had split from Canon Collins and the Campaign for Nuclear Disarmament on the issue of a civil disobedience campaign to force the government into unilateral nuclear disarmament. The Committee of 100 was formed and a number of respected artists and intellectuals put their names down for the Committee, to take collective responsibility for the campaign, among them Robert Bolt, Arnold Wesker and Sir Herbert Read.

I read that a demonstration was planned to go to the US Embassy in Grosvenor Square. I decided I must join them. I told no one in the theatre company, or at home, and joined the demonstration. The police blocked the street leading to the Embassy. Orders to disperse were given by the commissioner in charge. I looked around me to see what we would do. Some of the demonstrators started to sit down in the street. Then we all sat down. Vans came, the police picked us up and put us into them. We were taken to a magistrates' court and fined. I paid my fine and went straight back to the Queen's Theatre, where I talked to John Neville. Two weeks later, Neville and I joined another demonstration in Whitehall. Again we were ordered to disperse; again we refused and sat down. This time we were arrested. We were taken to Vine Street police station, locked up in a small room and then taken to court where we paid our fines and left to go back to the theatre.

It was spring 1961. I had my own flat now, off Gloucester Road, on the ground floor with a door that led down some iron steps into a communal garden. The telephone rang and Peter Hall asked me to come to Stratford to play Rosalind in *As You Like It*. Over the next weeks I studied and learned all my lines. I tramped along the soggy, springing paths in the woods around Wilks Water, the cottage in Hampshire given to my mother by Cousin Lucy, thinking over the play. Denne Gilkes had made the Studio at 18, The High Street, Stratford available for me again. Before going up for rehearsals I listened to an old recording of Dame Edith Evans and Michael playing one of the love scenes from *As You Like It*. Rosalind has long, incredibly quick-thinking, quick-witted speeches. Like a driver about to set off on a complicated cross-country drive to an unknown destination, I needed a really good map. Dame Edith, one might say, had recorded an Ordnance Survey of the Forest of Arden, if only for one scene. Her tempo, her phrasing, her through line on the dialogue, were superb. I copied everything I could, and committed it to memory. Next, I read every piece of Elizabethan prose I could lay my hands on, including the short stories of the time, particularly the story of Dick Whittington. I have never dared tell a journalist that I prepared for Shakespeare's *As You Like It* by reading 'Dick Whittington', but that is exactly what I did. The prose, which was the nearest window into the actual vocabulary and style of speaking in everyday life in the late sixteenth century made it possible for me to understand how a lively, interesting man or woman might talk.

Michael Elliott, our director, took me to lunch on the day of the first night. We had rehearsed for six weeks. I was nervous and keyed up, anxious about the first night, but looking forward to it. Michael was looking at me with the same grave eyes as my father. I thought he was going to thank me for my hard work, offer me words of encouragement. What he said shocked me.

'Vanessa, the whole production is going to be a failure. You won't give yourself up to the play and to what is happening. You are refusing to give *yourself* over, you are holding back. You've held back all through rehearsals, and if you don't go on stage tonight and give *all* of yourself to the play, the actors and the audience, we will have failed totally.'

The grilled plaice turned to sticky cotton wool in my mouth. My jaws continued to munch, but the saliva had stopped totally and I couldn't swallow, I was terrified. Then he said: 'That's all I have to say: if you can't do that there's no meaning to the play.'

John Barton, Peter Hall's co-director, gave me one of his notorious massages. It hurt horribly as I was so tense, his fingers were like steel rods punching away at my shoulders, back and neck. My mind was racing. I wanted to run after Michael and say 'Why now? Why do you tell me all this now, after six weeks?' But I couldn't. I respected Michael and trusted his direction of the play absolutely. Rosalind, which is one of the longest and most complex of Shakespeare's parts for an actress, longer than Cleopatra, had been making me more nervous than I realised. I was cautiously trying to control my performance, to get it right. With Michael's words burnt into my brain I realised that I had absolutely nothing to lose and everything to gain by going with the immediacy of the moment and the audience. It goes back to Jani Strasser's advice – if you keep controlling your poodles they can do so much and no more; you've got to let them off the leash. This isn't something you can suddenly do unless somebody gives you a very big jolt as Michael did. I dressed, went down to the wings, and took a leap into the unknown. All mental control and calculation vanished, all precautions, *how* I do this, *how* I say that. I threw myself into the moment of Rosalind's life, into Orlando's eyes, into the Forest of Arden. Around the giant oak in the dapple-shadowed clearing we danced in a chain, four men and four women, celebrating their love for each other. With *As You Like It* I rediscovered on a new level and in a different way the same sheer enjoyment and living of my parts that I'd felt in *A Touch Of The Sun*, and that alertness and immediacy has stayed with me in my acting to this day.

I doubt whether any other director would have had the courage, or the wisdom, to speak to me as he did only hours before the first performance. Only a director who had won the total confidence of his actors could have said such things, and only a man who cared so deeply about his work would have dared to take such a risk. There are people who will be important to work with throughout a career but if, as I did with Michael, you are lucky enough to work with them at a very important moment of development it will prove decisive. Michael was the same person with everybody, he loved his work and respected the theatre. He saw so much in *As You Like It*, and combined a complete conviction and thoughtful-ness in trying to bring out what he saw in the play that I found absolutely inspiring. He was very direct but when he gave advice or encouragement I trusted it completely which is very rare. Working with him so early in my professional life, and on a classic was crucial, and I certainly could not have played the part as I did without him. A great Italian actress once said to me about the director who found her and cast her in three of his films: 'He is my husband, my lover, my father, my son, and my brother.' I felt that way about Michael Elliott, with whom I worked three times. He changed my life.

Ian Bannen played Orlando, and I was, as every Rosalind becomes with her Orlando, in love with him. *As You Like It* was praised beyond praise. Michael Elliott's production struck a deep, responsive chord with audiences and critics, for there was not a shadow of cynicism in it, and that was already rare among directors of his generation. The word was that 'upstairs' in the offices of the administration the production was thought too sentimental. It was not in the least sentimental. Michael had understood the essence of the play. The dream of Orlando's older brother, which changes him, is the allegorical form of the story for all the characters, who discover their essential, true human nature, at odds with the inhuman world of the Court and Frederick, the usurper.

Peter Hall told me that *As You Like It* would transfer to the Aldwych in 1961, which at that time was the London home of the Stratford company, and asked me to play Katherina in *The Taming of the Shrew*. The BBC wanted to televise our production. Newspapers and magazines besieged me for interviews. I was almost saturated in a conspiracy of kindness and praise, which might have choked me for ever if I hadn't known that Michael Elliott would be watching our performance once or twice a week, and I wanted his notes and his opinion more than any praise. Having the chance to continue as Rosalind in *As You Like It* in London, then play her again on film, was exceptional as it meant that I could change and develop the part, add small touches. With classics – whether by Tennessee Williams, Ibsen or Shakespeare – I find it very necessary to be able to play the part more than once, which is rarely possible today since there is no longer a proper repertory system and rehearsal time is very short.

As I had made a leap as an actress, I took an irrevocable decision to make a leap into political life as well. Bertrand Russell and members of the Committee of 100 were arrested and charged with incitement to break the law when they spoke at a rally in Hyde Park in September 1961. John Morris, a member and organiser in the

Committee, rang me and asked if I would join the Committee to take the place of those who had been arrested. I agreed.

During that autumn and winter, I wrote to my father in New York. A large part of this letter describes my feelings at this point in my life.

My Darling Poppa . . . I go back to London on Sunday to take part in a discussion 'whether artists should involve themselves directly in politics' which is being televised in the new programme of Ken Tynan's on ABC TV called 'Tempo'. Similar to 'Monitor'. Lindsay Anderson and I versus Auberon Waugh and Noni Jabavu, a coloured woman who is editor of the 'New Strand' magazine.

Generally speaking I think that an artist has the same responsibility for thinking and acting politically as any other human being, but of course there are many qualifications to this statement . . . it is said that if Beethoven had joined the army during the Napoleonic wars he would never have written some of his most marvellous work, and the world would be poorer for it. That's true. But Beethoven lived at a time when it was possible to live and work more or less normally whatever wars or upheavals were going on around you. Conquerors needed music and drama in the capitals they occupied. It's a wonderful thing that art has this kind of Red Cross immunity. But Beethoven knew that life would be carrying on centuries after his death. *Anything* we create or work for in our ordinary lives can only be done for each other in the present. The only thing we can do for the future is to do all we can to make sure there is a future.

I want to act as well and as continuously as possible all my life, no holds barred; I want to play Imogen next year, and maybe St Joan the year after that, to play Rosalind all my life! But in the present situation I have to realise that there may not *be* another season at Stratford; it sounds fantastic and incredible; I can't really believe that I haven't necessarily got forty-odd more years of life, but I should be deluding myself if I was sure that I *had*.

Anyway, all this apart, I just can't help myself. The more I think, the more I read (arguments on both sides) the more convinced I am that unilateral disarmament for Britain is a *must – must, must*. And is the only minute hope we can have for a *beginning* which could conceivably make possible an ultimate world disarmament.

But darling, I won't go into details of why I think this.

I can promise you that my present actions concerned with the Committee of 100 are in no way reducing my capacity, will and concentration for acting. You told me that Dame Edith once said approximately 'That one must never let one's life outside the theatre become more important or demanding than one's imaginary life in the theatre' or one's work would suffer. I agreed with this at the time. Because if this does happen, it tends to make the theatre and acting seem too 'unreal' to be gone on with. There is this danger, and I have several times sensed it.

But the last two weeks or so have proved to me that on the contrary my work in the theatre and 'real life' have now marvellously become one. I am more aware and awake in my work and every day life.

When I play at night I not only feel happy, as I always have done, because I enjoy acting; I've always been far too self-indulgent in this as you probably know; but I feel a far greater joy, a longing to share everything with the audience, to give them all I can. I feel almost in love with them.

I used to feel tired and even slightly irritable if I had to do more than two different things during the day – such as writing letters, seeing and talking to someone I didn't particularly want to – I used to feel rather peevishly 'I do like having the day to *myself*'. You may be horrified but it was true. During the week up to and just after the Sunday sit down not only did I have a first night, but I saw and talked to at least five reporters-interviewers, Committee people etc. etc. a day, and wrote all the letters I could, answered questions of any kind as fully as I could, made countless telephone calls (which I am paying for) and answered countless calls; I am reading and thinking and living. Does this sound very silly? Most other people have done this all their lives but it's new for me. Now *no* amount of work can dismay me!

Last of all. I expect you have read a general account of what happened in the Square so I won't tell you in detail. I didn't get hurt as some people did. Shelagh [Delaney] and I, and some other girls, spent Sunday night in a cell of a police station in Ealing, of all places. We were sent there in a Black Maria, each sitting in a little upturned coffin-cupboard with the door closed. I was lucky to be with Shelagh throughout all this as we could keep each other's pecker up by joking and chattering. We were very cold that night on the floor of the cell, and very tired and dirty the next day. We waited until 4 o'clock at Marlborough Street [the magistrates' court], sitting in the corridors. None of it was really unpleasant, but being tired and hungry and dirty completely saps one of feelings, clear thoughts, or anything. The first thing I did when I got home was to have a bath and ring Mum up. Six of the organisers on the Committee were charged with the 1936 Incitement Act and will almost for sure get three months; but they are fighting the case as they were particularly charged with inciting people to charge or break the police barriers. And this is just not true. It is completely against the policy of the Committee for any such thing to be done. And besides we can all give evidence that this was not true.

97

Bob Bolt is in an open prison with the rest, Wesker, Michael Randle, Christopher Logue among others. And they are treated extremely well. But the prison authorities refuse to allow Bob, alone of all the others, to write, and I hear he is very het-up and worried as he must finish the Lawrence of Arabia script by tomorrow or probably be sued by Spiegel who is furious. He even applied to the Home Office and all he can get out of them is that if he would sign an agreement to keep the peace then he could write or leave prison or anything. Why he has been picked upon no one knows.

I'm so happy to hear rehearsals are going so well, hurray. Please give much love to Freddie and thank him for his nice letters. I can't write just yet as I have a mass of other stuff, letters, the discussion, a speech and a poetry reading Max and I are going to do this month.

Fondest, fondest love my dearest – Take care of yourself –
Your loving V.

My father kept all my letters. Alas, I have not kept all his, and I have not preserved his reply to my letter. But reply he did, and evidently he was even more worried than before. He had never fully recovered from his wartime experience with the People's Convention and I am certain he feared I was being used, as he had been used for purposes and a cause he could not believe in. I, on the other hand, could see nothing wrong in being used, provided I understood and believed in the cause for which one was used, which I did.

Monday
Darling, your letter, Express, came this morning, and I will answer it as best I can –

Firstly, I should explain that I have been on a Sub-Committee for arranging the Public Forum the Committee are holding next Sunday. Five speakers are dealing in specific detail with the aims and beliefs of the Committee of 100, and will be explaining why we feel it necessary to commit civil disobedience. The public will then be able to ask questions, and finally Russell will speak. This was an idea of mine, which I am very glad to have carried out, and is probably the most positive contribution I could ever make.

The reason I think this Forum is very important is that most people do not know exactly what we stand and hope for. This is partly due to misrepresentation of us by the political leaders and particularly the Press who are only interested in the sensational aspect, the sit-downs and arrests. *Also* many supporters are not clear in their heads either, and there is a definite tendency to be far more interested in sitting down than the reason why we sit down – I won't go into detail but you yourself probably don't know that many, not all of us, but many supporters and Lord Russell himself advocate a policy of neutralism for England – not to save our own skins but for many practical reasons, thought out in terms of practical politics. However most people think we are just making a cri-de-coeur, or that we naively and stupidly want the West to renounce nuclear warfare leaving Russia a monopoly on the Bomb. Until we can let everyone know exactly what we are sitting down for, we can't possibly expect them to join us or even sympathise.

I have read your last letter to me carefully to see what point in it I had not answered. I found your two main points and I feel that I answered them at great length, however I probably interpreted them differently so I will try and answer them again, and more specifically.

You say–

1)  That I have a divine gift, which is more important than heroism, and that I must do nothing to jeopardise or paralyse this gift.

2)  That I have made my point, and proved I am committed.

Answer to Number 1: I mainly interpreted this in terms of doing nothing to *paralyse* this gift, which is why I tried to explain that my awareness of all the life around me, political, personal, natural or theatrical, and my love for that life which is *why* I act after all, had been doubly *increased* since becoming more aware and involved with the present political situation. As I see it, very clearly, one's desire to act, and the juice, energy and feelings that prompt this desire, *could* be diminished by falling headlong into politics, Bomb, and Committee of 100. But they are not diminished and can never be. However, if one thinks of *jeopardise*, then there are several things to be clear about and beware of, I know.

Firstly, as I proved for myself last week, if I tag along to any or all of the various small demonstrations, the night previous to a Stratford perform-ance, I am very tired the next day, and in fact the performances the next day were not good. This was very wrong of me, and if I did it again, I would not only jeopardise one performance but certainly my work in general and my career in future. I talked to Corin about this, whose judgement and love I respect enormously as you do, and he cleared my mind on this point; but if I hadn't (however foolishly or wrongly) done this just once, I could not have realised so fully for *myself* how wrong and stupid I was.

Lord, I want to act and go on acting more than I can, or need say. Don't imagine there aren't many moments when I long for the personal comforts of body and mind that I could enjoy if I forgot about everything nuclear etc.; I believe I could contribute a good deal to the theatre; and that the theatre contributes something valuable to people; but having become really aware, intellectually as well as emotionally of the present situation – I can never go back – *How* I go forward is something I must work out bit by bit for myself, as I said earlier.

I could go on writing forever at this rate! But it's probably better that it should be by letter than a personal talk, for which there is never enough time, and when we might get too emotional!

I must stop now darling. I do hope I've been able to calm a few of your fears; though as I now realise that you disapprove of the civil disobedience campaign, I also realise that nothing short of me steering clear of the whole thing could completely reassure you. But don't worry about my ever becoming a crank. With my darling Corin, and sensible marvellous friends like Bob Bolt, and you, last but not least, there are enough people for me to discuss matters with to prevent me ever becoming the wild woman of Grenville Place!

Most enormous good luck for the next few days and for your opening. And always all love – V.

Dad was in New York playing in Graham Greene's *The Complaisant Lover*. He had been asked by Olivier to play *Uncle Vanya* that summer at the new Chichester Festival Theatre. Everyone had been sworn to secrecy, but it was understood that Chichester was to be the trial run for the launching of the National Theatre Company. Just before Christmas 1961 I wrote to Dad again from Wilks Water, trying to calm his fears about my commitment to the Committee of 100.

I came here on Wednesday and shan't leave until first thing Sunday. I got another cold and was feeling a bit nervous and depressed, so I cancelled everything and joined Mum here. A few days of walks and music and patchwork in the evenings have already made me feel peaceful and longing to start rehearsals again for 'As You'.

I was wanting to write you a proper letter for a long time. Particularly now. You may not have heard this but whether you haven't or will I want to tell you. I was in a bit of a state last Saturday – the 9th – when I was feeling very upset, and also feeling that I *must* go on the demonstration which would have meant missing two performances. This will shock you terribly and shocks me now I am clearer. I can only explain that I had to for two reasons:

1)  If I couldn't make this sacrifice for something I feel to be terribly important, how could I ever ask anyone else to; and how could I any longer believe there was a small hope of our success sometime in the future?

2)  None of the other 'names' were going for various reasons. Of course as soon as I'd had a talk with Peter and John Roberts to get this off

100

my chest, I realised that I couldn't dream of breaking my contract. So I didn't go, and the 'Sunday Times' asked me for an interview, which I gave them, hoping to get across to them that I felt the demonstration had *not* been a flop as the Minister of Home Affairs called it. The reporter was mainly interested in why I hadn't gone. We discussed responsibilities etc; and I said that you and I had always felt that under no circumstances *whatever* should one ever break a promise or contract, or irresponsibly avoid one's duty to the theatre. But that while actors and actresses of your generation would feel that under no circumstances *whatever* should one break a contract, I felt that there were certain conditions under which I would, albeit against every instinct and wish in me. However, this came out in the paper very differently 'my father has always urged me to never miss a performance or break a contract. But people of that generation would feel that way.' I felt terrible at the thought that you would read this, or anybody else, and think I meant such a thing. Well it was my own fault for giving an interview and I shan't again, but darling I just want to tell you not only that I never felt or said such a thing but that I do see now that I can be of far more use to the Committee if I continue to work as hard as I can in the theatre; and that it is important and more right for me if I do. There is no question of what I *want* to do. To put everything into the theatre for the rest of my life. It is just that for one thing I do not feel at all convinced that there will be all my life ahead of me, or ahead of *us*; and that believing in unilateral disarmament etc. etc., I could not be at peace with myself if I didn't join with other people to do something according to my beliefs. Anyway darling, please believe that I love and respect what you are and what you think, and that I love the theatre. Mum says you may be coming back in April and that you have been asked to go to Chichester. I'm so glad, and I'm longing to see you again.

Very much love my dearest and a happy happy Christmas.
Your loving Vanessa.

P.S. Bernard Levin has now taken me out twice, and red roses on the last night of 'The Shrew!' and is escorting me to Covent Garden on Saturday to see 'A Midsummer Night's Dream'. He is a very interesting person to talk to and I've enjoyed myself thoroughly, but alas! my heart is elsewhere engaged. So we'll have to have a splendid Shaw–Terry relationship.

Alas for Bernard Levin (whose heart is now safely engaged elsewhere, and who probably thanks his maker a thousand times for saving him from a fate worse than death, if indeed he so much as spares a thought for his youthful folly), my heart, and soon my hand, was engaged to Tony Richardson. When he came to see *As*

*You Like It* one night at the Aldwych he said I was the only actress who could play Shakespeare's heroines, and drove me off to supper in his red Ford Thunderbird.

# 10

Tony was rehearsing *A Midsummer Night's Dream* at the Royal Court, with Lynn as Helena and Corin as Lysander. Lynn was in her final year at Central School when Tony asked her to audition, and had been unsure whether she should accept the job. I thought it extremely important for her self-confidence, and remembering how Tony had turned me down for the film of *Look Back in Anger* because I wasn't ready, I told her that he would only offer the part if he was certain she was ready to take it on. Corin had joined the Royal Court from Cambridge as an assistant director. He was helping Tony to prepare the *Dream* when at the end of a long day's auditions Tony said, 'by the way, can you act?' Corin launched into Hotspur's speech, 'My liege, I did deny no prisoners,' and Tony interrupted him after a few lines, saying, 'Okay. You can play Lysander.' Almost all the cast were young, just out of drama school, and unknown: David Warner, Ronnie Barker, Nicol Williamson, Samantha Eggar, Rita Tushingham, James Bolam, Alfred Lynch. The critics who only five years before had ridiculed the Royal Court for introducing the kitchen sink into drama were now equally incensed that the home of the kitchen sink should be invaded by fairies and magic, and lampooned the efforts of Tony and his young cast mercilessly. Tony was absolutely indifferent to his own success or failure, but was very concerned for his young cast. He persuaded George Devine to direct them in a Sunday-night performance of *Twelfth Night* to cheer them up and take their minds off the bad notices.

Tony was twenty-seven when I first met him in 1961, setting aside our earlier brief encounters. He was incredibly lively, full of fun and I admired him immensely. I was attracted to his defiant and outspoken political views, fascinated by the unreserved way he thought and spoke about everything, and by the careless way he treated his own success, which was phenomenal. He always had three or four projects on the go simultaneously. At the time, besides rehearsing *A Midsummer Night's Dream*, he was preparing to shoot Alan Sillitoe's story, *The Loneliness of the Long Distance Runner*, and working on the script for a film of *Tom Jones*. He had made friends with the wrestler Joe Robinson, now an actor, who taught judo in a gym in Orchard Street. Tony and John Osborne, who both took judo classes with Joe, used to hurl each other to the floor in the Curzon Street offices of Woodfall, Tony's production company. One night Tony drove up to Stratford, exhausted after a long day's work, laid his head on my lap and closed his eyes. I was incredibly happy and moved that he needed rest and felt rested. Next morning, before he drove to London, he asked me to marry him. I was back in Denne Gilkes's studio, rehearsing Imogen in *Cymbeline*. I wasn't called for rehearsal until midday, so I lay in bed all morning thinking 'why?' but as the morning went on, still in bed, I changed to thinking 'why not?' I looked at my watch. It was ten minutes to twelve. I jumped out of bed, flung on my clothes, and raced out of the flat. Then I realised I should ring Tony, so I ran back upstairs and dialled his office in Curzon Street. He came straight on the line and I said 'Yes, yes, yes!'

George Devine and Jocelyn Herbert were our best man and best woman at the Register Office at Hammersmith Town Hall on 28 April 1962. We drank champagne, and Michael, Rachel, Corin and Lynn joined us all at Tony's home in Eaton Mews South. I did two performances of *As You Like It* and then we flew to Athens for two days, and on to Corfu where we walked, and found small cafés that served lobster and wine. All through the summer Jan, Tony's Polish driver, came and fetched me from Stratford and took me down to Dorset and Somerset where *Tom Jones* was being filmed. Rachel, George Devine, Dame Edith and countless other brilliant actors had parts in the film. It was a masterpiece.

By now I was fully participating in all the daily meetings of the Committee of 100 in their offices at Finsbury Park. We had planned a mass civil disobedience action around the entrances to the US Air Force base at Wethersfield in Essex. The leaflet we printed had a map of the base showing the entrances and feeder roads. This brought a Special Branch raid on the Committee offices. Returning to my flat after a performance at the theatre I found two Special Branch officers in plain clothes waiting for me. They asked to come

As Susan Thistlewood in Robert Shaw's superb play *Cato Street* at the Young Vic, 1971 (*above*); and (*right*) as Polly Peacham in Tony Richardson's production of Brecht's *The Threepenny Opera* at the Prince of Wales Theatre, 1972.

Tony and I off on our honeymoon, June 1962 (*above*); Natasha, just after she was born, 11 May 1963 – Tony took the picture (*top right*); and (*right*) Tasha and Joely aged four and three – I took this one.

On holiday with Tony in Mexico, 1963 (*right*); and (*below*) Joely trying my glasses, California, 1966 – luckily all my children have good eyesight.

With Michael in *Behind the Mask*. The portrait of Rachel, by Anthony Devas, is now in my flat in Chiswick (*above*); and (*right*) almost my favourite picture of Michael, leaving Shepperton Studios after a day's shooting on *Behind the Mask*.

in, and questioned me for two hours. Had I seen the map before? Had I agreed to this demonstration? Had I been present at meetings on such and such dates? I did not know that it was my right to demand a solicitor to be present before I answered any questions.

All the Committee members including myself were completely taken by surprise. We had not anticipated Special Branch intervention, and neither I nor anyone else at the Committee had sought, or been given any legal advice. Eager to assert my moral co-responsibility and commitment to the demonstration I gave a firm 'yes' to all the questions related to my own involvement in the decisions and the planning, and evaded questions concerning other Committee members with sudden lapses of memory. I rang the Committee later and went over to the offices the next day. Michael Randle, the Secretary, George Clark, Helen Allegranza, Pat Pottle and two other members were charged with offences under the Official Secrets Act. I was not charged even though I and other members wrote to the Attorney-General declaring that we were equally responsible with our friends. The trial took place at the Old Bailey. Many of us gave evidence as witnesses on our friends' behalf. Our testimony was entirely centred on the moral correctness of what had been done rather than fighting the Attorney-General on the grounds that the Official Secrets Act had not been broken and the five were wrongfully accused. One of our witnesses was a scientist who had been one of the inventors of radar. He gave good evidence about the dangers of misreading radar air warning signals, but none of it touched the issue of the breach of the Official Secrets Act.

Michael, George, Helen and others all received prison sentences in 1962. Helen Allegranza was sentenced to a year. On a cold, rainy day she was released from Holloway. We were outside the gates to greet her with flowers, hugs and a cup of tea. I saw her once after that; and much later I heard she had committed suicide. I went to visit Michael Randle in Wormwood Scrubs. He told me he was not allowed any political reading and the book by Mao Tse Tung I gave him was immediately confiscated after I left. By now I knew Bertrand Russell and his secretary Ralph Schoenman very well, and was being asked to speak at meetings. I was already a subscriber to *Peace News*, the pacifist weekly, and I began to read more widely. I became a member, and then honorary treasurer to

105

the Movement for Colonial Freedom. I met members of the Labour Party, including Arthur Greenwood, Judith Hart, Philip Noel-Baker and Fenner Brockway, a founder member of the Independent Labour Party. At a major sit-down demonstration in Victoria Street near Parliament Square, I suddenly saw my father in the crowd. He had come to check what I was doing and if I was all right.

The big question I could never answer to my satisfaction was whether to pay my fine or not. I knew that if I refused to pay I would go to prison, and if I went to prison I would miss performances and be fired. If I was fired I would not work again – my reputation would cease to exist as an actress and the press would not listen to what I had to say. On the other hand, the press never printed what I had to say anyway, only pictures and 'stories', so I need not have concerned myself with that. I had no method for making an analysis, no perspective except that of pacifism and protest. I saw nuclear weapons as a moral not a political question.

One Sunday I had a long talk with George Devine, Jocelyn Herbert and Tony Richardson about an advertisement I had been offered by Weston Biscuits. I was told that if I did it, all the money due to me could be paid directly to the Committee or to CND. I was going to accept. George Devine told me I must do no such thing. Everyone would know that if I was paid to lend my name to promote biscuits then I could be paid (although I wasn't) to lend my name to CND. My name's only value was the integrity of my convictions. If my convictions could be bought to promote Weston Biscuits, then the stand I had made for unilateral disarmament would be devalued. I was convinced that George was right, but I was still faced with the question: what was going to stop nuclear war? The clergymen and pacifists I met continually advised and always discussed the question from a moral standpoint. Then the logical question would be: how many moral people are there and will their protest be sufficient to stop nuclear war? I became increasingly convinced that sit-downs were inadequate. I read a lot about Mahatma Gandhi, and several articles from the USA and Canada about the history of non-violence. That summer of 1962 I read one of the volumes of Simone de Beauvoir's autobiography *La Force de l'âge* (The Prime of Life). Her life with Sartre and the political events she was involved in were engrossing. Her book opened political horizons for me that until that moment had been limited both by the pacifist and religious connections and influences of the nuclear disarmament movement, and by the narrow, insular perspective of the movement and its members. *The Prime of Life* explained a whole period of history I was completely ignorant of – the 1930s, the Spanish revolution and the Nazi occupation of France. For the first time I learned something about the political role of the Communist Party, and the political and philosophical discussions and disagreements amongst French intellectuals.

In autumn 1962 I was pregnant. Tony and I went to New York. He was directing Kim Stanley in a play by William Inge. I read Simone de Beauvoir's *She Came to Stay* and *The Mandarins*. One paragraph I remember, without having the book to hand: Nadine is taken for a holiday to Portugal by Henri. They stand on a hill looking at the lights of the town below, able to drink real coffee and eat fresh oranges once again. Henri is full of excitement at the sunset, the view and the good food. Nadine says she can think only of the actual life of the workers, unable to drink real coffee or participate in the kind of life which makes possible the luxury of enjoying a beautiful view. She tells him she finds the beautiful view and the enjoyment of it obscene.

Tony loved New York, saying it recharged his batteries. I liked it too but found I was looking at it through Nadine's eyes. The rounds of expensive meals paid for by United Artists, who were going to distribute *Tom Jones* and perhaps finance Tony's next film, the vast quantities of food and alcohol – whiskies first and then French wines – and endless discussions of film budgets running to millions of dollars began to drive me up the wall. I was restless and, not for the first time, made a resolution: I must work. So I took singing lessons. My teacher was highly recommended by Tammy Grimes, star of *The Unsinkable Molly Brown*. He insisted on his pupils' sucking in their breath 'Hee – hee – hee!' It was a far cry from Jani Strasser and his poodles. A friend of Tony's found me another teacher up on the East Side in a brownstone house full of old antiques. I went there every morning for a lesson, and then spent the rest of the day in the New York public library.

I began to devise a programme for a Sunday-night show at the Royal Court – *In the Interests of the State*, an historical guide for the modern agitator. My starting-point was the manifesto of one of the leaders of the English Peasants' Revolt of 1381, the priest John Ball. I had in mind that the end would be an excerpt from the Official Secrets trial of the Committee of 100 members. The project excited me intensely. I found my way empirically through my own history. The Peasants' Revolt in England; the revolution led by Cromwell and the struggle over private property and democratic rights between the two wings of the revolution; the question of censorship; the French Revolution; Tom Paine and the *Rights of Man*; the reaction led by Edmund Burke; the Irish revolution; the liberation struggle in Cyprus of the 1950s. I read and read, and was educating myself in the only way I knew. I studied books and microfilm of old documents at the public library and marvelled that I could have access to such material for no payment and without any red-tape obstructions. I felt Simone de Beauvoir was by my side. I ate lunches on my own in small cafés – hamburgers or chopped chicken liver on rye.

I wanted to devise a programme that would be the opposite to the Royal Shakespeare Company's *The Hollow Crown* – an entertainment with music which was basically a light-hearted anthology about the kings and queens of England. I had taken part in several performances at the Aldwych and found myself disliking it, and rejecting my own teenage adulation of the monarchy in the early 1950s. I wanted to discover the historical truth, and present it publicly.

*The New York Times*, unlike the English press, carried daily reports about Cuba, where Castro's revolution had been in power for three years and when Tony told me he had been invited to go to Cuba by ICAIC, the Cuban film industry established since the overthrow of the Batista dictatorship, I was on fire with excitement.

We flew first to Jamaica. Having directed *Luther* on Broadway, and then Talullah Bankhead in Tennessee Williams's *The Milk Train Doesn't Stop Here Anymore* immediately after, Tony was exhausted and wanted to have a few days' holiday before going to Cuba, where he would give talks and interviews. The island was more beautiful than anything I could have imagined, but the poverty of the shacks where Jamaicans lived was stark and very apparent. When we drove in a taxi-cab through the country roads or village streets, they looked at our taxi and at us, as tourists, with undisguised hostility. The hotel at Ocho Rios was extremely luxurious, and the Jamaicans who swept the white sands of the private beach were called 'boys' by the management, although they were adult men, well past boyhood. It was sickening and obscene. We moved on to Acapulco in Mexico. Vast billboards by the roadside, 'Pepsi-Cola Nada Mas'. Water-sprinklers whirred round softly, keeping the hotel grass green. One hundred yards across from the brand-new hotel, its *cabanas*, its pina-colada drinks, its tourist shop full of beautiful embroidered Mexican smocks and papier mâché bracelets, were the small shacks surrounded by fences and dust lacking both water and electricity. I hated to be living the life of a rich tourist at these people's expense, served and waited upon in the hotel, the restaurants and in the port by Mexicans who could not even afford to buy meat for their children. Those children had nothing at all. I felt guilty because I knew Tony needed this rest but I did not feel at all grateful for any of the luxury he was paying for. We went to the Mexican Embassy in Mexico City for our Cuban visas. The US government had stopped diplomatic relations with Castro's Cuba and was already announcing that severe penalties would be imposed on Americans who travelled there.

The first thing Tony and I saw when we arrived in Havana were the giant billboards on either side of the road. But instead of advertising Pepsi-Cola they urged people to learn to read. They urged mothers to learn about sanitation, hygiene and health precautions for their children: 'The mother, too, has her place in the revolution.' Then we saw the Hilton hotel that had been the pride of Batista's Havana. Cuba was under an economic blockade from the United States. It could not borrow money from the American-owned banks, and therefore could not buy urgently needed industrial machinery, tools, or spare parts for worn-out equipment. Food was rationed and the hotel had only two items on the menu, one of which was frogs' legs. There was no coffee, only hot chocolate. Visible on the near horizon, three and a half miles out to sea, was a huge American destroyer, the *Monroe*, its guns permanently trained upon Havana.

Before the revolution, there were only American films in Cuba. In a projection room at the Cuban Film Institute we watched the first Cuban feature film, *Las Doce Sillas* (The Twelve Chairs). We saw a documentary about 'Playa Giron', the defeat of Kennedy's invasion of Cuba at the Bay of Pigs, and *The Year of the Pencil*, a documentary intended to assist the literacy campaign – trains and truckloads of young students with books, pencils and paper going into the villages to teach reading and writing. In the film studio the technicians were working and improvising with equipment sent over from Czechoslovakia by the Soviet Union.

The former Country Club of Havana was now the building site for a new university, planned on the scale and the form of a medieval town in Italy. The former villas of the rich Cubans or American businessmen were now houses for orphans, small schools with 'house' mothers and fathers, students looking after the kids. An enormous effort was being made to provide a full primary and secondary education for the children and youth with new brightly coloured illustrated paperback reading primers with poems and stories by Cuban writers. We went up through the rain-sodden country roads to Ernest Hemingway's house, now maintained as a museum. Clean and quiet, with cretonne-covered sofas, his desk, his books, his bathroom with his weight recorded in pencil-marks day by day up the side of the door.

Our companions were young film workers in their mid-twenties, who drove us around and explained how they all took part in volunteer brigade teams to help cut the sugar cane, the only source of income for Cuba. They explained the history of the United Fruit Company – its transformation of Cuba in the last century into a one-crop economy, and an American colony. The Cubans were under siege from the Wall Street banks, the Pentagon and the CIA and, down on the south of the island at Guantánamo, a large US base. All the film workers were members of their street militia and carried rifles on a rota, alert to the constant attacks from small CIA-backed teams from Miami. Tony held a number of question-and-answer sessions with the film workers. We arranged for one of the young directors to come to London and train as his assistant on his next film.

This experience fundamentally transformed my political outlook. I had seen a society that had carried out a revolution to end the misery and the squalor of capitalist exploitation, and the domination of international finance capital. It had been wonderful to see the kids and the young students, who were teaching them, living in the spacious villas each of which now provided a decent house for some eighteen to twenty youngsters. The revolution had overthrown the brutal military police dictatorship of Batista. It had

110

opened the way for a socialist Cuba. It showed how the rest of the Caribbean and the states of South America might liberate millions from the hunger and destitution of the free-market system, all of it controlled and policed from those giant skyscrapers on Wall Street, the military bases and the domes of Washington. Pacifism was out of the question. The Cubans had to have their revolutionary militias and Army, and they needed all the support we could get for them. Otherwise, the *Yanquis* would certainly bring their destroyers and bombers in to try to regain control and reimpose a dictatorship of wealthy Cuban jet-set exiles and torturers.

I hated President Kennedy for ordering the invasion of the Bay of Pigs and I realised now why the Cubans had wanted the protection of missiles. I saw that while Soviet assistance had been on a small scale, without the Soviet Union the Cuban revolution would be destroyed. I thought of Hungary and Egypt and I worried to think that the Cubans might not get all the help they needed from Moscow. We came back to London in October 1962, filled with enthusiasm for what we had seen, and longing to share our experiences and impressions of Cuba with all our friends. What we found was a shock. George Devine and Alan Sillitoe were excited and wanted to help. But we were appalled by the shallow, insular attitudes of so many of our colleagues. Blank, uninterested looks of barely concealed hostility settled on their faces. I fumed and fretted, and could not fathom their reaction. Now I can recognise a process. It has to do with the power of images. Fidel Castro had led a national revolution in Cuba, but our friends knew nothing of the real Castro. What they thought they knew was nothing but an image, constructed by the imperialist propaganda machine. The image-makers concentrate much attention on the leaders of national revolutions, distorting their features, twisting their words, busily manufacturing an image of a demon or a madman. Every leader of a national liberation struggle has been subjected to this treatment: Gammel Abdel Nasser, Muammar Gadaffi, Yasser Arafat. Fidel Castro was no exception.

We had a house to live in now in St Peter's Square, Hammersmith, and I had several months' more pregnancy. I met George Devine in his office at the Court and gave him my script, *In the Interests of the State*. We cast it with George himself, Robert Stephens, Jack McGowran and myself. I directed rehearsals and we performed it on a Sunday in March. I remember George

111

standing with an umbrella as George V reviewing British troops in Dublin; Robert Stephens giving Lord Byron's maiden speech in the House of Lords denouncing Judge Jeffreys and the misery of English workers, and Shelley's *Mask of Anarchy*. I delivered a complacent Christmas Day broadcast speech by Elizabeth II, which I counterposed with radio reports of schoolchildren's demonstrations in Cyprus and the sounds of violence of the British troops in Kenya.

I was asked by Vera Brittain if I would accept the post of chairman of *Peace News*. I had tea with her in an apartment just 150 yards from Parliament Square and, thanking her for the invitation, explained that I was no longer a pacifist. Oppressed peoples needed armies and weapons against military attacks by Britain and the United States. I did not support Britain having nuclear weapons because I did not want them to be used against the Soviet Union.

A group of Labour Party members asked me if I would open the first museum of trade union history in Britain. I readily agreed. The new museum was near Wilks Water. Having spent a week in Norfolk with Nanny Randall making nightshirts for the baby, I went to Rachel's and planned to drive over on Saturday morning, 11 May, for the opening. At about four o'clock in the morning I woke up. I felt a periodic pain. By the time the sun rose at six the pains were regular, at about ten-minute intervals. I woke my mother, rang Jan, Tony's driver in London, rang the doctor, rang my trade union friends and apologised that I would not be able to attend the opening after all, I would have to drive to London and have my baby. They were very understanding and wished me good luck; I dictated a message to be read out. I dressed and walked around the small lake. It was a beautiful, sunny morning. The little Yorkshire terrier Marvellous, my present from Tony, scampered through the damp grass. I picked some violets and primroses and drove off to London at breakneck speed with Jan.

## 11

I had signed up some months before the birth with a Mrs Betty Parsons who was recommended by the National Childbirth Trust. 'Pains', according to Betty, were the contractions preceding and following the waters breaking, so that the neck of the womb could open. Contractions came in waves, short and shallow at first, with intervals between, later in almost continuous waves. I must breathe and pant in rhythm with the waves. Then my baby would have plenty of oxygen in her blood, and I wouldn't tense up and fight against the contractions. Only fear, and ignorance of the natural processes of our own bodies, made us fight what we had been taught to believe was unbearable pain, and so prolong our labours and tire ourselves out. 'Give me your wrist.' Betty grasped my wrist in both hands, twisting it in opposite directions, giving me the Chinese burn. 'That's pain,' she said. 'That's me hurting your body. That's destructive and painful. But contractions are creative, and they're *not* painful. Every contraction is opening the neck of your womb so that the baby can get out.'

She warned me that the Harley Street gynaecologist I was attending would not approve of the natural childbirth technique. She was right. He thought it a harmless eccentricity, something to be humoured. I was 2 stones overweight, with a craving for salty biscuits and ice-cold milk, but he never seemed concerned about that, and gave me no advice about my diet.

Why, in the third quarter of the twentieth century, and despite all the advances made by medical science, should attitudes to childbirth be so primitive, even downright inhuman? In the nursing home they shaved my pubic hair and gave me an enema. I'm told neither of these things is done today, but even now, mothers are sometimes anaesthetised from the waist down, which more often than not means that their bodies are torn, and have to be cut and stitched. And why, when there is so much evidence to suggest that the way a baby is handled when it is born will affect it for the rest of its life, should it have taken so long for natural childbirth methods such as Leboyer's, to gain acceptance? I was pleased, and rather surprised, when some weeks later the National Childbirth Trust asked me to speak at a press conference on breast-feeding. I couldn't think why they should need publicity, or why breast-feeding should need my support. I was even more surprised to find that the press attacked what I said at the conference and treated it sarcastically.

The nurses in the nursing home weren't inhuman, they were kind enough, and gentle, but they'd been trained to believe, as had the gynaecologist and all the doctors, that giving birth was the most painful experience a human being could have, and that their job was to administer gas or drugs to lessen the pain. This made it very hard to concentrate on breathing as Betty had taught me; half of my energy was absorbed in fending off the painkillers. 'So kind of you puff puff – quite unnecessary puff puff pant – no really, I don't need it thank you puff puff puff puff – please let me get on with it.' I shut my eyes and shut the nurses out, thinking of my little Yorkshire terrier, Marvellous, as he scampered through the long wet grass at Wilks Water, and panted like him.

Everyone suddenly burst out singing;
And I was filled with such delight
As prisoned birds must find in freedom,
Winging wildly across the white
Orchards and dark green fields; on – on – and out of sight.

Tasha was born at 5 o'clock that Saturday afternoon, 11 May 1963. From the crown of her head, whorls and spirals of hair moved like water over sand stirred by the wind. She smiled at five days old. I was always told, 'newborn babies don't smile, it's only wind,' but when Joely was born eighteen months later, and Carlo five years after that, I knew that a breast-fed baby, who is cuddled, kept clean and carried around is happy, and does smile.

I breast-fed Tasha and kept house for six months, helped by an Italian girl called Viola who lived with us at St Peter's Square. Tony rented a villa for a month in the South of France and we had a holiday of the kind I had never even dreamed of. Swimming pool, lavender, sun on hot stones, aioli, fireflies. The lavender steamed

114

into oil, the grapes crushed into wine. Lynny came over and sang all the latest songs for Tasha. I got up every two hours in the night to feed Tasha, while Tony prepared a film script, three plays for Broadway in the autumn and two plays for London in the spring. He read a book a day, laughed at the top of his voice as if he were almost choking to death, and clapped his hands with glee when Lynn and I sang 'Let Me Entertain You' and did cabaret turns for our guests. Lynn was a member of the National Theatre Company, under Laurence Olivier's direction, at the Old Vic. She had graduated from walking on to playing leading parts. Noel Coward directed her in a production of *Hay Fever* and admired her so much that he wrote his first and only television play for her.

Back in London I began to read the newspapers again. Nelson Mandela, Walter Sisulu, and the leaders of the African National Congress were on trial for their lives in Rivonia, South Africa. The leaders of the Labour Party denounced apartheid fiercely in their speeches. I thought that meant that they would boycott South Africa if they came to power in the next election. I wrote a song, 'Hanging on a Tree', and sang it in Trafalgar Square. I recorded it, together with a poem by Paul Eluard, 'Liberté j'écris ton nom', which I had seen pasted to a wall in Havana. The words of 'Hanging on a Tree' were published in *The Observer*, and a day or so after it appeared someone told me that a group of businessmen, headed by Sir Jock Campbell whom I had never met, had paid for an advertisement in *The Financial Times*, using my song as a text, to appeal for sanctions against South Africa. Even in those less inflationary days a full-page advertisement in *The Financial Times* cost a sizeable sum, and I think I may have wondered if there were not some more practical or better use to which the money might be put. If so, I could have spared myself the worry, because to everyone's surprise, not least Sir Jock Campbell's, *The Financial Times* refused to print it.

> From: Sir Jock Campbell
> Bucklebury House
> LONDON EC4
>
> 23rd January 1964

Dear Miss Redgrave,
I think you may have heard from David Astor that, having been deeply moved and impressed by the words of your song published in 'The

115

Observer,' I decided to try to get them published, in the form of an advertisement in the 'Financial Times.' Businessmen being usually more romantic it occurred to me that they might be influenced by your poem in a way which they are not by factual reporting from South Africa. Hence my choice of the 'Financial Times.' The whole thing has failed because, even after going so far as sending me a proof, and the Advertising Department having obtained editorial approval, somebody decided that the advertisement should not be accepted. I am very disappointed. I enclose a copy of the proof as a monument to the attempt! I sent all the facts to John Freeman, and I think he may say something about it in this week's 'New Statesman.'
Don't bother to reply to this,
Yours sincerely,
Jock Campbell.

Peter Finch and his Jamaican wife Yolanda joined the demonstration against apartheid, on the steps of St Martin-in-the-Fields. He and I were in the cast of *The Seagull* at the Queen's Theatre, he as Trigorin and I as Nina. I've played in *The Seagull* twice since 1964, as Nina in Sidney Lumet's film, and as Madame Arkadina, again in a production at the Queen's Theatre. There I had the almost indescribable pleasure of seeing my daughter Natasha playing Nina – 'my' part. But nothing could erase the memory of the excitement I felt at my first encounter with Chekhov's play. Peggy Ashcroft as Arkadina, my mother as Polina, young Peter McEnery as Constantin Gavrilovitch, George Devine as Dr Dorn. I would listen to George, especially Dorn's speech to Constantin at the end of Act I, almost every night. I did not see how his performance could be bettered. Like Peggy Ashcroft, he was one of my father's generation, whose opinion mattered more to my father than any other. And he had dedicated the whole of the last and best part of his life to bringing forward a new generation of writers and actors. Listening to Constantin Gavrilovitch's play, encouraging him because 'he saw something in it', something that all the others laughed to scorn because it made them uneasy, George *was* Dr Dorn.

Rehearsals of *The Seagull* seemed effortless. Peter Finch and I gave each other carte blanche to enter, move or exit wherever we wished. I was as happy as I had ever been, and longed for Tony to return from New York, where he had flown after our opening to rehearse *Arturo Ui*, so that we could begin work on our next production, *St Joan of the Stockyards*. 'What is so fascinating about Brecht,' Tony wrote, 'is that he makes each and every actor see what they themselves really are . . .'. There is much truth in that. Brecht's play, in the short time that I was associated with it, became a source for the development of my political consciousness. In the microcosm of the Chicago stockyards of the 1930s I learned for the first time how capitalism operated, and how the morality of Christian ideology actively assisted the exploitation of the poorest of the poor. That is not to deny the great bravery and courage of church leaders in South Africa like Bishop Desmond Tutu, or of Archbishop Romero who was gunned down by the Salvadorean death squads for preaching against the dictatorship. But by showing *how* and *why* capitalism worked, not just its cruelties and injustices, Brecht's play showed me that a morality which appealed for charity from the oppressor and patience from the oppressed was utterly utopian and reactionary. Thinking back to the 'romantic' instincts of businessmen, which my unknown friend Sir Jock Campbell had vouched for and I myself had subscribed to, I thought I had much to learn from that.

Donald Sutherland, a young Canadian actor, and Lionel Stander, a veteran of many a Hollywood gangster movie and a fine stage actor, joined the cast. With only four weeks to rehearse, and some of the cast like myself still playing in *The Seagull* in the evening, Tony enlisted the help of Lindsay Anderson, George Devine and Anthony Page, and soon every bar and lobby and corridor of the Queen's Theatre was filled with actors rehearsing *St Joan of the Stockyards* in triple shifts. Tony always turned to his colleagues – directors, writers, designers, actors – for advice, and always listened to what they said. Theatre is a collective art so a collective approach to problems is always the best way, and it was Tony's way. He never felt that his ego was under threat from listening to others, and in this he is almost unique amongst British directors.

It was hard and difficult work. To grasp what freezing cold and gnawing hunger does to human beings we had much detailed, physical work to do to break free from our 'stencils' – 'Please sir, may I have some more?' I was pregnant again, and congratulating myself on the extra energy that pregnancy seems to provide, when suddenly I started to haemorrhage. I stopped work for three days, had an injection, and the bleeding stopped. But as soon as I went

117

back to work it began again. Siobhan McKenna replaced me, and I went to bed for two weeks.

By the time I was back on my feet Tony was in America again, filming *The Loved One* in 1964. I went out to join him. Waugh had written the novel in 1947, but what Jessica Mitford called the 'American Way of Death' was still in business and doing a prosperous trade in 1964. Terry Southern, who scripted the film with Tony, took me to Forest Lawns. It wasn't called a cemetery; it was a 'resting place'. There, for a small fortune, the remains of the 'Loved One' could be laid to rest amidst porphyry statues of Philosophy, Wisdom and Love, watched over by Michelangelo's David or Phidias' Discobolos, in a copy of Annie Laurie's wee kirk or trysting bower. Or, if the relatives preferred, the ashes of the Loved One could be sealed in an amphora and placed in a marble niche in a marble mausoleum, lulled in perpetual sleep by piped music. For a suitable consideration they could provide an eternal flame, or, for a slightly reduced fee, a semi-eternal flame, a gas jet in an iron holder which would be turned on and lit by one of the 'guardians'. Terry told our guide that we were married and wished to book a resting place for my English mother. We were shown the coffins, ranging from the 'Imperial', lined with purple satin and costing $3000, to the 'Commodore', a modest but sturdy oak. We met the chief mortician. I was astonished. Waugh had exaggerated nothing. My mother would be embalmed so perfectly that with make-up, hair tongs and the mortician's expertise, she would look in death ten years younger than in life – for ever. It was astounding to find the funeral rites practised in Egypt 3000 years ago were still alive in the age of the computer and fast food.

I became firm friends with the lighting cameraman, Haskell Wexler, and his wife Marion, and through them I enrolled for a summer course at the University of California, Los Angeles. I chose political science, and for the next eight weeks buried my nose in books or sat in lectures with our course teacher from the Rand Institute. I was twenty-seven, a few years older than most of my fellow students, and felt alternately like Mrs Rip Van Winkle and a callow fifteen-year-old ignoramus. The other students were much better read than I, yet in discussion a narrow, conservative outlook prevailed. They seemed to accept everything they read in the papers or heard on the radio. This was soon put to the test. Early in August 1964 the Gulf of Tonkin incident hit the headlines, and almost to a man my fellow students believed the government and the newspapers' version of the affair. I couldn't. It was all too clear that this was a deliberate provocation. The US destroyer entered the 12-mile zone of North Vietnamese waters deliberately, the Vietnamese patrol boats fired warning shots to drive the ship out of their waters, and President Johnson declared that this was an act of war against the United States. He demanded and won a vote from Congress and the Senate for an enormous increase in funds, and tens of thousands of troops began to land on Vietnamese soil. A dictatorship as rotten, cruel and corrupt as the Batista regime in Cuba was to be kept in power by the American Army, without even the prospect of free elections. I studied every press report I could lay my hands on, amazed that editors and reporters without exception fell for the provocation and swallowed the State Department's explanations. Despite everything, I still believed that the duty of the press was to report the truth, and that by and large they did. I wanted to protest, and wrote an article saying that Johnson and the Pentagon were dragging America into full scale war against Vietnam, and had created a provocation to justify it. I wanted to send it to an American paper, but each day's reading chipped away at my faith in their objectivity, so I sent it to *Peace News* instead.

In the early mornings, while the dew was still on the grass, and not even Tony was awake, Tasha, aged fifteen months, and I bathed in the shallow end of the pool. Tony had heard of a young woman called Jan Stevens who could teach babies to swim, and soon she came every day with her eighteen-month-old daughter, Jolie. She explained to me that a baby's most natural environment for the first year of its life is water. The water had to be warmer than blood temperature, like a very warm bath. I watched Jan's daughter Jolie blowing bubbles, kicking and swimming under water with her eyes open. She wore tiny flippers to give her the propulsion her legs were not yet strong enough to provide with kicking. 'What happens if Tash falls in off the side by mistake?' I asked. 'Once she's confident and accustomed to the pool she won't be frightened,' Jan said. 'She'll just come up and hold on to the side. There'll be plenty of time for you to reach her. Just be sure you don't show her you're frightened. She'll soon learn how to climb out of the pool. We'll show her.' Jan was right. The pool was filled to within an inch of the brim, and in no time at all Tasha could climb out on her own. Jan became my firm friend, and before I left California I had invited her to come to London. She had given me an idea, for a school where every child would learn to swim as soon as it learned to walk. Jan's idea was so simple and so demonstrably right that I was sure it would be accepted wherever it was shown. Teachers like Jan, who extend our ideas of what children can do, and can teach them to do it, should be honoured everywhere.

I finished my thesis, and got a C. In the last weeks of filming *The Loved One* Tony rented a beach-house at Tranchas beach where enormous surfing waves crashed on the shore. I hurled myself into the rollers and was picked up and rolled over and over. I thought, my baby and I are one, tumbling in the water head over heels. She must have felt she was in a washing machine. But I reasoned that it would make me strong and healthy, which must be good for her after all she and I had been through in the first few weeks of her life inside me. And sometimes I would lie for hours in my room, listening to Tony and Tasha playing in the dunes.

I flew back to London in September 1964 for a television play, intending to return to California when I had finished it. But a general election was called and I decided to stay in London and do everything I could to help the Labour Party into power. I rang the constituency office in Hammersmith and asked what they would like me to do. There were three weeks for campaigning and my front room became the canvassing centre for the local ward. The party sent canvassers, I enlisted all my friends and fellow actors in the area who supported the Labour Party, and we worked night and day, pasting up cards and sending out election addresses. I knocked on doors from 9 am until 9 pm.

Labour's campaign song for that election was 'Thirteen Wasted Years' – the Conservatives had been in power since 1951. I thought it rather tame, and despite my faith in Labour and what they would do, I wondered why they chose to promote themselves as the party of efficiency rather than the party of socialism. Nevertheless I fervently wanted Labour to win, and was puzzled by the large numbers of housewives and old-age pensioners in the council flats who told me wearily and politely that the election of a Labour government would bring nothing they needed. 'It won't change anything,' they said, 'we'll still be living like this. Labour don't care any more than the Tories.' 'Oh, they *do*, I'm sure they do,' I protested, convinced I was speaking the truth. But as I listened to the Labour leaders on the platforms I was invited to share with them, I began to have my doubts. They said nothing to reassure housewives and pensioners about prices, the state of their flats, or their pensions. Nor did these politicians speak of unilateral nuclear disarmament or Vietnam. They spoke brightly, cheerfully, energetically, but in generalities. Perhaps, I thought, they were just not very good speakers, and would say more if they could.

So I buried my doubts and worked non-stop. At the count in the town hall we had a majority for Ivor Richards, our Labour candidate, of just over a thousand votes; we cheered him to the echo. I was invited to a post-election reception at the Labour Party headquarters. I danced with James Callaghan and George Brown. Prime Minister Harold Wilson made a speech thanking us all, and we cheered again until our throats were hoarse.

Tony had backed me all the way, and was full of encouragement for my campaigning. He persuaded the studio that all the post-synching for *The Loved One* must be done in London, so that he could be back by the time our second baby was born. Two weeks earlier then predicted I had to go into a nursing home in Welbeck Street and wait for my labour to begin, hoping that Tony would make it back in time. I clearly remember sitting in front of a gas fire, strumming a guitar and wondering if the chords might be heard inside my womb. There was not too much danger of Tony missing the birth as the injections I had been given to prevent a miscarriage had slowed everything to a standstill. Eventually I succumbed to the doctor's advice that the baby should be induced. Just when my labour began, Tony arrived, and stayed with me throughout. He was terrific, murmuring 'you look beautiful, you look like Monica Vitti.' I knew he thought the world of Monica Vitti, and so did I, so my morale soared immediately.

His back-rubbing was not so good, but he knew just what to say whenever I became discouraged because the labour was so much longer than Tasha's. And when finally I could push, he took pictures of the baby as she came out through my legs covered in the white protective grease of the womb like a cross-channel swimmer. The nurses felt embarrassed but he didn't give a damn and neither did I. I reached down between my legs and took her hand. I had things my way this time and put her straight to my breast. Her mouth opened instantly and she took the nipple in her lips and started to suck. The crumpled, wrinkled face began to fill out and the tiny, delicate, tendril-like fingers began to come open from the fist, like a sea-anemone. Joely Kim had arrived on 11 January 1965.

# 12

If I set aside my early stumbling efforts as Pamela in *Behind the Mask* in 1958, about which the least said is soonest mended, *Morgan, a Suitable Case for Treatment*, was my first big film, in 1965. 'What must I do?' I asked Tony. 'You must listen to what Karel says, and try to do everything he asks you,' Tony said. 'Remember, in the theatre everyone has eyes and can watch what they like. But in the cinema only the director has eyes, and they are the camera. What communicates through the camera is a *different substance* to that of the theatre.'

Karel Reisz and Tony had first met when they were making documentaries for Free Cinema in the late 1950s, and were old friends. Betsy Blair, Karel's wife, was one of the generation of artists who had left America because of the McCarthy witch-hunts. Karel had left Czechoslovakia after the Communist Party took power. Both of them were immensely well read and thoughtful, and set the pace for me politically. Karel taught me that when acting in a film, unlike the theatre, the moment is all important. One must never enter the scene with the mood of the previous scene or the previous day. It is wrong to imagine that acting before the camera should be in a lower key just because the camera is closer than the audience in the theatre. There has to be just as much energy and spontaneity as in life. The basic difference between film acting and stage acting is that more than half of the film is *made* in the editing. Both the director and actors can find that on viewing a rough-cut of the film some point they all thought needed to be brought out and explained from one scene in a sequence of scenes is already contained in the one scene and so the additional material is immediately cut away. Film acting is a process that demands the utmost understanding of the fact that any moment in life will contain more in it than any single person involved in it is

123

conscious of, and the actor or actress has to accept and use this all the time. It maybe that one scene that did not appear very significant in the actual filming, appears in the rough-cut and editing to be the *key* scene in the whole film. While everyone participating in the filming is playing their part a strange thing happens, independently of them the story and all their work takes on a life of its own which becomes clear in the course of editing.

All the rules of formal logic that are often and detrimentally applied to acting in the theatre become intolerable and damaging in film making. Michael described this to me once when he was telling me about a particular scene in the film of *The Quiet American* where he had thought he would approach it quietly and develop it into its emotional climax. Joseph Mankiewicz, the director, chose the opposite direction wanting him to start the scene at the emotional climax and end it quietly. This shows how in film you often go against, even invert, what might appear to be the normal craft of a scene. Just as life does not happen in a logical progression, so to try to impose such an order in film making has a totally lethal effect. In filming you have to play every scene as if it is the only scene, and I find this same approach helpful in the theatre. If you keep control of the formal plan you have made in your mind of how to approach your character you end up fighting against the life that the play gathers and develops independently of each individual's consciousness of the piece as a whole. The very nature of film making brings this out as part of the process but in the theatre the old notions of craft and logic often dominate with deadening effects.

Long before *Morgan* was released I began to get calls from producers and directors, and life seemed crammed with opportunity. Frederico Fellini sent a photographer to take pictures of me, looking mysterious amongst the cedars and statues in Chiswick Park. It was about this time that I received an invitation for lunch with a journalist from the Democratic Republic of Vietnam, and met him, his wife and a colleague of theirs in their flat in north London. US troops and weapons were pouring into Vietnam, with the official title, 'US Advice and Support Missions'. In February 1965 the US Air Force began bombing strategic targets – bridges, roads and railways – and all the civilians who lived and worked in those areas. About 25,000 US Army and Marine Corps soldiers were fighting with the South Vietnamese Army units. On 19 June

Air Vice-Marshal Nguyen Cao Ky seized power in a coup, the fourth in six months, and the United States had the man they wanted.

The journalist asked me if I would be willing to go to Vietnam and see the destruction caused by the US bombing. I would then be able to report back to the people and the press in Britain. But I was afraid to go, and told him so. I thought I would lose all prospects of a career in films, just when life seemed so promising, 'and if that were to happen,' I rationalised, 'I should be no use to you at all.' I had torn up my Labour Party card because the leadership under Wilson was backing Johnson's Vietnam policy all the way but there were no mass organisations or protests against the war yet, and I knew that if I went I would be fiercely attacked in the press. I wanted victory for the Vietnamese National Liberation Front, which of course was a very different thing from wanting 'peace' – everybody wanted peace – and I thought that if I went to Vietnam I would have to say so. I trusted neither the Labour Party nor the Communist Party, nor the clergymen, however sincere they were, and so I clung to my profession, feeling ashamed that I could not do what was asked of me, and that I was on unsteady ground both politically and in my personal life.

In 1965 Tony was filming Jean Genet's *Mademoiselle* in a village called Le Rat in the Corrèze, a poor, depopulated, densely wooded region in southern France. On the train with my two baby girls, travelling from Paris to Limoges, I sat opposite a plump French woman in a suit. She was talking animatedly to her companion, a businessman I thought. She talked for both of them, about business, the state of the currency, strikes, and the fate of the Republic, and as the train neared Limoges she concluded: 'Ainsi, je dirai à mon fils – Mon fils! La bataille a commencé et nous, nous devons préparer!' I was almost pinned in my seat by the force of her implacable bourgeois class consciousness. I made a note in my diary, and promised I would tell Tony. And then I forgot all about it. I was walled in with my own problems and my two small daughters, and her forbidding sentences simply evaporated like smoke trails in my memory.

Tony and I were now in difficulties in our marriage, facing problems we could not resolve. Both of us wanted to pursue our careers, and neither would have countenanced the suggestion that the other should do less. So we saw very little of each other. When

Tony told me he had two films to make with Jeanne Moreau, *Mademoiselle* and *The Sailor from Gibraltar*, I was delighted. When he fell in love with her I thought it was completely understandable. She was enchanting. The crew, the cast, the whole village were in love with her. But I felt miserable and excluded. Trying not to be 'in the way', not to be the passive object of sympathy and understanding from Tony's friends, I felt terribly in the way, and resented that it should be so.

I passed the days with Tasha and Joely, trundling the pushchair through the woods to pick wild strawberries, catching baby frogs for Tony's grass snakes. There were some happy times, but not many. Tony and I slept in different rooms. Neither of us knew any longer what to do for each other and I didn't know what to do with myself. I made eyes at a member of the crew, who was very soon joined by his wife. I was horrified by my own pain and dissatisfaction and terrified as I could see Tony experiencing the same emotions. The *Mademoiselle* production finished in Rome, where Tony had rented a villa on the Via Appia Antica. I had a one-night stand with a friend, both of us seeking consolation for our unhappiness, and stupidly confided in a friend of Tony's. I should have known he would make trouble, and he did. Pain and distrust settled between us like a wall of glass. We saw each other's lips move, but couldn't understand a word. Perhaps Tony understood me better than I understood him or myself. Each day I drove down to the seashore, played the juke-box and cried at the words of popular love songs.

I had become a founding member of the Society for Anglo-Chinese Understanding, and was invited to go to the People's Republic of China for one month as a delegate. The other delegates included Robert Bolt. I had studied Chinese for three months. Carrying a Leica camera, a tape-recorder and loads of film, I set off from Rome in a Czechoslovakian plane bound for Moscow. There I discovered I had no transit visa to allow me to stay the night. The young man from the Chinese Embassy explained that I would have to spend the night in the transit hotel at the airport, and wait there until 4 p.m. the following day, when my plane left for Peking. I cried myself to sleep over several glasses of vodka, and the next morning found I was staring at the ceiling, thinking of Tony. I started to write a letter, full of apologies, expressions of love, promises to be different, more loving, more understanding. By midday, having written, torn up, and rewritten page after page, tears flowing down my cheeks and all over the paper, I convinced myself that the only way to show him that I really loved him was to return immediately to Rome. Otherwise, I felt certain, our marriage would be finished by the time I came back. China must wait – I must save our marriage. Tears flowed again.

I grabbed my enormous trunk and lurched back to the airport. I couldn't understand how to use the telephone, and in any case I had no money, but a kind Russian produced a few kopecks from his pocket, put some coins in the machine, dialled and handed me the receiver. He must have been a genius to understand through my sobs and hiccups that I wanted the Chinese Embassy in the Sparrow Hills. In a moment my young attaché came on the line, and still sobbing I told him, 'I'm sorry, I can't go to China. Personal reasons. I'm so very sorry I can't go. My husband and children – very big problems. I'm sorry, I must go back to them.' The puzzled voice of my young friend promised to meet me in an hour. I ran round all the airline offices to find a plane. Air India had a flight to London that evening. I changed my ticket, got an endorsement from Aeroflot and ran back to meet the attaché. He was, of course, totally bewildered by this tearful young woman apologising over and over again and shaking his hand. We said goodbye. I found a $5 bill in my bag, enough to buy a piece of bread with red caviare from the buffet, and a cup of tea. I began to feel elated. By tea-time tomorrow I would be back in Rome with Tasha and Joely. Tony would laugh and clap his hands, and we'd make a fresh start.

In London the next morning I phoned the Society for Anglo-Chinese Understanding, feeling in my bones that my oblique references to 'family problems' were beyond all human understanding, whether Anglo or Chinese, but knowing I had to make my apologies, however futile. Back in Rome, I took a taxi down the Via Appia Antica and shouted, 'I'm back!' as I ran through the door of our villa. Tasha and Joely were having tea with the temporary nanny. Tony was still at the studios. I wondered whether to ring him there, decided against it, and busied myself playing with the children. Hours later Tony came in. He wasn't excited to see me. I should have kept to my plans and gone ahead with the visit to China, he said. Of course he was right. My return was not going to transform the problems in our relationship, but at that moment it was the last thing I wanted to hear.

We were to work together on a film for the first time – *The Sailor from Gibraltar* based on a novel by Marguerite Duras. I told myself we must not let our personal troubles affect our professional work, a promise I knew would be hard to keep considering the nature of the story. Jeanne Moreau was to play the lead, and Ian Bannen the man at the centre of the story. I had the role of his fiancée Sheila, a well-meaning Englishwoman who loses him to Jeanne Moreau. Filming was in the south near Paestum, 40 miles or so from Naples. My first day of shooting was a scene on a sand dune with Ian where he had to tell me he was in love and going to leave me. We had played Orlando and Rosalind together five years before at Stratford. We knew and trusted one another. I did the scene in a couple of takes, sobbing my heart out for both Sheila and myself.

I kept my promise and told myself that if I could complete the work well and professionally, I should have something to feel proud of. We moved to Florence. Our make-up department was in the bedroom of a house near the Duomo, and every morning I looked out at the swallows wheeling in the space above the rooftops with the restlessness that tells you that they will be leaving any day for Africa. I loved that hour in the make-up room before the first set-up, a time for testing out the opinions of those you are working with, hearing and discussing their problems and your own. I love the communal life and the collective work of film-making, and that hour in Florence with a paper cup of espresso from the bar below, a cigarette, a newspaper and Maria the hairdresser, was the most welcome time of the day. Maria was very good to me, and extremely good at her job. She watched my work, and one morning gave me a tip. I was standing close to the camera for the shot, and Maria told me to turn my look up to the sky, slightly away from the camera. I remembered how Lynn had told me that James Mason, after they had been working together for some weeks, gave her a tip. Always look into an arc lamp, he told her, just before a take. Your pupils will contract, and that's good for the camera. Tony had spotted Maria talking to me, and later that day he looked at me and thanked me for working so well. 'The film crew are impressed,' he said. 'They like you. They don't often bother to give actors advice.'

When the filming was over we spent a weekend in Athens

together, and discovered that we could still understand and like each other, laugh together, and have fun. I remember one thing he said to me about this time: 'The thing is, Vanessa, you're simply wonderful in an emergency, but life in between, all the small humdrum details are just as important. If you could only be reliable in small things you would be amazing. But that's exactly what you don't care for.'

We were thankful to find we were still friends and still respected one another. We made the decision then that in due course we would separate, and probably divorce, but for the moment we were in no haste to decide our fortune. In fact we stayed together for two more years, as parents united by love for our children. When the time came for us to separate and divorce, and I moved to a house on the other side of St Peter's Square. We worried about the effect our parting would have on Tasha and Joely. But we both knew that however it would grieve them, if we continued to care for each other that would sustain them in the long run.

Returning to London in 1966, I congratulated myself. 'I have survived a crisis in my life,' I thought. I had a new play to rehearse, *The Prime of Miss Jean Brodie*, based on the novel by Muriel Spark. The girls had a new nanny, Christina, who was sweet and serious and stayed with us for a long time. Peter Wood was our brilliant young director, whose production of *The Iceman Cometh* with Ian Bannen had held me enthralled for all its five hours' length, in 1957. As we began to rehearse, every omen seemed good. I started our long pre-London tour with a tweed suit, a bobbed wig and a genteel Morningside Edinburgh accent, assuming that Jean Brodie, the schoolmistress, would look like an ordinary teacher of her time and situation, only neater and prettier than most. I played her for two weeks like that, and both Peter and I knew we weren't 'there'. John and Penelope Osborne came to a matinée in Brighton, and when I told them my doubts, suggested that I drop the Scots accent for a while. No sooner had I done so that evening than I suddenly realised what was wrong. I stared at myself in the dressing-room mirror – that was not Jean Brodie. Jean Brodie was determined to mould her girls, her world in the shape of her fantasies – the Duce, her hero, D'Annunzio, the poet airman, General Franco, The Lady of Shalott – and so she would shape herself to fit her fantasies. She would dye her hair Titian red, like her adored pre-Raphaelite heroines, and loop it over her ears like

Anna Pavlova, her idol. Within the limits of her small teacher's salary she would wear clothes with a 'medieval' line. Peter, and our producer Donald Albery, understood what I was after, and ordered a new wig and costumes. Now I could restore the Morningside accent, and now Brodie had arrived. Our notices were splendid – for the play, the production, and the actors. That night I looked at an evening newspaper, for the first time in weeks. I was on the front page, photographed at our first-night party the night before. Next to my photograph was a report of a new US bombing offensive against Vietnam.

Michelangelo Antonioni asked me to be in his new film *Blow-Up* in 1966. I began filming by day, while playing every night at Wyndham's, with two matinées a week. Antonioni asked me to dye my hair black and shave it an inch from my hairline to give me a higher forehead. With Michelangelo the camera angle, its movement, the frame, the objects in the frame, their colour, position and movement, whether human or inanimate, told his story. The dialogue was of no great significance, or certainly of secondary importance. Trained as a dancer I was able to appreciate this. I learned to look sharply and precisely at the shapes and colours around me. Exact positions, angles of the body, the head and shoulders, exact tempo of movement were vital to him. I had never encountered such an eye in the cinema. In English and American films, colours and shapes were part of the decoration, appropriate, but only as background to the action. In Michelangelo's films they *were* the action. *Blow-Up* was about the unity and difference of essence and phenomena, the conflict between what *is*, objectively, and what is seen, heard or grasped by the individual. Much later, when I saw Joely in Peter Greenaway's film *Drowning by Numbers*, I thought he too was a director for whom everything, every shape and every object on the screen, told his story. I would only add that Michelangelo's ear, not for dialogue but for the sounds of nature and normally inanimate objects, was as subtle as his eye. The sound of the leaves rustling in *Blow-Up* and of the wind blowing cords against metal poles in *The Eclipse* are unforgettable.

On location, one day, I heard hoots, shouts and laughs, and Claude Watson, our first assistant, came running across the grass to me in Greenwich Park with a glass of champagne. 'You've won the Cannes Festival prize for the best actress.' It was for *Morgan, a Suitable Case for Treatment* and from that moment everything seemed to go mad. I was photographed, interviewed and invited to a non-stop round of parties and night-clubs. At Leslie Caron's one night I was warned by her secretary that a newsreel team from France was there to film 'a swinging London party'. Since I had always secretly considered myself rather out of the swim, for which I blamed my conventional middle-class education, I was hopelessly flattered and thrilled to think that, to the French at any rate, I was part of the 'swinging' set.

One night during the run of *The Prime of Miss Jean Brodie*, as I waited for my entrance into my classroom, schoolbooks under my arm, the other hand ready to open the door with a flourish – 'Good Morrrning little girrrls!' 'Good Morning, Miss Brodie!' – I wondered how is it that I actually know all these lines? How is it that they come out of my mouth every night? No sooner had I thought that, and run ahead in my mind to my first speech, than suddenly the whole thing seemed unfamiliar and far away to me. I realised that I had hardly thought about Brodie since our opening in May. A wave of fear swept over me and I recorded what I felt in my diary.

Through another performance and then the next day, all day, with a shaking stomach and trembling spine. I had a sleep on the divan in my dressing room which made me feel better, stronger that is, so that I was able to control my nerves. Tony rang me and told me to improvise or sing a song if I forgot my words, which made me laugh, and feel more determined to go on and *play*. Also, I forgot, dear Corin rang up, and he was helpful and reminded me to think of the situation and what I was after, rather than *words*, which of course is really good advice.

Wednesday, 7th September.
Panic all Tuesday as never before in my life. I was trembling all over with the effort to remember and keep going and the strain of feeling all this would crack up suddenly and I would go berserk on stage and have to leave or something. This morning I stayed in bed until 12 and went to John Henderson who gave me a shot of B12 and some Librium and promised me that by Saturday all would be well. Robin Fox, my agent, met me at Sheekey's and I couldn't eat I was so frightened. He had a ticket for the show, and all was well in fact, because I had a note from a father who has bought a ticket for his daughter's fifteenth birthday and wanted to bring her round to meet me. I sent a note saying of course, and felt better, thinking I just couldn't go mad and forget, or run away when it was someone's special treat . . .

It is easy enough, looking back, to diagnose some of the causes of my panic. Throughout the run of *Brodie* I was filming, first with Michelangelo, and then with Tony again, in a short film called *Red and Blue*. Work in the theatre, especially in the London West End theatre with eight performances a week, must be recreated every night, and replenished as often as possible with notes and sometimes rehearsal. With no time, and little energy to do otherwise, I was relying on memory to carry me through, and my crisis was a kind of inner rebellion against this. In fact I never did forget my lines, though for the rest of that run I felt that I was never more than one syllable away from a screaming, yawning abyss. Muscles in the face, lips and tongue have a 'memory', and when they have repeated certain sounds and movements a sufficient number of times *they* don't forget, even though the mind disclaims all knowledge of what comes next. But to stand upon a stage and to feel your lips forming words and your throat making sounds with no knowledge of them is – in Kierkegaard's famous phrase – a 'crisis in the life of an actress'. From *Brodie* I went to California to film *Camelot*, and thereafter I did nothing but films, never daring to set foot upon a stage, until 1969 when Michael Elliott persuaded me to play Gwendolen Harleth in an adaptation of 'Daniel Deronda' in Manchester.

Lynn and I were both nominated for Oscars that year, I for *Morgan* and she for *Georgy Girl*, and the press had a whale of a time playing two sisters against each other. I think Lynn would have been chosen, but as it happened Elizabeth Taylor, who had given an extraordinary performance in *Who's Afraid of Virginia Woolf?*, was awarded the Oscar. I saw *Georgy Girl* again recently, and was bowled over. Lynn has a unique quality in her acting, so comic and so vulnerable at the same time.

I also got a letter from Buckingham Palace asking if I would accept a CBE in the 1967 New Year's Honours which halted me in my tracks, but only for a moment. I didn't think I should accept. Why should I, who didn't agree with anything the British Empire was or had done, agree to be a 'Commander' of it? But I did accept, saying to myself that it was like the Cannes Film Festival award, or the *Evening Standard* award which I had been given for Katherina in *The Taming of the Shrew*, though deep down I knew it wasn't the same at all. I wore a leopardskin coat, which Tony had bought me that winter, and went to the Palace telling myself that I was following in my father's footsteps.

Every retreat exacts its own price, even if the bill is presented later. Given the invitation to go to Vietnam, I had clung to my profession as an actress. I had rationalised my decision at the time, and my fear of the consequences to my career, by saying that I could only serve such causes as Vietnam if I maintained my position as an actress, and to do that I must follow my career. That was my father's argument, in those anxious letters he sent me when I joined the Committee of 100, and it was persuasive. Indeed its logic, on its own terms, was irrefutable. But it was wrong. The source of all development in art is in nature, which art reflects, mirrors and criticises. That was why Aeschylus insisted that his epitaph should mention nothing except that he fought at the battle of Marathon. I had walled myself off from the source of my development, but I didn't know that and had no method for understanding it, except an empirical grasping for something which would make me feel stronger. 'A man who has no nature beyond himself,' Karl Marx wrote, 'is not a natural man.' And an actress who uses her profession, as I did, to shield herself from reality, runs the risk of finding that what she is doing seems totally unreal.

On the back lot at Warner Brothers where we filmed *Camelot* there were hundreds of daffodils and dozens of apple trees in blossom for the 'Lusty month of May', all planted and watered and timed to blossom at the beginning of January. Joshua Logan's excitement and enthusiasm, and the skills of hundreds of Warner's craftsmen and women, working for the last time on permanent contract, had transformed the back lot and the sound stages into an extraordinary series of *tableaux vivants*. Guinevere's dress was made of finely crocheted cream wool cobwebs, hung with bleached melon seeds, each cobweb with a sea-shell at the centre.

*Camelot* was the last film Warner Brothers made as a studio product. The Burbank studios went 'four walls' after that, which meant that television companies and Warner-financed films rented the space and hired their crews and personnel on a temporary basis. Carpenters, plasterers and painters in the scene dock, joiners and painters in the props department, tailors and cutters, seamstresses and embroiderers in the wardrobe block – all were fired. Generations of craftsmanship were destroyed, because craftsmanship requires continuity, and continuity meant trade union organisation, union rates, wages, sickness pay and holiday benefits. Of course there remained many highly skilled individuals whose skills were prized. But high craftsmanship and standards require time, and time is money, and the businesses that own and control television production care little or nothing about standards unless they can get them for nothing.

Franco Nero played Lancelot. He was the most beautiful man I had known, but so modest and shy about his looks that it only struck me after months of knowing him: 'That's the most handsome sight I've ever seen.' I loved the way he was on his guard, and kept his guard up all the time we were in Hollywood. The English he described as 'The most treacherous people in the world.' Their hugs, kisses and casual embraces were, he said, heartless, insincere and deceptive. 'You think Italians are always embracing? When they meet, yes. When they part, sometimes. But the English, who hardly nod or shake hands when you meet them, always their arms around you. Always ready to stab you.' We became great friends during the filming of *Camelot*, and when we parted at the end of the film, to meet again in Italy, he gave me a bracelet with a gold disc: 'Francesco e Vanessa – per sempre'.

# 13

Franco Nero was born on 23 November 1941 in a northern Italian village near the city of Parma. His father, Gabriele Sparanero, migrated from the South in the Thirties. With Ninetta, he had five children, Guglielmo, who died as a baby, Franco, Rafaele, Rosa and Patrizia. In 1967, when Franco took me to meet his family, they all lived in a flat in Parma. Ninetta brought a big bowl of *capellini in brodo* to the table. Her speciality, almond cake, was ready for us on the sideboard. Gabriele produced two bottles of his own wine to celebrate. All the tenants in the block had the use of a small cellar in the basement, and every September Gabriele went round all the markets, chose his grapes, and crushed and fermented them in the cellar. The wine was purple, 'with beaded bubbles winking at the brim', and was delicious. Some years later, Franco bought his parents a small villa covered with wistaria on the slopes of Velletri, in the hills outside Rome. Gabriele spent the last years of his life fulfilling his greatest ambition: digging, hoeing, spraying and pruning an acre or so of grape vines, working the earth and enjoying the produce of his labour.

Franco and I met the film director Elio Petri and agreed to act in his film *A Quiet Place in the Country*. Franco played a successful abstract artist who is driven mad by the commercialisation of his art and plans to murder his mistress, an art dealer. We filmed in a huge deserted villa about 20 miles from Vicenza and Padua. Franco and I rented a wing of the Casa Veronese, a villa surrounded by a farm, from two elderly spinsters, the Misses Veronese, and we spent about two months there, in May and June 1967. For Tasha's fourth birthday on 11 May we organised a farmhouse feast, with two baby goats roasted over the wood embers of the gigantic kitchen hearth. Along with Nanny Christina and baby Joely, who was two and a half, I erected giant scarecrows and obstacle courses on the grass of the small courtyard. The local children who joined our celebration thought we were crazy, but they accepted Tasha and Joely, taught them their games and rhyming songs and looked after them throughout our stay.

Franco and I had some thunderous rows and some wonderfully happy days together in Italy. Happiness was driving through the country roads in our white Mercedes at the end of the day's work, singing

> Mai, Mai, Mai
> Am – er – o
> Nessun altra come te
> Val – en – tin – a
> Val – en – tin – a

at the tops of our voices, or playing round after round of *bocce* at the dusty bar at the end of the track that led to our farm, or visiting the shooting range at a fair on Sunday, where Franco won five white doves. He played every game – soccer, pinball and table tennis – with fearsome intensity as if his life depended on winning, and I learned never to console him when he lost. 'It's only a *game*,' he would growl.

'Yes, but I'm sorry you lost.'

'What did I tell you? It's ONLY A GAME!'

The rows would blow up from nowhere, like sudden storms in the Adriatic. Or like an overture from Rossini that gets louder and louder. I was thankful for the many rooms in the Casa Veronese: there was always somewhere to hide or sulk. He is very obstinate and pig-headed, I thought, and congratulated myself again that I had been wise and sensible to resist the temptation to suggest that we might marry. Franco was very kind and gentle with the girls, but also reserved, as if he didn't want to trespass, and they were very disapproving of his fits of bad temper. He passionately wanted a child of his own, and I wanted a child with him. But neither of us wished to marry, and we both wanted to continue our careers.

All too soon *A Quiet Place in the Country* ended, and the girls and I piled into the white Mercedes with the five white doves, and returned to England, to Rachel's cottage in Hampshire. Franco returned to Rome, to the Via Monte del Gallo, near San Pietro.

Tony was filming *The Charge of the Light Brigade*, based on C. V.

136

This photograph by
Skrebnevski was taken
when I was filming
*Camelot* in 1966, and
used by Universal
Studios in 1967 for
*Isadora* (*right*); (*below*) as
Michelangelo
Antonioni's mysterious
lady in *Blow-Up*, 1966;
and (*bottom right*) playing
Leonie in *Morgan*, for
which I was awarded
the Best Actress Award
at the 1966 Cannes Film
Festival.

6 October 1966. Tony Richardson's *Red and Blue*. The songs were by Serge Bassiask (*top*); (*right*) Richard Attenborough's *Oh, What a Lovely War!* on Brighton Pier as Sylvia Pankhurst, 1968; and (*above*) Sydney Lumet directing me as Nina in his film of *The Seagull*, Stockholm, 1968.

In Yugoslavia, Rieka
Opera House, with Litz
Pisk and Karel Reisz
waiting for another
'take' on Isadora's
Beethoven 7th
Symphony (*right*);
(*below*) John
Schlesinger's film *Yanks*,
1977; (*bottom right*)
Hollywood tribute to the
great Fred Zinnemann,
1986. I was filming
*Second Serve*, Renée
Richards' story, for
CBS.

Jean Brodie and her 'little girls' Olivia Hussey and Vickery Turner, Wyndham's Theatre, London, 1966 (*top*); (*middle*) with David Hemmings in *Blow-Up*, 1967; and (*bottom*) with Daniel Barenboim and Zubin Mehta rehearsing *Pierrot le Fou* at the Royal Festival Hall, 1969. I was pregnant with Carlo.

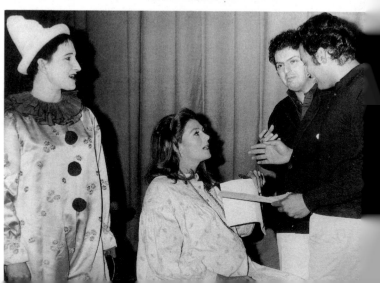

Wedgwood's history of the Crimean War, *The Reason Why?* I played Clarissa, the wife of Captain Morris, one of Cardigan's officers in the Light Brigade, who falls in love with Morris's best friend, Nolan, although she remains devoted to her husband. Whether this part of the story was based on truth or not I don't know. It was probably suggested by Henri Pierre Roche's *Jules et Jim*, which François Truffaut had filmed, and which had captivated Tony. We shot Clarissa's scenes in the garden of the hunting lodge near Rachel's cottage. At the bottom of this garden was a lake which Rachel and her dear friend John Fowler, the owner of the lodge, had restored, and beyond it was the Basingstoke canal, half choked with waterweed and rushes. Roger, the film's location caterer, parked his kitchen-wagon in the trees beside John Fowler's drive. Bernie, one of the 'sparks', wearing nothing but his heavy-duty gloves and a minute pair of denim shorts, waddled to and fro cursing obscenely and dissolving Fowler into helpless gurgles of laughter. They, and many others, all reappeared in Charles Wood's play about the film, *Veterans*. I doubt if any other director besides Tony has had two plays written about him in his lifetime: Charles Woods affectionate tribute, and John Osborne's *Hotel in Amsterdam*, which was malicious. I am certain that few directors have been so badly misjudged by the critics of their day. I find it astonishing and sad. *The Charge of the Light Brigade* was met with the same cavilling, carping, patronising dismissal as had greeted *The Loved One*. I thought it one of the best films about the British Empire and war ever made.

In August 1967, Franco, Joely, Tasha and I went for a month to the South of France. The trip was paid for by Universal, so that I could study dance sequences for Karel Reisz's film *Isadora*, about the life of Isadora Duncan, and have a holiday at the same time. I worked with the wonderful Litz Pisk and Anthony Bowles, the music director, about five hours a day, in a small village hall. For relaxation I played Franco's records, and bathed in the pool. My friend Jan Stevens, who had joined us from California with her daughter Jolie and her husband, saw both of the girls swimming under water with perfect ease, as she'd taught them.

In September, and all through autumn, we filmed *Isadora* in Yugoslavia. It was hard, gruelling work. In the evenings when we had 'wrapped' on the day's shoot, we rehearsed the dance sequences. I felt lucky to have even a 15 minute break, time enough to sit with Joely on my knee or comb Tasha's hair. Tasha was five, confident and self-possessed. Joely was very shy and had a sad, pensive look which touched me to the quick, and made me want to keep hugging her and stroking her to reassure myself that all was well. I loved the work but often wished I had more time to spend with them.

*Isadora* was ambitious. Imagine – the story of an American dancer who broke with the limitations of classical ballet to invent a new kind of dance, in which the dancer would not be miming and dancing to music, but would dance the music itself. A romantic communist, she denounced the greed and philistinism of Wall Street and went to Moscow at the invitation of the Bolshevik government, at a time when famine was knocking at the door of every family, to build a new school of dance for Soviet children – a scenario which no producer or studio would contemplate financing today. Not everything succeeded. Because our film tried to show the whole of Isadora Duncan's life, it left too narrow an angle for Esenin, one of the greatest poets of the twentieth century.

The Vietnam war marked a political awakening for many of my generation. In 1967 I organised a full-page advertisement in *The Times* demanding a halt to the bombing of North Vietnam, and peace talks with the National Liberation Front. Peter Brook and Geraint Evans had signed it, along with a number of scientists and bishops. James Cameron, the journalist, had also signed. He had just published a series of reports in the London *Evening Standard*, the first articles in the British press to expose the sheer savagery of the US government's war against the Vietnamese. Cameron was the only journalist in Britain at that time to challenge our 100 per cent pro-United States press coverage, and the Wilson government's total support for the US invasion of Vietnam.

In January 1968 *The Times* published a letter in which I pointed out how America's refusal to stop the bombing and talk to Hanoi and the National Liberation Front (despite repeated invitations to do so), and their disingenuous semantic arguments, showed that they had not given up blindly hoping for a military solution despite protestations to the contrary. I also wrote a letter about My Lai. An entire village was wantonly massacred in front of eye witnesses, yet every British newspaper referred, if at all, to the My Lai 'allegations', not massacre.

Above the entrance gate at Dachau near Munich you can still

read the words, *Arbeit Macht Frei*, 'work makes you free'. The architects of Dachau chose these words with sadistic, deliberate irony. For indeed, work that enables us to develop our skills and our talents *is* liberating. The Nazis knew this, just as they knew that slave labour, which was the purpose of their concentration camps, destroyed its victims by devouring their human identity. In Vietnam, General Westmoreland and the US forces turned whole villages into concentration camps, and called them 'pacification zones'. In the name of terms such as 'pacification' the most terrible atrocities were committed against the Vietnamese people. One of the most horrible was 'the butterfly', an anti-personnel bomb with scores of razor-sharp blades that propel and 'fly' when the bomb explodes. No surgery in the world can restore the human being who has been sliced in the head or the stomach by those steel slivers. During the Israeli invasion of Lebanon in 1982, the 'butterflies', left over from the Vietnam war and sold to Israel, flew again over the Palestinians and Lebanese, along with the 'clusters' and the phosphorus.

*Camelot* opened in Paris on 13 March 1968. Tariq Ali, a student member of the London-based Vietnam Solidarity Campaign, telephoned me. Would I wear a white headband as the Vietnamese did when in mourning for their dead at the première? It seemed to me an inadequate gesture of protest, even disrespectful, so I refused. But I did agree to lead the Vietnam Solidarity Campaign march to the US Embassy in Grosvenor Square on 17 March.

About 20,000 people came on the demonstration. The big Grosvenor Square hotels such as the Europa were doing a thriving business. Tourists and businessmen booked rooms and ordered champagne lunches so that they could enjoy a grandstand view. When we arrived we were surprised that the police let us in to the square. When most of the demonstrators were inside, the police put up cordons so that the exits were effectively blocked. Mounted police then charged with batons, and large numbers of the marchers were badly hurt by blows on the head or by the horses' hooves. That night, and all the next day, the press and the television had a field-day. The 'poor' horses were the favourite theme, with endless footage of policemen grooming them, and old ladies and children bringing carrots. Glass marbles, said to be offensive weapons, were produced. I was asked if I would appear on television to be interviewed by Ludovic Kennedy. Kennedy, a member of the Liberal Party and a notable campaigner for victims of injustice, was in no doubt on this occasion who the victims were. The police and the horses. At least, that was the line he put to me. I tried to explain as precisely and calmly as possible what had actually happened.

A few weeks later President Johnson announced that he would not be running for re-election and would be calling for a reduction in US bombing raids. I received a rather surprising telegram from the actor Robert Morley, congratulating me 'for the results of your efforts'. I certainly hadn't seen a connection between our demonstrations and the President's announcement, and although I did not feel as optimistic as Robert I was immensely grateful for his encouragement.

On 4 April 1968, Martin Luther King was assassinated. Some months earlier he had been at the Grosvenor Hotel in London for a television interview. I had wanted to ask about his mass civil disobedience marches for civil rights for the black American people, and his protest rallies against the Vietnam war. He answered my telephone call and said he was sorry there would not be time to see me; he was leaving for the United States in a few hours. His voice was strong and warm. We wished each other well and hoped we would meet soon. We never did.

King was under surveillance from the very beginning. But as his work developed he became a target, not only for individual racists, but for the US government. On 28 March 1968 he was in Memphis, Tennessee, marching in support of striking garbage collectors, both black and white. He had mobilised the masses of black America, and for the first time called on them to join their struggles with poor and low-paid white Americans. King had become politically dangerous, but exactly who was responsible for his assassination is not clear. We now know that the CIA was responsible for Nelson Mandela's capture in 1961. It was their agents who gave the South African security police the information that enabled them to arrest him. Soon we shall know the truth about King's murder.

It was at this time that I realised how futile it was to continue demanding that the Wilson government protest against the US invasion of Vietnam. The Labour government had completely tied itself both politically and economically to United States policy in Vietnam. At a mass rally in Trafalgar Square I rejected the slogans put forward by Tariq Ali and his Vietnam Solidarity Campaign (VSC). In my speech I called for the victory of the NLF and General Giap's armed forces, and the immediate withdrawal of American troops. I denounced the Wilson government and said we could not vote for them again.

I was never asked to speak at a VSC rally again. The British Communist Party's policy was for an end to the bombing and for peace talks, but on the basis of maintaining the North-South division that had been agreed by the Americans, French and British at the Geneva Conference in 1955. Tariq Ali's International Marxist Group, which had initiated the Vietnam Solidarity Campaign, preferred an unprincipled solidarity with the British Communist Party and the Labour and trade union centrists to principled support for the right of self-determination of the Vietnamese people, which meant concretely an end to the US puppet state of South Vietnam, and victory for the Vietnamese over the United States government armed forces. So the 'solidarity' of the VSC embraced any group prepared to swallow the line of the British Communist Party, but it most emphatically excluded anyone who shared my position. I could find no political party or group which shared my support for the Vietnamese national liberation struggle. I did not know where to go or what to do. I did not know then that a political party of Trotskyists, the Socialist Labour League, were calling for victory for the NLF. They wanted the defeat of the Wilson government, a general election and a political struggle to elect a Labour government pledged to socialist policies. When one of their members argued for this at a VSC rally, Ralph Schoenman, Bertrand Russell's secretary, tore the microphone away.

I read the news reports from France where hundreds of thousands of workers and students went on strike in May 1968, occupying the universities and factories, car plants and offices. On 4 June the French Treasury borrowed $745 million from the International Monetary Fund. At the end of the month, President Johnson announced US participation in an international 'paper-gold' plan and appealed to Americans to 'Buy American' and save the dollar. The United States government had an international crisis of enormous proportions on their hands. But I was unable to grasp the interconnections between this and all the political developments I read about, so I retreated and took refuge again in my professional work.

141

When I packed my bags and flew with Tasha and Joely to Sweden to play Nina in a film of Chekhov's *The Seagull*, I shut my mind to all that was taking place in the world. Sidney Lumet, his wife Gail and their children were in Stockholm with Simone Signoret, James Mason, David Warner and his girlfriend. Harry Andrews, Ronald Radd and our Russian adviser, Baroness Moura Budberg, Tony Walton, our designer, his girlfriend Jenny, and his daughter from his marriage to Julie Andrews, six-year-old Emma, were also there. I felt as if for the first time in my life, I was part of a community of real, true friends. It was idyllic. We shared our work, our free time, our thoughts, our meals, our children. We were isolated, as if in a time warp, dated August 1968.

The Soviet tanks invaded Czechoslovakia. We discussed the invasion, we watched it on television, and then forgot what we had seen. Only the house by the lake existed for us, and the lives of Councillor Sorin's household – the torments of Constantin, the jealousy of Arkadina. All of us were working for less pay than for any film we could remember, but we were so happy with our choice, and with those ten weeks, that when the journalists who arrived to interview us asked, 'What made you choose this part?' we burst out laughing and replied: 'We did it for the money!'

The script, director Sidney Lumet, and crew were all superb, and for an entire Swedish summer we had the luxury of escaping the distractions of daily life, and could concentrate entirely on what we were doing, and on each other. None of us wanted to leave or to see anyone from outside. We wanted to forget the countless problems we must all face soon. I read in Maria St Just's book *Five o'clock Angel* that Tennessee Williams was asked: 'What is happiness?' He answered, 'Insensitivity, I guess.' Yes, that summer we were all happy, insensitive to everything except ourselves and our enjoyment. Later this became a stern reminder of the price others must pay if artists seek happiness by retreating from the problems of the world. 'Life, liberty and the pursuit of happiness', says the American Constitution. Certainly the pursuit of happiness is a noble aim, and one which Benjamin Franklin and the founding fathers must have intended as a counter-blow to the awful New Testament morality of suffering which served the British ruling class so well. But life, and liberty, come first.

When I finally watched the film of *The Seagull* I found it exemplified for me the difference between film acting and theatre acting because strangely although I can't fault any of the component parts – the acting, atmosphere, lighting, camera work and direction are excellent – it remains a filmed theatre performance, a recorded piece of theatre even though it was filmed on location. A filmed theatre performance can be enthralling to watch and tremendously exciting, like the Olivier/Redgrave production of *Uncle Vanya* in 1964 which Michael appeared in and I still watch on video for his extraordinary performance but it does not set out to be a film. The two media of theatre and cinema are so different that a recorded piece of theatre does not become a film by being captured on celluloid, the independent life of the story does not come through and that is where *The Seagull* falls short as a film.

After *The Seagull* schedule, in the autumn, Simone and I flew to Paris, dropped our luggage at her little apartment in the 16th *arrondissement*, and went straight to the famous Olympia to hear her husband Yves Montand's song recital. The Olympia was packed. For the first time I heard the song of the Italian partisans, *Bella Ciao*:

> I woke up one morning
> Goodbye beauty, my beauty, my beauty, goodbye,
> I woke up one morning,
> My country was invaded.
>
> Oh Partisans, get me away!
>
> Goodbye beauty, my beauty, my beauty goodbye –
> Oh Partisans! Take me away!
> For now I'm going to die.

On 16 October I sat with Simone and Yves in their sitting-room and drafted the text for a telegram to the Soviet Ambassador in Paris. Five Soviet intellectuals were on trial in the USSR for protesting in Red Square against the Soviet invasion of Czechoslovakia. We rang Alain Resnais, the film director, and Jorge Semprun, the Spanish writer, close friends of the Montands. They came over and added their signatures. This is my translation of the French text; copies were also sent to the French news agency, France Press and United Press International.

Gathered together today, we decided to send you this telegram,

Monsieur Ambassador. Please convey our warmest congratulations to the Soviet people you represent here. It is with great encouragement that we realise there are still people in your country who have the courage to be heirs of the traditions which have amazed the world since 1905; legions of men and women, in opposition to the regiments of sheep in the world. We are referring of course to Pavel Litvinov, Larissa Daniel, Constantin Babitsky, Vladimir Delaunay, Vadim Dremliouga. It is very fortunate for the people of the Soviet Union that these five exist and that they are citizens of the Soviet Union. As it is fortunate for the American people that the Nine of Baltimore: Daniel Berrigan, Philip Berrigan, David Darst, John Hogan, Thomas Lewis, Marjorie Melville, Thomas Melville, George Mische, Mary Moylan, and also Doctor Spock, were born on American soil. As it is fortunate for France that Gabriel Peri d'Estienne d'Orves, Manouchian l'Arménien, Henri Martin and Maurice Audin were French.

We are sending a copy of this telegram to the newspapers, so that whether for bad or good motives, it will be published. That it should be published is the only thing that is important to us.

Signed: Yves Montand, Alain Resnais, Jorge Semprun, Vanessa Redgrave, Simone Signoret.

The nine Americans had been sentenced to prison for inciting young men to resist the Vietnam draft. Peri d'Orves and Manouchian were executed by the Nazis. Martin was imprisoned for refusing to fight the Viet Minh in Indo-China, Audin was imprisoned and murdered for denouncing French atrocities in Algeria.

All the French newspapers except the French Communist Party's *L'Humanité* published the statement. The *International Herald Tribune* published the first half, but cut the paragraph referring to the anti-Vietnam resisters, and to the French martyrs of the Nazis and the war for Algerian independence. After Simone rang the chief editor he published the full text, followed by an apology. And in England? Black-out. *The Times* made a brief reference to the telegram. I protested to the editor but received no answer. I could not understand why *The Times* would not print our letter, since they more than any paper had publicised the case of the Jewish dissidents who were imprisoned in the Soviet Union. And the names of the five signatories were surely of some weight, one way or another? *Le Figaro* published in full and I concluded that British imperialism was more gravely threatened by opposition to the Vietnam war and more conscious of the danger than their French allies. It never occurred to me that *Le Figaro* was glad to publish anything they deemed 'anti-communist', because of the political significance of the French Communist Party.

I loved and admired Simone and Yves. Simone was the most beautiful woman I had ever met, warm-hearted, loving and amusing. She was everything I had imagined her to be since I first saw her, as a girl, in *Casque d'Or*. Yves was the star of the most outstanding French film made since the war, Clouzot's *The Wages of Fear*. I envied them because they were not isolated, as I felt myself to be. French intellectuals in the cinema and theatre had been involved in political struggles for years, alongside writers like Simone de Beauvoir and her friends. During the May/June struggles in France in 1968, the Cannes Film Festival was brought to a halt by François Truffaut, Louis Malle, Jean-Luc Godard and Roman Polanski. Truffaut, and Godard whose films included *Quatre Cents Coups* and *A Bout de Souffle* were then at the height of their international fame. Since 1961, not one English intellectual of note had participated publicly in any rally or demonstration. Even in 1961, I remember two well-known English theatre directors wavering for a week before they could bring themselves to join the anti-nuclear-war rally. Peter Finch was the only famous actor besides myself who, to my knowledge, made a public protest after the Soweto massacre in South Africa. None of the British film-makers made films like *Z*, *State of Siege* or *L'Aveu* by Costa Gavras. Northern Ireland has been occupied by the British Army since 1969, but no film-maker in Britain has made a feature film taking the side of the Irish Republican movement, as Pontecorvo did when he supported the Algerians in *The Battle of Algiers*.

I had felt inspired when I read *My Life* by Isadora Duncan. In preparing for the film I read everything about her and by her, including her passionate statement about the Russian revolution and her commitment to the USSR, quoted in Gordon McVay's *Isadora and Esenin*:

For the second time in the world's history a great force has arisen to give capitalism, which stands for monstrous greed and villainy, one great blow. The dragon, man-eating, labour-exploiting, has here received his death-stroke. What matters it that in his final throes he has cast destruction about him? The radiant hero who smote him still lives, though enfeebled from the deadly struggle, and from him will be born a new world.

145

What had happened between 1921 and 1968? Why did the Communist Parties in Moscow, Britain and France refuse to call for the victory of the Vietnamese and the Algerians? Why had the Russian Communist Party degenerated so far as to order the invasion of Czechoslovakia, and the brutal repression of the 1968 reforms led by Dubcek, and the persecution and repression of its own intellectuals when they protested? Some people could tell me *what* had happened; none could explain *why*.

I left Yves Montand and Simone Signoret in Paris and returned to London in October 1968, once more conscious of my need for political struggle. Inspired by Litvinov, Daniel and their comrades and glimpsing an international connection in our struggle, I wrote to Jane Fonda. I had read about the anti-war work she was leading with Donald Sutherland in the United States, and decided I must initiate a similar campaign in Britain with the American GIs stationed on the giant USAF bases in East Anglia.

A return of political confidence, and the will to struggle. Perhaps my short stay in Paris with Simone and Yves, and the sense of hope I now found politically gave me the courage to work again in the theatre. Connections are never so simple and straightforward, but they are there none the less. Certainly the fact that Michael Elliott was directing *Daniel Deronda* encouraged me to take a step I had not dared to take since *The Prime of Miss Jean Brodie*. He, Caspar Wrede and Braham Murray had begun work in Manchester in a makeshift theatre whilst funds were being raised and plans drawn up for what would become a theatre in the Royal Exchange, the centre of Manchester's cotton trade in the nineteenth century. Michael's friend and colleague, the actor James Maxwell, had adapted *Daniel Deronda*, and I played Gwendolen Harleth. I made a copy of the first page of George Eliot's manuscript and kept it with me for protection. Her writing is small, neat and entirely legible, as clear as her mind. There are four or five corrections on the page, all certainly made in the course of composition, not as afterthoughts or revision. It is fascinating to look at that first page, the confident start of a process which would unravel through 2000 such pages. If I felt that I was stepping near the awful abyss which confronted me each night in *The Prime of Miss Jean Brodie*, I looked at George Eliot's handwriting and it steadied my nerves.

While in *Daniel Deronda* I took a large flat, with seven other members of the company, and cooked for them each night. Franco was working in Italy, and, to my great joy, I found I was pregnant. The baby we had both wanted was on its way. All in all I got through, and simply getting through was, in its way, a triumph. I would never feel the same fear of the stage again.

When our five-weeks' run in Manchester was over I packed my bags and headed straight for the farmhouse in Italy at Brendola and the Misses Veronese. Tasha was now six years old and Joely four.

On the morning of 21 July 1969, Tasha and Joely came down-stairs early with me to the kitchen. We made some breakfast and joined the elder Miss Veronese in front of her black-and-white television set. We half closed the wooden shutters to keep out the strong sunlight and saw Captain Neil Armstrong step out into the black sky on to the soft white powder of the moon. We watched, amazed. It was impossible, yet it was true. Outside, in the burning sunshine, the peasants Beppe, Angelo and Giovanni were moving the wagons off the fields. Their families didn't even eat meat once a week. Angelo's wife was my age, thirty-two years old, and she had four teeth missing. And out there in the black space beyond the earth, Captain Neil Armstrong was speaking to us as he climbed down a small ladder from the space module on to the moon.

The girls and I spent hours by the washing pool where the wives washed the clothes in cold water with bars of soap and wooden scrubbing boards, or in the courtyard, where the sweet corn was winnowed from the maize, the heads laid out to dry for fuel for the cooking stoves. We played games in the barns, and when we were thirsty walked through the field to the stream where a spring of cool, sweet water fell just above the waterwheel that drove the stone to crush the maize into polenta flour. In the cool evening we danced to music from our portable record player as the sun set. Corin came to stay, and Bob Regester, a dear friend with whom I shared some of my happiest and unhappiest times.

One afternoon, Tasha and Joely came and sat on my bed and asked why I didn't live with their father. They sobbed when I explained that we didn't love each other any more, but loved them. I assured them that both of us would always love them. I had convinced myself that children can face and understand such problems, so long as parents don't try to maintain a false and unhappy relationship by lying to conceal their unhappiness. How is it possible to tell children to speak the truth, however difficult, if the parents are living a lie? And yet the explanation even as I said it seemed to me inadequate. How could children accept the truth? They knew Tony and I still worked together, laughed together and respected each other. We dried our tears, went out and sprayed each other with the garden hose.

When Franco and my father joined us we travelled by busboat to Padua, down the ancient Brenta canal to Venice, Franco's favourite city, and saw the liquid glass twisting and twirling at Murano. One evening we heard an anguished cry from Michael. He had risen from a sofa and his legs had given way as he crossed the room. Franco took a photo of him that evening as we sat in the garden, and later Corin chose it for the front cover of Michael's auto-biography *In My Mind's Eye*, published in 1983. When I look at that photograph I see in Michael's eyes fear of the disease (Parkinson's) which, as yet unknown to him, had already attacked him.

We all flew home about six weeks before the baby was due. I had booked a midwife on the National Health Service through my doctor. I rang her at about 6 a.m. on the morning of 16 September 1969. Linda, our new nanny, drove Tasha and Joely across the river to Barnes to spend the day with Lynn and her family until the baby was born. Franco booked a flight to Rome immediately and fled from the house. I set to work with my doctor and the midwife, and the baby was born about four hours later. Immediately I rang Lynn and told her the news, and she drove right over. The girls came running up to my bedroom. I rang Franco to tell him we had a boy. He booked the next flight back to London, burst upstairs, opened the baby's nappy and kissed his little balls.

Betsy Reisz gave me a small album with gold letters stamped on the cover: THE DAY CARLO SPARANERO WAS BORN. Inside she had collected headlines from newspapers and magazines, all published on that day, 16 September 1969. These included:

ANGER IN US OVER NIXON'S ORDER TO RESUME BOMBING
AMERICANS TO PULL OUT 40,000 MORE TROOPS IN VIETNAM
TWO MILLION INDUSTRIAL WORKERS TO GO ON STRIKE IN ITALY THIS WEEK
VICTORY TO MRS GANDHI IN CALCUTTA
EVE OF ELECTION STRIKES ROCK WEST GERMANY
BAZOOKA MEN HIT ISRAELI VILLAGE
CHEERS FOR DUBCEK . . .

Next to these I pasted Franco's photographs of the new baby with Tasha and Joely cuddled in the bed next to their fat, happy mum. I published our boy's birth in *The Times'* birth column: 'Vanessa Redgrave and Franco Nero are happy to announce the birth of a baby boy.' The following Sunday the editor of the *Observer*, David Astor, denounced me for immorality. What was particularly immoral was that I was happy and unwed. My agent, Robin Fox, and his wife Angela were upset. They suggested that Robin and I should go to see David Astor at the *Observer* and ask for an apology in print. I don't remember the details of this meeting, but Robin must have said something acute and to the point, because the following Sunday another editorial expressed apologies for any distress and stated there had been a misunderstanding.

Carlo was five days old when I put him into a woven basket with handles and flew to Toledo where Franco was filming with Luis Buñuel. He was three weeks old when he lay in his Moses basket as I squatted on the floor with two students at the Royal College of Art, painting a large piece of canvas as a carpet for Yehudi Menuhin and Ravi Shankar to sit on when they played together on the violin and sitar at the Gandhi Memorial Concert in October 1969.

Tasha, Joely, Linda and I flew with the baby to Rome for Carnevale and Carlo's christening. The streets were full of children dressed as cowboys, queens, columbines and astronauts. We drove up into the hills of Tivoli to a boys' orphanage, where Carlo was christened by Friar Borromeo and we feasted in the refectory.

# 14

Writing your own history is an exacting test. There is a strong inclination to bend it to what you would like it to be. Memory is unreliable. I have to check all my dates rigorously, and when I do I find plenty of shocks and contradictions, and a few blank spots. This checking of dates and documents, diaries, letters and newspapers, starts a process in which the eclectic jumble of good and bad memories begins to disintegrate and form anew.

In early 1971, when filming *The Devils* with Ken Russell and pregnant with Franco's second child, I organised a meeting of the cast to discuss the government's Industrial Relations Bill. Our union, Equity, had circulated a document called *Our Profession in Peril*, protesting against the clauses in the legislation that would remove our right to a closed shop. I had heard that an organisation called the Liaison Committee for the Defence of Trade Unions was campaigning for a one-day strike against these new anti-union laws, so we passed a resolution that Equity should join the strike, and gathered signatures for a petition for a Special General Meeting.

On Sunday, my day off, I lay in bed, feeling terribly tired and in pain, but knowing I must get all the support I could for our resolution. I telephoned Robert Morley, who wished me luck and said he wasn't sure he could support a strike, but he promised to be at the meeting. The pains became worse and worse and I realised I was having a miscarriage. I cried bitterly, not knowing what I should do or what I had done wrong. I rang Franco in Rome, who was heartbroken, and that made me cry even more. I buried the baby that miscarried in the early hours of the morning in our garden at St Peter's Square and phoned my doctor. She came and soothed me, explaining I would never have miscarried if it hadn't been physically necessary. It was nature's method for preventing the birth of deformed or disabled babies. She took me to the Samaritan hospital for women to have the afterbirth removed and I stayed for a couple of days.

On the Sunday morning Corin came to fetch me and we went together to the Special General Meeting of Actors' Equity, at the Adelphi Theatre in Shaftesbury Avenue. Our motion was heavily defeated. The union's officers, Gerald Croasdell, the General Secretary, and the Council, were vehemently opposed to a strike, and argued that Equity should plead with the government for a special dispensation to permit it to keep a closed shop. Many of the members were sympathetic, but didn't believe that a one-day strike would be sufficient to deter the Heath government. But, by a large majority, they voted that the meeting had been necessary. And a few months later Corin was voted on to the Council.

In June I was filming *Mary, Queen of Scots* for producer Hal Wallis. Tasha and Joely came out to the set and Tasha carried my heavy queen's skirts and train, wanting to be useful and as thrilled to be on a film set as if it were her first visit. Joely was six years old and in her first year at the French Lycée. Tony wanted the girls to speak French fluently and thought the French education system was more disciplined and educational than that offered by English schools. On the days I wasn't filming we would pile into my Morris Traveller and Linda, our nanny, would drive us to the Lycée in South Kensington, Carlo strapped into the baby seat, the girls and I crammed into the back. I still couldn't drive. Later Timothy Dalton taught me to ride a motorcycle and for a year or so, to everyone's dismay, I weaved and wobbled through London's traffic on his old 250cc Suzuki. Later still a kind instructor from the British School of Motoring coaxed me into passing my driving test at my first attempt. In difficult situations, such as Hammersmith Broadway or Hyde Park Corner, he calmed his nerves and mine by speaking a strange language: 'Now Miss Redgrave, we'll wimble into the right-hand lane – signal first, if you please – then we'll womble up to the junction – oopsadaisy, easy does it . . . .'. I'm forever in his debt. But that came later.

Tim Dalton played Darnley in *Mary, Queen of Scots*. 'Let me not to the marriage of true minds, admit impediment.' But whatever fairy danced attendance at our first meeting decreed, contrarily, that there would be almost nothing we could agree on, and sure enough we have quarrelled ever since. This is not the steadiest basis for a relationship, but so long as it admits the possibility of reconciliation it is not a bad one either. One of the first arguments Timothy and I ever had was about a speech from Shakespeare's *Hamlet* – 'to be or not to be . . .'. He asked me, 'what do you think this means?' I told him, and we argued for about six hours. While we should have had a discussion rather then a row, it is nevertheless extremely stimulating to talk with another actor who cares so passionately and greatly to find out what a playwright means in a particular passage. It can also be extremely exasperating but Tim made me think, and over the years as we acted a great deal together in the film of *Agatha*, *The Taming Of the Shrew* and *Antony and Cleopatra* in 1986, and *A Touch Of The Poet* in 1988, the key note of our professional life has been our volatility and directness.

As time goes by fewer and fewer people will tell me what they really think of a performance and I have always valued the way Tim cared so much about my work that he'd talk for hours giving me strong criticism and explain what he felt was wrong. While this too would usually end in an argument, I knew that when he praised me it meant a great deal. He is a marvellous stage actor, and his performances as Petrucchio in *The Taming Of the Shrew* and Con Melody in *A Touch Of The Poet* were two of his finest. He also taught me to fish, and strangely enough, fishing, a pastime which lures many men away from their wives for a few hours of solitude, brought us together. His family come from Derbyshire, near Belper, and whenever we could we would walk along the streams in the Peak Park, which even now run, in Isaak Walton's phrase 'gin clear'. Or, more adventurously, we would pack knapsacks and set off on Tim's Suzuki for the boat to Ireland, to spend a week in County Mayo.

I have a cutting from the London *Evening Standard*. An interview by Leslie Edwards and a photograph taken on the set at Pinewood, during the filming of *Mary, Queen of Scots*. In the interview I spoke about the attacks of the Heath government on the working class. On the weekend of 11 June the Chairman of Upper Clyde Shipbuilders (UCS), Anthony Hopper, asked the Tory Secretary of State for Trade and Industry, John Davies, for £6 million to save the yards from bankruptcy. Davies refused: it was not the policy of Heath's government to rescue the 'lame ducks' of industry. On the following Monday Upper Clyde Shipbuilders was put into the

152

hands of the receiver. The 8500 men who worked in the four shipyards which made up the UCS consortium occupied the yards to defend their jobs, and the tens of thousands of jobs which depended on shipbuilding on the Upper Clyde. I went round the set and the Pinewood workshops and made a large collection for the occupation.

In the autumn, when I had finished this film, I flew to Los Angeles for some concert performances of Berlioz's *Béatrice et Bénédict* with the LA Symphony Orchestra. I met Shirley Sutherland, Donald's wife, Jane Fonda, and a number of her colleagues at a fund-raising reception at her beach house. I did not really know Jane until we worked together five years later, but I admired her greatly for her stand against the Vietnam war. We wrote to each other, sometimes telephoned, and felt close, because each of us knew the other's pressures and what it took to withstand them. Jane called her daughter Vanessa, after me, a compliment I cherished. I went down to San Diego where I met the organisers of a GI coffee-house, as well as some of the GIs based with the US Navy there, and interviewed them on tape. One group ran a theatre-cum-coffee-house in Los Angeles called the Haymarket, which had advertised a documentary film, *Fidel*. A group of armed Cuban *contras* had forced the organisers to lie on the floor, sprayed the place with gasoline and set it alight.

At this time Reagan was Governor of California, and schoolteachers were on strike. They were demanding better wages and more funds for the state schools. Basic necessities such as books and writing materials were almost non-existent. One of the teachers invited me to a strike meeting in a school in Watts.

On the second night of *Béatrice et Bénédict* there was an anti-war street theatre performance in the Plaza outside the building where the Academy Awards are given. The previous night the organisers had asked me to make an announcement from the stage. I told Zubin Mehta and Stacey Keach about this, and when I took my bow the next night, I invited the audience to watch the anti-war performance when they left the theatre. Some of the wealthy music patrons were far from pleased, but anti-war feeling ran high in Hollywood. The majority of intellectuals working in music and film were Jewish and opposed to both Reagan, as Governor of California, and President Nixon. They were appalled by the war, the increase in censorship, surveillance, phone-tapping and witch-hunting. Many of them had borne the brunt of state persecution in the 1950s during the McCarthy era.

With two English friends, a schoolteacher and a musician, I began to organise a GI newspaper and built up contacts with a number of GIs at Mildenhall and Bentwaters, the two biggest US Air Force bases in Britain. We were joined by three American graduates at Cambridge University. We leafleted the bases, and brought out several editions of a paper which we called *Peace*. We printed a small pamphlet, *A Guide to Military Rights*, which gave detailed advice on deferments, discharges, illegal seizure of a serviceman's property, search and seizure of mail and how to file complaints. I began receiving many letters from soldiers in Vietnam, encouraging me and supporting my anti-war protests. I no longer felt isolated, although I never met those men. One of the GIs on the base at Mildenhall gave me a carbon copy of a memo that was circulated by the commander at the base, warning the GIs not to make contact with us.

In 1971 I invited Barbara Dane, the American folk singer, to come to meet our GI group in a Cambridge hall we had hired. She sang, played guitar and talked, while someone wandered about taking photographs for the paper. Of course, thinking back, all those photographs must have gone straight to military intelligence. We knew about agents, we knew they must be around, but we were too green to take this threat seriously. Meetings took place once a week. I organised a benefit at the Lyceum Theatre in London, which got a big turnout and was filmed by Harlech Television. Jane Fonda sent a message on tape, which we played to the audience before the GIs came on stage to speak:

'show your solidarity with the long-suffering people of Vietnam by inundating the American army bases throughout Great Britain. There is one in Lakenheath, near Suffolk and the other in Brize Norton in Glouscestershire. Hold out your hands in friendship and support to those Americans thousands of miles from home who need your assistance to organise effectively against the war.'

Many of the GIs who came to the Lyceum were interviewed that day on the radio. They spoke of commanders who completely ignored intelligence reports and sent their men to certain death. Those who voiced criticism were sent to mental hospitals. One explained how desertion rates had soared to over 7000 a year by

1968. The poverty of the Vietnamese came as a shock to many of them. According to one GI, there were over seventy underground GI newspapers with a circulation of over 700,000. Dissenters were punished in the most cruel and brutal way. A GI could 'draw six months in the stockade for refusing a haircut after he'd had three haircuts that week'.

In summer 1971 a number of US airmen presented a petition to the United States Embassy calling for an end to the war in Vietnam. In the afternoon we held a concert in Victoria Park, Hackney in East London. Mia Farrow and I took part, along with musicians and other artistes, to pay tribute to these and all American servicemen who were resisting and protesting against the war in Vietnam.

On my birthday, 30 January 1972, I was invited to fly to Londonderry to take part in a Civil Rights protest march against the Conservative government's policy of internment. Men and boys were being arrested in their houses and kept in jail without trial. Bernadette Devlin had spent six months in prison the previous year, charged with inciting riots. In April 1969 she had become Member of Parliament for Mid-Ulster, with a huge vote from the Catholic working class, at the age of twenty-one. Her maiden speech, which by House of Commons tradition should have been on a non-controversial subject, followed by polite applause from MPs of all parties, had Tory and Unionist MPs baying for her blood, and Labour Members sitting in shocked silence. In 1969 the Labour government had sent the British Army into Northern Ireland, ostensibly to keep the peace and protect the Catholic population from loyalist violence. In reality they were there to make war on the Irish Republican movement.

I did not fly to Londonderry on the day that came to be known as 'Bloody Sunday'. Thirteen civilians, eight of them boys under twenty-one, were deliberately shot by British paratroopers. All were innocent victims of a calculated plan by the British Army High Command to provoke the IRA into battle on the streets of Derry and wipe them out. I flew to Newry the following Sunday, 6 February, to take part in a protest march against the massacre.

Bernadette Devlin and Eamonn McCann met me in Newry. We waited in a small bungalow until it was time to assemble for the march. Reports came in continually that leaders of the various political groups involved in the march were trying hard to stop a massive turnout and limit the numbers to a small show of silent protest. The *Sunday Press* carried a front-page article headlined: 'Newry wants no hooligans', saying,

last-minute orders issued by the organisers of today's Civil Rights March in Newry were 'Hooligans Out – Civil Rights In – Stop at the barricades'. There is to be no chanting, no singing, no hurling of words of abuse at the steel ring of British troops which now surrounds the town.

I thought this an insult to the dead of Bloody Sunday and to all the men and boys who defied the British troops, their racism and their brutality.

Helicopters buzzed overhead. Army officers shouted orders to disperse. The march was illegal and anyone taking part could be prosecuted and sent to jail for six months. No one knew what the Army might do, though we guessed that the large numbers of Members of Parliament and clergymen would prevent a shoot-out. We marched and dispersed at the army barricades. The organisers claimed a victory, because it was a peaceful march. But Bloody Sunday was a peaceful march until the British Army, on orders from Whitehall, opened fire on innocent, unarmed men and boys.

After interviews with press and television journalists from all over the world, Bernadette and I sat down with some other women, exhausted and drained. We talked about the politics of the different parties who had participated in the march. She was mistrustful and very critical of them. 'Why don't you tell everyone what you know, that these other groups are not to be trusted?' I asked her. Bernadette herself, unlike virtually all other Irish leaders, spoke frequently and publicly of the need to unite Catholic and Protestant workers. This was not a popular line, but it was absolutely right. And because Bernadette had real courage, and was unafraid to speak out against the British government and Army, she had immense support from the Irish people. On the other hand she did not believe, and neither did I at that time, that the English working class would ever support the liberation of the Irish.

On 24 March 1972 Edward Heath suspended parliament in Stormont and a police-military dictatorship was established in Northern Ireland. I offered to stand bail for a young man, Sean O'Toole, who was arrested and charged with incitement to riot in Whitehall on a February demonstration in London. Detective-Sergeant Ian Will opposed my surety in the court: 'She is passionately involved in demonstrations and civil disturbances and would not be acceptable as surety.' I felt cold and worn out and did not know what could be done politically. I did not support terrorism against civilians. I did support the Irish right to self-determination and their right to fight the British Army and choose their own methods. I could see no political road forward. I felt there was no party or group I could really trust, because none I had worked with or talked with had a perspective beyond protest or terrorism.

One of the political groups I knew well, a West Indian Black Power group, studied with C.L.R. James. He was in his seventies when I met him, a very cultivated, well-read man, whose knowledge of modern history far surpassed mine, or any of my acquaintances'. Author of a world-famous book about the revolution in Haiti, led by Toussaint L'Ouverture, *The Black Jacobins*, he had come to England from Trinidad in the Thirties with his friend Learie Constantine, the great cricketer. He himself had written books on cricket, which were much admired. He talked about Shakespeare with great love and insight, and one evening at my house, he entertained a gathering of writers, artists and actors with a fascinating two-hour talk on *King Lear*.

In our conversations, however, he said next to nothing about that period in his life when he had been a member of the Fourth International. Once, at a talk he gave in Ladbroke Grove, I recall his saying that he and Trotsky 'disagreed about the Negro question in America', and that he, James, had argued for separate organisations for black Americans. In his pamphlets, *Facing Reality* and *Every Cook can Govern*, he referred scathingly to Lenin, dismissing Trotsky as 'the comedian of the revolution'. The Soviet Union, he told me, was a capitalist country, 'state capitalist', ruled over by a Stalinist apparatus which had become a new exploiting class. The responsibility for that lay with Lenin and the Bolsheviks. The dictatorship of the Bolshevik Party produced Stalin and Stalinism. Persuasive as James was, I did not agree with him, and would have liked to argue, but lacked the knowledge and, more importantly, the will to do so. For the second time I had arrived at a political crisis in my life, and not recognising it for what it was, I reached out for what seemed to me a practical solution. All my good political intentions, or so I thought, had become compromised because political parties, political leaders, the political struggle itself, were hopelessly compromised. Very well, I thought, I must do something I know I *can* do, and something I believe is necessary. I'll build my nursery school.

Some time before, I had set up a charitable trust for children living in deprived areas, and all the money I earned from major films had gone into it. I found an architect, Rodney Fitch. Together with a schoolteacher friend, a Professor of Education at Brunel University and Jan Stevens, who came over from California with her husband Bob and her friend Jaime, we worked hard on the project, down to the last detail – non-slip surfaces for the area surrounding the pool, a plentiful supply of flippers for the children. Hammersmith and Fulham Council gave a piece of land, small but just large enough for the school and its swimming pool. Finally, on 16 September 1973, the Vanessa Redgrave Nursery School was officially handed over to the Inner London Education Authority.

It was Carlo's fourth birthday, which meant that he could attend the nursery school for one year before going to primary school. We now lived on the south side of St Peter's Square in a house that Franco had helped me to buy. He often came to London to work, sometimes for months at a time, because he was much in demand for films, both American and British; he also wanted to be with Carlo. I think these years of Carlo's childhood were difficult for Franco. For both of us, no doubt, but more difficult for him than for me. He was a loving father, a proud father, and sometimes a stern father. I fretted and fumed over Franco's demands, thinking: *I* look after Carlo, *I* know what's best.

All the while the political and economic situation in Britain was going from bad to worse. Heath and his chancellor Anthony Barber's notorious 'dash for growth' had let loose a surge of inflation. A large number of so-called 'secondary' banks failed. Britain was heading for a colossal slump. In the summer of 1972 five dockers in London were sent to Pentonville prison for refusing to obey a court order banning the picketing of a container company, Panalpina. The TUC threatened a general strike if they were not released, and the government retreated. The weekend before the strike was due to begin the official solicitor, a government officer whose function and whose very existence were almost unknown until that moment, was found to have constitutional powers to release the dockers, and duly did so. That autumn the

Tories brought in statutory wage controls, at a time when prices were soaring. I read the news and then drowned it in the pleasant oblivion of a bottle of cheap wine.

Corin had joined the Socialist Labour League in 1971. He was the first person I met who tried to analyse and explain political developments. The main problem, as he put it, was one of leadership. That I agreed with. Sometimes I listened, and argued, sometimes I got drunk and dogmatically repeated my old ideas. 'How can any leadership be trusted?' I asked. 'Why should you ask for guarantees?' he said. 'Did you ask for guarantees when you supported the Vietnamese against the Americans?' I launched into a long, slow, tortuous explanation.

I opposed the Americans because they had no right to be in Vietnam. The peasants, the real victims of the war, simply wanted to farm their land. They wanted neither capitalism nor communism.

I met the General Secretary of the Socialist Labour League, Gerry Healy, and was extremely interested in his ideas. Their daily paper, *Workers' Press*, was impressive. It made me think, instead of telling me what I already knew. Questions that I had never got an answer to were raised, discussed and answered. But for a year I stubbornly refused to accept what was staring me in the face. I drank more heavily, opening a bottle of cheap wine every morning to get the fuzzy obliteration of alcohol in order not to have to think. I carried on with my work. *The Trojan Women*, a film of a Euripides play, with Irene Papas and Geneviève Bujold, was directed by Michael Cacoyannis. He wanted an intense, supercharged performance, and was obviously very disappointed with my first efforts. So I gave him what he seemed to want, and he flung his arms around me. I felt like drinking a cup of hemlock. I was simulating emotion by entirely artificial means and, worse still, being praised for it. What happened next changed everything for me.

On 8 March 1973 a wave of car bombs blasted off outside New Scotland Yard in Victoria Street, London and, shortly afterwards, outside the Old Bailey. Bombs shattered windows and injured ordinary civilian passers-by in the street. The police and press claimed this terrorism was the responsibility of the IRA. I thought: if this *is* the IRA they are crazy. What was being done to the Irish was not the responsibility of ordinary British people, not British workers. The Tory government as attacking British as well as Irish workers. Could the bombings be a deliberate provocation? I had heard of such provocations in Italy, where fascists had planted bombs in Bologna railway station, killing seventy people, and then blamed the bombing on the anarchists on the left.

A group of Irish youths were arrested, taken to Ealing police station and refused permission to see solicitors. I knew they could be badly beaten, interrogated and forced to sign false confessions before solicitors were allowed near them. I telephoned anyone I could think of who would have sufficient weight to demand entry into the police cells. I rang Laurie Pavitt, a Labour MP. He said they were terrorists, and would not go. I rang Lord Soper, the leader of the Methodist Church and a Labour man, who had always opposed British colonial atrocities in Kenya and Malaya. He also refused. In desperation I turned to the Church of England. The Bishop of Southwark, Mervyn Stockwood – No. The Roman Catholic Church – No. I tried my local vicar – No. I pulled out the directory and found a small Catholic priory near Ealing. The priest who answered my call was very sympathetic. He said he would have to get permission from his superior, but he was prepared to go. When he went to the Ealing police station he was told to come back later. He did, and was at last permitted to see the youths. He rang me and said they were in not too bad a state and had been relieved to see him. I was telephoned and asked if I would go to the magistrates' court in Bow Street and offer bail for one of the girls. I said I would. Edna O'Brien was there too. Our offer of bail was refused.

I lay on the bed, drew the curtains, took the phone off the hook and stayed like that for a whole day. Thoughts raced through my head. These young Irish were in a political blind alley through no fault of their own. British workers were not to blame for the atrocities of the British military dictatorship. The military dictatorship in Northern Ireland was as dangerous for the British trade unions and posed as great a threat to basic democratic rights in Britain as in Ireland. Military and police intelligence would have a field-day with terrorist groups. Terror played right into their hands because they wanted terror. They needed terror to get agreement from the opposition in parliament for new repressive powers against the trade unions. They hadn't forgotten their defeat – Arthur Scargill's call for mass flying pickets during the coal strike of

1972. I felt as though we were on the brink of civil war.

My thoughts turned to Robert Shaw's play *Cato Street*, which I had co-produced, researched and performed in as Susan Thistlewood in November 1971 at the Young Vic Theatre in Waterloo. It was about a group of radicals, led by a craftsman Arthur Thistlewood, who were infiltrated by a secret agent working for the Home Office of the Tory government of 1819. The agent, Edwardes, working under orders from Lord Sidmouth, the Home Secretary, proposed a plan to assassinate the Tory Cabinet and provided the money to collect arms and ammunition for the attack. *Cato Street* told how the Home Office placed a notice in *The Times* stating that the entire Tory Cabinet would be dining at a house in Grosvenor Square on Wednesday evening, 23 February. This was a fake, published so that the agent, Edwardes, could bring arms to Cato Street and encourage Thistlewood's group to attack. Troops were alerted. They surrounded the house, arrested the group and seized the arms. All members of the group were hung, drawn and quartered and a savage round of repression, arrests and hangings ensued. The Whigs, the Liberal parliamentary opposition, muttered but agreed. The Home Office operation, known as the Cato Street conspiracy, had achieved its objective.

Robert Shaw wrote his play with ringing precision and hatred for Tory class oppression.

Susan Thistlewood's call, written by Robert Shaw and based on the trial records and execution speeches of Thistlewood and his comrades, returned to my ears – 'One generation passeth away and another generation cometh. Do you not identify at all with us my friends? Are we strangers to you?'

I realised at that moment that I had no other way to live except in a political struggle with a party that knew that a serious study of history is necessary if we are to gain understanding and prevent a recurrence of repression. I rang Corin and asked him to come to my home then and there. He came, and I told him I wanted to apply immediately to become a Trotskyist and a member of the Socialist Labour League.

# 15

I remember that day in 1973 so clearly when I sat down with Corin at the table of my sitting-room in 18, St Peter's Square. He gave me a Socialist Labour League pamphlet and a large brown volume from Lenin's collective works, volume 38, the *Philosophical Notebooks*.

In that edition, which I still have, there is a photograph of the reading-room in the Berne Library in Switzerland, where Lenin studied Hegel and made his notes in the last two years of his second period of exile, before the Russian revolution of 1917. In the preface by the editors, from the Institute of Marxism-Leninism of the Central Committee of the CPSU, there is an important observation:

It is no coincidence that Lenin devoted so much attention to philosophy, and above all, to Marxist dialectics, precisely during the First World War, a period in which all the contradictions of capitalism became extremely acute and a revolutionary crisis matured. Only materialist dialectics provided the basis for making a Marxist analysis of the contradictions of imperialism, revealing the imperialist character of the First World War, exposing the opportunism and social chauvinism of the leaders of the Second International and working out the strategy and tactics of the struggle of the proletariat.

Nothing is said in that preface about the post-revolutionary history of Lenin's philosophical notebooks, and about the fact that they remained unpublished in the Soviet Union until after Stalin's death. This is also, as the editors of my edition would say, 'no coincidence'. Stalin suppressed them, just as he suppressed the last notes and letters dictated by Lenin which came to be known as 'Lenin's Testament', because, even more than the latter, they would have revealed the whole character of Stalin's tyranny.

Consequently, there was no English translation of Volume 38 until 1961, eight years after Stalin's death. Only then could Gerry Healy, the founder of the Socialist Labour League, begin to study them. Now, Corin told me, all party members studied them, and he promised that in a few days' time we would read them together. I felt uncertain, and as I flicked through the pages I was awestruck. 'Logic,' I read, 'resembles grammar, being one thing for the beginner, and another thing for one who knows the language (and languages) and the spirit of language.' And then a quotation from Hegel: 'It is one thing to him who approaches logic and the sciences in general for the first time and another thing for him who comes back from the sciences to logic.' Next to this Lenin had written in the margin, 'Subtle and profound!' Yes, no doubt, but I was most certainly one who was approaching logic, not to speak of the sciences in general, for the first time, and I felt inadequate; I had had no education whatsoever either in the sciences or in philosophy.

The other book or rather pamphlet, which Corin gave me was *A Marxist Analysis of the Crisis*, and I fell on it as soon as he left. I must have read it through at least three times that day. It explained the connection between the economic crisis of 1971–2 and the post-war policies of the Bretton Woods Agreement of 1944; it discussed the connection between the dollar, no longer backed by gold, and the massive inflation in advanced capitalist countries. The capitalist countries were in a crisis that was driving them to seek the same solutions as German capital had sought after the Wall Street crash of 1929 – the destruction of the trade unions, racism and war.

I read and reread the paragraph on 'The USSR, China, and Eastern Europe'. It told how a political revolution against Stalinism, predicted and fought for by Trotsky and the Fourth International, had begun with the victory of the Red Army in the Second World War, *despite* the policies of Stalin. This was something entirely new to me. I hated Stalinism, but without giving it much thought I had believed until then that Stalin was the architect of his country's victory. The East German uprising in 1953, Khrushchev's secret speech on the crimes of Stalin at the 20th Party Congress in 1956, and the Hungarian revolution later that year; the Prague 'Spring' in 1968; the strikes in Poland in 1970 . . . all were expressions of a developing political revolution against Stalinist bureaucracy. Here was a party, the Socialist Labour League, which

163

defended the Soviet Union, unconditionally, and stood for the political revolution. It stood for the right to self-determination of all oppressed nationalities, including the Irish and the Palestinians. It was for a united, socialist Ireland. It criticised the individual terror campaigns of the IRA because they fostered divisions between workers instead of uniting them to fight the real enemy, the British state. But it defended the right of the IRA to fight British imperialism. It stood for a democratic, secular state of Palestine in which all religions, Muslim, Jewish and Christian, could live and work together, and it called for the victory of the Palestine Liberation Organisation. At the end, it presented a programme: for a social revolution to establish workers' power, based on soviets, which would develop all resources and productive forces, under social ownership, in a planned economy.

I put the pamphlet down after the third or fourth reading, and telephoned Corin. I said yes, I meant what I said, I want to become a member of the party. I was thirty-six years old. As I write this, I have been a member of this party for eighteen years. I can truthfully say that I remain absolutely convinced of the necessity of Marxism and that not for a single day has my conviction been shaken. On the contrary, it has grown deeper with experience and the passing of time. That this should be so I ascribe not to my own resoluteness and determination – though I think I can show those qualities when the occasion demands – but to the training and education I received from the party I joined, and from the man who led it for almost all those years, Gerry Healy.

The day after giving me the pamphlets Corin took me to the offices of the Socialist Labour League in Clapham, south London. Gerry Healy's office was on the ground floor, a small room, very simply furnished, with a plain wooden desk and some hard chairs. He greeted me warmly – he had been genuinely surprised when Corin told him I was interested in joining the party. We talked about the Heath government, how the League planned to hold a conference at the end of the year and adopt a new party name and constitution for the thousands of new members who would join in the coming months. At the end of our talk he said, 'So, I hope you'll consider joining too.' 'Can't I join now?' I asked, 'I've made up my mind already.' Gerry laughed, and said yes, of course, and turning to Corin said, 'So now Mary Queen of Scots has joined us.' We talked about the situation of the Irish, many of whom were held in

Category A isolation in British prisons, by order of the Home Secretary, Robert Carr. He knew that I had offered to guarantee bail for Dolores Price and her sister. 'That was courageous of you,' he said, 'to support those young Irish women.'

Gerry Healy was Irish himself, born in Ballybane in Galway in 1913. He went to sea in the Merchant Navy at the age of fourteen, and a year later joined the British Communist Party. As a seaman and a young communist, he became a courier for the Comintern, carrying messages to leaders of the German Communist Party in the cruel and dangerous days when Fascism was coming to power.

In 1936 he discovered by chance, looking at the Lloyd's shipping register, that oil from Batum in Soviet Georgia was being shipped to Barcelona via Genoa for the Spanish Republicans. But at Genoa the Soviet tankers were unloading half their cargo. So the USSR was supplying oil to Mussolini, which would be used to fuel the bombers Mussolini had sent to Spain to bombard the Republican forces. He went to Harry Pollitt, a very senior leader of the British Communist Party, and asked for an explanation. Pollitt sent him to William Joss, who headed the party's control commission. Joss said his questions was 'Trotskyite', and he would be expelled if he persisted with it. Gerry protested that he knew nothing of Trotsky and had never read a word he had written, but he wasn't prepared to drop his question. He was expelled, and there and then decided he had better make good the omission by reading Trotsky. And so he became a Trotskyist.

The next few weeks were among the most exhilarating of my life. It seemed to me that I learned more in that short space of time than in the whole of my previous existence. I travelled with Gerry to a meeting of car-workers at Cowley in Oxford. Many of the workers in the huge British Leyland car plant, including several shop stewards, had joined the Socialist Labour League. I was struck by the amount of time which Gerry devoted in his political report to international events, and to analysing every aspect of the world economic crisis. And by the long and thorough replies which he gave to the questions which followed his report. It was evident from the discussion that Gerry knew everything about the history of the factory at Cowley, about its trade union agreements, its working practices, and the many disputes which constantly arose there. He could sense the workers' mood as keenly as if he worked there himself. Yet he did not confine himself to questions concerning the car factory. Much of the discussion that day centred on events in Chile, where it was clear that the Allende government was about to be overthrown.

Soon after this Gerry asked if I would speak at a public meeting in London. I felt inadequate, but I knew I must speak on this question. There was terrible brutality in the Chilean coup. There had also been ample advance warning in the months before September. There had been the dress-rehearsal coup in June, after which the rebellious regiments had been sent back to barracks by Praz, the senior general in Allende's cabinet, without a single leader being brought to trial. The transport 'strike' had crippled the economy. All the big haulage firms had refused to carry out deliveries. Large meetings of factory workers and trade unionists in Santiago had demanded arms from the government, to defend themselves against the coup they knew was coming, and Allende had refused them. Allende himself died a courageous death, gunned down in his Presidential palace. His body was later exhumed from its anonymous grave in the suburbs of Santiago and reburied with dignity. That is right and fitting, but neither his bravery nor the courage of his followers should ever obscure the fact that it was the policies of his 'Popular Unity' government and their failure to disband and disarm the Chilean armed forces that opened the way to the counter-revolution, which destroyed not only that government, but hundreds of thousands of men and women.

In my speech I drew a parallel between the events in Chile and the situation in Britain. I said that Chile was not some Latin American 'banana republic' where the military regularly ruled, but a state with a forty-year history of constitutional, bourgeois democratic government. There were lessons to learn from the coup and there were those in Heath's government who would want to use the military against the working class if they were threatened with a socialist government.

I wrote to C.L.R. James, telling him that I had joined the Socialist Labour League. His reply was an education in itself. He did not approve of my joining any party as the very idea struck him as elitist; Marxism he saw no need for at all.

In August 1973 I worked again with Tony directing me as Cleopatra in *Antony and Cleopatra* at the Bankside, an open-air theatre run by Sam Wanamaker. After an interesting two and a half weeks the production ended in a thunderstorm in July. The water filled the tarpaulins covering the stage and audience. Although Sam bailed out water as fast as he could with a bucket, crying 'the show must go on', the show collapsed with the tarpaulins and the audience left, never to return.

That autumn, President Sadat of Egypt tried to reconquer the Egyptian lands seized by Israel in 1956. The Egyptian Army made a tremendous advance in a surprise attack. But then Brezhnev withdrew Soviet support and put pressure on Sadat to halt the offensive. The result was victory for Israel, and terrible losses for the Egyptian Army. The Arab states put up the price of oil, out of sheer necessity, following the example of the Americans, French, British, Germans and Japanese, who all sought the highest possible price for their commodities. Prior to the price increase, the differential between what the Arabs received, as producers, and what Western consumers paid, was 400 per cent. Such was the margin of profit for the Western oil corporations.

In Britain, the miners had voted for an overtime ban. Coal production was down by an estimated 20 per cent. Electricity workers were on strike. The cost of oil, following the embargo, had risen four-fold, from $3 to $12 a barrel. Winston S. Churchill, the Tory MP for Stretford, fulminated against 'an unholy alliance of miners and Arab Sheikhs', holding the country to ransom.

I was rehearsing Noel Coward's play *Design for Living*, when we held our founding conference on 4 November, at the Odeon Cinema in Hammersmith, transforming the Socialist Labour League into the Workers' Revolutionary Party. Three thousand members attended the conference. In addition to the daily newspaper, *Workers' Press*, there was a weekly paper for youth, *Keep Left*. The party had its own printing presses and publishing company, and a bookshop in Charlotte Street off the Tottenham Court Road.

*Design for Living* is a romantic comedy, about a triangular love affair between a woman and two men. Noel Coward wrote it in 1932 and played in it, with Alfred Lunt and Lynn Fontanne, in New York the following year. Strangely, it was not produced in London until 1939. In his introduction to the published version in *Play Parade*, Coward says that audiences found it 'unpleasant . . . these glib, over-articulate and amoral creatures force their lives into fantastic shapes and problems because they cannot help themselves'. *Not* a political play, unless in the sense that the Soviet poet, Mayakovsky, claimed that every poem is political, 'even a lyric about two lovers, hand in hand'. And yet I continually sensed, in those three characters twisting and turning as they tried to find relationships they really wanted, the social crisis of the period in which Coward conceived his play, which found its own peculiar expression in the political drama of the abdication of Edward VIII.

Coward's only recorded comment on the Stanislavsky method, as I remember from my father's book, *Mask or Face*, is scathing: 'Isn't that the little company who went away to the country to rehearse for two years, and found they weren't ready?' But my guess is that such sarcasm was a deflection. He was critical, very demanding, and highly intolerant of anything he considered slip-shod or unprofessional. An 'infinite capacity for taking pains' was contained in the seeming effortlessness of his performances. His best known mannerism, a very light, fluted, quick-fire delivery, was really not a mannerism so much as a method of thought and speech ideally suited to the performance of his own work and the comedies of Oscar Wilde. It is easily imitated and that is the problem with most performances of his work. In the few pro-ductions I had seen of his plays the cast imitated what they thought to be the Coward style, whereas what Coward wanted was the truth of human beings in certain circumstances. As I rehearsed *Design for Living* I tried to remember what Coward had said to me on the two occasions he had seen me in the theatre: 'Your work is completely truthful. There is not one false moment in it.'

The first thing the Stanislavsky method requires is research and study of the historical circumstances, customs and social life of the play and its characters, and there are few directors or actors who would not enthusiastically agree that the cast should do this work. However, a diligent study of the historical context, necessary as it is, and indeed invaluable as a source for the raw materials with which to build a character, cannot of itself bring out the essential life of a play. No amount of careful study can recreate the life of a century, a decade, or even a year ago, because that life has ceased to be. It has passed into our abstract memory. Yet we can find what was essential in that life which has passed, the life of the play, by turning to the present. The more the actor is engaged in trying to change the conditions of his or her life, to grasp the meaning of

Franco Nero and I in *A Quiet Place in the Country*, directed by Elio Petri, 1967 (*left*); with Franco, Tasha and Joely at the Cannes Film Festival, 1968 (*below*).

Franco in *Carmen*, 1967: Vittorio Storaro was cameraman.

Bertrand Russell's
ninetieth birthday
tribute at the Royal
Festival Hall, 23
November 1961.

Outside the Ministry of
Defence, Whitehall,
during the Committee of
100 civil disobedience
campaign for unilateral
nuclear disarmament,
1962 (*left*); and (*below*)
with Tariq Ali leading
the march to the US
Embassy against the war
in Vietnam, March
1968.

Gerry Healy of the
Workers Revolutionary
Party in 1974. He led
the International
Committee of the Fourth
International from 1953
until his death in 1989
(*above*); October 1974,
the WRP parliamentary
candidate for Newham
North-East, London, for
the second general
election that year (*right*);
and (*below*) speaking to
trade unionists in
Britain, spring 1978,
during the Israeli
invasion of Lebanon, the
Fifth War.

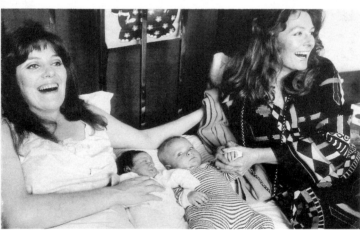

Natasha, Joely and
Carlo join Franco and
me filming *Drop Out* in
London, directed by
Tinto Brass (*above*);
January 1970 – Lynn's
daughter, Kelly, a few
days old, and Carlo at
four months (*left*); and
(*bottom*) Carlo and I in
1977, the year after
*Bugsy Malone*, at the
Young Socialists
Summer Fair.

problems and to analyse them, the more, in the course of rehearsal and performance, impressions will emerge. In further rehearsal and thinking these will become definite notions, which seem to have their own life. In fact they *do* have their own life. They reflect all that is essential now and all that was essential then in its clearest and most advanced form.

Every actor knows such moments, when it seems that someone else has taken possession of him. It is the union of the conscious with the unconscious. The problem is that everyone knows it when it happens, but artists spend most of their lives trying to understand *how* it happens, especially when they run into difficulties.

The actors will be surprised and look at each other with excitement. Suddenly the atmosphere of rehearsal becomes charged. All will know, even if few or none can understand how or why, that from somewhere a living truth has convinced them and made them convince each other and has taken physical shape in the thought and actions of the characters.

The week after the WRP's founding conference as I was coming out of the theatre after the first performance the street lights went out in a power cut. Next morning, Tuesday 13 November, the Home Secretary declared a state of emergency, giving the government powers to use troops to take over public utilities, transport and power supplies. It was the first time a national state of emergency had been declared since the end of the war. The Prime Minister, Edward Heath, announced that from 1 January 1974 industry would be put on a three-day week. It was on the same day that a number of British secondary banks, which had been lending money hand over fist in the credit boom the government had encouraged a year before, went broke and had to be bailed out.

Suddenly a wave of stories appeared in the national press about Arab terrorists at Heathrow airport armed with Soviet missiles, ready to shoot down civilian airliners. And, lo and behold, one January afternoon, tanks, armoured cars, army and police units occupied the airport perimeter and the area around Heathrow, setting up road blocks. Neither the Labour Party in parliament, nor the *Morning Star*, the paper of the British Communist Party, challenged the government story about Arab terrorists with Sam-7 missiles. We increased the print run of the *Workers' Press* from 15,000 to 20,000 copies a day, warning of the danger of police-military rule. We were denounced as scaremongers. But two years later, in 1976, two *Sunday Times* reporters, Stephen Fay and Roger Crozier, revealed – quoting sources which have never been denied or disproved – that several of the most senior army officers, city financiers and top civil servants were in favour of military intervention. At a meeting at No.10 Downing Street in early February 1974 Prime Minister Edward Heath had warned Joe Gormley, president of the National Union of Mineworkers, that this might be the consequence if the miners voted for an all-out strike. In February, the miners' Executive met to discuss the strike, with Gormley arguing heatedly against. But the vote was 8 to 1 in favour. Then, on 7 February, Heath called a general election.

At night I was playing *Design for Living* at the Phoenix, while rehearsing *October*, a play about the October socialist revolution of 1917, at the Oval House in Kennington. There were about forty professional actors and musicians working without a script. Many of us knew only the most elementary facts about the October revolution, so that much of our time was spent reading and discussing Trotsky's *History of the Russian Revolution*, improvising, then writing down the scenes we had sketched out. We had no funds for the production whatever, and in between our rehearsals, which lasted for about eight weeks though often for little more than two hours a day, we had to find costumes and props and construct a set, including an armoured car and the battleship *Aurora* whose gunshots signalled the beginning of the uprising.

Some of us were party members, most were not. Some had a certain professional reputation and experience, others were just beginning to make their way. Yet our cast became Lenin, Trotsky, Stalin, Zinoviev, Kamenev, Kerensky, Kornilov, and we peopled the hall with soldiers, sailors, workers and peasants in a way that was utterly convincing and completely transcended our own egos, inadequacies and different levels of professional experience and ability. We were united by an urgent political crisis. The miners were on strike, despite the attempts of the Labour Party to make them return to work, and the Tories were fighting the election on the slogan 'Who rules Britain?'

My experience with this play was to prove enormously valuable. I found, in the course of the run of *Design for Living*, that I was able to carry out my professional and artistic work and participate fully in the political life of my party. At an emergency Central Committee meeting, we had decided to put forward eight candidates in constituencies where there was a large Labour majority. In the country as a whole we would call for a Labour vote, and warn that if the Conservatives were allowed to return, they would come back with a dictatorship, based on the Army and the police. We chose eight constituencies, one each in Scotland, the North-East of England, the Midlands, and Wales, and four in London. The play *October*, was to be presented as the climax to our party's main election rally in the great hall of the Alexandra Palace, which seated about 4000 people. I was asked to be the party's candidate in Newham North-East, a large working-class district in the East End of London, between Canning Town, Barking and Dagenham. It was there that Eleanor Marx, Karl Marx's daughter, had organised the gas workers and thousands of the poorest-paid semi-skilled and unskilled workers in the last decade of the nineteenth century. Now the seat was held by Reg Prentice, Labour's shadow minister for education, a right-winger, with a huge majority for Labour. I accepted.

# 16

Our party members in Newham found a vacant shop in Green Street and rented it for three weeks for our election headquarters. Their families, friends and supporters supplied trestle tables and chairs, made cups of tea and sandwiches, and sat for hours cutting out columns of names and addresses on the electoral register and pasting them up into canvassing cards. The party press printed 65,000 election statements, and we folded each one and addressed it for the Post Office to collect each day. Electoral law in Britain gives a political party the right to a free post for its election addresses in a general election.

We had barely three weeks for the election campaign. Heath had dissolved parliament and set the election date within the bare minimum period allowed by law. By the end of the first week it seemed that every other house had a 'Vote Prentice, Vote Labour' sticker in its front window, but we soon found that Prentice and his policies were far from popular. Scarcely any householder had a good word to say either for the Labour Party or for their MP. We were on the streets from 6.30 every morning, outside the huge Ford car plant in Dagenham, the Tate & Lyle depot in Silvertown, the docks, the railway stations and the bus stops. We held open-air meetings on the High Street outside the supermarkets, indoor meetings in the colleges and hospitals. In the evenings we canvassed door to door, from six until nine o'clock. Our campaign grew in strength as the number of our canvassers and helpers grew. By the eve of the poll more than 800 had applied to join our party. We had canvassed every household in the borough at least once.

Again and again I was told: 'You are the only party that has bothered to come and see us.' A huge part of Newham consisted of rows of small terraced houses, split into bed-sitting-rooms and

172

rented out privately or from the Council. The average wage was about £20 a week, or £30 if the job was skilled. Wages in industry were held down by law, and prices were rising fast. Economic conditions were deteriorating rapidly, but prices, wages and unemployment were not the only subjects that workers talked about. In my election address I had warned about the plans for a military dictatorship in Britain. I said that the economic crisis could not possibly be resolved by parliament or through the ballot box, but only by building the Workers' Revolutionary Party as the means for the working class to take power. I called for Councils of Action, the occupation of factories, and a workers' militia to replace the standing army and the police. When I explained this programme at a press conference it evoked a largely hostile coverage. The *Guardian* said that the Workers' Revolutionary Party programme was 'alarmist', but in the front rooms of the terraced houses where I was invited for a talk and a cup of tea, and at the four public meetings we held in different wards in the constituency, people listened, asked questions, argued, and often agreed.

The Tory election theme was 'moderation versus extremism'. The miners were 'holding the country to ransom'. They were blamed for inflation, for the energy crisis, the three-day week, and the plight of pensioners and small children. The predominantly Tory newspapers ran stories about orphanages where children huddled in the dark during power cuts, and about old-age pensioners dying of hypothermia. Despite this it was evident that the Tory campaign was not succeeding. No one believed that the miners were to blame for the three-day week. Some dockers told us of oil tankers deliberately kept at anchor by the port authorities, unable to discharge their cargo.

On the day of the poll it rained, as it had done throughout the campaign. Our canvassing returns promised us about 1000 votes, and we pressed every car we could find into service to call on our supporters, and transport the pensioners amongst them to the polling stations. Soon after the close of poll I walked up to a door and was welcomed by a middle-aged worker who had promised to vote for me. 'I'm sorry,' he said, 'when I got there, I voted Labour. I was anxious and I wanted to make sure we kept the Tories out,' but he insisted on inviting me into his home. He said he still agreed with our manifesto, and had been so impressed with the way our party worked in the area that he wanted to join.

173

The Labour candidate won the Newham seat with a big majority over the Conservatives. I had just over 700 votes. In the country no party had an overall majority. The next day there was no formal announcement that the Palace had summoned Labour leader Harold Wilson, and as we walked down Oxford Street we saw a convoy of armoured cars with soldiers in full battledress crossing Oxford Circus into Regent Street. On Monday, 4 March 1974, Prime Minister Heath resigned, having failed to persuade the Liberals to support his government. Wilson became Prime Minister, and two days later Michael Foot met the miners' leaders at the Coal Board and settled their claim.

Wilson's government was unstable from the outset, not because it lacked an overall majority in parliament, but because the state security services and army intelligence were at work to destabilise it. In the North of Ireland, operation 'Clockwork Orange' was started. Its purpose was to change the leadership of all three parties at Westminster. A journalist on the *Investors' Chronicle* made a tour of officers' messes and wrote: 'The most serious fact is that one top general apparently took three months' leave of absence to write a manual on how and in what circumstances the army would take over.'

In July the *Evening News* published on its front page a statement by a retired army officer, General Sir Walter Walker. 'Perhaps the country might choose rule by the gun in preference to anarchy,' he commented. Walker was quite explicit: Britain needed a leader like Enoch Powell. He had spoken with officers who had fought in the Burma campaign and who were saying, 'What we want is a leader who will put forward fundamental democratic principles like rule by the gun under an army junta that the man in the street can follow.' In August *Peace News*, the pacifist weekly, published a memorandum by the founder of the SAS, Colonel David Stirling. He had founded a paramilitary strike-breaking organisation called 'Great Britain '75'. 'The immediate purpose of our project,' he wrote, 'is to provide on a volunteer basis the minimum manpower necessary to cope with the immediate crisis following a general strike or a near general strike, in the knowledge that the government of the day must welcome our initiative and would assume responsibility for our volunteer force and reinforce it as best it can.'

Alex Mitchell, on the editorial board of the *Workers' Press*, wrote an article headlined 'What is the CIA up to in Britain?' revealing that the former assistant deputy director of the CIA's planning department in Washington (the Department of Dirty Tricks) had been sent to London. With thirty or forty operatives the CIA was gaining information about the trade unions' left-wing organisations. The year's events brought another general election, on 10 October. Our meetings in the October election campaign in Newham were packed. I must have made a score of speeches in public since my first effort a year before, and although I had gained in confidence I still needed sheaves of notes to make a 20-minute speech. Gerry, who spoke after me, was the best political orator I have ever heard. He would use three or four cards, with at most two or three lines of notes on each card. He would invariably begin very quietly, as if thinking aloud, his hands thrust deep into the pockets of his jacket. Then, as his speech progressed, he would seem to summon all the force of his intellect and personality, binding himself and his audience. If it is said that Marxism is the conscious expression of the unconscious historical process, such a union could be observed for sure on those occasions when Gerry spoke to an audience of workers. Without rhetorical tricks or flourishes he would use the full range of his political vocabulary, expressing complex ideas in a way that everyone understood. I never saw an audience who did not respond.

It was a very busy period. My children suffered from the amount of time I had to spend away from them, Natasha and Joely the most. It was difficult for me but worse for them, and it would not have been possible without first of all Christina, then Linda and finally Silvana. Thanks to them there was always a caring loving young woman to take responsibility, listen to the children's problems and be there for them when I was unavailable. I had made Natasha a new bedroom with a small desk, because she now had so much homework. One night I sat by her bed, my knees on the floor, kissing and hugging her goodnight, having sung songs to Joely and Carlo in their bunks in the adjoining room. Natasha appealed to me to spend more time with her. I tried to explain that our political struggle was for her future, and that of all the children of her generation. She looked at me with a serious, sweet smile. 'But I need you *now*. I won't need you so much then.' It was true. She and Joely needed me. The time we spent, talking, laughing or playing together, was seldom long and always very precious. They naturally did not understand when I told them how many children could not live a happy life with their parents because of the injustice and cruelty of our society. Or rather, they did understand, but understanding did not lessen the loss they felt.

They understood my grief when Timothy Dalton broke off our relationship because I told him I was going to a big rally for trade unionists in Manchester one Sunday afternoon when he wanted me to stay with him. We had both been very much in love, and so it was all the worse that he could not accept what I was doing. I went to the rally and sang at a concert afterwards. I listened to the speeches and knew that I could not and would not give up. Since my early childhood I had been convinced that fascism, war and the destruction of peoples because of their race, religion or politics must never happen again. I cried coming back on the train, and again the next morning at breakfast. Tasha and Joely put their arms about me. I told them why I was crying and they comforted me.

I had been invited to work at the giant Ahmandon Theatre in Los Angeles, in a production of *Macbeth* with Charlton Heston. When I filled in the application for a work visa I wrote: 'I am a member of the Workers' Revolutionary Party – see file.' When I had tried and failed to get a visa before, a US Embassy official had simply pointed at the massive file on the desk in front of him which contained all the newspaper cuttings about my work in Britain against the Vietnam war. By 1974 when I went for an interview, Nixon had resigned and the Attorney-General, John Nutchell, had gone to prison. This time the Embassy interview was brief and the officer told me he would grant me a visa, 'when we hear from Frankfurt'. 'Does that mean I may not get one?' I asked. 'I can't tell you that. A waiver has been requested for you. Frankfurt will notify us.'

The visa I received was strictly limited to the run of the contract. Years later, when Joely went to school in California and I applied for a working visa that, too, was strictly limited to the few days specified in my application. I could not get a multiple entry visa until October 1983. To this day a figure or letter on my visa tells Immigration on entry to the United States that I am a 'waiver' person, which means that I am under surveillance at all ports of entry into America.

Before departing for LA in December 1974 I discussed with Gerry Healy our plan to buy a house and convert it into a school for the party, a college of Marxism. We wanted a house in the country with enough room for fifty students, lecture rooms and a library.

We decided that I would give four lectures on Marxism in Los Angeles to raise as much money as possible.

Joely, Tasha, Carlo and I spent the Christmas holiday in Tony's house above Sunset Boulevard, where he now lived permanently, astonished and delighted with the warmth of the Los Angeles weather, and the luck of having a small swimming pool. With Tony's help I found a school for Joely for the spring term, among the eucalyptus trees in the valley in north Los Angeles. Tasha had to leave us to return to St Paul's Girls' School in London. Tony had decided she should leave the French Lycée and have an English education, and that Joely would join her at St Paul's in the autumn term.

I was looking forward to working again with Peter Wood, who had directed me in *The Prime of Miss Jean Brodie* and with Charlton Heston as Macbeth. When Tasha flew back to London, Joely, Carlo and I settled down to our Californian life, which for me meant rehearsing *Macbeth* and preparing my four lectures on Marxism. In this way we saw in the New Year of 1975.

First rehearsals were lively and interesting. Charlton Heston, John Ireland and I were excited by Peter Wood's idea of the witches. They were embodied in the corpses of Cawdor's rebel army on the battlefield in Act I scene i, rising up from the stench and smoke of the battlefield to chant 'When shall we three meet again?' The assassins hired by Macbeth to murder Banquo, Fleance, Lady Macduff and her son were also the witches. It was a brilliant conception, connecting the witches with the violence and cruelty of war and Macbeth's superstitious despotism.

For all that, some fundamental concept was lacking through which to grasp the essence of the play as a whole. What is Macbeth's superstition? A company of actors may readily conclude it was the superstition of the age, and yet, less than half a century after *Macbeth* was written, no one believed in 'hobgoblins' or such creatures any more, according to contemporary observers of Cromwell's republic.

Scholars have debated over the dating of *Macbeth*. From internal evidence it seems likely that it was performed at the court of King James I of England and VI of Scotland, probably in 1606. Shakespeare's company then had a royal charter, and Malcolm, crowned King of Scotland at the play's end, was James's ancestor. In Act IV scene iii Malcolm describes the English king, Edward the Confessor, as having miraculous powers of healing:

and 'tis spoken
to the succeeding royalty he leaves
the healing benediction. With this strange virtue,
he hath a heavenly gift of prophecy.

James, though affecting to belittle his own healing and prophetic powers, made sure that his bishops promoted belief in both. He wrote a treatise on witchcraft and possession by evil spirits, *Daemonologie*, published in 1597, which became a rubric for religious and political persecution during his reign and his son's. James also murdered two Scottish nobles, the Ruthnen brothers, chieftains of the Gowrie clan. He arrived at their castle with a company of soldiers on a surprise visit, and requested dinner. After supper the two Ruthnen brothers were stabbed to death, and James declared he had been forced to kill them because they had attempted to assassinate him. He made his ministers sign their names to corroborate his story, but none of his contemporaries believed it. On 28 March 1606 Henry Garnet, Provincial of the Jesuit Society in England, was brought to trial indicted for complicity in the gunpowder plot. James was present in the court that day, incognito, disguised as a commoner. The more we read of James's rule, the more his features merge with those of Shakespeare's Scottish tyrant, Macbeth. 'Stands Scotland where it did?' asks Macduff, and Ross replies,

Alas! poor country,
Almost afraid to know itself; it cannot
Be called our mother, but our grave; where nothing
But who knows nothing, is once seen to smile.

*Macbeth* cannot be understood without a knowledge of this history. And yet that knowledge will not, of itself, bring the play to life. To do that, we must examine our own times. The poet Osip Mandelstam, for instance, called Stalin 'the Kremlin Highlander',* and indeed the play was never performed in the Soviet Union during Stalin's reign of terror. Stalin also liked to be present, unseen, at the trials of his victims. A recent Soviet documentary pointed out a small window high in the wall above the judges' bench in the hall where the Moscow trials were held, where an invisible Stalin could look down directly into the dock. If we had

*A double entendre, 'Highlander' also refering to Stalin's Georgian Nationality'.

discussed the simplest, most fundamental, everyday facts of political life, facts, so to speak, right under our noses, the essence of *Macbeth* would have emerged more clearly for us and for the audience. Memories of Nixon's downfall were still fresh, and there were many accounts of his last days in office. According to one witness, Nixon, abandoned by his former colleagues, wandered the corridors of the White House, praying to the portraits of his predecessors.

> Now, does he feel his title
> Hang loose upon him, like a giant's robe
> Upon a dwarfish thief.

But these are notes for the *Macbeth* that might have been, or for some future *Macbeth*. The *Macbeth* that filled every seat in the Ahmandon Theatre was bloody, bold and resolute – and essentially rather decent. One day, perhaps, I will get the chance to make another attempt.

I gave the four lectures on Marxism during my stay in Hollywood, and learned something of that town's political history. I met technicians who remembered the ferocious battles with police and strike-breakers in the 1930s, when the bosses tried to stamp out the unions in the studios. Many actors and writers who came to hear my lectures had been members or supporters of the Communist Party in the Forties and Fifties, and had suffered from the blacklist. A beautiful and talented actress, whose career had been blasted by the McCarthy purges, said I was brave to speak out. I tried to turn the compliment aside, because I spoke in the way I knew and had learned to speak in my party, and bravery didn't come into it, but I understood what she meant. When the purges began the Communist Party of America took a 'low profile' and told its members to do the same, claiming the Fifth Amendment or the First Amendment; it did not lead any political struggle against McCarthy. And so its members – who were courageous, or wanted to be – were abandoned politically with no movement to support them, and worse, with no clear theoretical lead to explain why they were being persecuted or what to do about it. I thought again of my father, how he had feared for me, and how cynically the Communist Party leaders had treated his questions when he had been blacklisted and went to them for advice.

The collections at my lectures and the many donations I received from film and theatre people in Hollywood came to more than $20,000, at least half the sum we needed to buy a house in the country and convert it into a full-time school of Marxism. One visit I remember with special pride and pleasure. It gave me a great deal of inward satisfaction at the time because Elliot Gould, who could be very funny and very helpful, would try to irritate me by answering my telephone calls – 'Hello, this is Groucho Marx.' So it was thrilling to sit with Groucho in his house and listen to this old gentleman, who was *very* funny and very courteous, talk about his battles with the studios. We told him why we wanted a school of Marxism in Britain. 'There's one thing I don't like about Britain,' he said. 'On second thoughts, there are several things. But the thing I least like is the monarchy.' He promised a donation, which never materialised, not because he changed his mind but because his affairs were complicated by a dispute, which broke out soon after his death, between his family and his companion.

We returned to England at the end of March 1975 where Natasha joined us again. We had missed each other terribly. I went up to Parwich in the Derbyshire Peak District to see White Meadows, a large, empty house, once a youth hostel, which Corin had found. It was half derelict, and would need a great deal of work to restore, but the dollars we had raised in America meant that we could buy it and do the work of restoration ourselves. We got planning permission from the Peak Park Planning Board and set about converting White Meadows into a school. One of our members was an architect. He was not young, so we booked a room for him in the nearby Bentley Brook Hotel. But when he saw that our younger members, workers in the building trade, were camping in the house itself so that they could start work at first light, he gallantly said to hell with the hotel, and joined them with his sleeping bag. Roy Battersby, who was to be warden of the school, camped there too, and the work proceeded at a terrific pace all summer. The derelict part of the building was gutted and in its place a canteen for sixty people took shape: a kitchen, a laundry, store rooms, and above, a flat for Battersby and his family. A new wing was added to the main part of the house, with a large dormitory above and a lecture room and library below. Carpets were laid, bathrooms and showers fitted and plumbed, and new wiring was installed throughout. We were all determined to open the school on 27 August and I enrolled for the first course. We had decided that it would be for our comrades in the entertainment unions.

Equity had been taken over by a right-wing leadership led by Marius Goring and Derek Bond, after the group who had led the union, the 'Campaign for Re-registration and Progress for Equity' (CRAPE) had lost the confidence of the membership. They had backed away completely from their main promise, which was to establish a branch and delegate structure in the union. This would have meant all members belonging to a branch, discussing policies in the branches, and electing delegates to an annual conference, which would then become the highest authority and policy-making body in the union. It would also have meant a battle with the right wing, who were determined to prevent the introduction of a branch structure at all costs.

It must have been at about this time that the national press, one of whose chief functions is to invent misleading labels, came up with a new term for right-wing trade unionists: they were called 'moderates'. Their opponents were 'extremists'. When you explain to someone that in Equity's constitution the Annual General Meeting has absolutely no powers whatever, and that whatever policy the members may decide at AGMs can be immediately overruled, or simply ignored by the Council, they are amazed. In fact, the only body in political life in Britain whose annual conference is as powerless, constitutionally, as Equity's, is the Tory Party. And that system was what the 'moderates' in Equity were seeking to preserve. There was only one area in which Equity's constitution gave the members the right to decide at AGM, and that was in the matter of the constitution itself. Union rules could only be changed by a two-thirds majority vote at an Annual General Meeting. This the new Council immediately set out to change. They announced a Special General Meeting for 12 October. A resolution would be put by the Council for powers to change rules by referendum, in a postal ballot.

We had organised a group in Equity, with the demand 'Keep Equity a Union and make it fight'. We went to the CRAPE group and suggested a joint campaign against Goring and Bond's group on the Council. We agreed a title for the campaign – 'Defend Equity! Defend the Union!' – based on a principle which both we and CRAPE would uphold, the right of members to make and change the rules of their union at their Annual General Meeting.

The postal ballot is not an alternative method of deciding issues within the democratic process, because the bureaucracy that governs Equity, as in the majority of trade unions, has absolute control over the presentation of the issue to be decided in a postal ballot. When the answer to a question can only be Yes or No, much depends on how the question is put, and in the selection of arguments for and against. Also, a postal ballot deprives members of the opportunity to debate, to ask questions and challenge their leaders, and only in that process can a matter be understood in its context and with all its implications, so that members can make an informed decision on which course of action to adopt.

In the summer of 1975, when I was filming *Murder on the Orient Express* at Elstree Studios with Sidney Lumet and a galaxy of stars playing Agatha Christie's murder suspects, Sidney suggested we should have only a half-hour lunch break, something which was unheard of at that time. I rang Equity, who sent the film organiser down, and the cast met in the lunch break. Around the table sat Sean Connery, Albert Finney, Rachel Roberts, Ingrid Bergman, Michael York, Jacqueline Bisset, Richard Widmark and Colin Blakeley. The organiser said it was up to us, we could make our own decision on whether to accept the half-hour lunch break or not. I said it was not only ourselves we were deciding for. I spoke of the economic crisis, the continuous attack on the unions, and the fact that Elstree Studios were soon to be closed. I said that if we, who, no doubt, had the power to refuse, said that we could manage without a full lunch-break, others would soon be forced to accept it, and we should have opened a door for all employers to increase the workload and thereby cut pay throughout the industry.

Our famous cast considered the question seriously, but since the organiser had said that they could accept the half-hour, and had disagreed with my view that there was a danger of our setting a precedent, they voted to accept. Almost immediately stories appeared in the press that Vanessa was causing trouble at Elstree on Sidney Lumet's film. It seemed most unlikely that any member of our cast would have volunteered such misinformation to the press, and I was forced to consider the possibility that someone from the union offices might have telephoned them. Sadly, my suspicions proved correct. There was indeed a regular two-way channel of communication between the press and Equity's offices for stories about me and my party.

I spent two weeks up at our college in August and September, and from 1975 to 1985 I went there for study at least two weeks every year. We worked from 9 a.m. to 1 p.m., from 3 p.m. to 6.30 p.m., and read and discussed questions that had arisen until the ten o'clock news on television. It was difficult but immensely exciting to learn to read, think and discuss the process by which the changes in the world of nature and social life are reflected in thought. The students included some who had studied at universities, some like myself who had had training in a profession, industrial workers, and young people who had never had the chance to get a real education in anything.

Tasha and Joely were both now at St Paul's Girls' School in Hammersmith. Carlo was in his first year at primary school. They had a new nanny, Silvana Sammassimo. She and Carlo spoke Italian together, and thanks to her he grew up as fluent in Italian as in English. As time went on she became my secretary, and then my agent and a dear friend. Corin had separated from his wife Deirdre, and for a while he lived in the basement of our house in St Peter's Square.

My party branch was in Central London, and when I wasn't filming I worked with the branch every day. We sold papers early in the morning outside the post office in Rathbone Place, and at hospitals and colleges. We delivered them to our daily readers before they went to work and at lunchtime. In the evenings we canvassed new readers, had pub sales and took our paper to sell to printworkers in Fleet Street. Every morning at eight o'clock we analysed political developments and made day-to-day decisions. At 9 a.m. the editorial board of the *Workers' Press* met to discuss the main stories, and analyse the news. The paper was still 'hot metal' at this time. It went on to the presses at lunchtime and was then sorted into parcels which went overnight to Scotland, the North-East, the Midlands and Wales. Comrades in London came into our centre in Clapham around midnight to collect the papers and take them to the main drops throughout London.

Early on Sunday morning, 26 September, I had a telephone call. One of our comrades said 'Get a copy of the *Observer* immediately.' I ran upstairs to the front door and found the newspaper lying on the mat. I saw my photograph and the headlines on the front page: 'Police Raid the Red House', with a photograph of White Meadows, our college. The report alleged that the WRP ran a military-style organisation at the college and that police had raided it the previous night looking for weapons in the grounds. About a hundred police with dogs and pocket flares had burst into the college as the students were having a cup of tea at about 10 p.m. They had no search warrant. They had confined Gerry to his study and searched all the students, including a couple of elderly women. One of the policemen had put his hand into a cupboard where we kept cleaning brushes and detergents, and pulled it out with five bullets in it. Apparently they were .22 bullets of the kind farmers use for shooting rabbits, but no one in the college had a gun, and the bullets could not have been in the cupboard unless someone had put them there deliberately.

I knew an enormous frame-up had taken place. As Marxists we were totally opposed to individual terror, which we regarded as the politics of despair. We were not terrorists, we did not carry, store or trade weapons. But, clearly, Marxist ideas were considered too dangerous to be tolerated.

The only previous political raid in Britain this century had been during the Second World War. The Communist Party offices in King Street, Covent Garden had been raided during the period of the Molotov–Ribbentrop pact. Later, during the war, some of the British Trotskyists had been raided, charged and tried for incitement because they defended the young 'Bevin Boys' from exploitation in the mines during the war.

It was clear to me and to our Political Committee that this organised provocation was directed by the state. We knew, since we were in the newspaper business, that the *Observer* front-page story could not have appeared in the first edition, which could be bought at about 10.30 p.m. on Saturday night in Fleet Street, unless the paper knew about the raid before it happened. The raid took place at 10 p.m., approximately half an hour before the *Observer* with its front-page story appeared on the streets.

Tasha and Joely spent that day and the night with Corin's wife Deirdre. They were very frightened because they dreaded what might be said to them at school the next day. They thought that everybody would be talking about them and asking questions. As it happened, happily, no one said anything about it at all. When the party or I myself am attacked in the newspapers for my politics I feel enormous pressure, and can be very hurt, but I do feel vulnerable when my children come under siege as well. It is worse for them than for me, and the children have always been incredibly supportive and strong.

All the television news programmes contacted our newspaper office and on Monday I agreed to appear on two of them, just after the main news at six o'clock in the evening. I would be interviewed first by Eamonn Andrews for ITV and next by Sue Lawley for the BBC. I met Eamonn Andrews, and we went on the air 'live'. I took a deep breath and warned the trade unions and Labour Party members that this organised frame-up of the WRP meant that we all faced a new and major struggle for our basic democratic rights. That Monday every single newspaper carried headlines and news stories about the police raid. Featured prominently were quotes from Peter Plouviez, Equity's General Secretary. Equity members were warned that they must defeat the Redgraves at the Special General Meeting which was to discuss the rule changes on 12 October.

On Thursday 2 October, I went up to Blackpool and joined other comrades who were getting signatures for our petition, 'Hands off the Workers' Revolutionary Party'. Jack Jones, General Secretary of the largest trade union in Britain, the Transport and General Workers' Union signed, and so did Communist Party trade unionists, including Jack Collins, leader of the Kent miners, and many others. Some of them telephoned the *Morning Star*, and said that they would cancel their subscriptions unless the paper took a united front position and defended our basic democratic rights. 'An injury to one is an injury to all', the fundamental historical position of the trade unions, was no empty catch-phrase. Workers, and many trade union leaders, knew that we had been framed.

In a few weeks about 7 million trade unionists had come to our defence. Most Equity members signed our petition. I remember my bitterness when two close actor friends of mine refused, but they were in the minority. Such incidents reminded me how sceptical middle-class people still were at that time, how full of illusions about 'British democracy'. 'If you call yourselves the Workers' *Revolutionary* Party,' said one, 'surely you must expect this kind of thing to happen to you.'

We worked night and day to collect signatures and to rally Equity members to the Coliseum Theatre on Sunday 12 October. The Coliseum was packed and the overflow had to be accommodated in another theatre. Press reporters and photographers were everywhere. Lord Olivier, then Sir Laurence, had appealed for the defeat of the 'extremists' in a letter to *The Times*. I remembered how he had been a guard on the Underground to help break the General Strike of 1926. In 1975, the acting élite – who had regular employment and close ties with judges, lawyers, newspaper proprietors and the armed services – lined up, with honourable exceptions, against 'The Redgraves'. The actors and actresses who suffered all the slings and arrows of our profession, including unemployment, low wages and constant humiliation, were on the whole distrustful of the Equity Council, who had never lifted a finger to change the terrible conditions in which most performers work.

Our General Secretary Plouviez spoke for the rule change. Corin and I led the opposition. Marius Goring, Nigel Davenport and their supporters failed to get their two-thirds majority – in spite of the police raid, the press witch-hunt, and the appeal by Sir Laurence Olivier.

Immediately after their defeat at the Coliseum Goring and Davenport took Equity's rule-book to court, where it was ruled that Equity's rules could be changed by referendum. We engaged a solicitor and a barrister and got the High Court decision over-turned on appeal. Then they went to the House of Lords, which overruled the Appeal Court.

In December 1975, 6000 trade unionists marched with us to Trafalgar Square. Robert Bolt, the playwright, who was at this time president of the Association of Cinema and Television Technicians' union, spoke on our platform along with other trade unionists. Some Labour MPs challenged Home Secretary James Callaghan in the House of Commons to declare whether or not there were grounds for prosecuting members of the Workers' Revolutionary Party. What happened, and how this provocation was organised, could only be exposed if we sued the *Observer* for libel. It was in the course of this libel case, which came into the High Court in October 1978, that we officially cleared our names and put on record the truth of our party's position on terrorism, and the truth of the role of the state and the Labour government in the police raid.

The strength of support we received indicated that a great many people, and many of them in the theatre profession, were very uneasy about the role of the press. This was particularly true for older people in the profession, like Rachel and Michael. As often happens, my marriage, family and career had taken me away from my parents, and then my intense involvement in political work in the seventies distanced me from them. I found it difficult to explain this work to Michael and Rachel initially, and they could not understand it but with the *Observer* case, they, like many others, supported our demand for basic democratic rights and were not deceived by the avalanche of articles in the press. In the late seventies and early eighties when Corin and Michael worked together on his autobiography the distance between us all closed again, and Michael became involved in both film and theatre projects organised by the party which meant that I had the tremendous pleasure of acting with him again in 1982.

# 17

Circle in the Square is a protected island in the middle of Manhattan's tempestuous theatrical seascape, and it is where plays and musicals sink, 'flop', or swim and become hits. At Circle in the Square the plays, some new, some revivals, run for two or three months, and the theatre has an audience which likes and understands what it is trying to do. It takes much dedication, imagination and knowledge of plays and audiences to build up a theatre like that in New York, and Theodore Mann has all those qualities and more. I first came to know him in 1975, when Tony and I asked if we could do Ibsen's *Lady from the Sea* there. Both of us were excited to try theatre in the round, and fortunately Ted was excited by us, so he made some space in his programme and we got down to business.

Since that time I've got to know Ted and his wife Ruth much better, and now when I go to New York I stay at their apartment on 7th Avenue. It is old and spacious, with high ceilings and lovely old brown furniture, and hot water pipes that hiss and gurgle through the night. It's very peaceful – for Manhattan – which means that it is shatteringly noisy from midnight till 4 a.m., when the garbage trucks load up with all the half-eaten sandwiches from the Carnegie Deli opposite. But in 1976 I rented a painter's apartment on 3rd Avenue, and for my thirty-ninth birthday I sat round a small wooden table with Carlo and Silvana, celebrating with a bowl of Rice Krispies. Once again we had had to leave Tasha behind in London, and this time Joely as well. Tasha stayed with her schoolfriend Elisa, and Joely with Corin's wife Deirdre and their two children, Jemma and Luke. Even though Deirdre was no longer with Corin, she very sweetly agreed to look after Joely for me.

*The Lady from the Sea* was my first appearance in New York, and

188

as things turned out, my only appearance until, fourteen years later, I played another 'Lady' in *Orpheus Descending*. There were plenty of offers in the 1960s to appear on Broadway, including the chance to work with Mike Nichols in *The Little Foxes*, but I turned them all down. I did not feel that playing in Broadway was a goal in my life, and what is more I felt certain I could do no good work under the kind of excessive pressure and hype I had seen at close quarters when Tony worked there soon after we were married. But to work at Circle in the Square, a theatre that depended on subsidy and could measure its success or failure in some other terms besides the weekly gross at the box office, was closer, in my experience to working at theatres like Stratford, Manchester Royal Exchange, or the Royal Court in London. I greatly admire the people who make theatre in America. The work of many American actors, directors, designers and companies like Steppenwolf for example, has been inspirational but the Broadway system can be very damaging. The West End today is becoming increasingly like Broadway; both places make it practically impossible for new plays to be performed unless there are several leading names in the cast. But Theodore Mann and his partner Paul Libin were from the generation whose creativity I had glimpsed back in 1955, and I was delighted to be working with Tony again.

Rehearsing with Tony is one of the greatest pleasures I know. He is very sharp and intelligent, and because he knows his own mind and has a very firm conception of what he wants, he really listens to others and is never afraid of asking or taking advice. He has an absolute scorn of playing safe, and can be very provocative. One day in rehearsals, Pat Hingle, our leading man, became exasperated with Ibsen's portrayal of Ellida. He simply couldn't tolerate her, and became more and more impatient with her suffering. Tony urged him to think of his own wife, whereupon Pat burst out: 'If she was my wife I'd hit her.' Tony was thoroughly delighted. He laughed and clapped his hands, as if this was the funniest joke he'd heard that year, and urged Pat to drop all restraint and do just that. 'Go on, hit Vanessa! Hit her hard! It'll do her good!' I have been hit a few times in my life, but no one had ever suggested this should happen, apart from Edith Evans when I was very small, and I waited anxiously for a box on my ears. But despite Tony's prompting it never came.

Ellida is Ibsen's most sensitive and profound exploration of a

189

woman's longing to discover and share fully in the life of her times. The play deals with the awful harm inflicted on women, especially married women, by the hypocritical morality and laws of bourgeois society. I identified very much with her yearning for the unknown, and for the freedom she had before marriage, when she was a lighthouse-keeper's daughter on the seashore. None the less I found many areas of the play very difficult to grasp, and as often happens when we don't fully understand something, I resorted to demonstrating what I thought the scene was about.

Tim Dalton and I had got back together again, and he came to New York from filming in Los Angeles with Mae West. He saw the play, and his criticism drove me to re-examine what I was doing. I realised that in demonstrating what was happening to Ellida I was avoiding the contradictions in her moments of development. I was acting what she knew, and avoiding all the things she did not know or understand. 'Science,' Engels says in *Dialectics of Nature*, 'has to investigate what we do not know.' And so, though it is not a science, does acting.

After the first night Tony and I went to a café, and his assistant went off to get the reviews. When Clive Barnes, the drama critic of the *New York Times*, said I was 'a child of nature', and praised Tony's production, we all heaved a sigh of relief and knew we had a success. I was contracted to play for twelve weeks, at $1000 a week, less than half what I had earned the last time I had worked with Tony in 1972 in *The Threepenny Opera* at the Prince of Wales' Theatre in London. I mention this remembering my father's advice to his mother, when she was old and in a nursing home in Stanmore. He sent her some school copybooks, suggesting that since she remembered so much about the theatre of her days it should be recorded. 'Don't write what you thought of this or that actor or actress,' he said, 'so much as what you were paid, working conditions, landladies, Sunday "train-calls" and the rest of it.' His father Roy died penniless, with only just enough to pay for a plain tombstone. Michael died with no savings in the bank and my mother at the age of eighty-one has to work as often as she can to pay the bills.

In the Sixties and early Seventies I had earned some large salaries for films, *Mary, Queen of Scots* and *The Devils*, which I had put into the Vanessa Redgrave Nursery School. I don't remember ever reading an article in the press which complained that I gave my money to a school. But from the time I joined the WRP in 1973 the press continually wrote: 'She gives all her money to the party', as if to warn employers not to hire me because they would have been subsidising the WRP, and, in fact, my earnings fell very considerably. For *Agatha*, co-starring with Dustin Hoffman, I was paid $50,000 (£25,000). From that I paid 10 per cent agent's commission, 60 per cent corporation tax, national insurance and PAYE for Silvana and Sandra Marsh, my secretary, which left about £7000 for the year to pay the bills. I paid my weekly subscription to the party, like every other member, and if I could lend a sum to the party for some special need, I did; it was always paid back. Franco has been a truly kind and generous friend, helping me to find work when I have been in difficulties. After we separated, Tony gave me about £200 a month to bring up the girls. I am proud of the men I loved, the fathers of my children. All of us despise professional women who drain their former husbands of money when they divorce, so we shared everything which is how it should be.

One night as I came into the Circle in the Square to get ready for the performance, Pam, one of the usherettes, who used to baby-sit for Carlo on her night off, gave me a book. 'You must read this – it should be made into a film and you should play Julia.' That night when I got home I read *Pentimento* from start to finish. Next day at the theatre I found a message that Fred Zinnemann wanted to see me. I telephoned his office the following morning and heard that he was casting for a film of *Julia* with Jane Fonda, and wanted to meet me.

Zinnemann was kind, but he was also extremely cautious. I decided to take the bull by the horns and told him I wanted to play the part of Julia. He gave me the script to take away and read. Julia's role was very small in the script, but that did nothing to affect my desire to play her. I rang my agent and told him if Zinnemann's office came through the answer was Yes, and he should accept their first offer without argument.

Julia, as described by Lillian Hellman, was a communist in outlook. Also, like Lillian, she was Jewish. She was one of millions of ordinary/extraordinary people who sacrificed everything to defeat German Fascism. I knew that *Julia* was a true story long before Lillian Hellman confirmed it. Every line in her book told me that. Not long before she died Lillian also told me that her own part in the story was true and I believed her. I did not meet her until

191

1984, but after I had done the film she revealed that she had insisted on my being cast as Julia. 'You're so like the lady in question, it's uncanny.' A controversy arose because Mary McCarthy and Martha Gellhorn accused Lillian Hellman of lying, saying that she stole Julia's story from an Englishwoman, Margaret Gardiner, and claimed it as her own. 'Every word she writes,' said Mary McCarthy, 'is a lie, including *and* and *the*.' Lillian began a libel action, but died before it came to court. No one can say what the outcome would have been, but one thing is sure: her story has survived, and will survive, as a compellingly truthful account of a woman's struggle against Fascism, long after the attacks by Lillian's opponents have been buried and forgotten.

The part of Julia became even smaller in the second and third version of Alvin Sargent's script, and many of the political references in the first draft were cut out. Fred asked me to discuss each new version with him. I told him I was sorry at what had been cut, not because it affected the size of my part, but because the political references were true, and taken directly from Lillian's book. Fred looked at me with his cautious eyes. 'But I *told* you it was not going to be a political film. Are you not happy with the script?' I assured him that I was very happy, and realised almost at once another reason for Fred's caution. Some of his greatest films had been made when the House Un-American Activities Committee was at work: *High Noon* with Gary Cooper, which no studio had wanted to finance and with a script by a blacklisted Hollywood screenwriter, had been considered possibly subversive by the Committee.

Fred gave me a photocopy of the *New York Times* front page on the day after the Nazis invaded Austria. As I read their correspondent's report from Vienna, I felt a painful twisting and clenching in my chest. 'Isn't it terrible how the Social Democrats refused to arm the workers against the Nazis?' I said. I had been reading Trotsky's essays and articles on the *Anschluss*, the Nazi annexation of Austria and knew that but for the policies of Stalin and the Social Democratic leaders the Nazis could never have taken power. Fred looked at me gravely. 'Better defeat than that the Socialists should have taken power.' Many Jewish people in his parents' generation, in Lenin's time, had joined communist parties. But Fred, and others, came to identify the crimes and anti-Semitic repressions of Stalinism with socialism and, by this route,

192

to think that the defeat of socialism was the lesser evil. Stalin's crimes, especially the Stalinist falsification of history, prevented his and my generation from knowing the truth of that history, or even wanting to read and discuss it.

I learned a great deal from Zinnemann, whose work I had admired ever since I saw *The Search* as a young girl, and later *From Here to Eternity*. Fred is a master storyteller with an expert control of his narrative. Two nights before Jane and I filmed the café scene where Julia and Lillian meet in Nazi-occupied Berlin, he asked us both to look at the scene for cuts. 'It's too long,' he said. 'Please give me your suggestions tomorrow.' That's the main scene of the film, I thought to myself, and approached the task with some reluctance. But when I looked at the script, trying to see the scene in the context of the whole film, I found that he was right: a lot could be cut, especially from Julia's lines. Fred was very pleased with my ideas, and I was excited that he trusted me enough to make my own cuts.

Jane and I had travelled along very different roads since the time we worked together with GIs against the Vietnam war. But we worked together on *Julia* in perfect harmony. Four years later in 1980 *Time* magazine wrote a feature article about me, to coincide with the screening of *Playing for Time*. As usual with such articles, they approached a number of fellow artists who had worked with me, including Jane. I knew her to be a generous friend, generous to other artists in a way that only actors who are confident in themselves and take pride in their work can be. I knew her to be very intelligent and perceptive. But her interview moved me to tears. I was astonished by what she had observed in me. I made a silent wish that I would one day have the chance to write about her with the same generosity and breadth of mind that she had shown to me.

In Paris, where most of *Julia* was filmed, I lived for some weeks with a Palestinian couple near Billancourt. They were students with very little money and their flat was tiny, one small living room with a gas stove, and an even smaller bedroom. One night they invited a friend to dinner, a Palestinian engineer living in Kuwait, who told me, in a voice choking with emotion and fatigue, of the treatment of Palestinians there. He spoke of the astonishing riches of the Kuwaiti sheikhs, with their palaces and Rolls-Royces.

We spoke of the siege of Tal al Zaatar, and how the young men, women, and children had to run a gauntlet of sniper fire when they crossed waste ground to fill their cans with water from the only pipe within reach of the camp, all other water having been cut off; and of the horror of the continual bombardment, day after day, month after month. The siege had begun in January 1976, and after many months, its sheer savagery had begun to penetrate the indifference of the European press. When the civil war in Lebanon had started it was portrayed in the British press as a fratricidal war between the Christians and Muslims, and their many sects. In fact, it was a war, first and foremost, of the rich against the poor, fascist feudal landowners against Lebanese poor peasants and workers organised in their trade unions. And side by side with the Lebanese poor were the Palestinians who had been driven to take refuge in the camps by the Israeli massacres in 1948, 1967 and 1973. The camp of Tal al Zaatar, the 'Hill of Thyme', was next to some of the largest factories in Beirut, which used the camp dwellers for cheap labour. The civil war began with a demonstration by Lebanese fishermen and trade unionists led by Ma'arouf Saad against Camille Chamoun, the feudal boss of the city port of Sidon and its fish-processing factories. The Sidon Lebanese battalion was ordered to fire on the demonstration, and a soldier's or a sniper's bullet killed Ma'arouf Saad. That was the flashpoint for the war.

In the Lebanese civil war the Palestinians, who had organised clinics and hospitals, schools and sanitation, factories and workshops where before there had been none, joined forces with the Lebanese poor and Kemal Jumblatt's Druze mountain farmers. Some of the rich merchant families, whether Muslim or Christian Druze, supported the Palestinians because their communities had suffered under the old French colonial regime. Opposing them were the Falangists, feudal absentee landlords and industrialists, Pierre Gemayel's Fascist Party and other feudal clans with their militia, all of whom had had acknowledged ties with Hitler, Mussolini and Franco. They laid siege to the Palestinians in Tal al Zaatar, and vowed to exterminate every man, woman and child.

What had happened at Tal al Zaatar was so hideous that I immediately wanted to do something to assist the situation, so I suggested to Gerry Healy that I should go to Lebanon, as Jane Fonda had gone to Vietnam, with a camera team and make a documentary about the Palestinians. He was enthusiastic and our proposal was agreed by the Political Committee.

As the tide of the war turned against the Falangists, the Syrian Army, which had been sent into Lebanon by decision of the Arab League as a peace-keeping force, was ordered to turn its guns on the Palestinians and destroy Tal al Zaatar. What the Falangists could never do on their own they now did, with the assistance of Syrian army detachments. The Palestinians kept silent, at least in public, about this treachery. They knew the Syrian masses still supported them. They knew too that Hafez Assad's regime twisted and turned, now stabbing them in the back, and the next moment offering support. Thousands of Palestinians were refugees in Syria, and many of their fighters were based there. Syrians, as Arabs, were their brothers and sisters, and they too had suffered bombardments, massacres and the seizure of their villages and pastures in the Golan Heights. I started to plan for the documentary in Paris in 1976, asking French artists if they would take part. I made contracts with film producers and technicians in Italy. Roy Battersby, who had directed many excellent television feature films and documentaries, agreed to direct and brought a first-class cameraman, Ivan Strasberg, into the project.

Back home I sat down with a sheet of paper and made some calculations. Our home at No. 18 St Peter's Square was a freehold and I had another house around the corner, which I had bought for Jan Stevens and her family when I built the nursery school. She had returned to California, having trained an English swimming instructor to take over her work. I could hope to get £40,000 for my home, and perhaps £25,000 for the other house. I found a small house near Ravenscourt Park, almost opposite Carlo's primary school, for £23,000. I managed to get a mortgage of £18,000 and we moved into 1 Ravenscourt Road. Now I had the money for *The Palestinian*.

Roy flew out to Lebanon about four weeks ahead of me in the spring of 1977. We had budgeted for a six-to-seven-week shooting schedule. Silvana would stay in the house with Tasha, who was now fourteen, Joely and Carlo. Tasha and Joely discussed plans for a new kitchen with me before I left. Our new house needed a proper kitchen and eating area and an outdoor lavatory. We agreed the girls would organise these while I was away. I told them it was unlikely that I would be able to telephone from Lebanon, because we would be constantly on the move. They were both frightened for me. Joely had great difficulty sleeping, sometimes lying awake for hours in the dark. I remembered how Rachel would sing me to sleep, so I sang her the lullaby from *A Midsummer Night's Dream*, trying to make her feel safe.

> You spotted snakes with double tongue,
> Thorny hedge-hogs be not seen;
> Newts, and blind-worms, do no wrong;
> Come not near our fairy queen.
> Philomel, with melody,
> Sing in our sweet lullaby;
> Lulla, lulla, lullaby; lulla, lulla, lullaby.
> Never harm, nor spell nor charm
> Come our lovely lady nigh.

It had been beautifully arranged by Jock Addison for Tony's production at the Royal Court Theatre, which was where I first met him.

# 18

The sunshine was hot and dazzling as I came out of the airport at
Beirut in May 1977. A group of women came to meet me, kissed me
and gave me some red carnations. They were from the General
Union of Palestinian Women. One was the widow of Hani
Jawharieh, the Palestinian cameraman who had been killed in the
mountains while filming during the war. She took me home and I
met her two small children. She told me how she and Hani had first
met, arranging the first exhibition of photographs organised by the
PLO to show the life of their people. She showed me the handful of
Palestinian earth she kept, and took me to the cemetery to see
Hani's grave. The pine trees stood warm and silent above row
upon row of graves, each covered with wreaths and palm leaves
and a large photograph of the martyr.

Roy Battersby, Ivan Strasberg our cameraman, and I were lent a
flat to stay in, and we sat down to discuss our schedule. There was
a Falangist conference in a few days' time and we agreed the crew
would go without me and try for an interview with Pierre
Gemayel, the Falangist strongman. Roy Battersby succeeded in
persuading him to do an interview for our film and this is what he
said:

Everything that happened in Lebanon was due to an intervention by
international communism. We were one of the happiest countries in the
world. Our people, the workers, the social laws. . . . Only Lebanon had
such liberty and democracy, no other Arab country. Naturally, that
challenged international communism to get rid of the government. So we
had to fight international communism. I think we overcame it, despite its
great strength.

Gemayel spoke in French, sitting in front of the Lebanese flag. He
continued:

I began life as a sportsman. I was Captain of the football team, President of the Lebanese Football Federation. We attended the 1936 Olympic Games in Berlin. I was impressed by the discipline there, by the bearing and sense of nation.

One of Gemayel's sons, Bashir, was head of the Falangist militia which had spearheaded the assault on the Palestinian camp at Tal al Zaatar in 1976, butchering women and children with disgusting savagery. But the Falangists could never have overcome Tal al Zaatar without the backing of the CIA, the Israelis, and the Syrian Army. The CIA funded Bashir Gemayel and Israeli 'advisers', trained the Falangists and coordinated the whole operation.

Kemal Jumblatt, leader of the Druze and Progressive Socialist Party, had been assassinated a few months before, because he and the Druze supported the Palestinians. No one knew who the assassin was, but everyone knew the CIA was behind the murder, because Jumblatt's people and his party were the strongest Lebanese opposition to the Falangists and the Kitaeb. The director of the CIA from January 1976 to January 1977 was George Bush. Our team got interviews with Bashir Gemayel and Danny Chamoun, and the Archbishop who headed the Christian Maronites. They and their colleagues stated they would kill every Palestinian child they could get their hands on and would welcome the destruction of every city in Lebanon.

I drove with our crew into the eastern zone of Beirut, now controlled by the Falangists. We had to keep a constant lookout for their militia. A month earlier a young nun had been kidnapped and murdered during a visit to her family in the eastern sector. We parked the car on a sandy road beside some deserted factories. Below us, mounds of rubble stretched to the perimeter of the city: 3500 men, women and children had been slaughtered there during the six-month siege of Tal al Zaatar. One thousand had been killed on a single day, the final day of the evacuation, as the Red Cross trucks waited at the checkpoints which were controlled by Syrian armed forces. We filmed there for about an hour, slowly panning the camera across the shattered cinder blocks, the remains of a mosque, twisted corrugated iron, and broken water pipes.

A few days later we met Abu Jaffar, one of the defenders of Tal al Zaatar. He sat on the floor of a small room with some eighteen-year-old boys in battle fatigues and about fifteen women, some Lebanese, some Palestinian, all of them in black. After a long discussion together, Abu Jaffar said: 'Now I am going to sing you Abu Jaffar's song of Tal al Zaatar.'

Oh Tal al Zaatar, you held out against an enemy
that came like a swarm of locusts.

I sing in honour of your brave heroes
who fought and faced rockets and bombs.

I will tell what happened, the truth
and I need no witness.

For from the first bullet to the last bomb
I was there.

The first day twenty thousand bombs fell
on civilians and soldiers alike.

On the second day there were fifteen thousand
bombs, and you could see the flames and smoke rising.

On the third day there was a lull while they
stopped for a rest, only to start again.

And the worse it got, the more like tigers
our heroes fought.

For two long months we lived through that
battle, and our hearts turned hard like stone.

We had no water and the food ran out.

And the children were thirsty and cried to
their mothers 'I want my Dad' until their
mouths were dry.

And mother says 'He'll be back in the morning,
I promise.'

And in the morning the boy asks again,
'Where's my Dad?'

And they tell him 'Your father is missing.'

And the girl asks her mother 'Where is my
brother?'

She says to her 'He is in the trenches.'

'Oh my son, he is fighting for honour and dignity,
in a few short hours he is learning the struggle
of a lifetime.'

199

So many young people were victims, so many
martyrs for heaven.

Every mother has to say 'Oh my son'
and the tears run down her cheeks.

And the girls say 'Oh my brother'
and visit his house in mourning.

Who can have guests anymore when you've
seen your son lying on the ground?

I had two sons, dearer to me than my sight.
They were so good, it's hard to believe.

Whenever I saw them it was like sunshine,
their cheeks were so rosy.

Yar Yar joined Patah and Thausy, the Democratic
Front. You'd say they were like a couple of tigers.

And they went to the mountains and they didn't
come back.

And that day, my heart broke.

Oh God, dear God, bring them back to me.
Bring back all our lost relatives. Oh God,
whom we worshipped.

It is God's will – the vine is growing but
we pick no grapes.

Oh God, oh merciful God, hear our prayers
and bring them back to us, these miserable
nights.

Oh Zaatar, the drab leaders who betrayed you,
now praise you for the way you fought.

They offered you a helping hand to stab you
in the back.

And I know for a fact they are conspiring
again, and those who were martyred live on.

His rough voice rose from his soul. The coal miners of Kentucky
and the old miners from the copper mines of Sicily sing their stories
in the same way. Harsh and deep from the throat they sing of their
tragedies, the fights, the low wages, the strikes, the deaths of their
sons on the picket lines.

*Antony and Cleopatra* in 1986, with Timothy Dalton, at Duncan Weldon's Theatre Royal, the Haymarket (*above*); and (*right*) as Katharina again, with Timothy Dalton as Petruchio, 1986.

*The Lady from the Sea*, directed by Michael Elliott, at the Round House, 1979. This was the last time I worked with Michael, a dear friend and a great director (*left*); *Design for Living*, 1974, produced by Bob Regester and directed by Michael Blakemore (*right*).

Guinevere marries King Arthur. John Trusscott, the designer, used candles and black velvet for an illusion of a great dark cathedral in *Camelot* (*left*); one day's work as Anne Boleyn with Robert Shaw in Fred Zinnemann's *A Man for All Season's* (*bottom left*). Corin played Roper, Thomas More's son-in-law; and (*below*) with Glenda Jackson as Queen Elizabeth in *Mary, Queen of Scots*, 1971.

Tony directed this 1973
production of *Antony and
Cleopatra* in Sam
Wanamaker's tent on
site of the sixteenth-
century Globe Theatre
(*above*).

nia Fenelon in
*for Time*, Arthur
's masterpiece for
'V about the
's orchestra in
witz (*above*); and
as Sara, with Ron
, in the 1983 PBS
about the Salem
ials, *Three
ns for Sara.*

The first night of Michael's *The Aspern Papers*, March 1984 with Christopher Reeve; and (*right*) as Cordelia at a benefit performance of *King Lear* in 1982 for the Young Socialists' Youth Training Centres. It was the last time we acted together.

With Rachel, Lynn, Tasha, Jemma, Carlo and Joely at Michael's funeral, March 1985. Joan Hirst, family friend and Michael's secretary is standing next to me.

There were about 500,000 Palestinians in Lebanon, living mostly in camps together with the poor Lebanese families. Before the war in 1976 there had been seven camps in Beirut. Now there were five. They were similar to the black townships like Soweto in South Africa. In fact, everything that Winnie Mandela wrote about her people under apartheid is true of the Palestinians in Lebanon, the West Bank and Gaza, and in Israel, with one essential difference: the Palestinians do not have the right to live in their own country, not even to be buried there.

We searched for Doctor Youssef. He and his one colleague, Doctor Labadi, had run the hospital in Tal al Zaatar throughout the six-month siege, and had trained a team of nurses to tend the 6000 casualties. We found him in a small clinic. On his desk beneath a glass top were photographs of fifteen boys and girls who had been lined up and shot in front of his eyes. He, too, would have been shot, but for one of the Syrian soldiers, a captain, who recognised Doctor Labadi and remembered that he had saved his life about a year before the siege. Doctor Youssef had seen the Falangists shoot his nurses while the Syrian forces stood by and watched. 'I'll not forget that moment. What is civilisation? These people consider themselves the representatives of European civilisation in the Middle East. I don't know if European opinion agrees with that. Maybe there is a new definition for civilisation? I don't know.'

In Bourj al Barajneh, Sabra and Chatila camps, we visited wounded fighters and children. The Palestine Red Crescent Society, the equivalent of the Red Cross, had built hospitals and clinics where they could receive therapy and be fitted with artificial limbs. We saw a tiny baby with pneumonia struggling for breath with an improvised humidifier made out of a cardboard box over her head. A six-year-old boy lay writhing on his back in a cot, his limbs shaking with uncontrollable spasms, his mouth twisted into a terrible smile. His entire family had been killed in the siege. The doctor introduced me to him, speaking with deep affection. 'We love Mohammed: we are his family and he is our brother.'

We walked down the narrow alleys between the houses and shacks in Sabra and Chatila, our guide introducing us to the families. When we said we were from Britain, a sixty-year-old woman invited us for a glass of tea. In the back of her home her daughter was stirring a pot, making sweets for their family business. She told us about life in Palestine under the British mandate. 'They took our fields, our flour and our food. They killed our men and our sons, and they took our land and gave it to the foreigners, the Jews.'

We went south to Sidon, the seaport where Queen Cleopatra of ancient Egypt built her fleet from the cedar trees of Lebanon. Here we met the commander of the joint Palestinian and Lebanese armed forces of the south, with his wife Princess Dina. In the ancient port of Tyre, a few miles further south, we met leaders of the Lebanese fishermen's union, all close comrades of the Palestinians. We gathered in a small group on the jetty, introduced ourselves, and began filming. 'This region of Lebanon was an absolute dictatorship before the war,' they told us. 'The Lebanese *Deuxième Bureau* was everywhere – if they caught you listening to a radio broadcast from a revolutionary country, they would take you away to prison. To organise a trade union that would fight for us was illegal, you would be arrested for that.' They told us that fishing had become almost impossible because the Israelis sank their best boats and patrolled the waters a few miles out to stop them fishing.

The PLO helped the Lebanese peasants form cooperatives, and provided funds and assistance for hospitals, welfare clinics and schools. They built small factories where young people could get skilled training and a weekly wage. The United Nations Relief and Rehabilitation Administration provided some schools which opened the door to a college education in the United States, and the PLO tried to provide the fees, since the majority of families could not afford such an education. Not many, even with the PLO's help, could send their children abroad. However, the UNNRRA schools taught English language and literature and we met very few Palestinian children in the camps who did not speak some English. I met a girl of fourteen in Bourj al Barajneh, and asked her what her favourite subject was. 'English,' she replied. 'And your favourite writer?' 'Shakespeare.' 'Will you read me something?' I asked. She sat there on the sofa, her hands folded on her lap, and began to recite:

Shall I compare thee to a summer's day?
Thou art more lovely and more temperate.
Rough winds do shake the darling buds of May
And summer's lease hath all too short a date. . . .

The children in the camps all belonged to the Cubs and the Flowers, Palestinian youth organisations. At weekends they studied Palestinian history, sang Palestinian songs and learned the old dances or performed their own sketches. They learned the embroidery of their Palestinian villages and how to shoot. They had to know how to defend their camps from attack, and they all hoped to take part in the struggle of their armed forces to liberate their country, and return to their parents' and their grandparents' homes in Palestine.

These young people of eleven or twelve were all politically conscious and could distinguish quite clearly the political ideology of Zionism from the Jews as an oppressed people. This could only be the result of an honest and advanced political outlook on the part of their teachers and parents.

When I first met Salah al Tammari he was playing football with some teenage boys in the early evening in Ain al Helwe refugee camp. After the game we sat on the grass and he spoke fast and passionately: 'Zionism is a racist movement. It's the same as Nazism. Nazism was not a threat against the Jews only, it was a threat against the whole world, against humanity. It was a *bad event* in the history of man.' He said 'bad event' with great emphasis. 'This event is being repeated. That's why Zionism is not a threat to Arabs only – it's a threat to the Jews themselves. Zionism is dangerous to Judaism itself. It's a racist movement. It seeks what differentiates the peoples of the world while we are in the epoch where we should seek what unites the peoples of the world.' Salah's outlook, as with all the Fateh political and military men we met in Lebanon, was reflected in the answer of a young girl of thirteen to my question: 'What would you do if you met a wounded Israeli soldier?' 'I would look after him and make his wounds better and I would explain to him that we are not against Jews, only against Zionism. I would explain that we need our homeland back and we would share it with the Jews. We could live together in a democratic state of Palestine.'

We slept at night on floors or cots, and drove on each morning. At breakfast one morning in Sidon we met Elias Shoufani and one of the Lebanese trade union leaders. Elias gave us an interview in a tiny villa as we waited for transport to go down the narrow road leading to the Crusader castle, Beaufort. 'The so-called South Lebanon,' he told me, 'is nothing more than an extension of the

Upper Galilee of Palestine. Geographically, ethnically, historically it has always been so. The Upper Galilee extends in Palestine, from the road linking Acre to Safad all the way to the Litani river. This is one block of mountains and it is the same all the way.'

He smiled at me. 'As my name Shoufani indicates, I am from this area near Sidon.' He was speaking of the Shouf mountains. 'My family lives south of the border, half of which is Lebanese and the other half is Palestinian. So how could I recognise a border, a line that was drawn in 1926, I think, by two imperialist powers, the French and the British? To split one clan into two halves – that is totally unacceptable to me.'

We stopped in Taib and Nabatiya. The few remaining Lebanese families welcomed us and showed us their houses, wrecked by shells. Some shell cases had Hebrew writing and some were made in the United States. The CIA funded a small Lebanese Army of fascists down south, commanded by Major Sammi Haddad. They seized control of some of the small villages. A schoolteacher told me how his village had been taken by the Kitaeb in 1976. Everyone was ordered into the main square. Then twelve young men were pulled out of the crowd, lined up against a wall and shot as an example of what would happen if the village refused to collaborate with the Lebanese fascists. He trembled as he spoke, reliving those days.

Here, two miles from the border between Lebanon and Israel, the night sky was full of heavy red rain as rockets poured into the Lebanese villages. Every night the shelling began. Dozens of 155mm and 175mm shells came over the border from Israel. At night as we moved from village to village or sheltered in a dug-out or cellar, the earth shook and thudded.

I visited the UN post on the border. The United Nations officer was pleasant, courteous and suntanned. 'Do you report to the United Nations how many rockets and shells are fired from Israel into Lebanon every night?' I asked him. The officer shook his head. 'What do you do then?' I asked. 'I'm trying to find some garlic I need for the dish I'm cooking this weekend,' he replied.

Refugees poured out of their houses, packing bundles and suitcases into cars and lorries to leave their homes. Seeing our camera they spoke angrily, some of the women crying. 'Israel! Israel! Look what they are doing!' The Israeli Defence Forces were using terror bombing and a scorched-earth policy. The aim was to force Lebanese civilians to leave their homes and land, and then invade. Everyone knew an invasion was coming. The families were frightened, but they spoke up with pride for the Palestinians, and they held on as long as they could until their homes were completely wrecked. I noticed that the nearer the front lines people were, the more courage and strength was shown by Palestinians and Lebanese alike.

We met Abu Jihad, and he gave an interview for our camera, and, last of all, we met PLO Chairman Yasser Arafat. He asked about our work and where we had been, then gave me an interview. He was extremely tired, but he spoke effortlessly, spontaneously, and his smile was warm and direct.

'We are not against Jews: we are against Zionism. And you remember that in the first slogan we gave we said that our aim is to establish our democratic Palestinian state where Muslims, Christians and Jews can live together – together. And I'm saying now, they are speaking of settlement. OK, I am saying why speak about settlements? Why not speak about living together, all of us in this homeland? I am offering this in the name of my people.

'Without a civilised, ideological theory you can't have victory. And I think that in the future, all the Jews will understand that we are fighting for them too.'

Arafat has been slandered and attacked more than any other leader of our time. His life is in constant danger from his assailants, yet I doubt if he has any personal enemies. In conversation – and that was all my interview was, a filmed conversation – he is absolutely unselfconscious and transparent, with a warmth that lights up his audience. Small wonder that when *The Palestinian* was shown in America and Britain, Zionist organisations did their utmost to prevent it from being screened.

# 19

I returned to London on a sunny June morning, and the children met me at the front door with a big 'Welcome Home' sign. Tasha had permed her hair, and was directing scenes from *West Side Story* at her girls' school, with all the boys' parts cut out. The fourteen-year-old girls danced and sang 'San Juan' and 'I feel pretty' with such gaiety and excitement that all the mothers, including me, got to their feet shouting 'Bravo!'

The editing of *The Palestinian* proceeded apace. We hired a Steenbeck editing-table and Battersby and the two editors worked into the night for weeks. In November the film was premièred at the London Film Festival on the South Bank and the Workers' Revolutionary Party held public meetings all over the country for trade unionists, students and young people to see the film.

Later in June I was invited to Los Angeles, Chicago and New York to do a publicity tour for *Julia*. I took cassettes of *The Palestinian* with me and invited a number of film-makers to private screenings. I also showed the film to various Public Broadcasting Service producers, who said they would lose their oil sponsors if they screened it. I took the film to CBS, who said it was their policy never to buy a film by an independent producer whom they had not commissioned. I pressed on higher up and was told that the film was 'not objective'. This was at a time when not one American or European network had shown a film about the Palestinians. I did the Mike Douglas TV show in Las Vegas.

From there I flew to San Francisco where Timothy Dalton and I sat spellbound in the Old Theatre watching my father in *Shakespeare's People*. Parkinson's disease had robbed him of his ability to learn new parts and his walk had become a shuffle. But he could still remember all his Shakespearian roles, and when he set foot on stage his muscles loosened and he stood upright. He played some

206

scenes from *Hamlet*, *As You Like it*, *Macbeth* and *King Lear*, and then he came forward to the podium and looked out:

> Shall I compare thee to a summer's day?
> Thou art more lovely and more temperate . . .

He could recite Shakespeare's best-known sonnet as if he had written it himself that afternoon, and made you forget you had ever heard the poem before. He was touring North America with the show that summer in 1977. There were five of them in it – Dad, David Dodimead, Philip Bowen, Rosalind Shanks and Rod Willmott. They spent a week in San Francisco, but in some places they only did three performances then would get back into their tour bus and travel to the next city.

An article appeared in the *New York Post*. One of the actors I had invited to a private video screening of *The Palestinian* had given the story to Liz Smith, the *Post* columnist. In February I had won the Golden Globe Award for *Julia*, and was nominated for an Academy Award as best supporting actress, and now the press all over the United States were running stories about my support for the PLO. Rabbi Meir Kahane's Jewish Defence League went to 20th-Century Fox and said they would cause every kind of problem unless Fox issued a statement that they would never employ me again.

In Los Angeles, my friends said that I was unlikely to win the Oscar, because of the press campaign against me. Sandra Marsh, my secretary, told me that a British producer was putting it about in the film community that I was a terrorist. She had saved me some news-cuttings, including a long report of a meeting of the Jewish Defence League in Los Angeles where one speaker had waved a fistful of dollars and asked: 'Who is willing to rid the world of a Jew-baiter?'

The day before the ceremony Howard Koch, chairman of the Academy Awards Committee, urged me not to say anything more than 'Thank You' if I won the Oscar. Then he explained the security arrangements. There would be armed plain-clothes security backstage and in the auditorium, and police sharp-shooters on the roof. I told Howard that I must reserve the right to say whatever I thought was right and necessary, and I thanked him for all the care he had taken with security. That evening I stayed in a hotel owned by an Arab-American businessman. A large reception room was packed with members of the Arab-American community in Los Angeles, who were there for a showing of *The Palestinian*. Waiters and kitchen staff stood in the aisles and doorways to watch. There had never been a film in the United States which showed the Palestinian-Arab cause, or a news report which allowed ordinary Palestinians to speak out. In our film many ordinary men, women and children spoke, with the directness and truth that only comes from the masses when the whole people is engaged in a struggle.

As we drove up to the Dorothy Chandler Pavilion for the 50th Academy Award ceremony, there were dense crowds behind police barriers. Opposite the theatre several hundred Arab-Americans stood waving the red, green, white and black Palestinian flag. On another pavement about twenty members of the Jewish Defence League were burning an effigy of myself. 'Arafat's whore', they called it, dancing and shouting around the smouldering heap.

Inside the artists' entrance a beautiful actress I recognised but had never met turned to me and came up and put her arms around me. The embrace was honest and warm, and she could have pretended not to see me. When we finally met properly, a year later, she told me of the poverty and suffering she had seen while on a publicity tour of Latin America. 'I wish I had the same courage as you,' she said, 'I wanted so much to speak out about what I saw, but I knew that my career would be destroyed if I did.'

I came into the auditorium and sat down. I had been given a seat next to the aisle, so I thought that I would probably get the Oscar that night. I thought of the Palestinians in the camps and the hospitals; and the socialist and communist Jews who were the first to be sent to the concentration camps. I thought of Lillian Hellman, categorised as a 'premature anti-fascist' by the FBI and blacklisted in the 1950s. I thought of all the American artists and workers in the film, TV and theatre industries who were persecuted because they were trade unionists, or communists, or Jews, or all three. John Travolta came into the centre of the stage, opened an envelope and read out my name. I got up from my seat, he gave me the Oscar, and this – verbatim – is what I said:

My dear colleagues – I thank you very, very much for this tribute to my work. I think that Jane Fonda and I have done the best work of our lives; and I think this was in part due to our director, Fred Zinnemann, and I also think it's in part because we believed in what we were expressing. Two women – out of the millions who gave their lives and were prepared to sacrifice everything in the fight against Fascist and racist Nazi Germany, and I salute you and I pay tribute to you and I think you should be very proud that in the last few weeks you have stood firm and refused to be intimidated by the threats of a small bunch of Zionist hoodlums whose behaviour is an insult to the stature of Jews all over the world, and to their great and heroic record of struggle against fascism and oppression.

And I salute that record, and I salute, salute all of you for having stood firm and dealt a final blow against that period when Nixon and McCarthy launched a world-wide witch-hunt against those who tried to express in their lives and their work a truth that they believed. I salute you and I thank you and I pledge to you that I will continue to fight against anti-Semitism and fascism. Thank you.

When I referred to the 'Zionist hoodlums', I meant of course the Jewish Defence League and their death threats. There was a round of booing from upstairs. And then enormous applause when I finished.

I received many letters of goodwill and support. Many of those who wrote were American and some were Jews. This letter, written in English, came from a Palestinian in Kuwait:

Struggler Vanessa Redgrave,
You'll stay as a candle in our hearts that lights our way and leads us to all what we want and we'll stay grateful to you for what you are doing for our cause which you believe in its justice.

I wish I could help you, but anyhow you realise that my conditions as a student decrease the possibility of offering the necessary help you deserve. Very, very much, at last, with my compliments to her who offers herself for the Palestinian problem and for the freedom problems in the world.

Dawood K. Almani, April 4, 1978.

I returned to London, kissed and hugged my children, and then left immediately for the Palestinian Film Festival in Baghdad. In March, Israel had invaded Lebanon. I met a number of our friends from the Palestinian Film Institute at the Festival, and they asked me to return to Lebanon and do interviews for a film of the invasion. So I flew to Beirut again and drove down South. Sidon was devastated and Tyre was very badly damaged. Whole apartment blocks and districts were mounds of rubble. Rescue teams were still pulling bodies out of the wreckage. The pools of water in the streets from shattered water mains were red with blood. The camp of Rashidiye had been evacuated, street upon street of ruins.

I interviewed a group of fighters, defending a hill position very close to a group of Israeli tanks, which included a girl of seventeen. I spoke to youngsters who had ambushed tanks and held them back for several hours before they were forced to retreat. I met the widows of two of my friends, both Palestinian cameramen. They had been surrounded by tanks where they stood in the middle of the road and shot on the spot, although they had no weapons and were holding a piece of white cloth to show they had surrendered.

The Israelis had now acquired a new five-mile deep strip of territory across the south of Lebanon. Thousands of civilians were dead and wounded, their homes, farms and workshops destroyed. No medicine, food supplies or aid were sent from America or Europe. There was no vote from the US Senate or Congress for economic sanctions against Israel. On the Security Council and in the UN Assembly, the United States and Britain blocked and vetoed all resolutions of condemnation. Cluster bombs and other weapons made in the United States and sold to the Israelis by authority of the US government were used in the invasion. In his memoirs, President Jimmy Carter complained about this: 'I was particularly disturbed because American weapons, including lethal cluster bombs, had been used in the operation; contrary to our agreement when they were sold.' Here was the former President of the United States actually admitting that the United States sells 'extremely lethal' weapons, which are specifically *anti-civilian* weapons (they were dropped on villages in the Vietnam war), claiming that a written agreement was made that they would not be used, and then complaining that they had been.

The news stories of the Israeli brutality, with more than 100,000 civilians injured and made homeless, forced the State Department to agree to a UN resolution calling for a United Nations peace-keeping force and the Israeli withdrawal from Lebanon. The IDF forces did not withdraw. They assembled a small army of Lebanese fascists under the command of Major Haddad as cover for their complete control of the area. The United Nations Intermediary

Forces in Lebanon (UNIFIL) when they arrived, never entered the area: 'No can see, no can hear, no can do.'

The Israelis claimed the invasion was provoked by a Fateh military operation in March against an Israeli army position near a beach outside Tel Aviv. Our party published a two-page statement which told the truth about that operation and paid tribute to the bravery of the Fateh fighters who led the assault. In our view the Palestinians had every right to pursue their armed struggle in their own country against the Israeli state. They had the same right as Mandela's African National Congress, whose armed wing, Umkonto We Sizwe, fought the apartheid state of South Africa. Mugabe and Nkomo's armies had the same right when they fought the colonial state of Rhodesia. The people of Nicaragua and the Sandinistas had the same right to fight for their liberation.

In June 1978 came the Annual General Meeting of British Actors' Equity. The resolutions presented by our 'Defend Equity, Defend the Union' faction included one to raise the minimum wage, which we won. Another resolution called for Equity to organise all the performers and hostesses who worked in the clubs, and also the young girls who were used in porno films which were, of course, non-union productions. This resolution for 100 per cent membership won a majority vote. We also presented a resolution on South Africa, and one condemning the Israeli invasion of Lebanon. I was the proposer and although we only needed twenty signatures for the resolution to be included on the agenda, we had seventy-three signatures of support. Our resolution called on Equity's Council to ban the sale of all tapes and filmed material to Israel and cancel all tours there. We asked the Council 'to instruct all members working in Israel to terminate their contracts and instruct the membership of Equity to refuse offers of work in Israel'.

The Council arranged the agenda in such a way that the motion was not even debated. But someone in Equity had sent the *Jewish Chronicle* in London a copy of the resolution. Three weeks before the AGM the *Jewish Chronicle* ran a story which was immediately taken up by *Variety* and the *Hollywood Reporter*: 'Redgrave calls for Boycott of Israel'. On 27 June the *Hollywood Reporter* ran a full-page advertisement from the Association of Motion Picture and Television Producers, the Producers' Guild of America and the Writers' Guild of America West:

To our colleagues,
We emphatically reaffirm our position against any blacklist, censorship, or boycott of artistes and their work. Just as 20th Century Fox was commended for its refusal to blacklist or boycott Vanessa Redgrave as an artiste because of her political position, so we unreservedly condemn her recent attempt to institute a blacklist boycott of the film industry and artistes of Israel. We consider this a threat to all of us. Therefore we call upon the entire entertainment industry to join in public support of this stated position.

My resolution was a cultural ban on English artistes working in Israel and English films being sold to Israel – no different from the official policy of British Actors' Equity on South Africa. We had always supported that policy and defended it whenever the right wing tried to abandon it. Of course it was not universally popular, especially amongst those actors who made a lot of money on South African tours and wanted to continue doing so. Some regularly ignored the ban, and one of their number took the union to court to have it overruled by law. Nevertheless, it was supported by the majority of members, and many unions, including the American artistes' unions, had a similar policy.

For all the reasons we supported a ban on British actors working in apartheid South Africa, we believed such a ban should apply to Israel. Palestinian trade unions were and are *illegal* in Israel. Palestinian writers, poets and musicians were, and are, censored and imprisoned on mere suspicion of being members of an illegal Palestinian organisation. Indeed *all* Palestinian organisations created by Palestinians are illegal: the General Union of Palestinian Workers, the General Union of Palestinian Women and the General Union of Palestinian Students. For us to take money in the state of Israel as English actors, dancers, directors or designers, was to take blood money, when our Palestinian brothers and sisters were being killed, imprisoned, censored and denied their cultural freedom of expression. But we categorically did *not* call for the banning of Israeli artistes, or seek to prevent them from working in England, the United States or anywhere else, or prevent their work being seen or sold. We sought, as trade unionists, to establish a unity of all artistes to defend the basic democratic rights of all workers in the entertainment industries. Whether Jew or Arab, black or Hispanic or white, we have a common identity, we are all exploited. But 'white' artistes especially have the duty to defend the basic democratic rights of Afro-Asian, Hispanic, Jewish or Arab artistes and workers, against racism and discrimination of any kind, whether racial, political or religious.

No genuine unity can be established if we pretend that we are all in the same situation, and if we deny that some artistes suffer more than others, because of their race, their politics, their religion or because they are gay.

On 6 June *Variety* reported that *The Palestinian* would be screened on 16 June at the Academy of Motion Picture Arts and Sciences in Los Angeles. The Academy cancelled the booking. The Workers' League sponsored two screenings of the film on 17 and 28 June at the Marc Ballroom in Union Square, New York. In May they had sponsored a screening at the University of California, Los Angeles (UCLA) which drew 4000 students. Theodore Bikel, President of American Actors' Equity, was quoted in the US press stating that he had read a transcript of *The Palestinian*, that Arafat called for the liquidation of Israel and that I had agreed. That was a lie. I wrote to Donald Grody, American Equity's secretary, pointing out that nowhere in the film was such a statement made, nor could Chairman Arafat have said such a thing, which was directly contrary to the policy of the PLO. Perhaps, I said, Theodore Bikel had been misquoted. If so, would he correct the reports?

At the screenings in New York, the auditoria were filled to capacity. The Jewish Defence League threw a bomb at the box office of a small independent cinema in Los Angeles, which had booked the film for two weeks. The owner, to his credit, did not cancel and ran the film as advertised.

Trotsky, more than once, quoted a proverb saying that a lie travels all round the world while truth is still struggling to pull its boots on. The saying is apt in a descriptive sense, but inadequate. The CIA and other Western intelligence services, including the Israeli intelligence service Mossad, have whole departments and networks for 'disinformation'. There is very little value placed on the truth in the media as a whole and this was why it was so important to show our film whenever possible, and why it was so difficult.

# 20

In October 1978, three years and eleven days after we had issued a writ for libel against the *Observer*, our case came to court. Our solicitors, Rubinstein Callingham, had briefed John Wilmers, QC as our leading counsel and John Previte as his junior. They warned us that it would be a difficult case to win, and we fully expected it to be so. Nevertheless, we felt bound to go ahead with it. We had been libelled as terrorists, and the police raid was an immediate result of the libel. Despite the petitions and protestations in our defence we still had to prove our case in law. Not to do so would make us fair game for any police informer, newspaper or police force to libel us again and raid us any time in the future. Moreover only by going to court and suing the *Observer* could we find out how and why their article had come to be published.

There was also another principle at stake. The history of the working-class movement is one of long and often bloody struggle to win democratic rights in parliament and in law. The WRP was a legal party, with rights like any other, democratic rights that had been fought for by previous generations. Some people, even some of our own members, thought we – who maintained that in a class-divided society there cannot be equality under the law – were naive to be going to court to defend ourselves. 'Don't you know you won't get justice in a law court?' We were not naive. We were defending the rights, not only of ourselves but of others.

On 30 November 1975, two months after our school was raided, the Prevention of Terrorism Act subtitled 'Temporary Provisions' which had been introduced in 1974 was renewed in an all-night sitting, with all-party support. And whilst our case was happening, the journalist Duncan Campbell and a former intelligence corps soldier, John Berry, were on trial under Section 2A of the Official Secrets Act of 1911 for an article in *Time Out* which exposed the monitoring of international communications by British Signal Intelligence.

There were six of us in court, all of whom had been named in the *Observer* article: Corin and I, Gerry, Roy Battersby, Roger Smith and Michael Harrigan. At four o'clock every afternoon, when the court rose, I ran to a waiting taxi and caught a train from Euston, arriving at the Royal Exchange Theatre in Manchester at seven o'clock, half an hour before my performance. I was working with Michael Elliott, playing Ellida again in Michael's new production of Ibsen's *The Lady from the Sea*. Every night after the performance I caught an overnight train back to London, to be at the law courts in the Strand by 9.30 a.m.

From the moment our counsel completed his examination-in-chief of Corin, and Colin Ross-Munro for the *Observer* began his cross-examination, we realised how much we, and not the *Observer*, were on trial. Corin was cross-examined for two and a half days, and throughout Ross-Munro scarcely mentioned the *Observer* article, the events it referred to or the allegations it made. One after another, he produced articles from our paper, *Workers' Press*, speeches and party resolutions, lifted out a sentence and asked Corin to explain it.

'The working class should take power?'

'Yes,' Corin said.

'And here, do you see, you advocate "a struggle for power"?'

'Yes.'

'By an armed uprising?'

'No,' Corin said, 'by peaceful, legal and constitutional means.'

It was during Mr Wilmers's examination-in-chief that Corin had said that our party's aim was for a socialist society, and we sought to achieve it by 'peaceful, legal and constitutional means'. There was a flurry of activity on Mr Ross-Munro's side of the court, as if a ferret had been let loose. Again and again he returned to this phrase, as if he expected each repetition to increase the jury's incredulity.

Mr Ross-Munro clearly intended to devote most of his questions to our articles and pamphlets, and our counsel objected several times, but the judge, Mr Justice O'Connor overruled him. He asked for an adjournment and suggested we take the matter to an immediate appeal, which we agreed to do, and Mr Wilmers put his objections to three Appeal Court judges presided over by Lord

Denning. But the Appeal Court ruled in our judge's favour, and so the pattern of the case was set. When it was my turn to take the witness-box I was asked about my attendance at the funeral of Maire Drumm, the Irish Republican leader who was murdered in her hospital bed by the British Army. I told the court that I was totally opposed to terrorism, but supported the Irish Republican Army's right to undertake military actions against the British Army and the Ulster Defence Force.

Most of my cross-examination was spent defending our party's position in support of the PLO and the Palestinians' right to self-determination, and my opposition to terrorism, such as acts of individual terror against civilians in other countries. But I supported the PLO's right to conduct military operations inside Israel, since their land had been illegally occupied by military force. The creation of the State of Israel in 1948 by the United Nations was in contravention of their own charter. They had no right to partition any part of Palestine. The Israeli government and Army had seized *all* of Palestine in 1948 and 1967. Since then it had refused countless times to obey UN resolutions, such as resolution 242, which calls on Israel to withdraw from the West Bank, the Gaza Strip and the Golan Heights.

I tried hard to remember the advice Mr Wilmers had given all of us before the case started – to make our answers as short as possible, preferably Yes or No, and to rely on him to come back with further questions if we felt the impression created by a short answer had been misleading. I tried, and on the whole I succeeded, but at times it was very difficult advice to follow.

At the beginning of the second week it was the turn of the police to be questioned. The first into the witness-box was Deputy Assistant Commissioner Victor Gilbert, who had headed the Special Branch in 1975. He submitted to the court a confidential report from the Metropolitan Police, dated 25 September 1975. There was some argument as to whether this should be admitted as evidence and made available to the court. This time, fortunately as it was to help our case enormously, Mr Wilmers won the argument, and the report was handed to the jury.

As Gilbert, then Walter Stansfield, Chief Constable of Derbyshire, and Colin Smith, the Observer journalist, took the stand and the contents of the report were revealed, the following chain of events culminating in the raid at 10 p.m. on 25 September and the

216

front page headline 'Police Raid The Red House' on 26 September became clear.

On Friday 24 September Scotland Yard received a call from David Astor to say that the *Observer* would be running an article on the activities of the WRP, and mentioned that 'reference had been made by their *informant* to Special Branch'. A meeting was held at the *Observer* offices between Gilbert, Astor and Smith. Gilbert stated he was instructed to have the meeting by Sir Robert Mark, the Chief Commissioner. The informant in question was an actress whom the *Observer* did not name to the police but stated would be named in the article on Sunday. Although it is now necessary for journalists to name their sources Gilbert did not seem bothered that her name was withheld. Irene Gorst, referred to only as a 'lady' and 'a former girlfriend of the WRP activist Corin Redgrave' alleged that Corin had made a remark 'to the effect that the WRP had a quantity of arms buried (or secreted) in the grounds of their Derbyshire establishment'. Gilbert's report stated that Special Branch had no 'collateral', that is firm evidence to support this allegation but that it would be investigated on the understanding that if any police action were contemplated that might spoil the effect of the *Observer* article on Sunday the police would liaise first with the editor of the newspaper. Gilbert notified relevant government departments about the article, the Security Service and Derbyshire police. It was understood that 'no overt action would be taken by any agency to destroy the impact of that story without prior reference to the editor of the *Observer*', he said.

A police raid was set in motion on the basis of an alleged remark by an unnamed lady for which Special Branch had no evidence. The Derbyshire police were to await confirmation that the allegations about the arms cache were going to be printed and then go into the school which they did with fourteen vehicles, two power generators, dogs, metal detectors, handcuffs, truncheons and flares soon after 10 p.m. on the Saturday night. By this time the *Observer* must have printed the front page story of the raid. Stansfield told the court that the school had been under constant police surveillance ever since it had been bought by the WRP.

Colin Smith told the court how Peter Plouviez, the General Secretary of British Actors Equity, had telephoned the *Observer* newsdesk and spoken to Robert Chesshyre who had then gone to meet him outside the Coliseum Theatre. The venue was Plouviez's suggestion, he refused to meet at either the *Observer* or Equity offices. It was Plouviez who told Chesshyre the Gorst story. Smith went on to tell the court that he had not contacted either Corin or myself or anyone else from the WRP to check Irene Gorst's story because, he said, she was frightened. Nor did Peter Plouviez contact us about the allegations made against us by a fellow member of Equity.

On the eleventh day of the case John Wilmers made his concluding speech. He reminded the jury that the *Observer* article had been published at the height of an IRA bombing campaign in Britain. Then he came to our policies, which had received so much attention from Mr Ross-Munro, especially our support for the Palestinians. Wilmers had fought behind enemy lines with the partisans in Italy in the last war, and he spoke from his own experiences, very movingly. He spoke quietly and modestly, as if the jury were sitting with him in his living room, asking them to see things from another point of view. 'It isn't popular to say that the Palestinians fight for their own land. Many of us would not think it right to support them when they carry the fight into Israel by measures which undoubtedly injure civilians. But ask yourselves this: is there just possibly another side to it?'

At the lunch break Corin and I with our friends walked into the public gardens at the back of the courts, where we could get a sandwich and a cup of tea. It was there, one day, early in the trial, that Corin showed me the opening chapters of Dickens's *Hard Times*, where the teacher browbeats a girl called Sissy Jupe in his class to give him the definition of a horse. I read it on the train going up to Manchester that afternoon, laughing out loud. Lawyers browbeat witnesses using the same formal logic: Yes or No, nothing else permitted.

On Wednesday 8 November the jury gave their verdict. The *Express* newspaper stated '£60,000 blow for Vanessa – actress proves she was libelled. The Judge orders her to pay massive costs.'

On 10 November *The Times* published a lengthy editorial:

the unfairness to the plaintiffs is that, though having shown to the satisfaction of the jury that the *Observer* article had been defamatory and wrong, they are now saddled with a bill for tens of thousands in costs. The Redgraves' action has demonstrated, not for the first time, the inequity of, in many respects, Britain's libel laws.

Corin and I spoke at a press conference on Friday, 11 November, to announce the launching of a £70,000 Appeal Fund. Corin said that the results of our case set a dangerous precedent, because it suggested that a newspaper could act on the information an 'informant' had brought it, which could be proved to be untrue, and yet the victim had to pay the costs of a libel action.

I learned a lot from the trial. We had proved our case and cleared the name of the Workers' Revolutionary Party. The jury were asked: 'Are all the words complained of substantially true?' They answered No. They were asked this question in respect of each of the six plaintiffs, one of whom, Gerry Healy, was only connected with the allegation about arms caches, and another who was only connected with the *Observer* allegations about Irene Gorst. Since the jury answered No in respect of all six plaintiffs, it followed the jury believed neither the 'arms caches' allegations nor the allegations about Miss Gorst.

We lost the case because the jury said our reputations were not materially damaged, a point of view Judge O'Connor emphatically agreed with.

Analysing the Special Branch report and the testimony given in court, it became clear that the Special Branch had been prepared to coordinate their activities to fit in with the *Observer*'s requirements and not only their activities but those of other government departments, ie the Home Office, police department, the Security Services MI5 and MI6.

The raid was authorised to give the article maximum credibility. No prosecution was ever brought against us. In fact the Attorney-General was obliged to state in December 1975 that he had no grounds for any prosecution. The Derbyshire police, whom we sued for wrongful entry, later settled the case with a statement that they accepted we were non-violent and had the same right to police protection as anyone else.

A Labour government had authorised this raid. At the same time as sections of MI5 were making strenuous efforts to overthrow the Wilson government, as Peter Wright shows in *Spycatcher*, the Home Secretary Roy Jenkins was authorising a provocation against the Workers' Revolutionary Party.

Now we had to raise the £70,000, so we launched an appeal for funds. To help this we organised a concert at the Lyceum Theatre. Our mother agreed to take part. What a relief, and what strength it gives you when you know that so many workers, youth, intellectuals from different generations will come forward to defend basic democratic rights – the rights of the trade unions, the rights of the working class to have trade unions, the rights of the Palestinians and all other oppressed peoples, the right to be a Marxist and not be witch-hunted or persecuted, and also, of course, the right to have a religious faith.

Gerry Healy and I went to Kuwait in April 1979 at the invitation of the Kuwait Cine Club to present a special screening of *The Palestinian*. We had a meeting with the Crown Prince, Sheikh Sa'ad-al-Sabah, and discussed our proposal to make a second documentary on the Palestinians living under Israeli military occupation in the West Bank and Gaza. He donated £25,000 towards the budget. We were driven out to Ahmadi to have lunch with the Governor, Sheikh Jaber. His colleagues took us on a tour around the gigantic petrol refinery which produced gas in icy temperatures in the middle of the blazing desert. We were welcomed by Kuwaitis and Palestinians and spoke at a special showing of our film in the PLO offices. Here we met for the first time Abu Jihad's brother and some of the women teachers in the General Union of Palestinian Women. From Kuwait, we went to the United Arab Emirates at the invitation of the Minister of Culture.

We met many young Palestinian girls who helped us to collect money for the new film. In the drawing-room of one of the wives of the ruler, I was introduced to Benazir Bhutto, whose father had recently been assassinated. On the last night of our visit we watched TV, extremely excited to see our film, knowing that the story of the Palestinians was being watched all over the Gulf.

We returned to London to take part in the general election campaign. I was a candidate again, this time in Moss Side, Manchester. Corin was standing as WRP candidate in Lambeth, an equally poverty-stricken area in south London. Workers were convinced that Labour would win, and I remember one building-site worker opening his eyes wide with disbelief when I told him the record of the Labour government had ensured Mrs Thatcher's victory at the polls. He told me he was prepared to bet me one pound that she wouldn't win. But she did. She had become the patron saint of the frustrated reactionary sections of the middle class, whose former Liberal and Labour votes now went to the

Tories, in support of Mrs Thatcher's policies of anti-trade unionism and anti-immigration. Thousands of workers did not vote at all or voted against Labour as a protest.

In June that year Michael Elliott brought his Manchester production of *The Lady from the Sea* to London. We performed at the Roundhouse Theatre, whose artistic director was Thelma Holt. Since we had shared digs when we both worked in *A Touch Of The Sun*, Thelma had done a lot of exciting work as an actress with Charles Marowitz at the Open Space. Thelma is practically unique in the British theatre; apart from Peter Daubeny I cannot think of anyone who has been so involved in bringing theatre work from other countries to England. When she was at the Roundhouse she opened its doors to every kind of event including concerts, unknown and established poets and musicians, and various benefits that we organised to finance our Youth Training Centres. She engages wholeheartedly and thoughtfully with her work and I admire her tremendously.

I was very glad to have the chance of working with Michael Elliott again, especially at the Roundhouse Theatre where seats were cheap compared with the West End: the arena stage established an immediate contact between audience and players. One night a woman came up to me after the performance and said: 'You know, your production made me feel so alive! I have never felt like this in the theatre before.' I took that as the greatest compliment to Michael Elliott and our cast of actors. Graham Crowden was wonderful to work with as Doctor Wangel. He was usually cast as a villain in films, but here he had the opportunity to immerse himself totally in the situation and the problems of his wife whom he dearly loved. I found his acting totally convincing; he always responded with open eyes and listening ears on stage, which meant we could really 'play' together.

That same month I received an invitation to the Moscow Film Festival. In my reply I thanked the organisers for their invitation and accepted it, on condition that they would recognise that I supported the right of Jews in the Soviet Union to emigrate to any country of their choice, including Israel. I never received a reply.

As a result of visiting Kuwait with Gerry for the special screening of *The Palestinian* at the Kuwait Cine Club we made a documentary called *Vanessa Talks To Farouk Abdul Azziz*. Farouk Abdul Azziz was the secretary of the Kuwait Cine Club and he wanted to interview me about my life. I discussed the idea with Corin and Gerry and we agreed that he could come to England and I would spend time with him doing the interview. The film had to be shot over a period of months because of both the cost and the time needed to do it, and we decided to include a scene that Dad and I could act in together. In the early spring of 1980 we went to Wilks Water and Michael and I did the scene from *King Lear* where he awakens from his madness and is reconciled with Cordelia. We filmed it by the little lake, and it was a marvellous experience. Michael played the scene extraordinarily – he had never played any leading Shakespearean role on film – and it was terribly moving to watch. I would act that very same scene with him the last time that we performed on stage together which was at the Roundhouse in October 1982 in a benefit for the Young Socialists' Youth Training Centres.

I will always remember him coming to see the finished documentary. He was stricken with Parkinson's but he walked out into the viewing room singing, and sang all the way home in the car. He was obviously extremely happy, and I asked him what he thought of *Vanessa*. He said that it was wonderful, and that now for the first time he could really understand the total relationship between my political life and acting.

# 21

*Playing for Time* was written for television by Arthur Miller, based on Fania Fenelon's autobiography. It is the story of the women's orchestra in the Nazi concentration camp at Auschwitz in Poland. All Miller's writing is superb, but historical subjects, the main events of our times, have inspired his best writing, and this story, in my view, is his masterpiece.

We were to rehearse in New York and film in Pennsylvania. I had given the script to Gerry, and before I left for New York he gave me three pages of notes. He said it was the best description of Fascism and Fascist ideology he had ever read, and advised me to pay close attention to all the physical details in Miller's script. Very good advice. From his knowledge of our history, and of the many men and women who had spent years in prisons and prison camps, Gerry knew how these physical details shaped their lives, expressing not only their suffering but their will to resist. He also reminded me that it is the present, the times we live in, which gives life to the past, stirs and activates the historical truth of the script.

Both of us knew that rehearsals would be a battle. Linda Yellen, our courageous producer, had stuck out her neck to cast me as Fania Fenelon, and now her decision was coming under fire. I arrived in New York to find a security guard posted outside the rehearsal rooms. Linda's office in downtown New York had been broken into by a gang who rushed the security and sprayed red paint on the walls. She herself was virtually in hiding in a friend's flat, and Bill Paley, the head of CBS television, had pickets outside his apartment block demanding my removal from the cast. Worst of all, Fania Fenelon herself was in the States on a speaking tour, denouncing my being cast to play her in the film.

I had met Fania Fenelon before going to New York in the CBS studios in Brompton Road, London, where I was to be interviewed by Mike Wallace for CBS's '60 Minutes' programme. She said I was too old for the part and Jane Fonda would have been more suitable. Jane certainly looked remarkably young, but as we are the same age I didn't think this objection should be taken seriously. Fania Fenelon declared that Yasser Arafat wanted to wipe out all Jews in Israel and sweep them into the sea. This was as big a lie as the infamous 'Protocols of Zion', and I said so. Then she compared casting me to play herself to hiring a member of the Ku Klux Klan to play Sammy Davis Junior, and I put the record straight on that. After the interview, we found ourselves sitting together in a small room, drinking cups of coffee and waiting for our transport home.

'Well,' she said, 'since you are playing me you had better know something about me.' She told me her father had been a member of the French Communist Party, which was the main organiser of the resistance, and that she herself had joined when she was twenty. Her job, as a cabaret singer, was to spy for the resistance. She sang in the cafés, entertaining and chatting with Nazi officers, gleaning every piece of information she could and passing it on to the resistance.

My car arrived and I offered her a lift. We stopped first at my home in Ravenscourt Road and I ran inside to get her a copy of the script, which she said she had never received. I found my copy of her book and brought it out to the car, asking her to sign it for me. She wrote: 'For Vanessa, with friendship, Fania Fenelon.' I promised I would do everything in my power to persuade CBS and Linda Yellen to engage her as adviser for the film, and I kept my word. CBS said they would, and Linda said they telephoned her but she never answered their calls. It was shortly after this while I was rehearsing in New York that she was touring the USA, denouncing me, my politics and acting.

In Harrisburg where we were to film, there was a tight security guard around the compound, a section of the Indiana Gap NATO Airforce base used in the Second World War to intern civilians. The barracks consisted of row upon row of wooden buildings. A chilling sight. They seemed almost identical to the wooden huts in Auschwitz. The citizens of Harrisburg, many of whom had been cast as extras in our film, had plenty to talk about, and plenty to worry about. Life had overshadowed the drama of our arrival. On 28 April 1980 a major accident had occurred at the nuclear plant at nearby Ten Mile Island, the worst disaster in nuclear power until

Chernobyl six years later. A meltdown had almost happened, as in the film *The China Syndrome*. Radioactive gas had escaped from the plant, contaminating a 10-mile radius around the power station. The accident radicalised all the local population. Talking to them I realised how swiftly ordinary people's views can change in response to such a shock. I doubt whether many of them were political before it happened, but it had made them realise that the government was not in the least concerned with their health or safety. I think this new political awareness combined with their desire to learn more about German Fascism was why they were keen to take part in our film.

Jane Alexander, Robin Bartlett, Marcelle Rosenblatt, Mady Kaplan, Melanie Styron, Marisa Berenson, Lenore Harris and I played the women in the orchestra. Shirley Knight was the Commandant, and Viveca Lindfors one of the guards. The day came when we were to have our heads shaved. When it was done we looked at the piles of hair on the floor; we looked at each other, and saw how we had been dehumanised, shorn of our identity. I have sometimes been complimented for cutting off my hair for *Playing for Time*, but in fact all of us did. This was the first time actresses had had their heads shaved in a film; the cast of the *Holocaust* television series wore special rubber skull-caps. As far as I was concerned, shaving our heads was one of those details which Gerry had asked me to pay close attention to: a tribute, albeit a very small one, to the millions of Jews, communists, gypsies and homosexuals who had been made to undergo this humiliation before they were killed. It made us understand their suffering more sharply.

For the first three weeks of the six-week shooting schedule we had a well-known and successful television director. During a rehearsal, before shooting had started, he said, 'This scene is rather melodramatic.' I was alarmed and could not understand how he could say this unless he was nervous or hostile to the entire story, because what was true of that scene was true of the whole script. In any event, our producers decided he must be replaced. Arthur Miller discovered that Daniel Mann was free. He was a great director, and a very generous man. With half the footage already in the can, and no budget to reshoot, he agreed to shoot the second half of the film. Each day's work was terrifying. We were frightened we should not do justice to Fania's story and to the memory of those who had died, and now we were frightened by the technical problem of having to complete so much footage each day, to finish the film on schedule. We, too, found we were playing for time, and this became a factor sharpening our consciousness of what each moment meant. We had to work well together, and we did. All the actresses told me they had been telephoned and written to with requests that they make a statement against my casting, but none of them had. Instead they all signed a press release saying that there should be no blacklisting and that they had been looking forward to working with me. Many had relatives who had been killed in the Holocaust, and some had family who had been blacklisted in the Fifties.

Later that year I went to Bahrain, and for the second time to Iraq. In Baghdad I met the film director Mohammed Shukri Jamil, who asked me to play the role of Gertrude Bell. She was one of those who were involved in setting up the British Mandate after 1918, putting King Faisal on the throne to serve British interests and crushing the Iraqi revolution of 1920. The Iraqis were brutally defeated, mainly because the British used their aeroplanes in a campaign of bombing and strafing villages and camps. They also used gas, from large quantities they had stockpiled after the war against Germany.

I spent some wonderful hours with Mounir Bashir, the director of the Baghdad Music Conservatory, who was gathering on cassette an archive of ancient music going back to the period of Nineveh and Babylon, 3000 years BC. I had heard Mounir himself play for the first time at a concert in Bahrain. His mastery of the twelve-stringed oud was extraordinary. It seemed to me I could hear a spider spinning her web, or frozen twigs thawing in spring, so delicate were the vibrations. Mounir's passion was to train his students in the knowledge of their own musical history, which was essential to their development as musicians. He travelled all over the country making recordings, always anxious to preserve what was there in case it should be lost for ever. In the oral music of the tribes, he said, he could trace connections with the music of the ancient civilisations of Assyria and Babylonia, later called Mesopotamia, and later still, Iraq.

I went to Iraq as I went to every Arab country, to give my support to the Palestinian struggle for the right to self-determination. I came to understand, as I had not understood before, how much this struggle means to the Arab peoples. Iraqis have always supported the Palestinians. In Kuwait, Saudi Arabia, Iraq, Libya and Syria I made many friends, and I will never forget their kindness and hospitality. Without their help *The Palestinian* and then *Occupied Palestine* would not have been financed or shown. I learned an important lesson – to have respect for the Arab peoples, be ready to learn, and never be hasty to judge on the basis of fixed categories such as 'right-wing' or 'left-wing'.

In March 1980 I was a guest at the General Popular Assembly at the Libyan Arab Socialist People's Jamahiriya, where I was introduced to a delegation of slender, beautiful women from the Polisario Front, the national liberation movement in Morocco. Every one of them looked too fragile for any physical work. Then they showed me a documentary of their struggle in the Sahara desert, and I saw these same women pitching tents, cooking, hauling metal water-wagons, feeding the children and the soldiers, always on the move. Every drop of water counted. I met with young Libyan women, students, some of them dressed like nuns, in cool, plain linen veils and tunics. They reminded me of young women in the Middle Ages and Renaissance who became abbesses, renowned poets and intellectuals. Selwa, a woman of my age who told me her story, was quite typical of her generation.

She had been a medical student in the Sixties, during the last years of the rule of King Idris of Libya. As the daughter of a privileged family, her education was exceptional. For most young people, and especially girls, education was minimal. Selwa was a supporter of President Gamal Abdel Nasser, and she agitated against US military bases in Libya. When the authorities discovered this her scholarship was cancelled. Her father was furious; he ordered her to stop busying herself in politics and concentrate on her studies. Somehow she managed to get a scholarship from President Nasser, worth £9 a week, to go and study for four years in

Cairo to learn to be a journalist. In 1964 Nasser told her there would be a revolution in Libya. She said, 'You're dreaming, all the men in Libya are cowards.' She was in Cairo in 1969, when the September 1st Libyan Revolution took place. All Libyan airports were closed, so she drove for five days to Benghazi, found some soldiers and asked them, 'Where are the leaders, I want to see them?' They took her to Colonel Muammar Gaddafi and the young men of the Revolutionary Command Council.

We travelled by bus for miles into the desert to a celebration in Taghrit, stopping only to wash our hands and drink coffee, and singing songs all the way. We arrived on a plain with windswept ridges so oxidised by the sun that the wind blew fine layers of rock off them. This was the scene of the famous battle when the Libyans, led by the legendary Omar al Mukhtar, the 'Lion of the Desert', armed only with rifles, had defeated Mussolini's armoured columns. We sat under an awning and watched the commemoration of this great victory, which was celebrated every year. Tanks rolled by, followed by armoured cars, and then a group of horsemen in the white Libyan toga and flat hat. The loudest applause was for a group of veterans from the war with Fascist Italy. Only five could take part in the ceremony that day. Mussolini's forces had massacred half the population of Libya, and it was rare now to see men and women of my father's generation, or even of mine.

That summer the European Parliament passed a resolution recognising the right of the Palestinians to self-determination. It also condemned as illegal Israeli settlements in the occupied territories and all 'modifications' in population and property in the West Bank, Gaza and the Golan Heights. In the autumn, on 17 September, Iraq invaded Iran. Our party central committee condemned the invasion and called on Iraq to withdraw. No matter what the rights or wrongs of the dispute over the Shatt al' Arab waterway, Iran, through revolution, had defeated the brutal tyranny of the Shah. The invasion would weaken their economy, as it would Iraq's, and undermine the cause of the Palestinians. The Americans, British and French publicly lamented the war, and privately got on with the lucrative trade in arms, hoping Iraq would deal a mortal blow to the Iranian revolution.

I was working night and day for the party, finding premises for youth training centres in London, Liverpool and Manchester. Our idea was to set up such centres in all the main towns in Britain, where school-leavers without jobs could find skilled training and also enjoy themselves socially. We opened our first two centres in January 1981, and very soon the press started a witch-hunt. *The Times*, the *Daily Express*, the *Daily Mail* and the *News of the World* ran stories about the centres, referring to 'bomb factories' and 'brain-washing'. In spring and summer, when there were riots in Brixton and Liverpool, some of the reports tried to make out that these were instigated by our youth centres. I was kept busy for several weeks answering these reports, and in almost every case I received an apology or the right to reply. By the time our centre in Glasgow opened we had got support from the Assistant Secretary of the Scottish Trades Union Congress, trades councils and branches, and sports people like Maurice Hope, the World Middleweight champion, and John Conteh.

That spring, 1981, I was in Nashville, Tennessee, shooting a television film for ABC called *My Body, My Child*. On the night of 4 May I was standing with a group of truck drivers, watching a scene I wasn't in and listening through the cab door to the driver's radio. Bobby Sands, on hunger strike in Northern Ireland's Maze prison, had died. It was the first item on the news. Those who were brought up, as I was, in Britain, reading the *Daily Mail* and listening to or watching the *Six o'clock News*, might find it hard to imagine or believe that a bunch of Tennessee truck drivers would bow their heads in respect and sorrow at this news, and that one of them would wipe a tear from his eye. But that was how it was. Next morning the *New York Daily Post*, a newspaper owned by Rupert Murdoch, whose papers in Britain vilified Bobby Sands and the hunger-strikers, had a banner headline with a black border: BOBBY SANDS, IRA MAN AND MEMBER OF PARLIAMENT, DIES IN MAZE PRISON, BELFAST. IRELAND MOURNS.

When the editor rang Murdoch for approval of his headline he must have reminded him that the *Post* has a large Irish-American readership. I cut the headline out, and when I got home I sellotaped it to my wall above my desk. It is there now. Soon it will be the eleventh anniversary of Bobby Sands's death. I'm sure there will be many who will commemorate him, a true hero of our time who wanted a United Socialist Republic of Ireland. He was not a terrorist, but fought as best he could, politically. Every British government, Tory or Labour, has denied the Irish their right to self-determination. We in Britain have a special responsibility to right that wrong, which has been the cause of so much tragedy and suffering.

Much more precious than the *Post* headline is the letter I have kept from Bobby Sands. It was written on toilet paper and smuggled out of the H-Block. Sands was a Member of Parliament, elected by the people of Derry whilst he was a prisoner. All his rights as a prisoner of war had been denied by the Thatcher government, which had refused him political status. As a Member of Parliament elected by a large majority he had no rights, nor had his electors, who could neither hear from him – except for the occasional message smuggled out – nor communicate with him. His letter is full of humour, courage and defiance.

Hiya! Vanessa,
How are ya? I'm sure you're a bit surprised to receive this little letter, but I'm sure that you recognise the good old H-Block writing paper. Well, anyway, I'm Bobby Sands, blanket man, H-Block 6. I'm not really writing to tell you about H-Block, Vanessa, as I'm more than sure you know as much about it as any one else, but all the same, things remain more or less the same here. We continue to resist here and they continue to torture us. Sometimes we make the mistake of saying 'the total boredom' that is very true most of the time, but there are times here when there is never a dull moment, so to speak, for if the screws aren't beating someone up, they're hosing someone down, searching remains nightmarish. Bedding as ever is damp, food cold and most times inedible. They've blocked up the windows and the flow of air is minimal, our view of the outside an eyesore of a few inches of barbed-wire. Bad and degrading searches remain the in-thing, you know the way it feels going into a dentist's surgery, well it feels about ten times worse when you walk naked into a group of screws armed with mirrors, torches and metal detectors, the tools of the searching trade and as they say 'they're only doing their job' God help us! Anyway, Vanessa, we don't know very much of how things are in England (or anywhere else for that matter), but we did hear that there were ten-thousand at the London march and after the reports of the Belfast march we were very pleased and morale is quite high. I'm putting a few wee odds and ends in along with this letter to you: perhaps you can use them for some of the papers or for leaflets. 'Sort of a direct from H-Block thing', anyway I'm also putting in five letters to other people, who we think may be interested in H-Block. We would appreciate it if perhaps you could pass them on to them, as they're in the film world, we can hardly get a letter to the Falls Road, let alone these people, so hope you could manage it. We're sort of pushing on the propaganda front and trying to get as many people as we can to tell them and explain to them about H-Block and Ireland. From in here all we can do is write some articles and letters, etc., when the situation permits, but we try. Well, no matter, if you wish or get the chance, you could drop us a note letting us know how things are with you. You could send it to the incident centre, 170 Falls Road, Belfast. Also (before I forget) if you can, could you send us the names and addresses of anyone you think would like to hear from us, or whom you think we could tell of H-Block, be they individuals or

organisations, come to think of it, you can add anyone at all approachable or unapproachable. Perhaps I'll be able to get you another letter again shortly to let you know how things are here. But anyway it's been nice writing to you and thanks to you from us all here for the great work yourself and your comrades have done for us and our people. Regards to everyone.

Sealadaigh Abu    See ya!

Bobby Sands

# 22

*Occupied Palestine* was completed in the summer of 1981. From September until spring the following year I did nothing but travel from one city to the next, showing the film or arranging for it to be seen, and speaking for the Palestinian cause. I was proud of *Occupied Palestine*, and I think even now, ten years later, when many remarkable films have been made about Palestine – for example Mei Masri's *Children of Fire* – that it stands amongst the best. It shows how the settlements in the occupied territories function, what a 'settler' is, what his or her mentality is. In one scene in *Occupied Palestine* we see a 'Park' where there was once a Palestinian village. A guide welcomes Americans and Canadians to look it over. They will receive cash and a house, together, of course, with Israeli citizenship, if they settle there. Water will be pumped from artesian wells, which once supplied the village, so that the 'Park' will be well irrigated. Barbed-wire and watchtowers will protect the 'Park' from those who once grazed their flocks, drew their water and tended their orchards on its slopes.

'Settlers', whether British, German, French, Dutch, Belgian or Romanian – many came from Romania during the Ceausescu regime – are reactionary individuals. I do not mean refugees, those who flee persecution, but those who after 1967 left Manchester or Johannesburg or somewhere in the States, to 'settle', as colonists, in the West Bank. It is not a case of nationality or religion, it is a question of racist mentality. They too, with guns and guard dogs, will live behind barbed wire. But they have all the rights. The Palestinians whose land they have taken have no rights at all.

In Jordan I was taken to the ancient Roman city of Jerash. My host, a deputy minister, showed me the theatre, and as we walked in the winter sunshine down Roman streets, long, long deserted, I thought of the Roman colonists and of their civilisation. I thought

Me as Julia and Jane
Fonda as Lillian
Hellman at Oxford
University, filming *Julia*
(*above*); and (*right*)
accepting the award for
Best Supporting Actress
for *Julia* at the 1977
Academy Awards.

With Dustin Hoffmann
in the RCA Club pool in
*Agatha*, 1978, the film
about Agatha Christie's
disappearence.

As Miss Jean Brodie in my dressing room, 1966 (*top left*); (*top right*) as an extra for Joshua Logan's *Camelot*; Guinevere in love with Arthur (*centre right*); Sylvia Pankhurst in Richard Attenborough's anti-war film *Oh, What a Lovely War*, 1968 (*bottom left*); acting for Sidney Lumet again in *Murder on the Orient Express*, 1974 (*centre*); and (*bottom right*) Julia says goodbye in the Berlin café.

*Playing for Time* (*top left*); *Agatha* (*centre*); as Olive Chancellor in Merchant-Ivory's film of *The Bostonians* (*top right*); Nora, the wife of Con Melody, in *A Touch of the Poet*, 1988 (*above*); Tennessee Williams' 'Lady' in Jimmy Nederlander's Broadway production, directed by Peter Hall (*middle*); and October 1990 with crew-cut hair again after *The Ballad of the Sad Café* and Lynn's scissors in *Whatever Happened to Baby Jane*.

*Ghosts*, with Adrian Dunbar as Oswald, at the Young Vic and Wyndhams, 1986-7 (*top*); Tennessee's 'Lady' again in *Orpheus Descending*, with Jean-Marc Barr, at the Haymarket, 1988 (*left*); and as Mrs Honey in Martin Sherman's *A Madhouse in Goa* at the Lyric, Hammersmith, 1989.

of Shelley's fable of an ancient empire buried beneath the desert sands and despite the beauty of the place and the warmth of the winter sun on pink stones, I was shivering.

Crown Prince Hassan met me in the Palace, and showed me on a screen a series of slides demonstrating how Israeli policy on the West Bank had reduced the Palestinian areas to tiny enclaves, dominated and engulfed by the settlements of 'greater Israel'. It was a very clear and objective presentation. I suggested that the Ministry of Culture should buy the rights to *Playing for Time* and screen it on Jordanian television. It had been banned in Israel, but if it were broadcast in Jordan Israelis could see it on their screens. One of the greatest tragedies of the whole conflict is that so much injury has been done to the Arab peoples, and there has been so much racialism that they do not feel they can show something like Fania Fenelon's story which proves again, not only the crime against the Jewish people, but the common identity of both peoples, suffering from the crimes of racialism and imperialism.

In the new year, 1982, I flew to Australia to speak at the premières of *Occupied Palestine* in Sydney, Melbourne, Canberra, Brisbane and Perth, and at public meetings sponsored by the Socialist Labour League, which at that time was affiliated to the International Committee of the Fourth International. I was guest speaker at the Australian Press Club, and the film drew large audiences everywhere. In Sydney, where the film was shown first, someone rang the caretaker of the town hall to say that a bomb had been planted: the police searched the place, and the mayor provided extra security. I rang a number of trade union leaders and asked if they would join me on the platform and help protect people's democratic right to see the film if they wished. They came, and the hall was packed. The Australian Congress of Trade Unions, under Robert Hawke's leadership, had a despicable record for abusing the rights of the Palestinians and Arab peoples, but that was by no means true of all the unions which made up the Congress, nor of their leaders. And Australian trade unions have a record second to none for defending democratic rights, including the right to free speech. So they came, and we spoke, and of course there was no bomb.

In all I spent six months on the road with *Occupied Palestine*, and during that time I spent seventeen nights at home. Tasha and Joely were nineteen and seventeen, almost grown up. Carlo was only twelve; I missed him terribly, and longed to hear him speak and hold him in my arms. Nothing can make up for the time you lose with your children, it only makes the time you have more precious. Our children see what we are doing and understand it, but sometimes they despair when things change slowly, or not at all.

One morning in March 1982 Silvana had telephoned me to tell me that I had been invited to perform in a series of concerts with the Boston Symphony Orchestra in honour of Stravinsky's centenary. I was in Venice playing Cosima in a six-part television film about Richard Wagner, with Richard Burton. Jessye Norman would sing Jocasta in the opera/oratorio *Oedipus Rex*, Seiji Osawa would conduct, and I would be the narrator, a role written and created by Jean Cocteau. I rang my agent in Los Angeles and said I was delighted. I learn a tremendous amount from working with musicians and dancers. Not in the matter of technique itself, which is of course quite different, but in studying their approach and seeing how they relate the problem of technique to the imaginative needs of their performance. Then I settled back to enjoy the false calm of a morning off in Venice, without tourists or motor-boats.

Back in London, the telephone rang by my bedside at 1 a.m. on 31 March. I was very annoyed to be woken and longed to go back to sleep, but the call was from the States, so I got out of bed and took it in the kitchen where it was cold and I should have to wake up. It was Bill Bewell, the BSO's musical director. He sounded very excited. He said, 'Vanessa, we had expected some protests, but nothing like this!' 'Like what, what's happened?' He said the BSO switchboard had been 'inundated' with phone-calls, and they had had dozens of letters protesting against my engagement for the Stravinsky concerts. He talked and talked, saying the same thing so often that I began to think something had happened that he didn't want to talk about. 'Supposing there's violence?'

I said phone-callers who threaten violence very rarely carry out their threats, and people who threaten bombs rarely plant them. I suggested that the BSO might make a statement, telling their subscribers that there had been protests but that they were sure their audiences would wish to see the concerts as planned, because it would be an exceptional artistic event. I had barely finished this when he interrupted: 'What will you do if they shoot you?' His question was so absurd that I almost laughed out loud. But I thought that might be taken rudely so I said something flat and positive like, 'Well, they won't, will they?' I said this was a political protest, and it was organised, but whoever was responsible obviously knew that a great orchestra like the Boston Symphony would not change its artistic plans; there would be neither bombs nor shooting, and at most perhaps one solitary picket. I talked for a long time and by the end of our conversation I thought I'd convinced him. Next evening when I came home there was a telephone message from my agent in Los Angeles, saying that the BSO had cancelled *Oedipus Rex*.

On the following day they issued a press release, with no mention of my name: 'The Boston Symphony Orchestra regret to announce that due to circumstances beyond their reasonable control, the concerts of Stravinsky's *Oedipus Rex* are cancelled . . .'. That was how my case against the BSO began.

A contract properly made is legally binding, but a *force majeure* clause in every contract permits an employer to cancel in case of flood, earthquare, fire or war, events which are presumed to be beyond his control. I rang lawyers in New York. I said I thought the BSO's reasons for cancelling my contract were political, so would they demand that the BSO reinstate my contract and resume their planned programme. I rang Mike Wallace at CBS, then I had a call from WRKO radio station in Boston, inviting me to fly there and talk to callers on the 'Jerry Williams Show'. ABC had invited me to do some publicity for *My Body, My Child* so fortunately I had a visa, otherwise I could not have gone. I flew to New York, and spoke on the 'Good Morning America' programme, saying I hoped the concerts would be rescheduled and that I had instructed lawyers to make this request for me. If they were not, it meant that blacklisting and political censorship of artists had come back to America. Then I flew to Boston and spoke with telephone callers on the 'Jerry Williams Show' for three hours. One of these, a violinist from the Boston Symphony called Jerome Rosen, said that a few members of the orchestra had signed a petition objecting to my appearance in the concert, but that they were shocked and upset to learn that it had been cancelled. He had been told by a member of the orchestra's management that their petition had nothing to do with the decision to cancel.

Jerry Williams:    How many members of the orchestra were upset?

| | |
|---|---|
| Jerome Rosen: | Well, you see, half the orchestra were on vacation at the time . . . |
| Jerry Williams: | So, there couldn't have been very many, obviously? |
| Jerome Rosen: | Do you mean upset at the cancellation, or . . . |
| Jerry Williams: | No, upset at the fact that Miss Redgrave was going to appear. |
| Jerome Rosen: | I think many of us were disturbed, but with little thought about what was really at stake, which is freedom of expression. I think most of us realised that many of us are Jews, who know our own history. Many of us are old enough to remember McCarthy in a more personal way, and the parallel was obvious and immediate. And as many people have said, the First Amendment in this country was not designed to protect popular opinions because popular opinions don't need protecting. It's the hard cases where you have to hold to the principle. |

After the broadcast I went to my hotel to meet Peter Sellars, who was to have directed *Oedipus Rex*. I was surprised to find a very young man of twenty-four, who was very thoughtful and very articulate. He, of course, had been at the meetings in Symphony Hall with the General Manager, Tom Morris, Bill Bewell, and the two press officers, Caroline Sandrig and Judith Gordon. I will always be grateful to Peter Sellars. He is one of those who, as Jerome Rosen said, knows that there are 'cases where you have to hold to the principle'. He told me the sequence of events as he knew them.

On 29 March Tom Morris had told Peter that they wanted to replace me, and that evening Peter told Morris that if they did fire me he would not direct *Oedipus Rex*. Asking Morris for his reasons, he was told that although no threats had been made, the BSO was afraid there would be. Morris told him the B'nai Brith were *considering* issuing a statement condemning my engagement. From the moment Peter refused to accept my being fired, the BSO had a problem. If they went ahead and fired me they knew he would resign and would speak out publicly. None the less, on the morning of 30 March Morris had my name removed from the artwork of a display advertisement that the press office were placing in the *New York Times* on 4 April. That same Tuesday Peter was told that the B'nai Brith had decided *not* to issue a statement. By late afternoon the BSO had still not received any threats, or any call from the Jewish Defence League. Peter's rehearsal in New York that Tuesday night was postponed. On Wednesday evening, 31 March, he was due to rehearse the chorus. Tom Morris called him and asked him once more for the record if he still refused to direct the concert without Vanessa Redgrave. Peter said he hadn't changed his mind, and that he was going to call the principal conductor of the BSO, Seiji Osawa, in Paris, and wanted to speak with the BSO trustees.

On Wednesday, 1 April he was told that a caller from the Jewish Defence League had telephoned and said he would be organising a picket. No one said that this caller had threatened violence, bloodshed or even any disturbance, but Morris told Peter that the call had absolutely clinched the cancellation of my contract. He also said he had visited Mr Jordan, the Boston Police Commissioner. Peter booked a conference call at the Symphony Hall offices with Seiji Osawa in Paris for that day, and told Seiji that he would resign if the BSO cancelled my contract. The press office then drafted their release, which was published the following day, 2 April.

There had been no threats of violence, bombs or bloodshed. The BSO had already decided to cancel my contract and fire me before Bill Bewell rang me in the middle of the night with his talk about floods of telephone calls and letters and his concern about my safety. No wonder that the more I tried to calm his fears the more he raised the ante – 'What will you do if they shoot you?' I had no means of knowing that his call was a hoax, a crude trick to try to frighten me into withdrawing voluntarily. Had he succeeded he could have gone to Peter Sellars and said, 'There's no problem, Vanessa's withdrawn, she doesn't want to do it, and you need have no scruples about directing without her.' When Peter heard that the B'nai Brith had decided not to make a statement he had assumed that meant that the BSO would proceed with the concert and with my contract, because B'nai Brith had respect in the community. On the contrary, they had decided not to make a statement because the BSO had told them they were going to fire me.

Alan Eisenberg, for American Actors' Equity, wrote to Tom Morris:

An orchestra of renown and standing such as the Boston Symphony should be a major champion of the artist's right to work and to espouse whatever political views he or she chooses. Your denial of Ms Redgrave's right to do both, poses a threat to the basic democratic principles we cherish and upon which art depends.

The Screen Actors' Guild also made a statement on my behalf. Then, on 6 April, Ed Asner, the star of the CBS 'Lou Grant' series, had his show cancelled: because of 'falling ratings', CBS said. But everyone knew that Ed was being victimised because he had led a fund-raising campaign for medical aid for Nicaragua and El Salvador, and had supported PATCO, the air traffic controllers' union which was in dispute with the Federal Government.

The BSO refused to reinstate the concerts. The Arab American Association in Washington said they would sponsor me to appear in a performance in Boston to help prove I could perform there without any public disorder. They booked the Orpheum Theatre for 29 April and I prepared a programme of songs and scenes from *As You Like It*, *The Seagull* and *Isadora*, with Phil Carnoff, a young actor Robin Bartlett had introduced me to. I rang Tennessee Williams and asked if he would join me, and read something from his own work. He said fine, he would read an essay called 'Misunderstanding of the Artist in Revolt'. We arranged to meet in the Ritz Carlton Hotel in Boston on 8 April.

I flew in from London that day and checked with the desk if Tennessee had arrived. They said, No, Mr Williams had not made a reservation. My heart sank. I knew there must have been great pressure on Tennessee not to come and read with me that day, and I supposed he must have bowed to it. My body felt heavy and exhausted. I sat down on the hotel bed, took a deep breath, drank a glass of water, and then the phone rang by my bedside. I picked it up and heard a warm, cheerful, deep southern voice. 'Vanessa? It's Tennessee.' 'Oh, Tennessee, where *are* you?' Distress does strange things to the voice, and I must have sounded like an anxious mother or a harassed schoolteacher, because Tennessee laughed and laughed until he had a coughing fit. 'I'm downstairs in the lobby of course, won't you come down?' 'Of *course* I'll come down,' I cried, and I really did cry, all the way downstairs in the elevator. When I saw Tennessee in a huge green chair in the quiet old lounge I cried my eyes out with joy, and he laughed and coughed. We hugged each other, ordered tea and muffins, and he said, 'You were right, they *all* phoned me and told me not to come, but damn it, here I am.' We gave two performances next day. A very small, orderly picket appeared for one hour, then shuffled off. A dozen policemen shifted from foot to foot in the foyer and on the pavement outside, with nothing to do but look at their watches. The press said practically nothing. Not one paper even mentioned that Tennessee Williams had come.

When he died the following year, his friends and fellow artistes paid him a tribute at Circle in the Square. They recalled Tennessee's definition of happiness – 'Insensitivity, I guess.' That is the key to Tennessee as a human being and as a writer. When he drank or took pills it was like Brick in *Cat on a Hot Tin Roof*, to hear 'a click in my head', to have a few hours' oblivion, because he could not bear the cruelty he saw in the world. His agent, Milton Goldman, was a very kind and noble man. When Tennessee died he wrote to tell me he had done his very utmost to stop him coming to Boston. He sent me a copy of the letter Tennessee sent him after the Boston performance. That was when I really cried. He wrote about the agony of the artist who feels he's alone, that no one is listening to him or seeing what he sees. That was why he had joined me in Boston, he said. Not because of my politics, but because I felt the suffering of human beings as an artist, and he did not want me to be alone in that.

It took two and a half years to get my case against the BSO into the Massachusetts court. It made some legal history and is a landmark in the struggle for civil rights, because, in the final judgment, it set a precedent for legalising blacklisting. To tell it in proper detail would require a whole book.

Many things were revealed in the process of 'discovery'. There had been exactly four letters protesting against my engagement by 1 April, when the BSO drew up their statement cancelling the concert. I found out that the Jewish Defence League member who had telephoned Symphony Hall saying he would organise a picket – the call that 'absolutely clinched' the cancellation of my contract, according to Tom Morris – had obligingly left his name and telephone number with the press office, the only JDL caller in history to do so. What is more, he was the only JDL member left in Boston. The others had gone to Israel with Rabbi Meir Kahane and joined the Fascist Kach movement.

Money was a problem. I borrowed heavily, and my lawyers allowed me to get deeply in debt with them so long as I paid them small sums fairly frequently. But even those small sums were hard to find. I discovered that my previous accountants had completely neglected my taxes; the Inland Revenue was now demanding large amounts that had been left unpaid, and for over a year I could get no work, owing to the publicity surrounding my case against the BSO. Things began to change in my favour when the BSO failed to get summary judgment to dismiss my case in 1983. Ismail Merchant rang asking me to play Olive Chancellor in a film of *The Bostonians*, with Christopher Reeve. He told me the Bank of Boston were putting money in the film and were pleased to hear I would be starring in it. But when Anthony Page wanted me to play in *Heartbreak House* at Circle in the Square, Ted Mann and Paul Libin said they couldn't engage me because of the BSO cancellation. They, too, depended on subscriptions, and if the BSO were unable to withstand political pressure and blackmail, they, a much smaller organisation, could not risk employing me.

The weekend before the case began, in 1983, I needed $150,000 to carry on and I had $20,000 in the bank. I telephoned the Washington embassy of the Royal Kingdom of Saudi Arabia and asked for Prince Bandar Bin Sultan's secretary. The ambassador came on the phone and invited me to see him and his family in Virginia. I flew up from Boston and we sat and talked, and I explained that without his help I would be forced to withdraw my case from the court for lack of money. I flew back to Boston with a cheque for $150,000 in my shoulder-bag.

For three weeks I was in the district court every day. Among my witnesses were Peter Sellars, Sidney Lumet, Ismail Merchant, Ted Mann, and my agent, Bruce Savan. Lillian Hellman had promised to appear as an expert witness for me on blacklisting. I had met her, at last, in the summer of 1983 in Martha's Vineyard, a fragile, indomitable woman who could hardly see and barely walk. She welcomed me, and we talked like sisters about the Rosenbergs, *Julia* and the BSO. Arthur Burnstein of the Jewish Defence League also gave evidence for me. A short, stocky, plain-spoken man, he said he had never threatened violence or bloodshed. He had said he would organise a picket, which was his democratic right. My dear friend Thelma Holt flew to Boston and told the court that during the visit to London of the Rustaveli company from Tbilisi, Georgia, soon after the Soviet invasion of Afghanistan, there had been bomb threats every night for ten days. Two busloads of police had arrived every evening at her theatre.

I would announce to the audience each night that we had received a threat. The people making the threats always told us when the bombs were to go off, shortly after the intermission began. So while people were filing out of the theatre for the interval the police went in and made their sweep. It was a bore for all of us and very expensive for the British police, but if we had cancelled, if we had given in to every nut who wanted his name in the papers, nothing could go on.

On 9 November 1983 the jury found that there were no causes beyond the reasonable control of the BSO to justify cancellation and awarded me $100,000 of consequential damages, ruling that the BSO caused 'foreseeable harm' to my career when they cancelled the concerts. They did not find for me on the separate issue of the abrogation of my civil rights, but a few days later they made legal history. They wrote a letter to the District Court judge, Robert E. Keaton, saying that they were indeed convinced that my civil rights had been abrogated by the BSO, but could find no way 'to express within the confines of the [questions put to us] and your explanation to us as to the parameters within which the law required we must decide'.

The judge overturned the jury's findings, and the award of $100,000 consequential damages. He ruled:

it is not illegal for a private entity to make a choice not to contract with an artist for a performance if its agents believe that the artist's appearance under their sponsorship would be interpreted by others as in some degree a political statement. Thus the BSO was entirely free not to make a contract with Redgrave for such reasons even though its agents considered her a superb actress and exceptionally qualified to perform as narrator in *Oedipus Rex*.

Therefore, Judge Keaton ruled in January 1985, the cancellation amounted to no more than standard breach of contract, and that an award of $100,000 damages would signify an attack on the constitutionally protected rights of the BSO.

The judge's ruling was staggering. It meant that all laws and provisions against discrimination were undermined. No employer would be obliged to employ someone, however qualified for the job in hand, or keep them in employment, if in the opinion of the employer or their agent to do so could be construed as 'a political statement'. Nor could it be illegal, beyond a 'standard breach of

241

contract', for an employer to make a political statement by firing someone.

I had no choice but to appeal. The Lawyers' Committee for Civil Rights of the Boston Bar Association, the Civil Liberties Union of Massachusetts, and finally the Attorney-General of Massachusetts himself, entered *amicus curiae* briefs on my behalf.

I announced my appeal at the Los Angeles Press Club on 21 March. Peter Feibleman, one of Lillian Hellman's executors, had joined me. Half an hour before the conference I had a call from Corin from a nursing home in Denham, in Buckinghamshire, to tell me that Michael had died. I wanted to cry and cancel the press conference, but I couldn't, and I knew that if I spoke I must speak strongly and well.

Michael had followed his political convictions in the Thirties. So had Lillian. She had kept hers until her death. He had lost all conviction until, already shaking with Parkinson's disease, he had made his way to a rally in Hyde Park where I was speaking and, standing well away at the back of the crowd, unnoticed by anyone, had found, he told Corin, that he liked the 'revolutionary flavour' of what he had heard. The night before he died, struggling for breath and shaking with fever, he took Corin's hand and whispered, 'You put the wind in my sails.'

I thought of Michael, and felt him with me, knowing he would want me to take a deep breath and speak as well as I could. So I did.

# 23

The Bostonians in 1983, was my first film with Merchant-Ivory Productions, since then I have done *The Ballad Of The Sad Café*, and I am now working on my third, *Howard's End*. I was immensely grateful for the work, in the midst of the BSO case, but I approached the job with some fear. Corin had read most of Henry James as had the majority of his generation who studied English at Cambridge University and attended Dr Leavis's lectures. My father was a devotee. He had faithfully and very creatively adapted James' novella *The Aspern Papers* for the stage, and his bookshelves were lined with Leon Edel's editions of James' letters, novels, and countless studies of James. But I was far from devoted. Every time I picked up a novel James' spiteful verdict on Ibsen – 'yet I feel, to the pitch of almost intolerable boredom, the presence and stirring of life' – rang in my ears, coming back, like a boomerang, to James himself, or rather to my response to his writing. Life there undeniably was in his portrait of Olive Chancellor, the sensitive and highly prejudiced view of a brother towards his sister, Alice James. He writes cynically, and often maliciously, yet touched in spite of himself at the fate of those middle-class women, treated like pariahs by their contemporaries, who set their faces against the mores of their society and campaigned for women's right to education and the vote, and often for women's rights in the factories. Reading James' novel, and Ruth Prawer Jhabvala's very good script, I felt his prejudice all the time in conflict with his artistry as a writer, and the fact that despite himself he was drawn towards the woman he portrayed.

'Forget the novel,' James Ivory told his cast, two or three times a day during our first days of shooting, 'we're not filming the novel, but a story by Ruth Jhabvala.' We had some friendly arguments about that. I could see why he said it, and I could imagine how it would try a director's patience to be told that such and such a scene 'worked' better in the novel, often because an actor would be disappointed to discover how much shorter his role was in the script than in the original. Nevertheless I could not forget the novel, simply because it seemed to me that I must understand James' very contradictory view of Olive Chancellor. Some arguments in filming can be debilitating. Ours were invigorating, and I could spring out of bed, looking forward to each day's work. I loved Madeleine Potter, who played Verena. And Christopher Reeve was a joy to work with, dedicated and full of ideas. He's a wonderful actor, very inventive and immediate. He became a good friend, and in 1984 we played together again in my father's adaptation of *The Aspern Papers* with Wendy Hiller.

*The Aspern Papers* was a wonderful experience. It is an extremely well-written play because Michael had a real feeling for the story. James does not explain very much, and Michael strengthened all kinds of human touches in the writing of the play that you might easily miss on a first reading of the novella itself. I was delighted when I finally convinced Christopher to play Henry Jarvis. I felt that casting an American in the part was important. Michael was very quiet when he met Chris, and looked at him intently, wondering how this very tall and muscular man would appear as Henry Jarvis. Before we brought the play into London, Michael spent a lot of time with us and I valued being able to share the production with him professionally. When he came to the first performance he sat in a box and Rachel said that at the end he waved his arms and clapped his hands above his head in admiration. He thought Christopher was a truly fine actor which meant a lot to us both particularly before the play opened when the British press tried to put Christopher down. Christopher has worked in the theatre since he was fifteen, long before he became known to British journalists as Superman, and he continues to work in the theatre today. But out of ignorance they presented him simply as 'Superman' assuming that he had never acted in the theatre before. He is a fine stage actor, and when we opened he rightly received unanimously good reviews. The critics agreed with Michael.

Shortly before he died Michael had seen Natasha as Ophelia in *Hamlet* at the Young Vic Theatre in Waterloo. The Young Vic's policy at that time was to present classic plays for school and college students so the Saturday matinees were boisterous affairs, with a good deal of whistling and giggling from sixteen-year-old kids who probably thought they had better things to do on a Saturday afternoon than watch Shakespeare and be bored. Michael's wheelchair was parked in an aisle, and he was surrounded on all sides by teenage schoolchildren. Tasha's was the sweetest, dearest, most affectionate Ophelia I had ever seen. Her 'mad scene' was not mad, but so grief-stricken at the horrors she had seen that her nerves gave way, and to the adults around her she appeared mad. It struck a chord with the Young Vic audience, who watched and listened in silence, totally concentrated, and applauded and cheered at the end. Michael said almost nothing as we drove back to the nursing home, but I knew from long experience that that was a good sign. When he was most absorbed he lapsed into long, impenetrable silences, and a look of deep melancholy, even boredom, settled on his face. It was exasperating for those who didn't know him well, but we knew that it meant he was turning something over and over in his mind. His grandchildren saw him very little, yet they loved him for his gentleness, and the way his eyes would follow them round the room. As we reached Denham he said, after a pause which lasted almost the length of the journey, 'She's a true actress.'

Michael had been moved into a clinic, run by the Licensed Victuallers' Association – a jolly place for retired publicans where all the patients could get cut-price drinks. No hospital could afford to have him because his disease was incurable, and to keep him in a bed would mean depriving another patient. The acute shortage of hospital beds caused by the Tory government's cuts in funding meant that there was a crisis in the National Health Service. The nurses welcomed him back and wheeled him to his room, teasing him about his 'outing', and helping him to undress. He shared a room with an elderly retired publican, who had kept a pub in Whitechapel in wartime, and remembered all Michael's films like *The Way to the Stars* and *The Dam Busters*. I tucked him up in bed, kissed him goodnight, and wished him 'Happy birthday' for the following Tuesday, his seventy-seventh birthday, when I should be back in America.

Parkinson's disease had muffled his voice almost to a whisper, and at times he could not speak at all. His greatest tragedy was that people would talk to him as if his mind was disabled. Because he often could not reply quickly, or at all, or stopped in mid-sentence,

245

they spoke to him as if he were a retarded child. I have seen many cases of retarded children, with disabilities which have their origin in a chemical breakdown in the system. Even in the most severe cases, given proper medical and above all human treatment, such children can develop their mental abilities to a degree not commonly imagined. If, however, they are shut away in institutions and tied to their beds for lack of staff, or out of sheer bureaucratic ignorance, they become hopelessly handicapped. Professor Watkins, the leading neurological surgeon at the London Hospital who had taken a close interest in Michael, explained that 'the more input the better. People hallucinate when they don't have enough input or stimulus from outside. Human beings are social beings. Without discussion, walks, activities, videos, they lose their human faculties.'

March went out like a lion and the daffodils in Mortlake crematorium tossed to and fro in the wind. But Michael's funeral was a celebration. Cecil Beaton's wonderful photograph of his Antony, the best theatre portrait I ever saw, lay propped against his coffin in the chapel. His friends and colleagues sang or spoke poems in his mourning. Natasha read Perdita's speech from *The Winter's Tale* – 'My fairest friend, I would I had some flowers now o' the spring . . .'. Ian McKellan spoke Milton's 'Lycidas' and the final, famous couplet,

> At last he rose and twitched his mantle blue:
> Tomorrow to fresh woods, and pastures new.

never sounded so fresh and hopeful. Ian Charleson, a beautiful, sensitive actor, who died in 1990 after a heroic struggle with AIDS, and who had a special place in the affections of his colleagues, sang Sky Masterson's solo from *Guys and Dolls*,

> My time of day is the dark time,
> A couple of deals before dawn . . .

It was Michael's favourite song. Walking the streets at night in a black overcoat and black felt hat, calling on his friends at two o'clock in the morning and coming home just before dawn, was his favourite occupation. Yehudi Menuhin and his wife Diana came, and afterwards Diana told me a story.

I always loved your father and I told him everything. People said he was aloof and difficult to know, but not me. I could say anything to him. So when I met Yehudi, Michael was the first person I wanted to tell. I went to his dressing room at the theatre and said, 'I'm in love with Menuhin and I want to bring him round to meet you. Can I?' 'Oh no, no, no,' Michael said, 'you can't. Please don't.' 'Why ever not?' I asked. 'Because he's a genius,' Michael said, 'and I won't be able to talk to him.' 'Don't be silly,' I told him, 'you're quite a genius yourself, and I can still talk to you.'

In April 1985 I was on the road again. The miners had returned to work after their year-long strike, betrayed by the Labour leaders and TUC, but not defeated. But now a terrible toll of reprisals began, in which the government, the courts and the Coal Board, did their utmost to take their revenge on the miners, and smash their union. Thirty miners were in jail, and more than 700 had been sacked. Their offences ranged from manslaughter, in the case of Russell Jones and Dean Shankland who were jailed for life, to the most trivial charge of trespassing on Coal Board property. But whatever their charges or their sentences, their real offence, in the eyes of their accusers, was that of fighting for their jobs, their families and their communities, and loyalty to their union, the National Union of Mineworkers, and to the trade union movement and the working class as a whole. They were victims of class warfare, and those who were in jail were political prisoners. If you said that to a member of the front bench of the shadow cabinet, or to a leader of the TUC he would roll his eyes heavenwards, or turn on his heels and walk away. The very concept of classes and class warfare had become anathema to the bosses of the labour and trade union movement, who preached a vision of classless harmony called 'new realism'. But it was true, and if you wanted confirmation of that from the horse's mouth, you need only have listened to the seventy-year-old American Scot, Ian MacGregor, brought over to Britain for a huge fee to run the Coal Board after the retirement of Derek Ezra. On the day after the miners were forced back to work in March 1985 MacGregor said, 'People are now discovering the price of insubordination and insurrection and boy! are we going to give it them.'

I set out with a camera crew and a reporter to visit all the mining communities in Britain and talk to the miners' wives. Our central committee had asked me to make a film about the women, because their movement, the miners' wives' support groups, was one of

247

the most remarkable political developments of the strike. They had sustained the strike for twelve months. They had travelled up and down the country for demonstrations and meetings. They had spoken on public platforms. They had travelled abroad, to speak and to raise funds. They had seen how other workers lived and struggled. And they had learned that Britain, under Margaret Thatcher, had become a police state.

Liz French, whose husband Terry, from Betteshanger Colliery in Kent had been jailed for five years, told me how it had begun. 'He'd been picketing in Warwickshire and when he came home, he said, "You wouldn't believe the kickings we're getting." Now me, personally, I was saying to Terry, come on, six of one, half a dozen of the other, but he said "what you've been seeing on television isn't half and half. Television hasn't shown you what they're doing. It's too busy making us out to be criminals and thugs."' And then, Liz said, the police moved into their communities in Deal and Aylsham and the women were shocked. 'You couldn't walk down this street. The police stopped you on every corner, where were you going, what were you doing, who were you married to? And then they came bursting into your home, trampling down your fence, knocking down your door, accusing your men of crimes they'd never committed. We experienced the police state, and it was frightening.'

In Barnsley I interviewed Anne Scargill, and then went back to her home to meet her husband and daughter. Arthur's home was modest, warm and welcoming. He told me there had been three attempts on his life during the strike. In no instance were arrests made or charges brought by the police. Arthur himself had been arrested for picketing at Orgreave in Yorkshire. He led the miners from the front, picketing with them, being arrested with them, and for that, besides his other very great qualities of leadership, he had retained their support and loyalty against the most sustained onslaught that had been waged against a trade union and its leader in our times.

I visited James Waddell, a young married miner from Kent, in prison on Sheppey Island. Outside the prison an enormous site was being scraped and bulldozed for another high-security wing. We met in the canteen which was unusual, and had a cup of tea at a plastic-topped table in a room full of other men and their relatives. He told me it was impossible to get *Newsline*, our party's daily paper, although we were posting it to him. He was allowed only the *Sun* or the *Daily Express*. I looked at James, who was young enough to be my son, knowing that when he came out he would be unable to get a job down the pit, which had been his life ever since he left the Royal Marines. He would be blacklisted by every employer in the country. In a short while every colliery in Kent would be closed and Betteshanger Colliery would be turned into a yacht marina or a leisure centre and families like James Waddell's, who had come down from Scotland in the 1930s in search of work, would be at a dead end. James knew this and explained it very well. He had fought for jobs, for his family, and now he was in a high-security prison on Sheppey Island.

I learned a lot during the making of this film. The more I listened to the miners' wives, mothers and daughters, the more it became clear that their main concern was for the men, like James and Terry, who were in jail, and the hundreds of miners who had been sacked. The party was preparing a march, from Edinburgh, Liverpool and Swansea to a rally at Alexandra Pavilion , against unemployment and the cheap labour schemes for youth, and as soon as I returned to London I wrote a letter to the Political Committee suggesting that the main demands of the march should be to release the jailed miners, and for the sacked miners to have their jobs back. Gerry agreed, and formulated a new proposal for the Central Committee, a concept in which the particular case of the jailed miner would be connected to the universal threat of mass unemployment, the destruction of industries and skills and the exploitation of young people, denied the right to join a trade union.

Political parties are tested, and prove themselves in a very concrete way at times of great social and political conflict. Elections and opinion polls provide one kind of test, but a very imperfect one. This is chiefly because opinion polls are now governed exclusively by the needs of the party in power. But it is also because every poll, no matter how 'objectively' the pollster approaches the task, addresses its sample of opinions as a passive object. It is incapable of analysing the changes in large masses of people, connected to one another in a struggle, or of listening to *their* questions. It is certain that no opinion poll could have detected the changes in the influence of the Workers' Revolutionary Party amongst decisive groups of workers and working-class communities in 1985.

But the miners' strike provided a test of another kind. Many workers joined the Labour Party in 1984 and '85, realising that their struggle was political, and wanting to become politically active. But far more significant was the number of miners and politically conscious workers who left the Labour Party, tearing up their cards in protest at Labour's refusal to back the strike. These workers and their wives, the vanguard, not in the sense of an élite but in terms of their political development, were searching for an alternative. And they now turned to the Workers' Revolutionary Party. Not to the Communist Party – which was conducting a half-open, half-clandestine campaign against Arthur Scargill, lamenting the NUM's decision not to ballot for a strike, and calling more and more publicly for a return to work – but to the WRP.

This was the situation for which Gerry had spent his life working, teaching and preparing. The party had a full-time college of Marxist education. We possessed a printing factory in Runcorn with £750,000 worth of plant and equipment. Astmoor Litho, our printing works, could produce a quarter of a million copies of *Newsline* each day, with full-colour printing superior to that of any Fleet Street newspaper. We produced a steady stream of books and pamphlets, with six bookshops in the largest cities. Youth Training, the movement sponsored by the Young Socialists, had eight youth centres. In Britain we had a political alliance, a united front with the most progressive elements in the Labour Party. Internationally we supported every revolutionary movement and national liberation struggle and had firm political alliances with all the most important trends and tendencies in such movements.

On 1 July 1985, the day after our rally at Alexandra Pavilion, the British state struck out at the WRP, unleashing an attack which it had prepared for a long time. Gerry's secretary, a woman who had been at his side politically for almost twenty years, disappeared. She left a letter with two of her comrades who had been preparing this 'bombshell' for the past nine months, accusing Gerry of sexually assaulting women in the party. The Political Committee rightly concluded that the letter was a provocation. The following day the second bombshell exploded. Mrs Gibson, who was in charge of the party's finance department, announced that two large bills had arrived for a total of £49,000, and the bailiffs were at the door because the party had no funds to pay them. This was strange, because Mrs Gibson and her companions in the finance office had been supplying weekly accounts which showed the party to be solvent, and all its companies in credit. Subsequently, they openly boasted that all the accounts presented to Gerry and the Political Committee had been falsified in order to create the worst possible financial crisis, and one of them signed a statement to this effect. For the time being, however, they offered no explanation.

Corin was voted to take charge of the finance department. He found £250,000 of unpaid bills and every bank account in deficit. He
also found forged copies of title deeds to party property in the finance office. The forgeries had blanked out entries on the charge sheets showing that the properties, unknown to the party, had been mortgaged to the hilt. The true copies of the title deeds were now, of course, in the vaults of the bank which had mortgaged them. He discovered that, unknown to any party committee, Mrs Gibson had promised the party's accountant that the WRP would redeem itself from insolvency by selling all its principal assets.

We raised, almost immediately, £100,000 in donations from party
members and supporters to pay off the most pressing debts. Corin, together with a sub-committee of members including Gerry, put the financial affairs of the party companies on a sounder footing. Credit, which had been refused by almost every company we traded with, was restored. The worst of our financial crisis, in the short term, was overcome. This was what the state feared. Gerry still commanded great support in the party ranks. The members knew that he more than anyone had built the party and that his opponents, university lecturers who only yesterday had voted with him for every decision, had built nothing at all. Moreover his work was still intact: no premises had been sold, the party held on to all its assets.

Now, in September 1985, *agents provocateurs* in the party began to do their work more openly. By October they had organised internationally, in sections of the ICFI (International Committee of the Fourth International) and here in Britain entire branches began to withhold subscriptions and dues. An emergency Central Committee meeting was summoned for 12 October by Mike Banda, the party's General Secretary, who had firmly opposed the provocations at first, but now had changed sides and headed the opposition. On the day of this meeting Banda and others had organised a mob of 200 members to descend on the party centre, demanding Gerry's expulsion and the resignation of the Political Committee which supported him. Three-quarters of the mob set up camp in the main warehouse, with loudspeakers to relay the proceedings of the Central Committee to them. Banda addressed them before the meeting began, urging 'restraint' and 'political maturity'. A small group was dispatched to Gerry's flat in Clapham High Street, with orders to seize him and frog-march him down to the centre, to face a show trial, and run the gauntlet of a lynch mob in the warehouse. We had found some temporary accommodation for him, and the raiding party came away empty-handed. For the next three months he changed addresses frequently. Twice before, in 1982 and '83, he had been the target of assassination attempts, and for the remainder of his life he would be in continual danger.

Corin had put forward a financial report for the Central Committee on 12 October, showing how for the past three years a group of five Central Committee members – Gibson, Bruce, Jennings, Cowen and Harris – had manipulated the party's finances, forging signatures on documents, mortgaging properties and contracting huge debts, without the knowledge of the party or the approval of any of its committees. He demanded that his report should be given to every party member, and charges be brought against these members who had wrecked the party's finances. A minority of twelve members supported him. But the Central Committee refused to consider his report or circulate it to the party. (The following year it was published in full in the *Marxist Review*, and submitted in evidence to the Companies Court under Mr Justice Harman.)

Two weeks later, on 26 October, the party was split. We called an emergency conference at the Great Western Hotel in Paddington and asked all members to attend who supported the policies and principles of the party and International Committee, and opposed the witch-hunt and the slanders against Gerry. More than half the members came, and two sections of the International Committee, in Greece and Spain, sent delegates and messages of unanimous support. The majority of the old Central Committee called their own conference, then proceeded to invite the press to the party centre in Clapham offering stories of sex and violence, for which, of course, they found a ready market. The technique is a familiar one and is used by state security agencies in every country. The FBI used agents to plant electronic bugs on Martin Luther King in order to compile a dossier of scandal and 'immorality' against him. Winnie Mandela has faced the same kind of attack from agents of BOSS, the South African Bureau of Security Services. In our case the state security services had a dual purpose: their stories were intended to discredit Gerry and the party he had built, and to create a climate in which any attempt on his life could be attributed to the blind, incomprehensible vendetta of 'Trotskyists'. The stories also served as a cover for the liquidation of all the resources which he had built. In a short while the printing presses were sold, the party headquarters, and the youth training centres. It was a lucrative process and large sums of money changed hands. Our centre at Clapham was sold in 1987 for £166,000. The following day it changed hands again, for £488,000. In the era of Thatcher and Reagan, when billions of dollars of fictitious value could be accumulated through junk bonds, mortgage bonds and interest-rate swaps, such transactions hardly raised an eyebrow.

Social being determines social consciousness. The morality of Thatcherism, a gospel according to which 'there is no such thing as society, there is only the individual', had percolated into our party, borne in on the flood tide of easy money which had swamped the middle classes. A revolutionary party is built on the devotion and self-sacrifice of its members, who work long hours, forgoing their own comfort and their families', often risking all chance of promotion in their work, and sometimes their jobs as well. Only a high level of theoretical understanding will sustain them, enabling them to see their goal clearly when the conditions for achieving it are most difficult and contradictory. That was why Gerry had placed such emphasis on theoretical training and the study of materialist dialectics. From that vantage point he had predicted a split in the party in 1981, four years before it happened. When it began to unfold he recognised it before any of us, and realised, before we did, that it was the work of the state.

In 1987 I was watching the television news with Gerry at my house in West Road, Clapham, where Gerry lived and worked for the last four years of his life and which I had bought in 1985. The government were fighting a battle in the Australian courts to ban the publication of *Spycatcher* by Peter Wright, an ex-MI5 agent. I sent off to a friend in America for copies of the book and there on page 360 was Wright's account of MI5's attack on the Workers' Revolutionary Party. He described a crucial meeting in 1972, when

Michael Hanley, the Director-General, ordered a major shift in the agency's resources and manpower from K branch, which dealt with counter-espionage against the Soviet Union, to F branch, which was responsible for 'domestic subversion', meaning political parties in Britain, including the Workers' Revolutionary Party. An argument had developed between Wright and a senior officer, John Jones, concerning the best method of spying on the WRP. Jones favoured electronic surveillance, Wright preferred to use agents. In point of fact both methods were employed. Every office in our party headquarters in Clapham was bugged, and agents were sent into the party, and recruited from amongst the membership.

All through the autumn and early winter of 1985 and during the most hectic days of the split in our party I was working at the Queen's Theatre playing Madame Arkadina in Chekhov's *The Seagull*. The production had begun at the Lyric Theatre in Hammersmith, with Samantha Eggar and John Hurt as Arkadina and Trigorin, but as they could not transfer with the production to the West End, Jonathan Pryce and I took over. Natasha played Nina in both productions. We only had about two weeks' rehearsal with the new cast, and I will always remember our first read through. Natasha's eyes were lit up with excitement throughout, and afterwards she said, 'Oh what a wonderful read through that was.' I was so happy to see her proud of me. Sadly we had very little dialogue together on stage. 'What is it like to be acting with your daughter?' I was asked. I had to restrain myself from raving on and on about her performance, which might have seemed somewhat too partial. But in truth I did not see how it could be bettered. I had read and thought a good deal about Olga Knipper, Chekhov's wife, who created the part. She had a trace of a Friesian accent, which hinted at her German origins, and she was fiercely independent, and sometimes disrespectful, even of Stanislavsky. Natasha's voice compels you to listen, which is a great gift. But more than that, she made you believe in what she saw in Trigorin, which was of course more than he saw in himself. And what does she see in herself? Nina's extraordinary soliloquy in the fourth act – 'I am a seagull' – is impossible if the actress sees only Nina's own estimation of herself, as an untrained *ingénue* in provincial theatre, finding herself out of her depth in parts that are beyond her powers. What wrecks the lives of Nina and Konstantin is not the cruel limitation of their own talent, or their capacity to mistakenly love the best in others, but the restrictions their society set upon all creativity, which meant that *The Seagull* was booed off the stage at its first performance. Our production, however, was praised to the skies, and in spring of the following year I was awarded the Olivier/Observer Prize for my performance as Arkadina.

*Homo sum, et nihil humanum alienum puto.* Marcus Aurelius' epigram should be a compulsory text, engraved on every magistrate's bench. I thought of it as I read Reneé Richards extraordinary, courageous autobiography. Linda Yellen our producer on *Playing For Time* had sent me the book, and a script based upon it, for a CBS film to be shot in January 1986. Linda's note said that it would be a 20-day shooting period, and though I had had to refuse the chance to play *The Seagull* in New York, which was a great disappointment as I would have loved Natasha's performance to be seen on Broadway, I knew, as I read Reneé's story, that this was something I wanted to do very much. Reneé, when she was a man, ranked amongst the best hundred tennis players in the world. But as she grew up she realised she had a problem which was not psychological but physiological: she was a woman, trapped inside the body of a man, and if she was to become herself she had to change, not her mind, as many in the medical profession attempted to persuade her, but her body. Reading her story I realised how many of my notions of what is normal, or healthy were based on ignorance and fear, and I was alarmed. If I, who thought myself an unprejudiced person, could have been guilty of such stereotyped thinking, how much more so someone whose ignorance was regularly played upon by politicians, judges and the press?

I spent a happy and fascinating evening with Reneé after we had completed shooting *Second Serve*. It wasn't that I had planned not to meet her before, it simply happened that way. I was glad of that because it made me re-read her book and concentrate upon what she was writing about. If I had met her before shooting I might have been tempted to copy what I saw, or thought I saw in her. Linda and Tony Page, our director, arranged a meeting, before we started filming, with a Los Angeles group of transsexuals. They told me how commonly they were treated as outcasts or untouchables, and how many of them had lost their jobs after they had had their operations. It was amazing, they said, how many spurious reasons and excuses were forthcoming for firing them, to explain why they, as women, could not perform the job they had been doing as men, jobs which they remained every bit as capable of after their operations as before.

Forrest Stewart was my coach for the tennis scenes, one of the best tennis teachers in Los Angeles, though no one, not even he, could make me into a shadow of the tennis player Joely had become. All the while I was learning from him I was conscious of her critical eye. But my height and my build helped a lot, and Forrest, like every great teacher, including my beloved Litz Pisk, taught me what was essential. How I should move, and how I should think.

I'd asked for my friend Peter Owen, an expert wig maker, to make my wigs, and he, I, and Del Ecevedo, George C Scott's make-up artist, talked late into the night experimenting to find out how my appearance as Dick – Reneé as a man – could carry conviction in close-ups. The general consensus was that I should wear a wig as Dick, and my own hair as Reneé, so Peter made a number of different men's wigs and we camera tested them.

And then, when we'd broken for lunch, and Linda, Tony and the crew had gone for a meal, I sat with Peter staring at my unconvincing silhouette, profile and rear-view in the three-sided mirror and said 'Let's go for it. Cut off my hair!' Neither of us had agreed with the general consensus, and now I felt sure we were right. Peter explained that almost every man who has a head of hair, has more or less, a widow's peak, so he shaved my forehead at the temples to give me one. Two other things, he said, distinguish a man's head and neck from a woman's: the Adam's apple, and two prominent occipital bones at the base of the skull. Unusually, I have a slight Adam's apple, so that distinction was no problem. And with my shirt collar turned up I could disguise the back of my neck. Linda Yellen had suggested I should have brown eyes, and I remembered how Laurence Naismith, when we were shooting *Camelot* had wanted green eyes for Merlin and had come back from an optometrist in San Fernando Valley with a pair of perfect emerald green contact lenses. Luckily he was still there, and soon I had brown lenses.

Dick, it seemed to me, would have been slow to speak his thoughts, not 'chatty' or talkative, precisely because he thought such a lot. Conversely, when I played a scene with Alice Krige in the first serious love affair which Dick had, I thought of the enormous physical and spiritual exuberance some very young men have when in love, especially those who are most silent and uncommunicative.

Twenty days of hard work. *Second Serve* was shown in America soon after we'd completed filming, and besides all the commotion and the hundreds of pictures of me with cropped hair and beard stubble as Dick, it was very well received. I was nominated for an Emmy award. But to my great disappointment the film was never shown in Britain. Neither the BBC or ITV companies would buy it, and I can only suppose that some prejudice against the subject must have influenced their decision. A pity, if it were so, because the film served, in a small way, to overcome the fear and ignorance which surrounds transsexuality.

# 24

There are certain parts which haunt you, teasing your imagination, daring you to play them again. Cleopatra is one. My first attempt had been interrupted by what insurers describe as *force majeure*, the cloudburst that swamped Sam Wanamaker's tent theatre on Bankside. I waited twelve years before my next attempt. It began well enough. Tim Dalton and I sat down with Duncan Weldon and planned a season at the Haymarket in which we would play *Antony and Cleopatra* and *The Taming of the Shrew* in repertory. In 1986 it was almost impossible to find an impresario who would risk producing a straight play in the West End with a company of twenty-two actors. But Duncan agreed. Having crossed that bridge we decided that anything was possible and embarked on rehearsals at the Chiswick Social Club in high spirits. I had moved from the house in Ravenscourt Road to a flat in a mansion block on Chiswick High Road. I loved my new flat, which had nice rooms for Carlo and Joely, and relished the thought of walking a mere fifty yards down the road to rehearsals. It had been a cold winter, and the first morning of rehearsal in February was also the first whiff of spring.

By the time we were about to open, in April, for a six week pre-London season at Theatre Clwyd in North Wales, I was in despair. I had chosen a long blonde wig, which in everyone's opinion except mine, was a disaster, and I was using it to hide from the audience. Kika Markham, Corin's second wife, played Octavia. She remembers coming into my dressing room and seeing me covering my face with plague spots. Apparently I said they were freckles. Tim and I had reached a natural pause in our relationship, but I could not recognise it at the time, and there was sadness and tension between us. The local papers were absolutely scathing about our first performance. Actors usually dismiss their notices in

258

provincial papers in the belief that their praise is too easily won and their criticism too uninformed to matter, but in this case we had an uncomfortable feeling that the *North Wales Echo* was right.

I sent an SOS to Corin, who came up the next night with Gerry. Next morning we had a discussion over breakfast. Corin talked about Fulvia, Antony's first wife, whose death is reported in the second scene of the play. He rolled the name around his tongue, and conjured up such a caricature of Fulvia that I began to laugh, imagining all the reasons why Cleopatra loathed this Roman matriarch. We talked about why Cleopatra insists on a naval battle with Octavius, and why she is called a 'gypsy'. He said I should read Prosper Mérimée's 'Carmen', the short story that inspired the opera. I felt better. I sent my long wig back to London, and asked for Arkadina's wig from *The Seagull* to be sent up. It was only a stop-gap, but it had tight red curls on top, a step in the right direction.

We were in Clwyd when the news of the Chernobyl meltdown came through. All that week figures in Roman armour and Eastern gauzes, Jacobean ruffs, ribbons and garters, gathered round the television in the green-room, as the stories came through of gallant efforts by Soviet helicopter pilots and firemen to prevent the catastrophe from spreading further. Outside, the sun shone, and great grey rainclouds sent their shadows racing across the hills. Spring had come late, with a burst of bluebells.

It was hard to believe, in all the din of rushing water from the melted snow, and the lambs bleating on the hillsides, that such beautiful country was being poisoned every minute by the Chernobyl disaster. The Ministry of Defence in Whitehall put out a statement and statistics designed to prove that whatever increases in radiation had taken place were acceptably below the danger level. A rumour that the alarm outside the North Wales reactor had been activated was hushed up. But the townspeople in Clwyd knew better. They lived in the shadow of nuclear power. They had relatives or friends in Cumbria, near the nuclear plant at Sellafield, where stories persisted of uncommonly high levels of leukaemia amongst children, and where fish-and-chip shops have notices in the window saying 'No *local* fish sold here'. Many had friends or family who were hill farmers, and who knew that their sheep and cattle would be storing radiation in their bones and milk because with every fall of rain it would be building up in the soil and the grass.

There was something else to note in the television film from Chernobyl. Gorbachev had demanded a full inquiry, and was said to be furious at the attempts which had been made, in the first days after the meltdown, to prevent the news from breaking out. I wasn't present at our Political Committee's meetings at this time, but I followed the way *Newsline* reported the Chernobyl accident. I couldn't understand why, after the first few days, the reports tapered off. Then came an editorial defending the right of the Soviet Union to have nuclear weapons. I thought yes, of course, our party has always supported that right, but why is this being asserted now – why now? Corin told me that Sheila Torrance, our general secretary after the split in 1985, had criticised the paper's first attempts at reporting the accident, saying they simply followed the line of the Fleet Street press, which was magnifying the disaster because it opposed the Soviet Union's right to develop nuclear power and nuclear weapons. I couldn't understand this line of reasoning. It seemed self-evident that the only people with an interest in minimising the Chernobyl disaster were those Stalinist bureaucrats in the government and the state planning industry departments, whether in Moscow or the Ukraine, whose negligence had helped to create it. But for the moment I simply filed these questions at the back of my mind, to return to them later.

Something had changed, though. In May the Soviet Film-Makers' Union elected Elem Klimov as their new general secretary. Many of his films had been banned under the previous regime. And then in June the Soviet Writers' Union held a conference and removed more than a third of the old leadership. Georgy Markov, the union's first secretary since 1971, was replaced by Vladimir Karpov, the sixty-four-year-old editor of *Novy Mir*, who had been a prisoner in Stalin's gulags. Yevtushenko, Bulat Okhudzhava and Bella Akhmadulina were on the new 63-member secretariat.

In August we were playing *Antony* and *The Taming of the Shrew* at the Haymarket. Somehow we had survived, with good reviews and excellent audiences, and Tim's Petruchio was brilliant. David Thacker, whose work at the Young Vic I had seen and liked with Natasha and then with Corin in *The Crucible*, came to see our productions. Margot Leicester, his wife, was playing Charmian, and was pregnant. The question had arisen whether we should tour with *Antony*. It was impossible to continue at the Haymarket, although we were playing to capacity, because Jack Lemmon was following us in *A Long Day's Journey into Night*. I badly wanted to go on and play on tour, even though we had had a hard time making something good of our productions. I felt sure there was still much room for improvement in my own performance as Cleopatra. But I couldn't bear to re-rehearse with a new Charmian, because I couldn't see how she could be bettered, especially in Charmian's immensely difficult scene after Cleopatra's death.

It was then that David Thacker suggested we do a play at the Young Vic, and I proposed Ibsen's *Ghosts*. I knew very little about the play. *Ghosts* had been neglected in my lifetime and one of the stupidest assumptions behind its neglect was that Ibsen's knowledge of the effects of venereal disease was inaccurate, and therefore made the play 'irrelevant' to modern audiences. I remembered that Michael was going to play Oswald at the Old Vic in a season he would have shared with Robert Donat, which was cancelled when the war broke out in 1939. But two events had made me think about Ibsen. The first was Chernobyl and Gorbachev's insistence that the truth of the disaster be made known. 'When you go out to fight for the truth you should put on a new coat,' says Stockman in *The Enemy of the People*. Stanislavsky describes in his memoirs how this line brought the audience to its feet one night when the 1905 revolution against the Tsar was at its height. And in Stalin's time every political opponent was labelled an 'enemy of the people'.

The second thing that made me think about Ibsen, and particularly about *Ghosts*, was my dear friend Bob Regester's death from AIDS. Bob had many friends who loved him. Natasha was with him when he died. But it was terrible to know that hundreds of people would have to battle, not only against the disease, but against the ignorance and fear which were being deliberately stoked up against homosexuals and bisexuals.

In August I read reports of Gorbachev's visit to Khabarovsk, in the east of the USSR. 'Those who are unwilling to change must go,' he said, and demanded that Communist Party officials should be 'more open in their dealings, more self-critical, and more democratic'. Gerry was convinced that *perestroika* and *glasnost*, the twin policies which had been proclaimed at the 27th Congress of the CPSU in April 1986, were the forms within which a political

261

revolution against the Stalinist bureaucracy was unfolding. It would not be long, he thought, before we saw the rehabilitation of Leon Trotsky in the Soviet Union.

But the more he argued on our Political Committee that a political revolution was under way, breaking up Stalinism and Stalinist dogma, the more we encountered a wall of opposition. For us it was axiomatic that we must intervene to the utmost of our ability in these great changes in the Soviet Union, supporting them in every way we could. For our opponents *perestroika* amounted to nothing more than a counter-revolution, carried out by the political descendants of Stalin. For supporting *perestroika* Gerry and I were accused of 'capitulating to Stalinism'. We realised that the split we had made before had been incomplete.

*Ghosts* transferred from the Young Vic, where it played for six weeks 'in the round' to Wyndham's Theatre in the Charing Cross Road, for a limited run of twelve weeks, and then a week at the National Theatre in Oslo. I had spent several weeks before and during the rehearsal period studying Ibsen and the conditions in which *Ghosts* was first performed: before an invited audience, in a drawing room in Bloomsbury. Ibsen was a socialist, and his first champion in England was Marx's daughter, Eleanor Marx Aveling. It was for this reason, I felt sure, that the first official reaction to his play was fear and loathing. And the other reason was imperial arrogance. If there was one thing the English of the 1880s and 1890s hated even more than being preached to it was being preached to by a representative of a very small nation on the outer fringe of European civilisation.

I began to learn Norwegian, by no means well enough to translate Ibsen's play, but enough to realise that we could not use any of the existing translations without falling into assumptions about Ibsen's meaning which might not be correct. I persuaded the Young Vic to commission a literal translation and to have a Norwegian scholar present throughout the rehearsal so that the whole cast could work collectively on the translation and could check every phrase and nuance against the original. We were taken to task for this by the critic of *The Financial Times*, who besides finding our production 'soporific' (I suppose that meant he fell asleep after an early supper), thought our collective approach to the text too egalitarian by half. In point of fact it had nothing to do with egalitarianism. But it concentrated our attention on Ibsen's text, and that was a good starting point for work each day.

I am certain that this approach contributed to the success of the production, the most successful run of any play by Ibsen in the West End. But above all it was the spirit of the times, in which the 'new thinking' proclaimed by Gorbachev stirred our audiences and made them consider aspects of our own society in a new light. Oswald's 'Give me the sun!' had a new urgency and conviction. Mrs Alving's horror at lies 'creeping like ghosts behind the words in newspapers' had an immediacy for the audience as well as for me.

In March Thelma Holt invited me to accompany her to the Soviet Union. She had been asked to produce an international festival at the National Theatre on the South Bank. Peter Stein's Schaubuhne Teater were coming in May with Eugene O'Neill's *The Hairy Ape*, Ingmar Bergman's Royal Dramatic Theatre from Stockholm would arrive in June, the Ninagawa Company would appear in September, and she wanted a Soviet production for October. The new Minister of Culture had invited her to Moscow, Riga and Armenia to see for herself and choose a production.

Riga was buzzing with vitality. There was a new exhibition of posters, extremely sharp and satirical, against the bureaucracy, and a brilliant documentary film directed by Yuri Podnicks, *It Isn't Easy to be Young*. Thelma and I scuttled along icy pavements, seeing every production we could, five in three days. The most exceptional was at the Rainis Theatre, *A Day is Longer than a Century*, based on the novel by Chingis Aytmatov. It was brilliantly staged, adapting cinematic techniques of 'cross-fading' and 'mixing', from the desert sands on the edge of a military space complex in Tajikistan today, to a space module hurtling through the galaxy in search of life on another planet, to one of Stalin's gulags fifty years ago where prisoners were building the railroad. It was playing in repertoire with a stock production of Schiller's *Elizabeth*, quite typical of the type of work which found favour in the pre-*perestroika* period.

On the road from the airport to Yerevan, the capital of Armenia, we asked our driver to stop for a moment so we could get out and look across at Mount Ararat. It was a grey, cloudy day. Everything was 'normal', said our driver. And there was Ararat, the ancient mountain of Armenia, except that it wasn't Armenian, and no Armenian could climb about its crags without a visa. The frontier of

Turkey had advanced in the 1915–19 war, devouring a large chunk of Armenia and the Armenian people. It seemed to me I could see eagles high in the clouds around the peaks where Noah's ark had settled and where Noah had planted the first vine from which sprang Armenian grapes.

The streets of Yerevan were grey and desperately neglected. The Stalinists on the Central Committee of the Armenian CP still controlled everything. They held all the top and middle-rung posts in industry, culture, sport and tourism, and they used their control to feather their own nests. They toasted Gorbachev, hung his portrait above their desks, voting with both hands for all his resolutions and carrying out none of them, except those laws which enabled them to make their own deals abroad.

Our young interpreter, who spoke excellent English, took us to see his father, and that was how we came to meet Gevorg Emin, the greatest living poet of Armenia, and latest in a centuries-old tradition. This short, rock-sturdy man, nearly seventy years old, was trained as an hydraulic engineer, and began to write poety in 1940. In the preface to the American edition of his work he wrote 'These poems are my true autobiography.' I began to read 'Ararat', 'Thaw' and 'Small', and could not stop, horrified by my ignorance and thrilled by the sense of discovery which comes when another human being opens your eyes and ears, telling you what you did not know and revealing that what you thought you knew amounted to very little. What exhilaration, what excitement, when you read a poem and think 'I am not alone'. Gevorg Emin wrote 'Small' to describe his people, and himself too.

> Small, yes
> you have compressed us,
> world, into a diamond.
>
> Small,
> you have dispersed us,
> scattered us like stars
> We are everywhere
> in your vision.
>
> Small,
> but our borders stretch
> from Pyrragan Telescopes
> to the moon

With Gerry and Selwa Abu Khadr in Kuwait, 1979 (*right*); Gerry and I backstage at the Sovremennik Prisoners' March, Moscow, with Marina Nielova and the cast of *The Steep Route*, about women prisoner's in Stalin's Gulag, February 1989 (*centre*); and (*below*) January 1991, two days before the end of the UN deadline and the start of the war against Iraq, at a public meeting for Symposium 1990 in tribute to Gerry Healy.

Corin and I outside the
Law Courts in London
in 1978 during the
hearings of our libel case
against *The Observer*
(*above*); playing
Arkadina, the famous
actress, with Natasha as
Nina, the would-be
actress, in Chekhov's
*The Seagull* at the
Queen's Theatre, 1985
(*right*).

Me, Joely and Tasha,
summer 1990 (*right*); a
family snap of Lynn and
me; and (*below*) a walk
on Hampstead Heath
one Sunday in summer
1990 with Rachel and
Carlo, nearly twenty
years old.

Lynn as Masha, me as Olga and Jemma as Irina in *Three Sisters* at the
Queen's Theatre, directed by Robert Sturua.

from Houssaran backwards
to Urarth

Small as the growth
of marvellous uranium
Which cannot be broken down
put out, or consumed.

Artashes, Gevorg's son, was a wonderful host, discussing and explaining everything, showing us how modern artists work in Yerevan. Making our way through a half-completed building we found a group of young people screen-printing posters and recording music. Their mood was in sharp contrast to the subdued and demoralised atmosphere in the theatre. There we were shown a film, made two years before, of Shakespeare's *Coriolanus*, with a superb performance in the leading role. We could not understand why the director and producer never referred to this fine actor by name and had great difficulty remembering it when asked. Later we learned from one of the cast that he had been banished to a small town.

The theatre director invited us for a special performance. 'Will Gevorg be there?' I asked Artashes; time was racing by and we badly wanted to meet him again. He would not be invited, Artashes told us, unless we asked for an invitation for him. So we asked and he came, and sat with us in our box, together with Ramaz Tchikvadze's wife Natasha who had come by train from Tbilisi, to meet us. We noticed how the directorate treated Gevorg and his wife as non-persons, as if they simply were not there. There and then Thelma proposed that we invite Gevorg to a poets' platform at the National Theatre in October, as part of the International Festival, and I promised to read his poems in English.

With one exception, *Autobus* by a Bulgarian author, the productions in Yerevan were poor, and the actors themselves were the first to acknowledge it. It was immensely difficult to choose a production for London but we narrowed it down to a choice between the brilliantly staged and acted Latvian production, *A Day is Longer than a Century*, and a far more modest production by the Mayakovsky Theatre Company in Moscow of a story by Boris Vasiliev, *Tomorrow was War*. It showed a group of boys and girls in their final year at high school in 1940–1. Stalinist persecution was at its height and reached right into the lives of these schoolchildren and their parents, bringing tragedy and a new consciousness of what, in spite of Stalin's crimes, they would fight to defend against the Nazis. The audience wept in recognition of these children, their parents, most of them about to be killed in the 'tomorrow' which was war, and despite the brilliance of the Riga production, we felt we must choose Vasiliev's play. Thelma announced our choice to Mikhail Ulyanov at the Actors' Club in Gorky Street, and I suggested that when the production arrived at the National Theatre in October, I would read the simultaneous translation.

And so it came about that my first job at the National Theatre was working in their sound-booth. My father was one of the very few actors in Britain who had consistently championed the idea of a national theatre during the Forties and Fifties, at a time when most actors and directors dismissed the need for such a centre. He led the company, with Olivier, in their first season at the Old Vic, and gave his last performances in London at the Lyttelton Theatre, directed by Harold Pinter, in 1979. I, on the other hand, was never offered a season at the National Theatre, and as I settled down to work in the sound-booth it crossed my mind, as Rosa Dartle might have said, to wonder why. But not for long. I would not have exchanged this job for anything. In fact, a month before, I was offered a job which I would have preferred to anything but this, in a film with Woody Allen. I longed to work with him, and still do, but I had promised the Mayakovsky that I would speak the live translation, and I knew I must keep my promise.

The Schaubuhne company was preceded by an immense reputation. So were Bergman's company and the Ninagawa. But London theatre-goers knew nothing of the Mayakovsky company, or of their author Boris Vasiliev, and only a very few seats were sold in advance. The National Theatre management were sceptical about this new work by a company which had never travelled outside the Soviet Union, and did not seem inclined to rouse themselves into publicising it. I remembered how, years ago, we had all turned out to meet the Moscow Art Theatre at Stansted airport, so I sat down by the telephone and rang everyone I could find. Peggy Ashcroft, Anthony Quayle, Tim Dalton, Kenneth Branagh and I met the company at Liverpool Street station off the boat train from Harwich, and that earned a picture in the London *Standard*. Michael Billington chaired an excellent, lively conversation-cum-interview with Vasiliev and the Mayakovsky's director,

Nikolai Goncharov. It all helped to sell tickets, as did my name on the poster. But in the end the company made its own success. The audience at their first performance warmed to them slowly, slowly, these very accomplished but modest young actors. An audience will cheer and stamp a virtuoso, a showman who astounds them with his skills, and sometimes they will take him to their hearts. These actors were neither virtuosi nor showmen, but they had something more rare, a total trust in the truth of what they were performing. At the end the applause was slow to begin, and grew slowly, wave upon wave, until the whole audience was standing. The last three performances were sold out, and to everyone's delight and astonishment, including mine, the Mayakovsky company was second only to the Ninagawa in popularity that season.

I visited the Soviet Union three times in 1987. Each time I had prepared a list of people whom I wanted to meet – historians, writers, artists – and every assistance was given me to meet them. I took books by Trotsky, none of which were published or available in the USSR, and no one ever opened my baggage or suggested I should not give them to Soviet friends to read. The Lubyanka still housed the KGB, and within the KGB were many who were working for a return to the time of Stalin and Brezhnev. Undoubtedly they followed my activities in Moscow and reported on them. But much more evident was the surveillance of the CIA. 'Hi,' said my new friend, in the lift of the National Hotel near Red Square, 'I used to work for *Ramparts*. Remember *Ramparts*?' I did indeed, and remembered how infested that magazine was with agents from Langley, Virginia, so 'Yes, I do remember *Ramparts*,' I replied with a big grin, and my new-found 'friend' grinned from ear to ear, and attached himself like a leech. I remembered an old gentleman in the Army telling me that the way to deal with leeches was to burn them with the end of your cigar, but I didn't think Langley, Virginia would take kindly to such treatment, so I used politeness instead, and said 'no, thank you' with deadly courtesy to all his invitations.

My second visit, in June, was to the Moscow International Film Festival, as a guest of the Film-Workers' Union. They had prepared a centre at Dom Kino, their club, for all their foreign guests. In the hall a seminar was about to begin. Vladimir Posner sat in one of the simultaneous-translation booths with Alla Pugacheva, the rock star. Stanley Kramer, Robert de Niro and Gregory Peck sat in the audience. Professor Yuri Afanasiev was on the platform, as was Mikhail Shatrov the playwright. When the discussion began I approached the microphone and was about to speak when someone tugged my sleeve from behind. 'Please let me speak first,' he asked. *'Please.'* As it was clear that he was burning with impatience to say something, I said, 'Please, go ahead.' It was Sasha Oskaldov. His film *The Commissar* had been shot in the 1960s with Rolan Bykov as a Jewish carpenter whose family shelters a young pregnant commissar in the Civil War. Soon after his film was completed he was fired from MosFilm, and had been banned from directing ever since. One of the highlights of this festival was a special screening of banned films, and Oskaldov demanded that his film should be included. When my turn came to speak I backed him up. Within a few moments Elem Klimov announced from the platform that the timetable would be altered so that Oskaldov's film could be shown that afternoon. It was an exhilarating taste of the new Soviet democracy in action.

Before I left London Gerry had urged me to see Mikhail Filippovich Shatrov. We had read excerpts from his plays in translation and we knew that his was one of the most powerful voices in the political revolution. Gerry had selected two books to give him; Trotsky's *The Stalin School of Falsification*, and a book by the great Soviet philosopher Evald Ilyenkov, *Leninist Dialectics and the Metaphysics of Neo-Positivism*, which we ourselves had translated and published in English.

We drove, my dear young friend Leila who taught English and I, through the leafy lanes to a small wooden bungalow, Shatrov's dacha at Peredelkino. He was fifty-five that year, short, grey-haired and hardly ever smiling. He welcomed me with great warmth, and immediately, without so much as two sentences of small-talk politenesses, began to talk about the reasons for my visit. Born in 1932, Shatrov's life was a paradigm of the entire era encompassing the struggle, with all its tragedies, against Stalinism. His parents were leading revolutionaries, his uncle was Alexei Rykov, one of the leading Bolsheviks in Lenin and Trotsky's time. Shatrov's father was shot in 1937. His mother was arrested in 1949. Not long ago she found herself standing in a queue at a supermarket behind a very tall man. When he turned round, she was face to face with her former torturer, who had fractured her skull in the Lubyanka prison.

We visited Pasternak's grave. The cemetery was full of trees, a jungle of tangled briars and weeds. One well-worn, narrow footpath led through the mass of undergrowth to a small square plot with a stone and railings. 'We have weeded it, you see,' said Mikhail Filippovich. Pasternak had been officially rehabilitated that year. Gesturing around him at the graveyard, and then at Pasternak's tomb, he said: 'It's like this, *perestroika*. A continual struggle against the weeds.'

As we parted he promised to do everything necessary for Gerry and me to obtain visas for a visit in November at the time of the seventieth anniversary of the revolution. His eyes shone when I presented him with Trotsky's book. It was published in the Soviet Union, with an introduction by Professor Vitali Startsev, two years later, but at this time it was still banned and unobtainable. Shatrov knew of it, and knew that it contained the definitive answer to all the Stalinist falsifications and distortions against Trotsky. Of Ilyenkov he said, 'He influenced me and my friends more than any other philosopher.'

It was bitterly cold in November, but Gerry flatly refused to wear the fur hat I had bought him. He had prepared himself for weeks for this visit. The foremost Trotskyist of his time, he was coming to the Soviet Union, where for sixty years Trotsky had been anathematised, his family and secretaries all murdered, and millions had perished in the mass killings of 'Trotskyite-Zinovievite agents of fascism,' 'saboteurs', 'wreckers', 'terrorists' and 'mad dogs'. He was watchful and alert, both tense and relaxed, every second of our visit. At the anniversary parade where only portraits of Lenin appeared, he was very critical, saying 'there are still some blank spots here'. I was feeling fairly euphoric and could not understand why he said it or why he returned to it that evening after a performance of Shatrov's *The Dictatorship of Conscience*. I thought at first he was disappointed that there were no portraits of Trotsky, but he brushed that aside, as if to say of course he hadn't expected that. But Lenin on his own? Without Marx, Engels, Trotsky or Stalin, what could that mean?

He lectured before an audience of historians, professors and lecturers at the Moscow Institute of State Archives. But he didn't choose to talk about Trotsky. He invariably approached every task and every problem from the standpoint of philosophy and on this occasion chose as his starting point the fact that the latest Soviet dictionary of philosophy omits the category of 'semblance', which in Lenin's explanation of the dialectical process of cognition is given great attention and which Gerry considered to be of crucial methodological importance.

The next morning we went to the Vakhtangov Theatre in the Arbat to see the first public preview of Mikhail Shatrov's *The Peace of Brest-Litovsk*. It had been banned in the Soviet Union since it was first written in 1969. Here, for the first time since 1927, Lenin was portrayed on the stage as a human being of flesh and blood. No special lights announced his appearance. Here, also for the first time, the whole of Lenin's Central Committee were presented, likewise as human beings, and when Lenin argued, in a minority against the majority amongst them, he won the argument not by fiat or command, nor by superhuman intelligence, but by the democratic weapons of political argument and persuasion. We were astonished by the force and vitality of the acting – Ulyanov as Lenin, Filipenko as Bukharin and Lanovoy as Trotsky – and by Robert Sturua's direction. There and then we decided to do everything in our power to bring the company to London.

I walked up a flight of rickety wooden steps to a tiny studio. Our guide was a dear friend, the great actor Sergei Yursky. Our host was a painter; Yursky was determined to introduce us to him and to show us some paintings which none but the artist's closest friends had seen. Pyotr Belov was a scenic designer by profession who had spent most of his working life designing sets for the Red Army Theatre. In his spare time, and only for his own pleasure, he took his easel to the woods and fields outside Moscow and painted landscapes. He must have been a very handsome young man, as I could see from an early self-portrait. A happy young man for the most part, who enjoyed his work and did it very well.

Almost everyone you meet in the Soviet Union has lost a father, or a mother, or grandparents, aunts or uncles in the wave of terror, or in the post-war purges, or in the war itself. But there are those, and Pyotr's family was one, whose lives were blessedly unscathed by the repressions. Nothing in his work until 1984 seemed to indicate the painter he has now become. But in that year he had a heart attack, and in convalescence he began to paint allegories against Stalin. In one, the familiar features of Stalin, head and shoulders, are seen peering impassively at an hour-glass. Everything looks normal and composed except – look closer – these are not grains of sand but tiny human skulls.

I wanted Pyotr Belov to design a production of *Orpheus Descending* by Tennessee Williams, which I was planning to do the following year, and we talked of arranging an exhibition of his work in London, but he died the following spring of a second heart attack.

We flew back to London on 10 November, and Corin drove to meet us. 'There are more real Trotskyists in the Soviet Union than I have met anywhere in my life,' Gerry said as we landed.

# 25

In simple arithmetic, two plus two invariably equals four. In higher mathematics it is not necessarily so. In acting, if acting is to be creative, the rules of simple arithmetic and their logical expression, the law of identity – $A=A$ – do not suffice, and the actor who relies upon them will be limited to producing Stanislavsky's 'stencils'. Stanislavsky's teachings, in this respect, may be compared to higher mathematics, in which the rules of simple arithmetic are contained, terminated, superseded, and simultaneously preserved. In political life and struggle, formal logic, a method of thinking in fixed opposites, is dangerous and even downright reactionary: 'A clock without a spring', Trotsky called it. The spring is dialectics. This problem preoccupied all his attention in the last period of his life, during 1939 and 1940.

The same problem had presented itself very acutely in November 1987, the day before Gerry and I left for Moscow. Savas Michael, secretary of the Greek section and of our International Committee, telephoned London urging us to call off our visit. Gorbachev had delivered his speech in the Kremlin, commemorating the seventieth anniversary of the October revolution, and it was reported in the press and on television that he had attacked Trotsky. 'It's not safe for you to go,' Savas Michael said. We were not inclined to heed his advice. It was true, Gorbachev *had* criticised Trotsky, and also Bukharin, repeating many of the old Stalinist lies about them. They constituted the form of his speech, but within it a new and powerful content was stirring. He announced that a commission had been set up, under the Politbureau, to investigate the crimes of Stalin and the Stalinist Comintern. Dialectics here, therefore, was 'the teaching which shows how opposites can be, and how they happen to be – how they become – identical, becoming transformed into one another'.

The old, historical past, sixty years of Stalinist lies and distortions, was contained within the living immediate present, as a unity of opposites. But the dominant opposite was now the new. Three months after Gorbachev's speech the first results of the Commission investigating Stalin's crimes were announced. Bukharin, Rykov, Christian Rakovsky and all the victims of the 1938 Moscow trials were rehabilitated.

Two other decisions were made at this time, February 1988, which we considered crucially important, and which determined much of my activity in the months that followed. The first was the decision to withdraw Soviet troops from Afghanistan, after a decade of occupation which had claimed hundreds of thousands of lives, including those of 50,000 Soviet servicemen. The second was the declaration by Gorbachev recognising the PLO as the sole legitimate leadership representing the Palestinian people, and calling on Israel to withdraw from the occupied territories, the West Bank, Gaza and the Golan Heights, which it had annexed since the 1967 war, in defiance of every resolution of the United Nations.

In March I organised a concert at the Adelphi Theatre in aid of the Arab Women's Association. It was a great success, raising £100,000 for children and orphans in the occupied territories. Nigel Kennedy played an unaccompanied Bach partita, the most beautiful sound imaginable. Julia Migenes and Kris Kristofferson sang. My friend Katharina Wolpe, the daughter of Stefan Wolpe, whose compositions, along with all the Viennese School of Alban Berg, were banned under the Nazis, played Scriabin. And Elisabeth Welch sang 'It had to be you'.

Elisabeth is a remarkable singer, and a woman for whom I have the greatest admiration. She will be found in any gathering of artists who have come together for a purpose which is good and necessary.

'Oh Lord, it's you, Vanessa,' she says, 'what is it this time?' And before I have completed three sentences she interrupts, 'OK. Count me in.' She has never refused, from the first time I asked her to sing at the Roundhouse in a cabaret to raise funds for youth training. The last occasion was in Leningrad, to raise funds for rebuilding the Russian Theatre Workers' Union, whose fine old building and Actors' Club in Gorky Street had been burned to the ground in what was suspected to be an arson attack. There I discovered the secret of Elisabeth's beauty, which is that she never goes to bed. In the white nights of Leningrad she sat up every night till four o'clock in the morning, talking and singing.

I learned a lot from the Adelphi concert. It was a charity concert, without political speeches or statements, as it was required to be by law if it was to raise funds for a registered charity. And yet, gathered together at the Adelphi were Arab and Jewish artistes together with artistes from Europe and America, united for one cause: the children who were the victims of the Zionist occupation. That was an achievement of great practical and political signific-ance. For what brought them together, and singled out this cause as the common aim of their endeavours, was the *intifada*, the Palestinian uprising in the West Bank and Gaza, with sticks and stones confronting the enemy, a war machine armed with all the most modern sophisticated weapons.

In Ramallah and Nablus, and in every town and village of the occupied territories, committees of young men and women had sprung up, which organised the *intifada* with leaflets distributed to the whole population. They were the heart of the intifada. Its political head was Khalil al-Wazir, 'Abu Jihad', Deputy Com-mander of the Palestinian armed forces, and second in command to Chairman Arafat.

I had known Abu Jihad and his family for eleven years, since we had met in the Beka'a valley in Lebanon, in Beirut and in Tunis. There are men, and he was one, whose every breath, thought and action are dedicated to the liberation of the oppressed, not only his own people, but the poor and oppressed of all nations. Every fighter in every national liberation struggle loved Khalil al-Wazir. He was an internationalist in every drop of his blood, and through his leadership, and Yasser Arafat's, the PLO was recognised in all continents and languages as the friend, ally and teacher of all who were struggling for their freedom.

I gasped and cried aloud when I heard he had been assassinated. It was 16 April 1988 and I could hear the radio announcement on the landing outside my front door, where workmen were repairing the stairway.

'In the early hours of the morning . . . a group of gunmen . . . at his home in Tunis . . .'.

I flew immediately to Tunis to pay my respects to Um Jihad and her children. Hanan, her daughter, showed me what had

274

happened. Her father had been shot before her eyes. The little boy, the youngest child, was asleep in his cot in his parents' bedroom when the assassins raked over his cot with sub-machine-guns. It was 48 hours before he could sleep again. The assassins spoke French and Hebrew. There were sixteen of them. They shot Abu Jihad's two bodyguards and a gardener, and rushed the house. He managed to reach his pistol to defend himself and the women and children but they got him before he could fire, and pumped scores of bullets into his body. When they left, Um Jihad and Hanan ran out on to the balcony and screamed for help. The house was in the diplomatic quarter of Tunis, and no one came. Every telephone line in the surrounding area had been cut, and Um Jihad had to walk almost a mile before she could telephone for an ambulance.

Um Jihad sent me a message to read at the memorial meeting we held at the Chelsea Town Hall on 8 May. Talal al Nasry spoke for the General Union of Iraqi Students in Britain. Another speaker was David Kitson, who had been imprisoned for almost twenty years in Pretoria as a founder member of the African National Congress, and a founder of Umkonto We Sizwe, the ANC's armed struggle section; also Mohammed Arif, for the Afro-Asian Solidarity Committee, and Harpal Brar, for the Indian Workers' Association. Gerry spoke for the Marxist Party. He recalled the time when he had first met Abu Jihad, in the Beka'a in 1976. And then a later occasion, in Beirut, when Abu Jihad had asked him to give lectures on dialectical materialism to a group of military cadres in Al Fateh. His voice rose in pitch and urgency as he spoke about the assassins. They escaped by sea. It must have been a major international operation, he said, involving not only the Israelis but the Americans, providing radar cover, and an electronic blackout. 'Why was our brother so lightly guarded?' he asked, 'Why? Two men and an old gardener.' In a situation like the present, 'they will always strike at the leadership'.

When Gerry spoke of a revolutionary situation, he meant not only the intifada but, above all, the political revolution in the Soviet Union: 'I've fought for this political revolution for fifty-two years, and now it's under way, and it interacts within the Gaza strip and the West Bank.'

The more I thought of this connection, the more I realised that the key to the whole situation, both for the Palestinian revolution and for the struggle against anti-Semitism, lay in the political

275

revolution against Stalinism. For years I had wrestled with this problem, which in its starkest and simplest form may be expressed thus: You are against the persecution and oppression of Jews? Then you must support Israel, because Israel is the Jewish state! You are against the oppression and persecution of the Palestinian Arab people, and you condemn Israeli occupation and demand a Palestinian state? Then you must be anti-Semitic! This simple syllogism torments the consciousness of millions. It is false through and through, and every honest person knows it, if only instinctively, to be wrong. But it is one thing to know it, and another thing to be able to prove, in practice, that the struggle against anti-Semitism and for the self-determination of the Palestinians are one and the same, and that they form a single whole. For that, something more than honesty is needed. A thorough knowledge of history is essential, especially the history of the seventy-four years since the October 1917 revolution, whose first decree and declaration was for the right of all oppressed nations to their self-determination

For the next five months, from April until August 1988, I devoted almost all my time and energy to preparing an international concert and conference in Moscow opposing the Israeli occupation of the West Bank and Gaza. There were to be two organising principles – an end to the occupation, and opposition to all forms of racism, including anti-Semitism. Why Moscow? I found myself thinking again and again about Sasha Oskaldov whose film *The Commissar* had been banned for twenty years. But why was it banned? It told a story of the Civil War, when the 'White' armies of Deniken, Yudenich, Wrangel and Kolchak terrorised the country. Everywhere these armies rampaged, they slaughtered Jewish communities in an orgy of revenge against the revolution.

Gerry's speech at our meeting in tribute to Abu Jihad, Oskaldov's film, and the anxiety we both found when we visited Moscow in May that year about the activities of the fascist organisation Pamyat – these were the parts I could now reassemble in a new whole, from which came the idea for the assembly and concert in Moscow against the occupation.

As I began to rehearse Tennessee Williams's *Orpheus Descending* that autumn, I read everything I could find about Sicilian immigration to the Southern States of America. I listened to recordings of Kentucky coal miners and Sicilian copper miners and farmhands. I played them to Peter Hall who was astonished, as I was, by the similarity of their themes and expressions, and even of their rhythms and cadences.

In *Orpheus Descending* Tennessee, at the height of his powers as a poet of the theatre, concentrated all his fear and hatred of oppression. The Klan that set fire to the 'Wop', Lady Torrance's father, was the same Klan that lynched and burned 'Niggers', and the same that daubed swastikas on the doors of Jews.

I spent a weekend with Franco and Carlo on the seashore outside Rome and asked Salvatore, a friend from Naples, about the songs that Tennessee mentions in his play. Salvatore had never read Tennessee Williams, or seen his plays. He had never even heard of him. We were sitting in a tiny garden, surrounded by bamboo bushes and oleander. I told him the names of the songs, 'Cor Ingrata', 'Come le Rose', not even sure that they actually existed or had ever been sung.

'These songs are in your play?' Salvatore looked at me with sudden, keen interest.

'Yes, they are, but I don't know them, and I don't know where to find them.'

'This is a very great writer indeed,' Salvatore said.

'Oh yes, he is, but why do you say that?'

'Because he understands a people who have had to leave their country. They long to return. People think when they hear these songs they are just love songs. No. They are so popular because they express people's love of their land, their homes, their history, their longing and their love for what they have lost.'

So there I was, on the first day of rehearsal, near the Chelsea Embankment, loaded down, as I always am at rehearsal, with as many bags as a pack-horse could carry, filled with books, papers and memorabilia, out of which I triumphantly produced the song-sheets of 'Cor Ingrata' and 'Come le Rose'. Peter was thrilled. Then I gave him a cassette of a musician playing the *marranzano*, a Sicilian instrument which you hold between your teeth and twang with your fingers. It originated in North Africa, and I know of no instrument other than the mandoline that has such a range of expression, with both male and female tonalities. Alas, the score for Peter's production was electronic, from a synthesiser. It was a powerful score, creating an atmosphere of oppression and fear which served the play well. But however remarkable a synthesiser is, it cannot in all its range of sounds reproduce the sound of the *marranzano* or the mandoline.

I worked at this problem, not finding the answer until we re-rehearsed *Orpheus* for the Broadway production the following summer. I paid a call on Hugo D'Alton the great mandoline teacher, in his home above Kenwood on Hampstead Heath. He and his wife Micky understood my determination to learn the instrument, despite the terribly slow progress I made. I consider myself quite musical, and I like to think my fingers can learn new movements, even at fifty. I had learned the cello for John Schlesinger's film of *Yanks*. Many people had patted me on the back for my accomplishment, and not all their compliments were patronising, I thought. But the mandoline tortured me and I tortured it. I became exhausted with the effort, and one night I slumped fast asleep in Hugo's sitting-room, and woke up next morning in his spare bedroom. But despite all, I knew that if I could play a few phrases of 'Cor Ingrata', the sound of a real mandoline would bring a note of the true heartbeat of Sicily.

Lady Torrance was the most difficult part I had ever played and I needed all Peter's help and encouragement. He is an alarming man to work with, if ever you stop to think that his calendar is filled from here until 1999. Then, momentarily, your efforts and those of your company shrink before the vast space of his activity. But his commitment and his concentration are inspiring. In the second week of our pre-London tour, at Bath, I spoke to Tony on the telephone. He loved the play and had directed its first production in England at the Royal Court, with Lea Padovani, in 1959. He had not been to see me in Bath, but Tasha had, and I knew she must have given Tony a full report. He was laconic. He considered the play almost impossible, but he knew how much I wanted it to succeed so he didn't say anything too deflating. But then he added, as an afterthought, 'I hear you're not playing her Italian, you must be out of your mind.'

I paused for a full minute.

'Hello. Are you there?'

'Yes,' I said wearily. As a matter of fact I was croaking. My voice often gives way in the first week of performance, what with the tension, and the shameful habit of smoking too many cigarettes. And I was trying to expand the range of my voice as Lady Torrance, hoping to find some new notes in my upper register.

278

'You must be out of your mind,' he said again. He was not being helpful.

'She's an immigrant,' I replied, 'but she came over on the boat with her father as a child. She should speak Italian?'

'Of course,' Tony persisted. 'You must be out of your mind.'

I really loathed this expression at third hearing. 'I'll think about it,' I said.

'You better had,' said Tony, laughing. 'Tennessee wrote the part for Anna Magnani.'

'You know that?'

'Of course. He was with me all through rehearsal.'

It was Saturday, the last performance in Bath. Next stop Cardiff. I rang Corin.

'Tony says Lady should be played Italian. He says Tennessee wrote the part for Anna Magnani. I don't think so, do you?'

'Of course not,' Corin said. 'She came over on the boat with her father as a child. Naturally she'd speak American.'

'Ye-es,' I said, 'that's what I thought.'

On the train to Cardiff I pored over the text. Why was she called 'Lady' Torrance? Because 'Lady' is the English translation of 'Madonna'. I looked hard for signposts, turns of phrase, expressions which would prove Tony right or wrong. The train to Cardiff takes an hour and fifty minutes, but when we reached Newport, eight miles from Cardiff I was no nearer to finding an answer. As the train pulled into our station I realised that there was only one way to find out. If you want to learn to swim, you must get into the water.

There was an hour scheduled for rehearsal on stage before our first performance. Without telling anyone or explaining what I was doing I began to speak in an Italian accent. I noticed a few of my fellow actors registering silent looks of surprise and shock. After fifteen minutes we had to stop for a technical adjustment and Peter came up on stage.

'I think I must go on trying it this way,' I explained.

'Yes, I think you must,' he answered, with his sexy and engaging smile. At the end of the performance he said,

'Yes, you *must*. Something is releasing in you that is Lady, that wasn't coming out before.'

The company divided sharply on the question, as companies do, getting deeply involved in each other's acting problems. But I knew that the only issue now was to get my Italian accent right, using definite Sicilian expressions.

Maria St Just, who was Tennessee's dearest woman friend and his executor, and one of the best people to turn to for advice and good, clear, detailed suggestions, was also encouraging.

'You must talk a lot of Italian, the more the better, then people will understand completely. That's how we Russians are. We talk English, but all the time we use our Russian blessings and exclamations, and we talk to ourselves in Russian when we're alone.'

For good measure she rang Franco Zeffirelli and got him to sing 'Come le Rose' to me over the telephone late that night.

It had been a fearful week. One night at Bath, during the performance, I heard from a desperate Franco – my Franco – that Carlo had been in a car accident and was in hospital. Every accident I had ever seen in Rome swam in front of my vision and I almost fainted. Tasha and Joely flew out the next morning and promised to let me know immediately if I must leave the play. Peter was wonderfully understanding; he assured me I must go and miss a performance if necessary. That evening the girls telephoned. Carlo was in hospital, badly cut, and with possible concussion. He had been sitting in the back seat of the car and had been thrown out through the back windscreen on to the road. I shuddered to think what impact the crash must have had to force Carlo, 6 feet 3 inches tall, twenty years old and weighing 12½ stone through the rear windscreen, and how near we were to losing him. But he was all right, the girls said, and promised me his cuts would heal and they did. Carlo spent two years at the Centro Sperimentale in Rome studying to be a director and scriptwriter. When he, Natasha and Joely were growing up the fact that we had split families seemed to mean that whenever I had free time and could be with them it coincided with the children rightfully going off to spend their holidays with their fathers in Italy and America. We dealt with this by never arguing about it but accepting it, and it meant that over the years they not only had some wonderful times with their fathers but I was also very good friends with both Tony and Franco.

I first met Gennady Abramov at the Actors' Club in Gorky Street in November 1987. A young man tapped me on the shoulder as I was telephoning. 'Are you Vanessa Redgrave?' He had the most beautiful eyes and looked much as I had pictured Daniel Deronda, George Eliot's hero. I asked him if there was a Jewish theatre in Moscow. There was a group, he said, but they had no theatre, and they were not rehearsing.

By May the following year they had a theatre, out in the Moscow suburbs, on Warsaw Boulevard. Gennady and their director, Alexander Levenbyk, welcomed us and introduced us to the company. The three oldest actors in the troupe had been in Stalin's gulags, up by the White Sea Canal. Specially selected Jews, they said, were put in charge of the Jewish prisoners. 'They were the worst of all.' When Emanuel Nelin, the eldest of the troupe, had returned from the war, decorated for bravery, he had auditioned for the great actor and teacher Solomon Mikhoels, still wearing his army uniform and boots. The great Mikhoels put a gramophone record on the turntable. 'Show me what emotions are aroused in you by this music.' The tune was very stirring, Emanuel said, but he could think of nothing except throwing hand-grenades at German tanks, so he got up and mimed that. Mikhoels accepted him. He spent two years at his school and then joined his company.

Then, in 1948, the pogroms began again. Every Jewish theatre, museum and cultural centre was closed down. Mikhoels was assassinated in what was called, officially, a car accident. Nelin and Lefkovitch were imprisoned, along with many other Jewish artists. Svetlana Alliluyeva, Stalin's daughter, writes about this terrible period in her memoirs, *Twenty Letters to a Friend*. Thousands of Jews were arrested, tortured and shot, charged with membership of an illegal 'Zionist Centre'. At exactly the same time as this was happening in the Soviet Union, Communist Party newspapers abroad, on Stalin's orders, were denouncing Palestinian Arabs as 'Fascists' and applauding Palestinian Jews as 'freedom fighters'.

After 1956 the artists were released from the gulags. But still they were not permitted to form their own theatres and companies, so they worked together privately in their homes striving to keep alive a great tradition. Individually they worked wherever they could: in cabaret, TV or radio. When we met in May, the actors were paid a weekly salary by Moskonsert, as variety artistes. It was certainly an advance on pre-*perestroika* days when they had no regular income at all, but there was still a long way to go. The company had no funds, no lights, no costumes. 'We must tell Ulyanov about this,' we said, 'he'll do something.' Indeed as

President of the Theatre Workers Union he did. When we returned in November the company had self-accounting status, and could keep a large percentage of their box-office income for their own purposes. They had a name The Moscow Jewish Theatre Company: *Shalom*, and a show, *The Train to Happiness* by their resident writer Arkhady Khait, based on stories by Isaak Babel, which told, in songs and sketches the history of their people from pre-revolutionary times until the present. There and then they staged a performance for us, but it was interrupted by a power cut so we came back a few days later and saw the second half. 'You must come to London,' we urged, 'with the Vakhtangov.'

That was how the Soviet Theatre season came about, which my company presented at the Lyric Theatre Hammersmith in February 1989. Both companies were a revelation to London audiences. Robert Sturua's work had been seen in a legendary production of *Richard III* by the Rustaveli Company some years before, and all who knew something of theatre history had heard of the Vakhtangov. But Soviet Jewish Theatre? *Shalom* were a sensation.

All through the summer of 1989 faxes and telephone calls hummed to and fro between New York and London, arguing whether or not our production of *Orpheus* should descend on Broadway. Frank Rich had reviewed our London opening in *The New York Times*, saying that I was a great actress and how shameful it was that I had not been asked to appear on Broadway, because I supported the Palestine Liberation Organisation. Jimmy Nederlander saw the review and decided he wanted me, and Peter's production, for one of his theatres. I was in hard financial difficulties and knew that the first salary that was proposed would only make my problems worse. But I wanted to go, not only because I believed in our production and passionately loved Tennessee's play, but because I thought Frank Rich was right – to be invited to play on Broadway would, in its way, strike a blow against the victimisation and censorship of artistes which was the great danger of the judgment in the case of the Boston Symphony Orchestra. When the Supreme Court in Washington finally refused my leave to appeal, I was even more firmly of that opinion.

In July, August and September I played a three-month season at the Apollo on Shaftesbury Avenue in Martin Sherman's *A Madhouse in Goa*, and for at least part of that time Joely and I worked next door to one another, she at the Lyric Theatre in *Steel Magnolias*.

It was not perhaps as great a pleasure as working together in the same play, but it felt good all the same. I longed to work with Joely. Twice I have almost done so, but neither time did I succeed, first because she fell ill, and the next time because she had second thoughts. Joely is fiercely independent, and wants to do things in her own time and in her own way. In 1985 she played my character as a young woman in the film *Wetherby*, and won a BAFTA Award for it. But that was that. I was proud of this independence. I saw her performance three times, in her mid-week matinée, and I knew how good she was. It gives me enormous pleasure to watch both Natasha and Joely on stage. I really think they are exceptional actresses, and so even if they were not my daughters I would be thrilled by their work.

Dr Swee Chai Ang came to our theatre between shows to talk to the cast. She had been in the Gaza hospital through the siege of Beirut and then during the massacres of the Palestinians in the Sabra and Chatila camps. She had been a doctor for UNRWA for a year, and now toured the world, raising funds for medical aid for the Palestinians. I had invited her to speak to the cast because we were discussing amongst ourselves a midnight benefit perform- ance of *A Madhouse in Goa* in aid of the Arab Women's Association and Centre Point, a charity for the homeless in London. A young member of our cast whom I liked and respected very much could not accept my explanations of the Palestinians' cause. He was Jewish, and had been taught many untrue things, not all of which he believed, about the PLO. I found I could not convince him, but I felt sure that Dr Swee could, and so it proved. Together we raised some funds in that midnight performance, and the money the AWA received went to buy an operating table for the Gaza hospital.

It was finally agreed that I should go with *Orpheus* to New York, yet more proof, I thought, of the great political changes brought about by *perestroika* and the intifada. On the day that bookings opened our producer Liz McCann came into rehearsal and announced that there were queues all round the block. I had not changed my views, but, clearly, a lot of people were changing theirs. Almost every American I met and talked to had been profoundly impressed by Chairman Arafat's speech at Geneva the previous November, accepting the State of Israel, calling for a two-state solution, with an independent Palestinian State in the

West Bank and Gaza, and renouncing terrorism in the name of the
PLO. Many of the young Americans who were queuing at the Neil
Simon Theatre wrote notes, looking forward to the production,
glad that I was coming and saying 'We agree with your political
convictions.' I had long known that many would agree with my
political support for the Palestinians if they could only know what I
really said and did, instead of the half-truths and lies in the press.
For a year I had only given interviews to newspapers and
magazines whose editors and journalists had signed an agreement
I had drawn up with my solicitor. The document stated that there
should be no political questions or political comments from the
editor or sub-editor, and that I had the right to see the copy or to be
given a tape of a recorded interview. Some journalists and editors
refused to sign this, which was fine. Others wrote articles saying
that I was attacking their rights and freedom of speech, which was
nonsense. They were free to write anything they wanted about me.
They had the time, the money and the space to print truth or lies
about me. They were only denied the right to waste my time and
misrepresent what I said to them.

That document has served its purpose well, on the whole. It
provides a basis for mutual trust and, I dare say, it protects those
journalists who want to write something decent and objective but
have been told by their editors to 'get' me. I deeply regret the two
or three occasions I have waived the agreement, accepting a
verbal promise from the editor that, whilst their house-rules forbid
signing to any preconditions, they guarantee that the 'spirit' of my
document will be adhered to. Every time I have been mis-
represented, and abused into the bargain.

I had dreaded going to New York. The night before I left I felt
tired in mind and body, ruefully reminding myself that I had not
had a day off for over a year, since *Orpheus Descending* opened in
London. I loved the company and I was proud of our new
production, but as I said goodbye to the girls I felt a great hollow of
loneliness inside my chest and at the airport a wave of self-pity
almost drowned me. I clung to the promise that Carlo would be
with me, and that held me up. He was there for my opening, and a
few days later we had our own celebration for his twenty-first
birthday in the Seventh Avenue apartment that Ted Mann had lent
me. As things turned out, it was a very happy time. Carlo was at
the New York Film School, and to mark his 21st birthday the family

all met up at Tony's in Los Angeles. It was one of the happiest days of my life. Franco came from Italy, and Natasha and Joely flew in. Everyone was delighted to be there, and both fathers were proud not only of their children but also of their friendship. It was a great day for us all.

The political revolution in the Soviet Union was spreading throughout Eastern Europe. Honecker, the East German leader, demanded Soviet tanks to crush the mass demonstrations in Leipzig, Dresden and East Berlin, and Gorbachev refused. For forty years the Berlin Wall had stood as a monument to Stalinist repression, a symbol of the reactionary utopian fantasy that socialism could be built in a single country. At midnight on 9 October 1989 the wall was being torn down.

I began to work at break-neck speed for a concert called *The Wall Breaks* which would celebrate the collapse of the Berlin Wall and pay tribute to all the victims of Stalin's repressions. The Nederlander organisation agreed to let me take the Marquis Theatre on 10 December. That gave us five weeks to pull together what would normally take five months. I telephoned Mikhail Shatrov in Moscow. Would he come and speak on behalf of the Memorial society? The Memorial Society for the Victims of Stalin's Repressions had held its founding conference in January 1989 although it had begun to organise before then. One of its most important aims is to collect all the evidence, written and oral, concerning Stalin's victims. It has many branches in the USSR. Gerry and I had met its leading members, including Professor Lev Ponomariev in May the previous year. We had organised a concert in aid of Memorial in London in November 1988, which raised £5000. And in spring 1989, during our last visit together to Moscow, I had been made an honorary member.

Shatrov agreed to come. Ekaterina Maximova and Vladimir Vasiliev said that they would dance *Elegy* by Rachmaninov. I began work with a group of students from the Circle in the Square on scenes from Vasiliev's play, *Tomorrow was War*. We assembled an extraordinary cast for the concert: Joanne Woodward, Christopher Reeve, Sigourney Weaver, the Manhattan String Quartet, Raul Julia, Harvey Fierstein, Alan Ginsberg and Dimitri Shostakovitch Junior.

Lynn agreed to come and play Masha, in a scene from *Three*

*Sisters*, with me as Olga, Sigourney as Irina, and Chris Reeve as Vershinin. On the night of 10 December every seat at the Marquis was sold.

# 26

Gerry Healy died on 14 December 1989, aged seventy-six. I wrote an obituary for him, which was published in the *Guardian*. I sat on the divan in my underground dressing room at the Neil Simon Theatre trying, in a few lines, to do some justice to a unique life, a human being of exceptional courage and integrity.

In his book *The Great Game* Leopold Trepper, the leader of the 'Red Orchestra', the Soviet spy ring which operated in Nazi Germany, paid tribute to the Trotskyists as the only political group who fought Stalin and Stalinism. He explained that it was their theoretical outlook and breadth of mind that enabled them to understand and withstand the terror, the mass purges, the falsification of everything Lenin and the Bolsheviks stood for. I thought of that as I wrote about Gerry.

Since the time I joined the party I had met many members who were exceptionally gifted and able, and sincerely devoted to socialist ideals. But I also noticed how many intellectuals and academics, despite the great advantage of their education, lived a life in which their thinking became almost petrified. For want of any real effort to develop creatively, their thinking became dominated by old dogma and quite a lot of mysticism. But Gerry never let a day go by without some serious study of philosophy backed up by his constant interest in developments in science which could throw new light on the law-governed processes in nature and society, and how they are reflected in dialectical thought. He never sought relaxation: he had no 'private life' of the kind so often yearned for by bureaucrats and professional politicians. At the same time, I have never laughed so much as with Gerry. The main point was that Gerry never said or did anything for personal advantage. His life was a single piece of steel, and that was why he was feared and hated by the state and by all political opportunists.

We held a meeting in his memory at the Adelphi Theatre in March 1990. Um Jihad, at whose husband's memorial Gerry had spoken two years before, sent a beautiful message of support and condolence. James Waddell, the miner from Kent whom I had met in prison on the Isle of Sheppey, spoke on the platform. Feisal Oweida, the PLO representative in London was there and Mikhail Shatrov, Robert Sturua, Mariana Belov, Alexander Levenbyk and Galina Vollchek came from the Soviet Union. Ken Livingstone, the Labour MP for Brent East and former leader of the Greater London Council, spoke about his friendship with Gerry and the support he had given when the state moved against the GLC. And then Livingstone came to the state attacks against Gerry and the party he led.

I haven't the slightest doubt that the upheavals which split apart the Workers' Revolutionary Party were not some accident or a clash of personalities. They were a sustained and deliberate decision by MI5 to smash that organisation, because they feared it was becoming too pivotal in terms of domestic policies, linking too many international struggles with progressive elements both inside and outside the British Labour movement. Nothing that I have seen causes me to question that basic assumption, and it may very well be that one day we will see the evidence drawn out that shows the work of MI5 agents that was put into actually damaging and trying to roll back so much of what had been done.

These few words had a profound effect upon the audience. I knew that great pressure would be put on Livingstone to retract his remarks. But I also felt confident that he had an independent spirit which might well resist such pressure. He speaks with a clowning, self-deprecating irony, which is a useful weapon in debate but sometimes masks the seriousness of what he is saying. But when he spoke about MI5 it was without a hint of irony or sarcasm. It was considered and deliberate. And, above all, what he said was true.

I flew to Florida a week later to film *Orpheus Descending* for CNN. I became convinced that Tennessee had really written for the cinema. In a very large theatre his story and his words become stretched out and distorted no matter how brilliant the production. But on camera, where you can play at the speed and tempo of light, everything falls into place. Kevin Anderson and I had worked well together in the play, but we both worked twice as well in the film. Kevin's great quality as an actor is the inner life you can see in his eyes and hear when he speaks. Miriam Margolyes played Vee Talbot, the Sheriff's wife. She had played the same part in our London production at the Haymarket. But now I was very struck by her playing of the 'visions', and the remarkable way she showed the mysticism and the poetry of a human being who is tormented by the cruelty of the society she lives in.

In April I returned to England, to East Grinstead in Sussex, where we had booked a hotel for a week for our symposium on the historical truth of the 1920s and 1930s in the USSR. Besides the historians, the brilliant Soviet eye surgeon Sviatoslav Fedorov came. There was the thin, frail figure of Nadezhada Joffe, eighty years old and one of the first signatories to the platform of the Left opposition in 1926. There was Ivan Vrachev and his wife Rebecca Boguslavskaya. He had joined the Bolshevik Party when he was sixteen and at the age of twenty-four was one of the delegates from the Transcaucasus, who signed the December 1922 treaty which founded the Union of Soviet Socialist Republics. There were members of the Academy of Sciences, and the young members of Memorial. There was Keti Dolidzhe, the woman film director from Georgia, and the actor Sergei Yursky. There was the editor of *Znamya*, Grigory Baklanov, Otto Latsis of *Kommunist* and Andrei Karaulov from *Ogonyok*.

In discussion at the symposium, all kinds of dogmatic views would arise, and fall apart as more objective reports overcame them. And all the way through, the ninety-two-year-old Ivan Vrachev would intervene, 'No, this is what happened, I was there!'

Taken as a whole, the reports presented at the symposium, many of them based on documents never before released from state archives, provided a new understanding of the nature of the problems that faced the Soviet Union, and the objective sources that gave rise to the bureaucratisation of the party. Some of the members of Memorial were convinced that Lenin was responsible for the crimes of Stalin, a view held by many Western historians and academics. I would say that this is the most terrible of all the historical lies perpetrated by Stalin and the bureaucracy. The Soviet historians' extremely detailed and thoughtful studies proved that this was not the case. What was most striking to me was how the symposium clarified so many of our contemporary problems. It became clear that they had their source in the 1920s and 1930s and that only an honest and scientific examination of the truth of that period could help to clarify their exact nature. At the close it was agreed by all that this work must continue, and a further symposium be held the following year. We, for our part, decided to invite Ivan Vrachev and his wife to give a series of lectures in Athens, Greece and London.

In the first week of May I set off to Leningrad to film a 'mini-series' for CNN about the young Catherine the Great. Leningrad was the most beautiful city I had ever seen. I marvelled at how its long classic streets, laid out by Peter the Great and all but destroyed by the Nazis, had been reconstructed, stone for stone. I read a wonderful account of this in Vladimir Posner's autobiography, *Breaking with Illusions*. No international treaty, such as had saved Rome from bombardment, protected Leningrad. The Nazis spared nothing when they invaded Russia, and the Soviets knew that all the treasures of the Winter Palace would be looted and Leningrad razed to the ground if the siege were broken. A Red Army commissar chose a woman attendant to take charge of hiding the treasures and making sketches of the Winter Palace so that it could be rebuilt. She was a small, very ordinary-looking woman who sat at a door collecting tickets, and not one of the millions of visitors before the war would have given her a second glance. But the commissar had noticed that she spoke two or three languages, and found out that she had been an aristocrat and a member of the Tsar's court before the revolution. He told her to choose three assistants, and to tell no one where she was hiding the treasures. After the war Posner asked her if she had never been tempted – times were so hard – to take just one of the priceless treasures and smuggle it out to the international art market. After all, she alone knew where all the objects were and no one could have found out. She said nothing, but looked at Posner with withering contempt.

At the Pribaltiskaya Hotel I found to my great delight that Franco was also playing in *The Young Catherine*. I was feeling tired, and constantly unwell from the attentions of a tiresome amoeba I had picked up in the water. Foolishly, I had overlooked the advice of Leningraders not to drink from the tap. Franco always travels with an entire pharmacopoeia in his trunk, and that helped somewhat. Looking after his needs, with boxes of pasta sent out by the production office, helped to distract me from mine.

Times were hard now in Leningrad. *Perestroika* was entering a period of protracted crisis and struggle. Shops were becoming emptier and every necessity was in short supply. The bureaucracy was deliberately choking the supply of food and everyday supplies, conducting a war of attrition against Gorbachev and the political revolution. I was organising a concert in the October Hall to raise funds for the Theatre Workers' Union, with a brilliant young musician called Sergei Kuryokhin, and his group 'Pop Mechanica'. Elisabeth Welch had come over, as had Maria Farandouri from Greece, and Patti Allinson from New York. One morning before the concert my friend Professor Startsev from Leningrad University took them on a tour of the Winter Palace, reconstructing step by step and blow by blow the storming of the Palace by Bolshevik troops at the climax of the 1917 revolution. As usual there were hundreds of visitors and tourists in the Palace that day, with their official guides, winding their way through the immense buildings. As they heard Professor Startsev they detached themselves from their guides and soon, like the Pied Piper of Hamelin, he had gathered a huge audience which followed him around, straining to catch his account.

From Leningrad to London, and two days later to Austin, Texas, where I arrived in June 1990 on a 'starry, starry night' in the middle of a wooden town on Willie Nelson's ranch. As I walked down the street of Willie's film town I saw lights and heard the strains of music. Three of India's top musicians, the Khan family, were seated on the porch of what was to become Miss Amelia's Sad Café, singing a long cadenza from a thirteenth-century Indian song:

> Somethin's still alive here in the country,
> somethin' sweet and wild!
> People loved each other,
> but now it's sick with neon.

Austin and its surrounding area was reputed to be the liberal region of Texas. Oil money had endowed a university and stocked it with some priceless manuscripts. I sat in the reading room for a couple of days studying Carson McCullers' typed manuscript, written and sent to *Harper's Magazine* in 1940. I was struck by the number of deleted paragraphs, scored through by the editor perhaps for length, perhaps for political reasons. The two races, black and white, bound by poverty, trapped with debt, the divisions between them maintained by that narrow but un-traversable margin on this side of which stood the white foreman, or shopkeeper, who can keep his family only as long as he takes the food out of the mouth of the black migrant worker or the fourteen-year-old cotton-mill hand. That was the Sad Café – and that was also 'Miss Amelia', the woman who fought like a man, who mercilessly made those who worked for her pay their ever-increasing debt, the same woman who culled and distilled wild herbs and flowers to cure the ailments and diseases produced by hard unceasing labour in the cotton mill. Just as a ballad will only tell you a few very simple but essential facts like 'Old Meg she was a gipsy', so Carson McCullers draws a very simple picture of the extraordinarily strange Miss Amelia. She does not explain, and so bearing the ballad of the title in mind I thought I should make very simple clear choices about how to play Miss Amelia, and I discussed each one with Simon. I had to make a choice about her appearance, and I am still not sure I made the right one. Carson McCullers specifically writes that she has dark hair but I thought I should have as little disguise as possible in the part. Given the fact that I am blonde and basically fair with blue eyes I decided to go for looking like a real straw-headed Southerner. I wanted to make Miss Amelia look as her father might have done when he was a young boy.

Again bearing in mind the lack of explanation in the book, I did not change my clothes as you normally would to mark the passing of time. I thought it should be more like a cartoon image so that Miss Amelia's presented looking one way as if to say this is how she looks and always will until something very significant happens in the story which it does when she changes out of her dungarees and wears a red dress to mark the fact that she becomes a woman.

I wanted her to appear to have remained rather like a 12- or 13-year-old boy emotionally. She was trained by her father to work like a boy to take over the business and the farm, and that is how she is. But she is also a woman. She is rather shy, awkward and her instincts tell her to hit out at people although she holds back some of the time. Her reactions are young and immediate; her hatred, and her love, are absolute. She has stopped developing and reacts with a readiness to fight like a teenager. When she is betrayed by Cousin Lymon in the fight with Marion Macey it is as though everything she ever cared for has died. Her life becomes tragic. And like a child without defences or the ability to dissemble she bawls and cries and cries for her loss when the fight ends. Like all human beings Miss Amelia is full of contradictory tendencies. Specifically she has been reared as a boy and yet she is a woman, and her father has taught her to squeeze the local people for their last penny. And yet the same poverty that drives her to keep others poor also produces a fellow feeling in her for their suffering. And so she heals them with her herbs.

Ismail Merchant came down periodically to give Simon Callow encouragement. It was Simon's first film as director. He was wonderful with the actors, and spent considerable time explaining the life and the background of each of the townsfolk who witnessed the strange love story of that café. He wanted the townspeople to be the main protagonists of the story, along with Miss Amelia, Marion Macey, Cousin Lymon and the Reverend Willis.

Ismail is unusual indeed in today's world. Whatever the circumstances, and wherever the location, he will seek out and find all the most rare and gifted people and bring them together, from the girl that feeds and tends the mule to the mysterious investors and academics whom he draws into each of his fascinating projects. For instance George Burns, who coached me for the Georgian dialect and accents of Miss Amelia, lectured in the English department at Austin University. Not only that, he knew how to wiggle and flap his ears and made an electrical device that, placed behind Cork Hubbert's ears, produced a wiggle for the camera that convinced all spectators that Cousin Lymon could flap his ears.

Early one August morning we heard news that Iraq had invaded Kuwait. I had been following the press closely and had read the reports of the Geneva OPEC meetings, especially the joint statement by the Saudi and Iraqi oil ministers agreeing that Kuwait must cut back on its massive over-production of oil.

Suddenly the US President, George Bush, announced that massive airlifts of US troops were on their way to Saudi Arabia, and the United Nations Security Council passed a resolution demanding the withdrawal of Iraqi troops from Kuwait.

It was not until late in September that *The New York Times* published the transcript of the 25 July meeting in Baghdad between the US Ambassador April Glaspie and Saddam Hussein. In the transcript, which was leaked to the ABC TV network, April Glaspie gave the green light to the President of Iraq to take whatever action Iraq considered necessary in an inter-Arab question, assuring Saddam Hussein that the United States would not intervene. In March 1991 Ms Glaspie maintained before a Senate Committee that the transcript did not accurately reflect her conversation with Saddam Hussein. Several committee members and most of the press were incredulous, especially since the State Department placed a thirty-year ban on her contemporary notes of the meeting.

It became clear that the American and British governments wanted war, for every peace initiative was failing. US planes were in the air heading for the Saudi Kingdom before the State Department requested permission for them to land. Suddenly Saddam Hussein was the 'Hitler' of the Middle East, and the governments of the United States and Britain presented them-selves as the liberators of Kuwait. The United Nations was used as a cover for all-out military attack on an Arab country and permanent occupation of the Arab lands.

I was unconditionally opposed to the Iraqi occupation of Kuwait, and also unconditionally opposed to a war against Iraq. Millions of ordinary people in the United States and Europe and in the Middle East were politically ambushed for a short but crucial period. They were denied information and the means to express their political views; the British and Americans feared that the example of the Palestinian intifada would be followed throughout the Middle East on the same scale and with the same speed as the revolution in Eastern Europe.

By now I was in the midst of rehearsal of a new production of Anton Chekhov's *Three Sisters* directed by Robert Sturua. Months earlier, Thelma Holt had suggested that I should work with Robert, who wanted to do *The Cherry Orchard*. But so did Tony Richardson. It seemed best therefore to consider another play. At the time Joely was out of work and it occurred to me she would be the most exceptional Irina, youngest of the three Prozorov sisters. Later, after *The Wall Breaks*, I suggested to Lynn that she might like to play Masha and I could play Olga. Thelma Holt, our producer, and Robert both liked the idea. The financiers were ready to put up money on the three Redgraves. As it turned out, Joely was offered a marvellous film and was released to play a role opposite Melanie Griffiths. I rang up Corin's daughter Jemma, and asked if she would agree to play Irina. Both of us knew that half the best chances an actress gets are when another actress has dropped out. Maggie Smith and I were continually picking up parts that one or the other had been offered first, and very glad I was that some of them came my way.

I was thrilled at the chance to work with Lynn and for us to have more time together. When she had decided to move to the United States in the early seventies I virtually lost touch with her. Once in a while she would telephone me, and once in a while, on a very rapid visit to Los Angeles, I would visit her and her home. Her daughter Kelly had lived with me in Chiswick for a year while she finished at the American school in London, and that had helped Lynn and me to see more of each other, because it made Lynn come to London more often.

We had only five weeks for rehearsals and Robert usually never rehearsed for less than ten. Our rehearsals began as usual around the table, with our scripts in front of us. We had an exceptional cast, and we all looked at Robert with great expectations. He spoke very little at the beginning. 'The play is set when it was written in 1901, but we live, think and act as if it were now. It would be good if we succeeded in making people in the audience think about their own lives, what they are doing with their lives; some are helping others, some are only living for themselves.'

I read two sentences: 'Father died exactly a year ago today – the fifth of May, your Saint's day, Irina.' Robert stopped me. 'Olga loved her father, but she's already forgotten him, she's forgotten that day. Some people say "Thank goodness we forgot!" Others say "How terrible." To Olga it's a terrible shock.' So the reading continued, very slowly, continually stopping so that we could analyse the context of the words.

When it came to the doctor presenting the silver samovar as a present to Irina, Robert explained that Olga was horrified. Love mustn't be connected with presents or it is debased. She is afraid that Irina will accept the present and become corrupted. There was not one line that Robert had not analysed. All his decisions were deeply thought out and all of them surprising and quite contradictory, just as in life, especially in the life Chekhov understood and wanted to write about.

When we began physically to 'block' the first act we stopped as often as we had during the reading. Every physical action had been prepared, and very often it was in contradiction to the inner thought of the previous moment. Again, just like life.

Some of the actors became concerned – 'Supposing I don't want to do this?' one queried. 'Then you would have to get another director,' Robert replied, calmly and with a big smile. There were several moments when an actor protested, not used to this way of working. One of them said, 'The trouble is his ideas are so brilliant!' which I found hilarious: most of the time we would all be happy to have that kind of trouble. I was trained to follow a director's concept, and I was perturbed. I could see problems if even one of the cast were unwilling to really give all he had to adapt himself and his ideas to Robert's. But Robert stayed calm, concentrated and enthusiastic, and the detail of his work demanded all the concentration we possessed. Lynn, Jemma and I were exhausted after the day's work. We would not go out to eat. As days passed we found ourselves using the tea-breaks and the lunch-breaks to think, discuss and explore every moment of the day. Robert noticed immediately concentration slipped and we took in deep breaths of excitement and nerves, knowing that his attention would miss nothing.

The first time I saw Act II assembled and run through, which was not until the end of the third week, I was absolutely lost in the world I saw before me. Every moment and every movement was rich with life and full of changes. Not for one moment could I anticipate what would happen or what would be said. There was no inevitable dread familiarity that settles so often in the theatre. I was not watching Lynn, Stuart, Lenny, Phoebe, Aden or Adrian or Jemma or Graham 'being good', but real people, Chekhov's people.

After the first run-through of Acts I and II we felt quite pleased. We all looked at Robert. 'Quite good, but rather bad,' he said. He is the only director I have worked with who can say 'bad' and you know he means it, but do not feel crushed.

In the last week he asked us all to make cuts. Some of us moaned, some pretended to be cheerful, but we all came up with cuts in our lines. To my surprise it was good to make cuts so very late in rehearsal. I had a copy of the play in Russian, as did Robert and his assistant Helen Molchanov. We had agreed quite early in rehearsal that our translation, like other published translations, was far too wordy and in a very English way did not get directly to the issue, as

Chekhov always did. Chekhov's sentences were short and very direct. Olga does not speak much. However, I found that the shortened version was all the sharper. Once again I forced myself to speak faster than I could think at first. Ellen Terry's advice in her autobiography remained correct. Actors speak too slowly, and the truth of the characters in *Three Sisters* is that they are often saying the first thing that comes into their heads without thinking. To play this, and the full content of the moment, required a great deal of work, and total concentration. Furthermore, Robert's method of work did not create conditions in which the actor can feel satisfied with what he or she is doing.

I made a few notes in my script of Robert's advice on the day of our press night, 11 December 1990. One note was for Lynn: 'Masha is crying like an unfortunate child who has been hit.' Lynn was wonderful. First because she worked to do everything that Robert wanted, second because she did not once attempt to portray Masha in a sympathetic light. Masha didn't care what anyone thought of her, and neither did Lynn. She didn't cry romantically, or beautifully or tragically. She cried just like a small child who has been hit – wailing and shrieking and as if her nose was running, and saliva spurting, and she needed a mother who would wipe her face and put her on her knee – only there was no longer such a mother.

Jemma was also remarkable, and she, too, worked to do everything Robert wanted. In all the rehearsals and in all the performances of a fourteen-week run I never heard one false note in her voice. That is the highest praise I would ever hope to receive myself.

For my own part, during our two-weeks' performances at the Yvonne Arnaud Theatre in Guildford I became concerned that I was 'acting'. I made some changes largely because Joely came and said to me afterwards, 'Do you think this Olga is really a schoolteacher?' After a few days Robert wrote me a letter:

After our conversation you did not begin to play yourself in the given situation, you are far more interesting. Instead you are playing a school-mistress – a rather ordinary, even dull person. Whilst Olga is an unusual character – a romantic, full of illusions, who believes that good will conquer evil. She wants to bring everyone happiness and good fortune. In order to do that she is prepared to sacrifice herself. She is how you created her. Her actions are different to those of humdrum people . . .

what you were doing before our conversation was unusual and at the same time painfully familiar. Portraying a woman, open to the world, full of a passionate desire to help everyone, to sacrifice everything for the sake of others. I do not know what has happened, it is either the pains of creation or labour pains – but I beg you to believe me that the way you used to play Olga was a *chef d'oeuvre* . . .

Well, enough said. I abandoned playing 'the school-mistress', the 'stencil' of the 'schoolteacher'. Robert, Lynn and Jemma were happy, and I found a new conviction in what I was doing.

Robert's last words on the press night were:

This play for a lifetime has been performed in a bad mood [I think he meant a tragic or mournful mood], which is why it has never worked. These people like life. The actors say they like life. You must fight, not just for yourselves, you are fighting for others. Maintain the main freedom you have. The heroes want to live, they deserve happiness from the smallest events. They want happiness, not to be afraid of life.

In Guildford, one of Jemma's friends overheard a married couple: 'Just like life,' the wife said. 'I hope *not*,' exclaimed her husband. One director said to me after a performance, 'I hope you're very proud of this production.' Another said, 'Fifty per cent I liked, fifty per cent I hated.' I took both as compliments. The reviews from the drama critics were 50 per cent ecstatic, and 50 per cent did not like us. One critic wrote: 'Thank goodness *Three Sisters* never got to Moscow.' Thelma Holt put that one on a board outside the Queen's Theatre.

On the morning of 13 January 1991 I flew to Barcelona and spoke at a peace rally of about 60,000, who marched through the narrow streets of the seaport, bearing banners: 'No war! For peace! US troops out of the Gulf!' On the same day there were enormous demonstrations in London, Berlin and in the United States. In Rome about 150,000 people demonstrated.

I spoke at another public meeting in the evening, a memorial tribute to Gerry. That meeting was packed, with all seats taken and many standing. The next morning I got to the airport and bought *La Vanguardia*, which carried a headline on its report of the anti-war rally: 'Vanessa supports Saddam Hussein'. The UN deadline for Iraq's withdrawal from Kuwait was the following day, 15 January. I rang *La Vanguardia*, and then Corin, who spoke to the newspaper's political editor. He got their agreement to publish a correction by way of a letter. But *La Vanguardia*'s headline was landing on news-desks around the world, and this was the way all the news media treated those who were against war. 'If you don't support us, you support Saddam Hussein.' I was totally opposed to the war, and to the destruction of Iraq and the Iraqi people. I was also opposed to the invasion of Kuwait and had called for the withdrawal of Iraqi troops. But I knew that the Kuwaiti people would not be liberated by the war. They would be in a worse situation, and when the war brought back the Emir, the democratic forces in Kuwait would be prevented from achieving any of their objectives, such as the right to have political parties and contend in elections for government.

The saturation bombing of Iraq began. If one counted the sorties from Saudi Arabia it was simple to calculate how many civilians must be dying. Even if only one died in each, 100,000 such sorties would kill that number of civilians. The British press and television became intolerable to watch, read and listen to. Racist caricatures in the newspapers, and so very few voices in opposition. Systematic destruction of Iraq was proceeding, and the anti-war demonstrations which still took place got no publicity at all. Seven trade unions in Britain, including the National Union of Journalists and the Fire Brigades' Union, declared themselves against the war.

A hail of fuel-fire and cluster-bombs was drowning the land and the people of Iraq in blood. Still efforts were being made to find a way to a cease-fire and a peaceful solution. Never before had the drive for war been so cynically and inhumanly indifferent to the loss of human life – whether civilian or military, and of whatever nationality. I am sure I was far from alone as I sat late at night watching the panels of experts enjoying their reports in the TV programmes, thinking how atrocious it is to see beings, dressed like men and women, completely unconcerned about sending soldiers to die, or killing civilians. If these governments and their thirsty media spokesmen gave any thought either to 'our boys' or to the Arab people there would have been no war, and a solution would have been found by the Arab people themselves and some of their leaders.

Now I believe that people in the United States and Europe will realise the truth about this war. We are not living in the age of the lie. The fact that nevertheless so many lies are being told only proves to my mind that the present governments are extremely frightened of their own people. I remember the cries that went up when Mandela spoke in the United States in February 1990. When he spoke of the poverty, the hunger and the racist violence, young and old Americans, black and white, cried out: 'Same here! Same here!'

As I played in *Three Sisters* in our closing weeks, and spoke Olga's lines, 'Our sorrows will turn into happiness for those that come after us. Peace and happiness will come to the earth. They will think kindly of us and they will thank us,' I cried for and with all those who will not see happiness again: for the painful reality of the suffering of those who are alive, for what Marx called 'man's inhumanity to man'. But I also see the opposite to all this cruelty and suffering – millions of human beings who do not accept that life should be like this for anyone. We want peace and we only need to know the truth, and will go on insisting on the truth, so that we can ensure that all oppressed peoples have justice and a real human life. The key to this lies in our history. As long as we do not know our history we cannot solve our problems. So, you see, what Chekhov wrote in 1901 in the *Three Sisters* is very much what millions of people feel today, ninety years later: 'We must see more and know more.' We must know the truth.

# Index

Abramov, Gennady 280–1
Actors' Studio 57–8, 59, 76
Adelphie Theatre 151, 273–4, 288
*Admirable Crichton, The* (Barrie) 22
Aeschylus 133
Afanasiev, Professor Yuri 268
Afghanistan 240, 273
Agate, James 87
Ahmandon Theatre, Los Angeles 176
Ainley, Henry 86
Akhmadulina, Bella 260
al Mukhtar, Omar 228
al Nasry, Talal 275
Al Tammari, Salah 203
Albery, Donald 130
Aldwych Theatre 95
Alexander, Jane 225
Algeria 144
Ali, Tariq 141
Allegranza, Helen 105
Allen, Woody 266
Allende, Salvador 166
Alliluyeva, Svetlana 281
Allinson, Patti 291
*All's Well That Ends Well* (Shakespeare) 89
Almani, Dawood K. 209
Amos (Israeli student) 54, 55, 72
Amos, Jill 68
Anderson, J.P. ('Grandpa Andy') 84
Anderson, Kevin 288–9
Anderson, Lindsay 21, 96, 117
Anderson, Margaret ('Daisy', née Scudamore,
    VR's grandmother) 13–14, 59–60, 80, 84, 87
Andrews, Eamonn 185
Andrews, Harry 142
Angelo (at Brendola) 147
*Anna Karenina* (Tolstoy) 35
Antonioni, Michelangelo 130
*Antony and Cleopatra* (Shakespeare) 42, 43
    *see also under* Redgrave, Vanessa, STAGE
    APPEARANCES
Apollo Theatre 282
Arafat, Yasser 49, 111, 205, 213, 223, 274, 283
Arif, Mohammed 275
Armenia 263
Armstrong, Neil 147
*As You Like It* (Shakespeare) 3
    *see also under* Redgrave, Vanessa, STAGE
    APPEARANCES

Ashcroft, Dame Peggy 42, 52, 55, 70, 116, 266
Asner, Ed 238
*Aspern Papers The* (James) 243, 244
Assad, Hafez 195
Astor, David 115, 149, 217
Audin, Maurice 144
Austin, Texas 291
Austria 192
*Autobus* 265
Aytmatov, Chingis 263

Babel, Isaak 282
Babitsky, Constantin 144
Baklanov, Grigory 289
Baksi, Joe 34
Ball, John 108
Ballet Rambert 36–7
Banda, Mike 251–2
Bandar Bin Sultan, Prince 240
Bankhead, Tallulah 108
Bannen, Ian 95, 128, 129
Barber, Anthony 158
Barker, Ronnie 103
Barnes, Clive 190
Bartlett, Robin 225, 238
Barton, John 93–4
Bashir, Mounir 226
Bates, Alan 59
Batista, Fulgencio 108, 110, 119
Battersby, Roy 180, 195, 197, 206, 215
*Battle of Algiers, The* 145
Baylis, Lilian 2
Beaton, Cecil 246
Beaumont, Hugh ('Binkie') 83–4
Beauvoir, Simone de 106–7, 108, 145
*Beggar's Opera, The* 50, 51
Beirut 283
Bell, Gertrude 226
Belov, Mariana 288
Belov, Pyotr 270–1
Benedetti, Prof. Jean 74
Beppe (at Brendola) 147
Berenson, Marisa 225
Berg, Alban 273
Bergman, Ingmar 263, 266
Bergman, Ingrid 182
Bernhardt, Sarah 60
Bernie (film electrician) 137
Berrigan, Daniel 144

Berrigan, Philip 144
Berry, John 214
Bevin, Ernest 18
Bewell, Bill 234, 236, 237
Bhutto, Benazir 220
Bikel, Theodore 213
Billington, Michael 266
Birdie (cook) 33
Bish, George 198
Bisset, Jacqueline 182
Black Jacobins, The (James) 157
Blair, Betsy (Reisz) 123, 148
Blake, William 90
Blakely, Colin 182
Blood Wedding (Lorca) 71–2
Blunt, Anthony 22
Boguslavskaya, Rebecca 289–90
Bolam, James 103
Bolshoi Ballet 62
Bolt, Robert 90, 91, 92, 98, 100, 126, 186
Bond, Derek 181
Booth, Shirley 57
Borromeo, Friar 149
Bourj al Barajneh 201, 202
Bowen, Philip 207
Bowles, Anthony 137
Bradley, Buddy 52
Branagh, Kenneth 266
Branch, Mrs 78
Brando, Marlon 57
Brar, Harpal 275
Breaking with Illusions (Pozner) 290
Brecht, Bertolt 59, 116–17
Brendola 135–6, 147–8
Brezhnev, Leonid 167
Bridgewater, Leslie 40
Brittain, Vera 112
Brockway, Fenner 106
Brook, Peter 138
Brown, George 121
Browne, Maria 35, 44
Budberg, Baroness Moura 142
Bujold, Geneviève 159
Bukharin, Nikolai 270, 272–3
Burgess, Guy 22
Burns, George 293
Burnstein, Arthur 240
Burton, Richard 41–2, 70, 234
Bush, Alan 24
Bush, George 293
Buñuel, Luis 149
Bykov, Rolan 268
Byron, Lord 29

Cacoyannis, Michael 159
Callaghan, James 121, 186
Callow, Simon 292, 293
Cameron, James 138
Campbell, Duncan 214
Campbell, Sir Jock 115–16, 117
'Carmen' (Mérimée) 259
Carnoff, Phil 238
Caron, Leslie 131
Carr, Ralph 42

Carr, Robert 165
Carr, Sylvia 42
Carten, Kenneth 73
Carter, Jimmy 210
Casque d'Or 145
Castro, Fidel 108. 111
Cat on a Hot Tin Roof (Williams) 239
Cato Street (Robert Shaw) 41, 161
Chamberlain, Neville 2, 63
Chamoun, Camille 194
Chamoun, Danny 198
Charleson, Ian 246
Chatila camp 201, 283
Chekhov, Anton 296–7, 300
   see also play titles and under Redgrave, Vanessa,
      STAGE APPEARANCES
Chekhov, Michael 54
Cherry Orchard The (Chekhov) 85, 294
Chesshyre, Robert 217–18
Chichester Festival Theatre 100
Children of Fire 232
'Children's Hour' 15
Chile 166
China 126–7
China Sydrome, The 225
Christina (nanny) 129, 135, 175
Churchill, Sir Winston 5, 18, 20, 21, 24, 26
Churchill, Winston S. 167
Cilento, Diane 56
Cinderella 14
Circle on the Square 188–9, 240, 285
Clark, George 105
Clark, John 32
Clark, Kelly 295
Clurman, Harold 56–7
Cocteau, Jean 234
Coliseum Theatre 185, 186, 217–18
Collins, Jack 185
Collins, Canon John 92
Come Back Little Sheba 57
'Come le Rose' 277–8
Commissar, The 268, 276
Complaisant Lover, The (Green) 100
Connery, Sean 182
Constantine, Sir Learie 157
Conteh, John 229
Cooper, Gary 192
'Core 'Ngrato' 277–8
Coriolanus (Shakespeare) 265
   see also under Redgrave, Vanessa, STAGE
      APPEARANCES
Costa-Gavras 145
Country Wife, The (Wycherley) 3
Coward, Noël 51, 52, 115, 167–8
   Play Parade 167–8
Cripps, Sir Stafford 32
Cristo si è fermato a Eboli (Levi) 45
Croasdell, Gerald 151
Croft, Stephen 16
Crowden, Graham 221
Crozier, Roger 170
Crucible, The (Miller) 61
Cruickshank, Andrew 92
Crutchley, Rosalie 59

Cuba 108–11, 119
*Curtain Up* (Streatfield) 15
Czechoslovakia 142, 143, 146

Dachau 138–9
*Daily Express* 218, 228
*Daily Herald* 20–1
*Daily Mail* 19, 20, 21, 28, 34, 46, 228, 229
*Daily Worker* 22, 25
D'Alton, Hugo and Micky 278
Dalton, Timothy 151–2, 176, 190, 206, 258, 260, 266
Dane, Barbara 154
Daniel, Larissa 144, 146
Darst, David 144
Daubeny, Peter 221
Davenport, Nigel 186
Davies, John 152
*Day is Longer than a Century, A* 263, 265
de Niro, Robert 268
Delaney, Shelagh 97
Delaunay, Vladimir 144
Dench, Judi 68, 70, 71
Denham film studios 24
Denning, Lord 215–16
Devine, George 28, 50, 53, 54, 59, 60, 76, 103, 104, 106, 111–12, 116, 117
Devine, Sophie 28
Devlin, Bernadette 155, 156
*Diary of Anne Frank, The* 58
Dickens, Charles 65
*Dictatorship of Conscience, The* (Shatrov) 269
Dina, Princess 202
Dinely Studios 76
Disney, Walt 38
*Doce Sillas, Las* 109
Dodimead, David 207
Dolidzhe, Keti 289
Domingo, Placido 87
Donat, Robert 261
Douglas, Mike 206
Dremliouga, Vadim 144
*Drowning by Numbers* 130
Drumm, Maire 216
Dubcek, Alexander 146
*Duke in Darkness, The* 13
Duncan, Isadora 138, 145
Dunham, Joanna 92
Duras, Marguerite 128
Dutt, Rajani Palme 20

Ecevedo, Del 256
*Eclipse, The* 130
Eden, Sir Anthony 63–4
Edward the Confessor, King 177–8
*Edward II* (Marlowe) 55
Edward VIII, King 168
Edwardes (in Cato Street conspiracy) 161
Edwards, Geoffrey 80
Edwards, Leslie 152
Edwards, Mr 27–8
Eggar, Samantha 103, 254
Eisenberg, Alan 237–8
Eliot, George 146, 281
*Elizabeth* (Schiller) 263

Elizabeth II, Queen 112
Ella (housemaid) 33
Elliott, Michael 93–5, 132, 146, 215, 221
Emin, Artashes 264, 265
Emin, Gevorg 264–5
*Encore* 59, 62
*Enemy of the People, The* (Ibsen) 261
Engels, Friedrich
    *Dialectics of Nature* 190
English Stage Company 42, 59–61
Esenin (?) 138
Evans, Dame Edith 3, 24, 89, 93, 96–7, 104, 189
Evans, Geraint 138
*Evening News* 174
*Evening Standard* 132, 138, 152, 266
*Every Cook can Govern* (James) 157
Ezra, Derek 247

*Facing Reality* (James) 157
Faisal, King of Iraq 226
Farandouri, Maria 291
Farron, Stoker 7
Farrow, Mia 155
Fay, Stephen 170
Fedorov, Sviatoslav 289
Feibleman, Peter 242
Fellini, Federico 124
Fenelon, Fania 223–6, 233
*Fidel* 153
Fierstein, Harvey 285
*Figaro, Le* 144–5
Filipenko 270
*Financial Times* 115–16, 262
Finch, Peter 116, 145
Finch, Yolanda 116
Finney, Albert 182
Fitch, Rodney 158
*Five O'Clock Angel* (St Just) 142
Fogazzaro, Antonio 45–6
Fonda, Jane 146, 153, 154, 191, 193, 194, 208, 223
Fonteyn, Dame Margot 36–7, 38
Foot, Michael 174
*Force de l'âge, La* (Beauvoir) 106–7
Forster, E.M. 24
*Fountains of Bakshisarai* 62
Fowler, John 137
Fox, Angela 149
Fox, Mrs (wardrobe mistress) 70
Fox, Robin 131, 149
Franciosa, Tony 57
Franco, Francisco 194
Franco (met on school trip to Italy) 44
Franklin, Benjamin 142
Freeman, John 116
French, Liz 248
French, Terry 248, 249
Frinton Summer Theatre 76, 78–80
*From Here to Eternity* 193

Gaddafi, Muammar 111, 227
Gandhi, Mahatma 106
Gardiner, Margaret 192
Garibaldi, Giuseppe 48–9
Garrick, David 57
Gaskell, Elizabeth 65

Gazzara, Ben 57
Gellhorn, Martha 192
Gemayel, Bashir 198
Gemayel, Pierre 194, 197
*Georgy Girl* 132
Gerö, Ernö 63
Giap, General 141
Gibson, Mrs 250–1, 252
Gielgud, Sir John 41
Gilbert, Deputy Assistant Commissioner Victor 216, 217
Gilkes, David 104
Gilkes, Denne 89, 93
Giovanni (at Brendola) 147
Glascot, Miss 28–9, 33
Glaspie, April 293–4
Glover, Julian 90
Glyndebourne Opera House 50
Godard, Jean-Luc 145
Goldman, Milton 239
Goller, Dr 81
Goncharov, Nikolai 267
Goodwin, Clive 59
Gorbachev, Mikhail 260, 261, 263, 264, 272, 273, 285, 291
Gordon, Judith 236
Gordon, Ruth 3
Goring, Marius 181, 186
Gormley, Joe 170
Gorst, Irene 217, 218, 219
Gould, Elliot 180
Grainger, Gawn 79, 80
Grasberg, Alan 285
*Great Game, The* (Trepper) 287
Greenaway, Peter 130
Greenwood, Arthur 106
Griffiths, Melanie 294
Grimes, Tammy 107
Grody, Donald 213
Group Theatre 56–7
*Guardian* 63, 65, 173, 287
*Guide to Military Rights, A* 154
Guinness, Alec 3, 37
Guinness, Matthew 28
Guthrie, Tyrone 89
*Guys and Dolls* 246
Gwynn, Michael 59, 84

Haddad, Major Sammi 204, 210
Haigh, Kenneth 59, 60
*Hairy Ape, The* (O'Neill) 263
Hall, Peter 92, 95, 277
*Hamlet* (Shakespeare) 86, 152
Hanley, Michael 254
*Hard Times* (Dickens) 218
Harding, Oliver 73
Harlech Television 154
Harman, Mr Justice 252
Harmer Brown, Maître 72–3
*Harper's Magazine* 291
Harrigan, Michael 215
Harris, Julie 57
Harris, Lenore 225
Hart, Judith 106

Hassan, Crown Prince of Jordan 233
*Hatful of Rain, A* 57
Hawke, Robert 233
*Hay Fever* (Coward) 115
Haymarket, Los Angeles 153
Haymarket Theatre, London 258, 261, 289
Healy, Gerry 159, 164–6, 175, 194, 222, 250–3, 259, 268, 285, 298
  at memorial meeting for Abu Jihad 275, 276
  death 287–8
  in Kuwait 220
  and Lenin's writings 163
  and miners 249
  in Moscow 269–71, 285
  and *Observer* case 219
  and *Playing for Time* 223, 225
  as public speaker 175
  and Soviet Union 261–2
  and White Meadows 176, 184
*Heartbreak House* (Shaw) 240
Heath, Edward 156, 158, 169, 170, 172, 174
*Hedda Gabler* (Ibsen) 42
Heflin, Van 57
Hegel, Friedrich 162, 163
Hellman, Lillian 17, 191–2, 208, 240, 242
Hemingway, Ernest 110
Henderson, John 131
*Henry IV Part I* (Shakespeare) 31, 39
*Henry V* (Shakespeare) 39
Hepburn, Audrey 37
Herbert, A.P. 28
Herbert, Jocelyn 28, 104, 106
Herzen, Alexander 48, 48–9
Heston, Charlton 176, 177
*High Noon* 192
Hiller, Wendy 244
Hingle, Pat 189
Hitchcock, Alfred 3
Hitler, Adolf 2, 11, 24, 25, 63, 194
Hoar, Peter 76
Hobson, Harold 60
Hoffman, Dustin 191
Hogan, John 144
*Hollow Crown, The* 108
*Hollywood Reporter* 211
*Holocaust* 225
Holt, Thelma 83, 221, 240, 263, 265, 266, 294, 298
Honecker, Erich 285
Hoover, J. Edgar 89
Hope, Maurice 229
Hopper, Anthony 152
*Hotel in Amsterdam* (Osborne) 137
Howard, Leslie 24
Hubbert, Cork 293
*Humanité, L'* 144
Hungary 62–3, 64–6, 163
Hurst, Brian Desmond 80
Hurt, John 254

Ibsen, Henrik 189–90, 243, 261, 263
*Iceman Cometh, The* (O'Neill) 129
Idris, King of Libya 227
*Illustrated London News* 82
Ilyenkov, Evald 268, 269
Inge, William 107

*International Herald Tribune* 144
*Investors' Chronicle* 174
Iran 228
Iraq 293–4, 298–9
Ireland 164
  *see also* Northern Ireland
Ireland, John 177
*Isadora and Esenin* (McVay) 145
Israel 139, 204, 209–12, 273, 283
*It Isn't Easy to be Young* 263
Italia Conti Stage School for Children 15
Ivory, James 243

Jabavu, Noni 96
Jaber, Sheikh 220
Jaffar, Abu 198–200
Jaime (friend of Han Stevens) 158
James, Alice 243
James, C.L.R. 157, 166
James, Henry 243–4
James I (VI), King 177–8
  *Daemonologie* 178
Jamil, Mohammed Shukri 226
Jan (driver) 104, 112
*Jane Eyre* (Brontë) 17
Jawharieh, Hani 197
*Jaws* 41
Jenkins, Roy 219
Jerash 232
*Jewish Chronicle* 211
Jhabvala, Ruth Prawer 243
Jihad, Abu (Khalil al-Wazir) 205, 274–5, 276
Jihad, Um 288
  and family 274–5
Joffe, Nadezhda 289
Johnson, Lyndon 119, 125, 140, 141
Jones, Jack 185
Jones, John 254
Jones, Russell 247
Jordan, Police Commissioner 237
Joseph, Stephen 78
Joss, William 165
*Jules et Jim* 137
Julia, Raul 285
Jumblatt, Kemal 194, 198

Kahane, Rabbi Meir 207, 239
Kalin, Tasha 35–6, 43–5
*Kapital, Das* (Marx) 36
Kaplan, Mady 225
Karaulov, Andrei 289
Karpov, Vladimir 260
Keach, Stacey 153
Keaton, Robert E. 241
Kempson, Beatrice ('Beanie', née Ashwell, VR's grandmother) 2, 6, 7
Kempson, Eric (VR's grandfather) 2, 6, 7–10, 15, 42
Kempson, Joan (VR's aunt) 15, 16
Kempson, Lucy Wedgwood ('Cousin Lucy') 4–6, 10, 16, 42, 61, 65, 66, 67, 93
Kempson, Nicholas (VR's uncle) 5–6, 9
Kempson, Rachel (Lady Redgrave, VR's mother) 1–7, 9, 10–11, 12, 32–3, 51–2, 65, 69, 73, 84, 85, 104, 112, 137, 196

as actress 39, 42–3, 116
and *Aspern Papers, The* 244
and English Stage Company 59
in Lyceum concert 219
marriage to Michael 2–3
and politics 20, 24, 26, 186–7
at Stratford 39–43
and Vic School 54
visit to Soviet Union 87
and VR as actress 38, 53
Kempson, Robin (VR's uncle) 5–6, 7–8, 92
Kennedy, John Fitzgerald 109, 111
Kennedy, Ludovic 139–40
Kennedy, Nigel 273
Kenneth (chauffeur) 33
Kenyatta, Jomo 48
Khabarobvsk 261
Khait, Arkady 282
Khan family (musicians) 291
Khrushchev, Nikita 163
Kierkegaard, Søren 132
Kilimov, Elem 260
King, David 41
*King Lear* (Shakespeare) 42, 157, 222
King, Martin Luther 140, 252–3
Kitson, David 275
Klimov, Elem 268
Knight, Esmond 92
Knight, Shirley 225
Knipper, Olga 254
Koch, Howard 207
*Kommunist* 289
Kramer, Stanley 268
Krasker, Robert 47
Krige, Alice 256
Kristofferson, Kris 273
Kuryokhin, Sergei 291
Kuwait 293–4, 298–9

Labadi, Dr 201
*Lady Vanishes, The* 3
Lanovoy 270
*Lark, The* (Anouilh) 57
Latsis, Otto 289
*Lavender Hill Mob, The* 37
Lawley, Sue 185
Lawrence, Gertrude 52
*Lawrence of Arabia* 98
Laye, Evelyn 14
Lean, Sir David 36
Leavis, F.R. 243
Lebanon 139, 194, 194–5, 197–205, 209–11
Lederer, Lajos 65
Lefkovitch 281
Leicester, Margot 260
Leighton, Margaret 92
Leila (friend in Moscow) 268
Lemmon, Jack 261
Lenin, V.I. 25–6, 157, 269–70, 289
  'Lenin's Testament' 162–3
  *Philosophical Notebooks* 162
  *Socialism and War* 21
Leningrad 273–4, 290
*Leninist Dialectics and the Metaphysics of Neo-Positivism* (Ilyenkov) 268

Levenbyk, Alexander 281, 288
Levi, Carlo 45
Levin, Bernard 100
Lewis, Dr 33
Lewis, Thomas 144
'Liberté, j'écris ton nom' (Eluard) 115
Libin, Paul 189, 240
Linda (nanny) 148, 149, 151, 175
Lindfors, Viveca 225
*Little Folks* 30
*Little Foxes, The* (Hellman) 189
Littlewood, Joan 55–6
Litvinov, Pavel 144, 146
Liverpool Playhouse 40, 84
Livingstone, Ken 288
Logan, Joshua 133
Logue, Christopher 98
London Theatre Centre 54
*Loneliness of the Long Distance Runner, The* 104
*Long Day's Journey into Night, A* (O'Neill) 261
*Look Back in Anger* (Osborne) 60–1, 80, 103
Loraine, Robert 86
Los Angeles 176–7
    Symphony Orchestra 153
'Lou Grant' 238
Louis, Joe 33
Lousada, Anthony 28
L'Ouverture, Toussaint 157
*Loved One, The* 118, 120, 121, 137
*Love's Labour's Lost* (Shakespeare) 42
Lumet, Gail 142
Lumet, Sidney 116, 142, 182, 240
*Luther* 108
Lyceum Theatre 154, 219
*Lycidas* (Milton) 246
Lynch, Alfred 103
Lyric Theatre, Hammersmith 42, 254
Lyric Theatre, Shaftesbury Avenue 282
Lyttelton Theatre 266

McBean, Angus 38
McCann, Eamonn 155
McCann, Liz 283
McCarthy, Joseph 61, 123, 153, 179, 209, 236
McCarthy, Mary 192
McCullers, Carson 291–2
McCulloch, Derek ('Uncle Mac') 15
McEnery, Peter 116
McGowran, Jack 111
MacGregor, Ian 247
McKellen, Ian 246
McKenna, Siobhan 118
McMaster, Anew 39
*Mademoiselle* 125
Magnani, Anna 279
Malcolm, King of Scotland 177
Malle, Louis 145
*Man called Intrepid, A* 5
*Mandarins, The* (Beauvoir) 107
Mandela, Nelson 115, 140, 211, 300
Mandela, Winnie 201, 253
Mandelstam, Osip 178
Manhattan String Quartet 285
Mankiewicz, Joseph 47, 124
Mann, Daniel 225

Mann, Ruth 188
Mann, Theodore (Ted) 188, 189, 240, 284
Manouchian l' Armenien 144
Marcus Aurelius 255
Margolyes, Miriam 289
Maria (hairdresser) 128
Mark, Sir Robert 217
Markham, Kika 258
Markov, Georgy 260
Marowitz, Charles 221
Marquis Theatre 285–6
Marsh, Sandra 191, 207
Martin, Henri 144
Marvellous (dog) 112, 114
Marx, Eleanor (later Aveling) 171, 262
Marx, Groucho 180
Marx, Karl 133, 300
*Marxist Analysis of the Crisis, A* 163
*Marxist Review* 252
Mary (housemaid) 33
Mason, James 128, 142
Masri, Mei 232
Maximova, Ekaterina 285
Maxwell, James 146
Mayakovsky, Vladimir 168
Mayakovsky Theatre Company 265–6, 267
Mazzini, Giuseppe 48
Mehta, Zubin 153
Melville, Marjorie 144
Melville, Thomas 144
Menuhin, Diana 246–7
Menuhin, Yehudi 149, 246–7
Merchant, Ismail 240, 293
*Merchant of Venice, The* (Shakespeare) 70
Merchant-Ivory Productions 243
Mexico 109
Michael, Savas 272
*Midsummer Night's Dream, A* (Shakespeare) 101,
    103, 196
    *see also under* Redgrave, Vanessa, STAGE
    APPEARANCES
*Mie Prigioni, Le* (Pellico) 46
Migenes, Julia 273
Mikhoels, Solomon 281
*Milk Train Doesn't Stop Here Any More, The*
    (Williams) 108
Miller, Arthur 76, 225
Minetti, Dida 48
Minetti family 45–6
Mische, George 144
*Miss Julie* (Strindberg) 84
'Misunderstanding of the Artist in Revolt'
    (Williams) 238–9
Mitchell, Alex 174
Mitchell, John 176
Mitford, Jessica 118
Moiseiwitsch, Tanya 40
Molchanov, Helen 296
Monroe, Marilyn 76
*Monroe* (US destroyer) 109
Montand, Yves 143–5, 146
More O'Ferrall, George 80
Moreau, Jeanne 126, 128
Morley, Robert, 140, 150
*Morning Star* 169, 185

Morris, John 96
Morris, Tom 236, 237, 239
Moscow Art Theatre Company 56, 74, 85–6, 87, 266
Moscow Jewish Theatre Company (*Shalom*) 282
Moylan, Mary 144
Mugabe, Robert 211
*Mulberry Bush, The* (Wilson) 61, 65
Murch, Pauline 79–80
Murdoch, Rupert 229
Murray, Braham 146
Mussolini, Benito 165, 194, 228
My Lai 138
*My Life* (Duncan) 145

Nabatiya 204
Nagy, Imre 64–5
Naismith, Laurence 256
Napoleon I, Emperor 29
Nasser, Gamal Abdel 63–4, 111, 227
National Theatre, London 265, 266
    Company 115
National Theatre, Oslo 262
Nederlander, Jimmie 282
Neil Simon Theatre, New York 284, 287
Nelin, Emanuel 281
Nelson, Dr Mary 38
Nelson, Willie 291
Nero, Franco 134, 135–6, 137, 146–50 *passim*, 158, 191, 277, 280, 285, 290
Nesbit, E. 35
Neville, John 92
New Lindsey Theatre 56
*New Statesman* 25, 116
*New York Daily Post* 229
*New York Post* 207
*New York Times* 108, 190, 192, 236, 282, 293
*News Chronicle* 21, 23–4
*News of the World* 17, 21, 228
*Newsline* 248–9, 250, 260
Newton, Robert 36
Nguyen Cao Ky 125
Nicaragua 211, 238
Nichols, Mike 189
Ninagawa Company 263, 266, 267
Nixon, Richard 153, 176, 179, 209
Nkomo, Joshua 211
Noel-Baker, Philip 106
Norman, Jessye 234
*North Wales Echo* 259
Northern Ireland 145, 155–7, 159–60
*Novy Mir* 260

O'Brien, Edna 160
*Observer, The* 60, 65, 115–16, 149, 183, 184, 214–19
O'Casey, Sean 56
O'Connor, Mr Justice 215, 219
*Oedipus Rex* (Stravinsky) 234–5, 236
*Ogonyok* 289
Okhudzhava, Bulat 260
Old Vic Theatre 115, 261, 266
    Company 1, 2–3, 54
    see also Young Vic Theatre
*Oliver Twist* 36

Olivier, Lord (Sir Laurence) 1, 3, 42, 89, 100, 115, 185–6, 266
Olympia (Paris theatre) 143
*On the Waterfront* 58
Open Space Theatre 221
Orpheum Theatre, Boston 238
Osawa, Seiji 234, 237
Osborne, John 104, 129, 137
Obsorne, Penelope 129
Oskaldov, Sasha 268, 270, 276
O'Toole, Sean 156
*Our Island Story* 28–9
Oweida, Feisal 288
Owen, Peter 256
Owen, Robert 9
Owers, Mr (gardener) 33
*Oxford Book of English Verse* 53

Padovani, Lea 278
Page, Anthony 117, 240
Page, Genevieve 36
Page, Tony 255, 256
Palestine 164
Paley, Bill 223
Pam (usherette) 191
Papas, Irene 159
Paris 143, 193
Parsons, Betty 113–14
*Passato e Pensieri* (Herzen) 48–9
Pasternak, Boris 269
Pavitt, Laurie 160
*Peace* 154
*Peace of Brest-Litovsk, The* (Shatrov) 270
*Peace News* 105, 112, 119, 174
Peacock, William 41
Peck, Gregory 268
Pellico, Silvio 46
*Pentimento* (Hellman) 191
Peri d'Estienne d'Orves, Gabriel 144
Petri, Elio 135
Petöfi Circle 62
Phoenix Theatre 170
*Piccolo mondo antico* (Fogazzaro) 45–6
*Picture Post* 3
*Pilgrim's Progress, The* (Bunyan) 10–11
Pinter, Harold 266
Pisk, Litz 54, 137, 256
Plouviez, Peter 185, 186, 217–18
Podwicks, Yuri 263
Polanski, Roman 145
Pollitt, Harry 165
Ponomariev, Professor Lev 285
Pontecorvo, 145
Posner, Vladimir 267
Potter, Madeleine 244
Pottle, Pat 105
Powell, Enoch 174
Pozner, Vladimir 290
Praz, General 166
Prentice, Reg 171, 172
Previte, John 214
Price sisters 165
*Prince of Wales*, HMS 7
Prince of Wales' Theatre 190
Pritt, D.N. 25, 26

Pryce, Jonathan 254
Pugacheva, Alla 267–8
*Punch* 67

'Q' Theatre 42
Quayle, Anthony 42, 266
Queen's Gate School 80, 85
Queen's Theatre 84, 92, 117, 254, 298
*Quiet American, The* 46–7, 73, 80, 124

Radd, Ronald 142
Rainis Theatre, Riga 263
Rakovsky, Christian 273
Rambert, Dame Marie 36–7
*Ramparts* 67
Randall, George 30
Randall, Kathleen ('Nanny Randall') 10, 12, 13,
    15, 17, 18, 19, 20, 30–2, 38, 81, 112
Randle, Michael 98, 105
Rashidiye 210
Rathbone, Eleanor 61, 65
Read, Sir Herbert 92
Reagan, Ronald 153
*Reason Why, The* (Woodham-Smith) 136–7
Red Army Theatre 270
Redgrave, Corin (VR's brother) 84–5, 104, 147,
    180, 183, 222, 271
    on acting versus politics 99, 100
    as candidate for Lambeth 220–1
    childhood 1–18 *passim*, 28, 32, 33–4, 90
    in *Crucible, The* 260
    and Equity 151, 186
    and Henry James 243
    and Michael's death 242
    and *Newsline* 260
    and *Observer* case 215, 217–19
    and *Orpheus Descending* 279
    and parents 21, 24, 52, 148, 187
    and Socialist Labour League 159, 161, 162–4
    at Stratford 39–43
    and theatre 55–6, 103, 131, 259, 260
    visits VR at Frinton 79
    and Workers' Revolutionary Party funds 251–2
Redgrave, Daisy *see* Anderson, Margaret
Redgrave, Deirdre 183, 184, 188
Redgrave, Jemma 188, 294–8
Redgrave, Lady *see* Kempson, Rachel
Redgrave, Luke 188
Redgrave Lynn (VR's sister) 11, 12, 15, 18, 32, 33,
    42, 52, 85, 103, 104, 114–15, 128, 132, 148,
    285–6, 294–8
Redgrave, Michael (VR's father)
    and Actors' Studio 58
    *Actor's Ways and Means, An* 43, 74
    acts with VR 82, 222
    and *As You Like It* 93
    and *Aspern Papers, The*, 243, 244
    and *Beggar's Opera, The* 48
    death 242
    Diana Menuhin on 247
    on filming 124
    and *Ghosts* 261
    illness and death 222, 245–6
    *In My Mind's Eye* 148
    and marriage to Rachel 2–3

Mask or Face 168
    and money 33, 76, 190
    as musician 51–2
    on Natasha as actress 244–5
    and National Theatre 266
    and People's Convention 22–6, 98
    as photographer 47
    and politics 21–3, 186–7
    popularity as actor 3, 27, 28, 33
    and *Quiet American, The* 46–7, 73
    recording of 'A New World Will Be Born' 22, 23
    in *Shakespeare's People* 206–7
    as Shylock 43
    and *Sleeping Prince, The* 65
    in Soviet Union 89
    at Stratford 39–40, 43, 86–7
    and *The Tiger and the Horse* 90
    on Theatre Workshop 55
    and *Tiger at the Gates* 56
    and *Touch of the Sun, A* 82–4
    and Ulanova 62
    and *Uncle Vanya* 100, 143
    and Vic School 54
    visit to Soviet Union 87
    and VR as actress 79, 80
    and VR's birth 1
    and VR's childhood 6–7, 12, 13, 32, 38, 45
    VR's letters to 96–101
    and VR's political activities 106
    and Workers' Music Association 22, 23
Redgrave, Roy (VR's grandfather) 190
Redgrave, Vanessa
    and Actors' Equity 181–2
    and *Anschluss* 192
    in Armenia 263–4
    in Australia 233
    awards won 76, 130–1, 132, 207–9, 255
    in Bahrain 226, 227
    and Berlin Wall concert 285–6
    birth 1
    and Boston Symphony Orchestra 234–42, 282
    as candidate for Moss Side 220–1
    as candidate for Newham North-East 171, 172–
    4
    and Carlo *see* Sparanero, Carlo
    at Central School of Drama 52–4, 59, 61–3, 68–
    75
    and Chernobyl 259–60, 261
    childhood and family life 1–18, 30–4
    and Committee of 100 92, 95–100, 104–7, 108,
    133
    and concert for Arab Women's Association
    273–4
    in Cuba 109–11
    and Czechoslovakia, invasion of 142–3
    dance classes 36–8
    early political influences and views 45–9, 63–7
    education 28–30, 34–8, 44–5
    and *Encore* magazine 59
    and Equity 181–2, 185–6
    first journeys abroad 43–4, 45–6
    in France 137
    and Franco Nero *see* Nero, Franco
    at Frinton Summer Theatre 76, 78–80
    and IRA (Irish Republican Army) 155–6, 159–
    60, 216, 229–31

in Iraq 226–7
in Italy 135–6, 147–9
in Jamacia 108–9
and Jewish Defence League 207–9, 213, 237, 239, 240
and Joely *see* Richardson, Joely Kim
in Jordan 232–3
in Kuwait 220, 221
and Labour Party 120–1, 125
in Lebanon 197–205, 209–10
lectures on Marxism 177, 179–80
in Leningrad 290–1
in Libya 227–8
in Los Angeles 118–20, 153
and Marxist college (White Meadows) 176–7, 180, 183–5
and Memorial Society for the Victims of Stalin's Repressions 285–6
in Mexico 109
and miners 247–50
and money 190–1, 239–40
and Moscow Film Festival 221
move to Chiswick 27
and Movement for Colonial Freedom 106
and Natasha *see* Richardson, Natasha
in New York 57–8, 107–8, 188–9 223–4 283–6
and Newry protest march 155–6
and *Observer* 183, 186–7, 214–19
and Oscar ceremony 207–9
and Palestinians 194–5, 197–205, 207–11, 212, 216, 218, 220, 226–9, 232–3, 275–6, 281, 283–4
and parents *see* Kempson, Rachel; Redgrave, Michael
in Paris 143–6
and *Peace News* 112
and planned visit to China 126–9
and PLO (Palestine Liberation Organisation) 282
in Saudi Arabia 227
in school plays 35, 38
singing lessons 50–1
and Socialist Labour League 141, 159, 161, 162–6, 233
in Soviet Union 263, 267–71, 290–1
at Stratford 39–43, 86–7
in Syria 227
in Texas 291–3
and Timothy Dalton *see* Dalton, Timothy
and Tony Richardson *see* Richardson, Tony
and UCLA summer course 118–20
and US Air Force bases in UK 154–5
and Vanessa Redgrave Nursery School 158, 190–1
and Vietnam Solidarity Campaign 139, 141
and White Meadows 180
and Workers' Revolutionary Party 169, 173, 176, 183–6, 191, 219, 228, 247, 248–54

FILMS

*Agatha* 152, 191
*Ballad of the Sad Café, The* (Miss Amelia) 243, 291–3
*Behind the Mask* (Paula) 80–1, 123
*Blow-up* 130

*Bostonians, The* (Olive Chancellor) 240, 243–4
*Camelot* 256
*Charge of the Light Brigade, The* (Clarissa) 136–7
*Devils, The* 150, 190
film on miners' wives 247–50
film on Richard Wagner 234
*Howard's End* 243
*Isadora* (Isadora Duncan) 137–8
*Julia* (Julia) 191–3, 206, 240
*Mary, Queen of Scots* (Mary) 151, 152, 190
*Morgan, a Suitable Case for Treatment* 123, 124, 130
*Murder on the Orient Express* 182
*My Body, My Child* 229, 235
*Occupied Palestine* 227, 232–3
*Orpheus Descending* (Lady Torrance) 288–9
*Palestinians, The* 194–5, 205, 206, 207, 208, 213, 220, 227
*Playing for Time* 193, 223, 233
*Quiet Place in the Country, A* 135–6
*Red and Blue* 132
*Seagull, The* (Nina) 116, 142–3
*Second Serve* 255–7
*Trojan Women, The* 159
*Vanessa Talks to Farouk Abdul Azziz* 221–2
*Wetherby* 283
*Yanks* 278
*Young Catherine, The* 290

STAGE APPEARANCES

*Antony and Cleopatra* (Cleopatra) 166–7, 258–9, 260–1
appearances at Orpheum theatre, Boston 238
*As You Like It* (Rosalind) 93–5, 101–2, 104
*Béatrice et Bénédict* 153
*Camelot* 132, 133–4, 139
*Cato Street* (Susan Thistlewood) 41, 161
*Coriolanus* (Valeria) 89
*Cymbeline* (Imogen) 104
*Daniel Deronda* (Gwendolen Hareth) 132, 146
*Design for Living* 167–8, 170
*Ghosts* 152, 261, 262–3
*In the Interests of the State* 107–8, 111–12
*King Lear* (Cordelia) 222
*Lady from the Sea, The* (Bolette) 92
*Lady from the Sea, The* (Ellida) 188–90, 215, 221
*Macbeth* 176–9
*Madhouse in Goa, A* 282, 283
*Midsummer Night's Dream* (Helena) 85, 89
*Mother Goose* (Jack) 87–8
*October* 170–1
*Orpheus Descending* (Lady Torrance) 73, 189, 271, 276–80, 282, 283–4
*Othello* (walk-on) 89
*Prime of Miss Jean Brodie, The* (Miss Brodie) 129, 131, 132, 146, 177
*Sailor from Gibraltar, The* (Sheila) 126, 128
*Saint Joan* (Joan) 38, 41, 80
*Seagull, The* (Madame Arkadina) 116, 254–5, 259
*Seagull, The* (Nina) 116–17
*Taming of the Shrew,* (Katherina) 95, 101, 132, 152, 258, 260
*Three Sisters, The* (Olga) 285–6, 293–8, 300
*Threepenny Opera* 190

*Tiger and the Horse, The* (Stella) 90–2
*Toad of Toad Hall* (Mole) 35
*Touch of the Poet, A* 152
*Touch of the Sun, A* 38, 82–4, 84, 85, 91, 94
*Wall Breaks, The* 294
*Wizard of Oz, The* (Tin Man) 35

WRITINGS

'Hanging on a Tree' 115–16
'In the Interests of the State' 107–8, 111–12
obituary of Gerry Healy 287
Reed, Sir Carol 3
Rees, Evellyn 54
Reeve, Christopher 240, 244, 285, 286
Regester, Bob 147, 261
Reisz, Karel 123
*Reluctant Debutante, The* (Douglas-Home) 79
*Resistible Rise of Arturo Ui, The* (Brecht) 116
Resnais, Alain 143–4
Rhodesia 211
Rich, Frank 282
*Richard II* (Shakespeare) 39, 40–1, 54–5
*Richard III* (Shakespeare) 42, 57, 282
Richard, Ivor 121
Richards, Renée (Dick) 255–7
Richardson, Joely Kim (VR's daughter) 17, 126,
  127, 135–8, 142, 149, 188, 256, 258
  birth 114, 121–2
  and Carlo 280, 285
  in *Drowning by Numbers* 130
  education 151, 177, 183
  in *Miss Julie* 84
  and parents' separation 129, 147–8
  relationship with VR 175–6, 184, 195–6, 233–4.
    283
  in *Steel Magnolias* 282–3
  in *Three Sisters, The* 294, 297
  in *Wetherby* 283
Richardson, Natasha ('Tasha', VR's daughter) 17,
  126, 127, 135–8, 142, 147–9, 151, 175–6, 184,
  188, 195, 206
  birth 113–15, 121
  and Bob Regester 261
  and Carlo 280, 285
  at Central School 70
  education 177, 183
  learns to swim as baby 119–20
  at Michael's funeral 246
  as Nina in *The Seagull* 116, 254–5
  and *Orpheus Descending* 278
  and parents' separation 129, 147–9
  relationship with VR 175–6, 180, 233–4, 283
  at Young Vic 244–5, 260
Richardson, Tony 60, 90, 101–32 *passim*, 136–7,
  147–8, 166, 177, 188–91 *passim*, 278–9, 280,
  284–5, 294
Riga 263
*Ring Round the Moon* (Anouilh) 70
Roberts, John 100
Roberts, Rachel 182
Robeson, Paul 47–8, 61, 87, 89
Robeson, Susan 87
Robinson, Joe 104
Roger (film caterer) 137

Romeo and Juliet (ballet) 62
*Romeo and Juliet* (Shakespeare) 39
Romero, Archbishop Oscar 117
Roose Evans, James 61–2
Rosen, Jerome 235–6
Rosenberg, Julius and Ethel 47, 240
Rosenblatt, Marcelle 225
Ross-Munro, Colin 215, 218
Roundhouse Theatre 221, 222, 273
Royal Court Theatre 42, 59–61 76, 103, 107, 111–
  12, 189, 196, 278
Royal Dramatic Theatre, Stockholm 263, 266
Royal Exchange Theatre, Manchester 189, 215
Royal Shakespeare Company 108
Rubinstein Callingham 214
Russell, Bertrand 92, 95–6, 98, 99, 105, 141
Russell, Ken 150
Rustaveli Company 240, 282
Rykov, Alexei 268, 273

Sa'ad-al-Sabah, Sheikh 220
Saad, Ma'arouf 194
Sabra camp 201, 283
Sadat, Anwar 167
Saddam Hussein 293–4, 298–9
Sadlers Wells Theatre 85
Sadoff, Fred 58, 71
Saint, Eva Marie 58
St James's Theatre 42
*Saint Joan* (Shaw) 42
  *see also under* Redgrave, Vanessa, STAGE
    APPEARANCES
*St Joan of the Stockyards* (Brecht) 117
St Just, Maria 280
Saint-Denis, Michel 50, 53–4
*Salopian*, HMS 6
Salvador, El 238
Salvatore (friend from Naples) 277
Salvini, Tommaso 74–5
Sambalini, Dr 48
Sammassimo, Silvana 175, 183, 188, 191, 195, 234
Sandrig, Caroline 236
Sands, Bobby 229–31
Sarah (schoolfriend) 44–5
Sargent, Alvin 192
Sartre, Jean-Paul 106
Saudi Arabia 240, 293, 299
Savan, Bruce 240
Saville Theatre 84
Scargill, Anne 248
Scargill, Arthur 160–1, 248, 250
Schaubühne 263, 266
Schildkraut, Joseph 58
Schoenman, Ralph 105, 141
Scudamore, Daisy *see* Anderson, Margaret
Scudamore, Fortunatus Augustus 14
Scudamore, Lionel 14
Scudamore, William 13
*Seagull, The* (Chekhov) 84
*Search, The* 193
Sellars, Peter 236–7, 240
Selwa (Libyan woman) 227
Semprun, Jorge 143–4
Shaftesbury, Lord 65

Shakespeare Memorial Theatre, Stratford *see* Stratford
Shakespeare, William 87, 157, 202
  *see also play titles and under* Redgrave, Vanessa, STAGE APPEARANCES
Shankar, Ravi 149
Shankland, Dean 247
Shanks, Rosalind 207
Shatrov, Mikhail 268–9, 285, 288
Shave, Dulcie 1, 3, 4, 10
Shaw, George Bernard 61
  *see also play titles*
Shaw, Glen Byam 53, 80, 89, 92
Shaw, Robert 41, 42, 56, 161
*She Came to Stay* (Beauvoir) 107
Shelley, Percy Bysshe 29, 233
'Shipwreck' 16
Shostakovitch, Dimitri, Jr 285
Shoufani, Elias 203–4
Sidmouth, Lord 161
Sidon 201, 209
Signoret, Simone 142, 143–5, 146
Sillitoe, Alan 111
Sisulu, Walter 115
*Sleeping Prince, The* (Rattigan) 65
'Small' (Emin) 264–5
Smith, Colin 216, 217, 218
Smith, Liz 207
Smith, Maggie 295
Smith, Roger 215
Soper, Lord 160
South Africa 115–16, 117, 145, 201, 211, 212
Southern, Terry 118
Soviet Union 62–3, 64, 89–90, 143, 144, 157
Soweto 201
Spalding, Miss 34
Sparanero, Carlo (VR's son) 114, 148–9, 151, 158, 175, 177, 183, 188, 191, 195, 233–4, 258, 277, 280, 284–5
Sparanero family 135
Spark, Muriel 129
Spiegel, Sam 98
Spock, Dr Benjamin 144
*Spycatcher* (Wright) 219, 253–4
Squire, Ronald 83–4
Squire, Ursula 83–4
Stalin, Joseph 24, 25, 63, 90, 157, 162–3, 178, 192–3, 260, 265-6, 270, 272–3, 281, 287, 289–90
*Stalin School of Falsification, The* (Trotsky) 268, 269
*Stalky & Co* (Kipling) 35
Stander, Lionel 117
Stanislavsky, Konstantin 56–8, 73–5, 81, 168, 254, 261, 272
  *Actor Prepares, An* 74
Stanley, Kim 107
Stansfield, Walter 216
*Stars Look Down, The* 3
Startsev, Professor Mikhail 269, 291
Stein, Peter 263
Stephens, Robert 59, 111–12
Stephenson, William 5
Steppenwolf 189
Stevens, Bob 158
Stevens, Jan 119–20, 137, 158, 195
Stevens, Jolie 119, 137

Stewart, Forrest 256
Stiebel, Victor 73
Stirling, Colonel David 174
Stock, Mrs 65
Stockwood, Bishop Mervyn 160
Strasberg, Ivan 195, 197
Strasberg, Lee 57–8, 76
Strasberg, Susan 58
Strasser, Irene 50
Strasser, Jani 50–1, 53, 94, 107
Stratford 40–2, 52, 62, 85, 86–7, 89, 93, 189
Stravinsky, Igor 234
Sturua, Robert, 270, 282, 288, 294, 295–8
Styron, Melanie 225
Sue (at Central School) 71
Sue (schoolfriend) 44–5
*Sunday Empire News* 21
*Sunday Press* 156
*Sunday Times, The* 60, 170
Sutherland, Donald 117, 146
Sutherland, Shirley 153
*Swan Lake* 62
Swee Chai Ang, Dr 283
Sydney 233
Syria 195

Taghrit 228
Taib 204
Tal al Zaatar 193–5, 198–201
Tanqueray, Paul 68–9
Tassarty, Mlle Eleanor 43, 44
Taylor, Elizabeth 132
Tchikvadze, Natasha 265
*Tempest, The* (Shakespeare) 39
'Tempo' (TV programme) 96
Tennent, H.M. 90
Terry, Ellen 53, 297
Terry Juveniles 14–15
Thacker, David 260, 261
Thatcher, Margaret 220–1, 248
Theatr Clwyd 258
Theatre Workshop 54–5
Thistlewood, Arthur and Susan 161
Thorndike, Dame Sybil 43
*Three Sisters, The* (Chekhov) 85
  *see also under* Redgrave, Vanessa, STAGE APPEARANCES
*Thunder Rock* (Ardrey) 2
Thurburn, Gwyneth 52–3, 65
  *Voice and Speech* 53
*Tiger at the Gates* (Giraudoux) 56
*Time* 193
*Time Out* 214
*Times, The* 61, 66, 138, 144, 218, 228
*Tom Jones* 104, 107
*Tomorrow was War* (Vasiliev) 265–6, 285
Topolski, Feliks 20
Torrance, Sheila 260
*Train to Happiness, The* (Khait) 282
Travolta, John 208
Trepper, Leopold 287
Trevelyan family 28
'Trolley Song, The' 51–2
Trotsky, Leon 157, 163, 165, 213, 262, 267, 268, 269, 270, 272

*History of the Russian Revolution* 170
Truffaut, François 137, 145
*Turquoise*, HMS 6
Tushingham, Rita 103
Tutu, Bishop Desmond 117
*Twelfth Night* (Shakespeare) 103
*Twenty Letters to a Friend* (Alliluyeva) 281
Tynan, Kenneth 60, 87, 96
Tyre 202, 209

Ulanova, Galina 62
Ulyanov, Mikhail 266, 270
*Uncle Vanya* (Chekhov) 85, 86, 100, 143
United Arab Emirates 220
United Artists 107
Universal Studios 137
University of California, Los Angeles 118
Ure, Mary 60

Vakhtangov Theatre 270
*Vanguardia, La* 298–9
*Variety* 211, 213
Vasiliev, Boris 265, 266
Vasiliev, Vladimir 285
Vaughan Williams, Ralph 24
Venice 148, 234
*Venture, The* 22
Veronese, Misses 135, 147
*Veterans* (Wood) 137
Vietnam 119, 124, 124–5, 130, 133, 138–41, 138–9, 144, 155, 159, 193
*View from the Bridge, A* (Miller) 57, 76
Viola (home help) 114
Vitti, Monica 121
Vollchek, Galina 288
*Volpone* (Jonson) 56
Vrachev, Ivan 289–90

Waddell, James 248–9, 288
*Wages of Fear, The* 145
Walker, General Sir Walter 174
Wallace, Mike 223, 235
Wallach, Eli 57
Wallis, Hal 151
Walsh, Kay 36
Walton, Emma 142
Walton, Tony 142
Wanamaker, Sam 90, 166–7, 258
*War and Peace* (Tolstoy) 35
Warner, David 103, 142
Warner Brothers 133–4
Watkins, Professor 246
Watson, Claude 130
Waugh, Auberon 96
Waugh, Evelyn 118

Weaver, Sigourney 285–6
Webb, Beatrice 61
Wedgwood, Henry Allen 10
Wedgwood, Josiah 10
Welch, Elisabeth 273–4, 291
Weldon, Duncan 258
Wellington, Duke of 29
Wesker, Arnold 92, 98
West, Mae 190
*West Side Story* 206
Westmacott, Caroline 28
Westmoreland, General 139
Wexler, Haskell 118
Wexler, Marion 118
*Who's Afraid of Virginia Woolf?* 132
Widmark, Richard 182
Wilde, Oscar 168
Will, Det. -Seg Ian 156–7
Williams, Jerry 235–6
Williams, Tennessee 142, 238–9, 277, 279, 280, 288
Williamson, Nicol 103
Willmott, Rod 207
Wilmers, John, QC 214, 215–16, 218
Wilson, Harold 121, 125, 174
Windmill Theatre 52
Winters, Shelley 57
*Winter's Tale, The* (Shakespeare) 246
Wolpe, Katharina 273
Wolpe, Stefan 273
Wood, Charles 137
Wood, Peter 129, 130, 177
Woodcock, Bruce 33–4
Woodfall 104
Woodward, Joanne 285
*Workers' Press* 159, 169, 174, 183, 215
Wrede, Caspar 146
Wright, Peter 64, 219, 253–4
Wyndham's Theatre 68, 76, 130, 262
Wynyard, Diana 83, 85
Wyse, John 39

*Year of the Pencil, The* 109–10
Yellen, Linda 223, 224, 255, 256
Yerevan 263–5
Yevtushenko, Yevgeny 260
York, Michael 182
Young Vic Theatre 53, 161, 244–5, 260, 261, 262
    School 50, 53
Youssef, Dr 201
Yursky, Sergei 289
Yvonne Arnaud Theatre 297

Zeffirelli, Franco 280
Zinnemann, Fred 191–2, 193, 208
*Znamya* 289